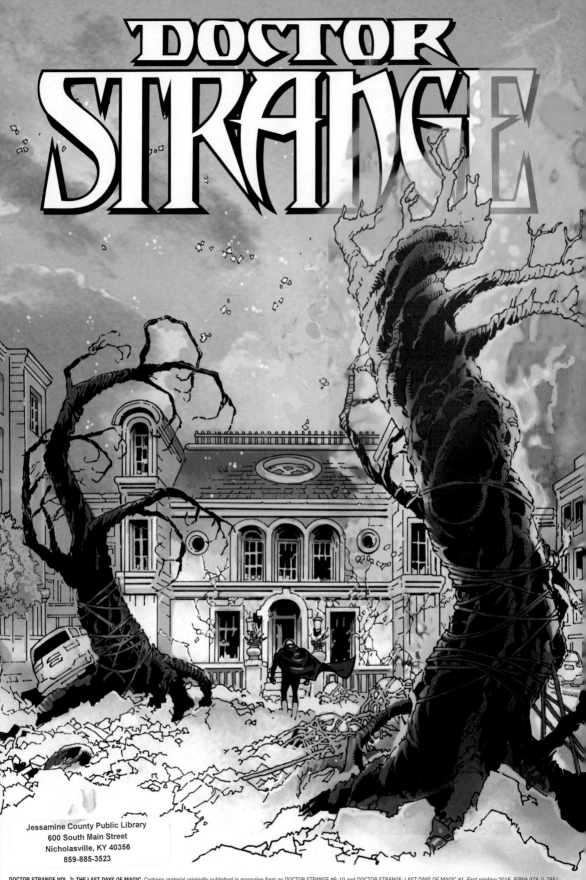

DOCTOR STRANGE

DOCTOR STRANGE VOL. 2: THE LAST DAYS OF MAGIC. Contains material originally published in magazine form as DOCTOR STRANGE #6-10 and DOCTOR STRANGE: LAST DAYS OF MAGIC #1. First printing 2016. ISBN# 978-0-7851-9517-7. Published by MARVEL WORLDWIDE, INC., a subsidiary of MARVEL ENTERTAINMENT, LLC. OFFICE OF PUBLICATION: 135 West 50th Street, New York, NY 10020. Copyright © 2016 MARVEL No similarity between any of the names, characters, persons, and/or institutions in this magazine with those of any living or dead person or institution is intended, and any such similarity which may exist is purely coincidental. **Printed in the U.S.A.** ALAN FINE, President, Marvel Entertainment; DAN BUCKLEY, President, TV, Publishing & Brand Management; JOE QUESADA, Chief Creative Officer; TOM BREVOORT, SVP of Publishing; DAVID BOGART, SVP of Business Affairs & Operations, Publishing & Partnership; C.B. CEBULSKI, VP of Brand Management & Development, Asia; DAVID GABRIEL, SVP of Sales & Marketing, Publishing; JEFF YOUNGQUIST, VP of Production & Special Projects; DAN CARR, Executive Director of Publishing Technology; ALEX MORALES, Director of Publishing Operations; SUSAN CRESPI, Production Manager; STAN LEE, Chairman Emeritus. For information regarding advertising in Marvel Comics or on Marvel.com, please contact Vit DeBellis, Integrated Sales Manager, at vdebellis@marvel.com. For Marvel subscription inquiries, please call 888-511-5480. **Manufactured between 8/5/2016 and 9/19/2016 by LSC COMMUNICATIONS INC., ROANOKE, VA, USA.**

10 9 8 7 6 5 4 3 2 1

DOCTOR STRANGE

The Last Days of Magic

Jason Aaron
WRITER

Chris Bachalo
PENCILER/COLORIST

TIM TOWNSEND, AL VEY, MARK IRWIN,
JOHN LIVESAY, WAYNE FAUCHER,
VICTOR OLAZABA & JAIME MENDOZA
INKERS

CHRIS BACHALO, JAVA TARTAGLIA
& ANTONIO FABELA
WITH RAIN BEREDO
COLORISTS

"A Day Without Magic"

MIKE DEODATO, JORGE FORNÉS,
KEV WALKER & KEVIN NOWLAN
ARTISTS

RAIN BEREDO &
KEVIN NOWLAN
COLORISTS

CHRIS BACHALO & TIM TOWNSEND
COVER ART

The Last Days of Magic #1

Zelma Stanton Framing Sequence
JASON AARON
WRITER

LEONARDO ROMERO
ARTIST

JORDIE BELLAIRE
COLORIST

Doctor Voodoo
GERRY DUGGAN
WRITER

DANILO BEYRUTH
ARTIST

DAN BROWN
COLORIST

The Wu
JAMES ROBINSON
WRITER

MIKE PERKINS
ARTIST

ANDY TROY
COLORIST

MIKE PERKINS
& ANDY TROY
COVER ART

VC'S CORY PETIT
LETTERER

CHARLES BEACHAM
ASSISTANT EDITOR

DARREN SHAN
ASSOCIATE EDITOR

NICK LOWE
& EMILY SHAW
EDITORS

DOCTOR STRANGE CREATED BY STAN LEE & STEVE DITKO

COLLECTION EDITOR: JENNIFER GRÜNWALD
ASSOCIATE EDITOR: SARAH BRUNSTAD
EDITOR, SPECIAL PROJECTS: MARK D. BEAZLEY
VP, PRODUCTION & SPECIAL PROJECTS: JEFF YOUNGQUIST
SVP PRINT, SALES & MARKETING: DAVID GABRIEL
BOOK DESIGNER: JAY BOWEN

EDITOR IN CHIEF: AXEL ALONSO
CHIEF CREATIVE OFFICER: JOE QUESADA
PUBLISHER: DAN BUCKLEY
EXECUTIVE PRODUCER: ALAN FINE

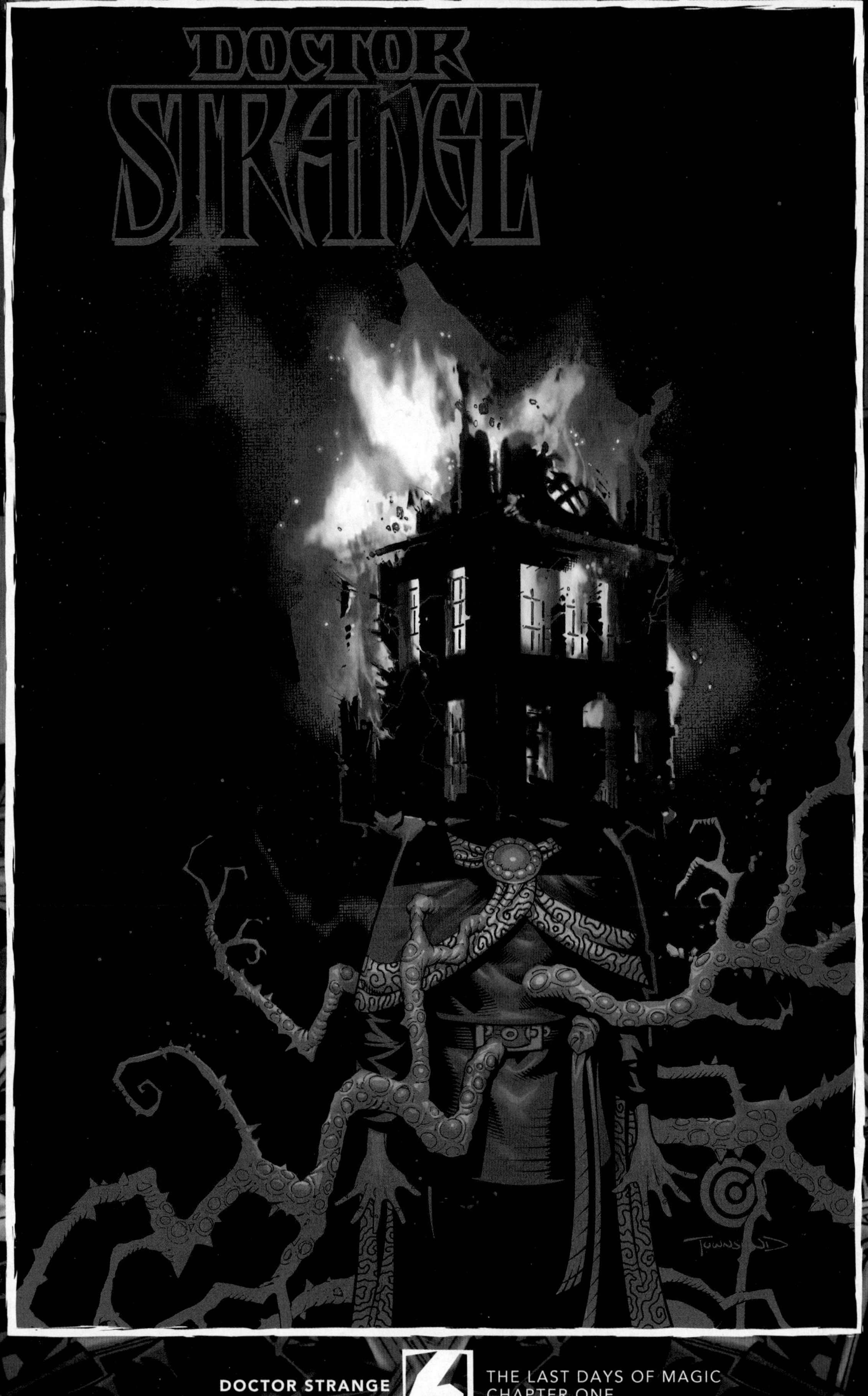
DOCTOR
STRANGE
TOWNSEND

DOCTOR STRANGE THE LAST DAYS OF MAGIC
CHAPTER ONE

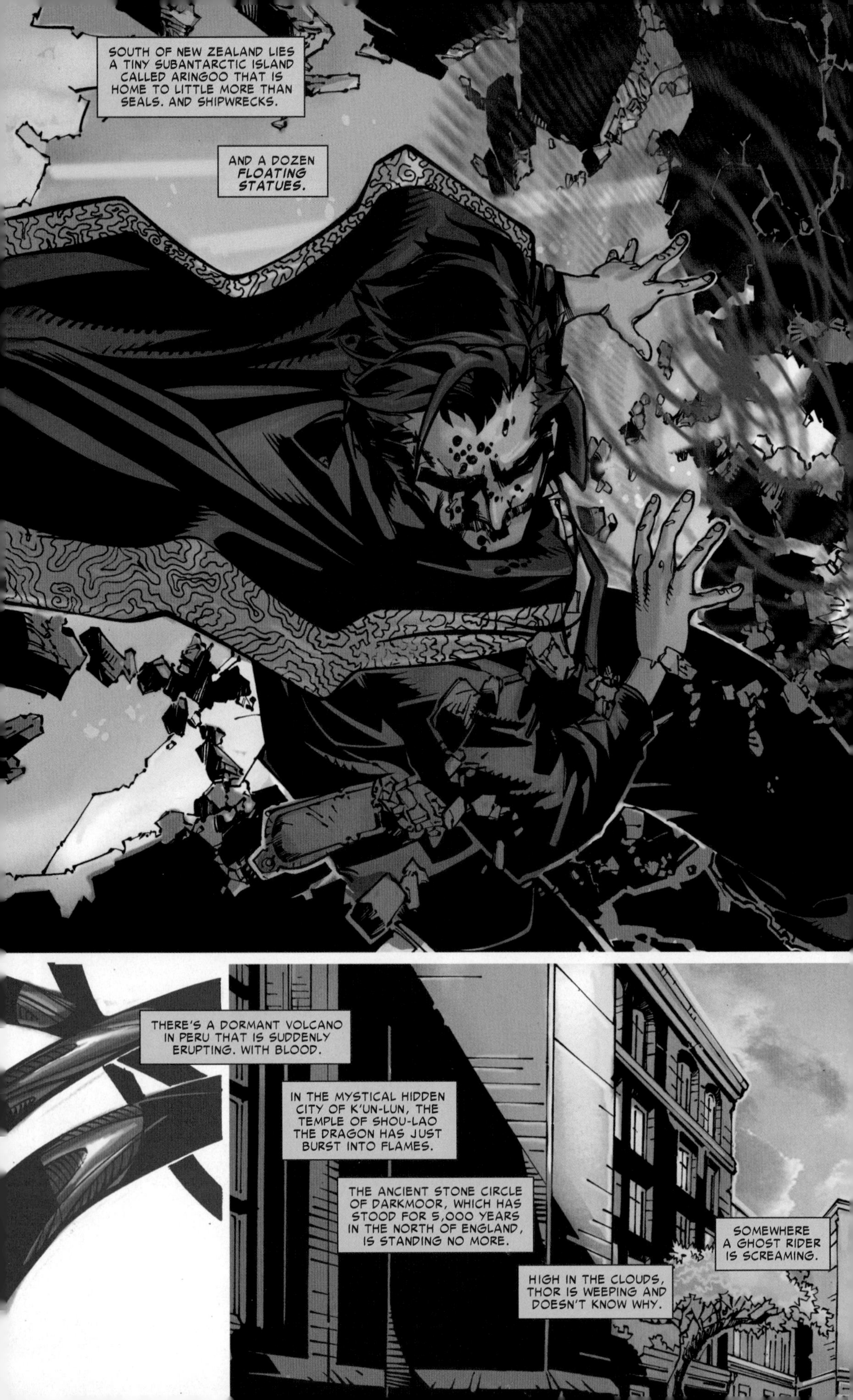
SOUTH OF NEW ZEALAND LIES A TINY SUBANTARCTIC ISLAND CALLED ARINGOO THAT IS HOME TO LITTLE MORE THAN SEALS. AND SHIPWRECKS.
AND A DOZEN *FLOATING STATUES.*
THERE'S A DORMANT VOLCANO IN PERU THAT IS SUDDENLY ERUPTING. WITH BLOOD.
IN THE MYSTICAL HIDDEN CITY OF K'UN-LUN, THE TEMPLE OF SHOU-LAO THE DRAGON HAS JUST BURST INTO FLAMES.
THE ANCIENT STONE CIRCLE OF DARKMOOR, WHICH HAS STOOD FOR 5,000 YEARS IN THE NORTH OF ENGLAND, IS STANDING NO MORE.
SOMEWHERE A GHOST RIDER IS SCREAMING.
HIGH IN THE CLOUDS, THOR IS WEEPING AND DOESN'T KNOW WHY.

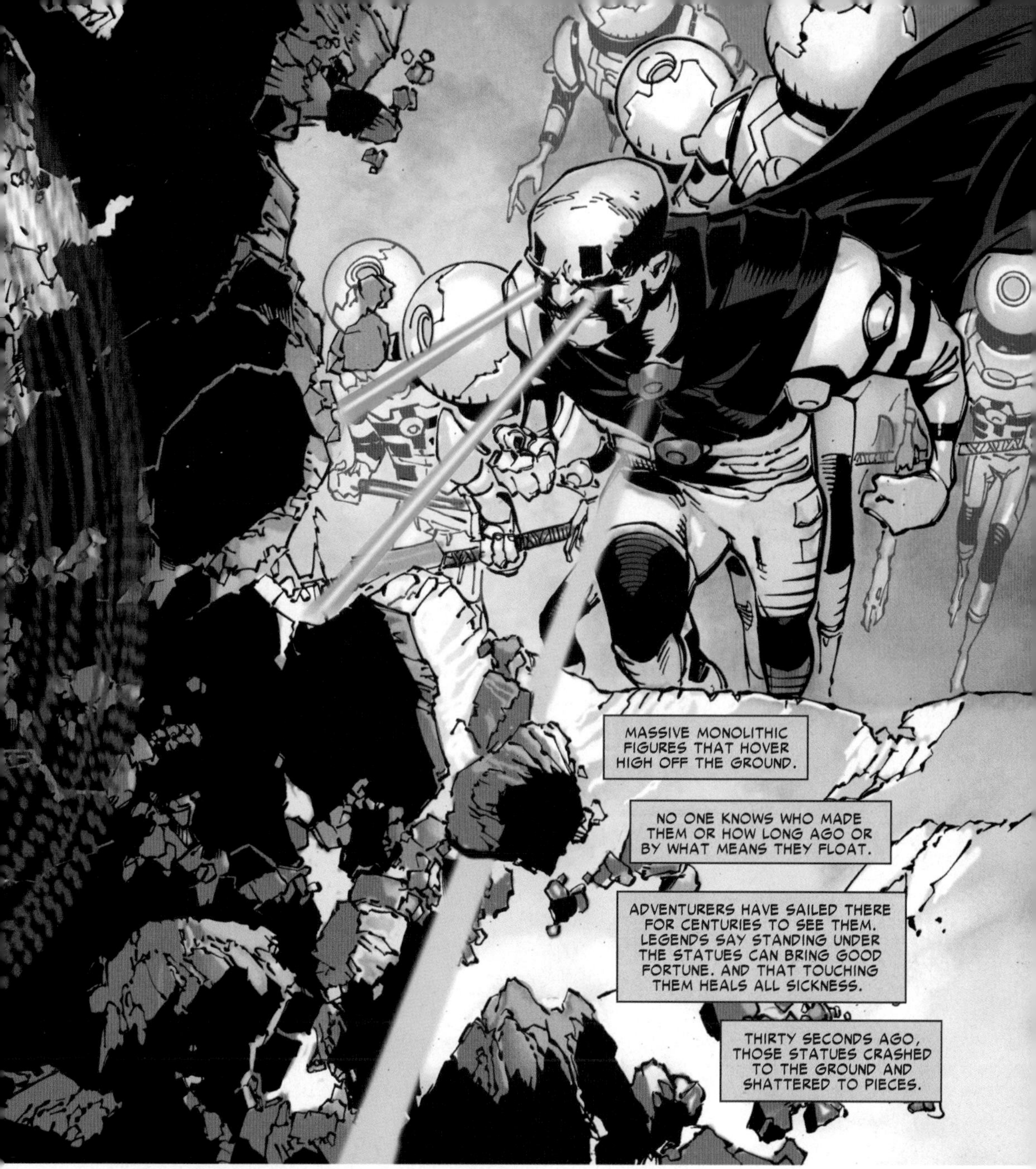
MASSIVE MONOLITHIC FIGURES THAT HOVER HIGH OFF THE GROUND.
NO ONE KNOWS WHO MADE THEM OR HOW LONG AGO OR BY WHAT MEANS THEY FLOAT.
ADVENTURERS HAVE SAILED THERE FOR CENTURIES TO SEE THEM. LEGENDS SAY STANDING UNDER THE STATUES CAN BRING GOOD FORTUNE. AND THAT TOUCHING THEM HEALS ALL SICKNESS.
THIRTY SECONDS AGO, THOSE STATUES CRASHED TO THE GROUND AND SHATTERED TO PIECES.

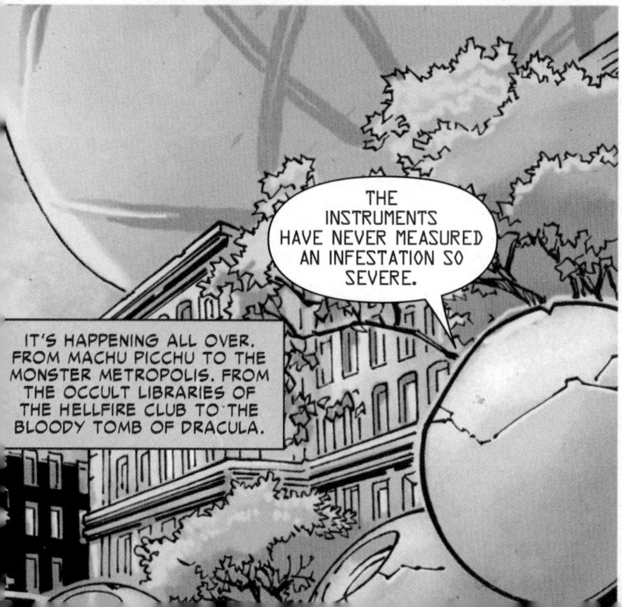
THE INSTRUMENTS HAVE NEVER MEASURED AN INFESTATION SO SEVERE.
IT'S HAPPENING ALL OVER. FROM MACHU PICCHU TO THE MONSTER METROPOLIS. FROM THE OCCULT LIBRARIES OF THE HELLFIRE CLUB TO THE BLOODY TOMB OF DRACULA.

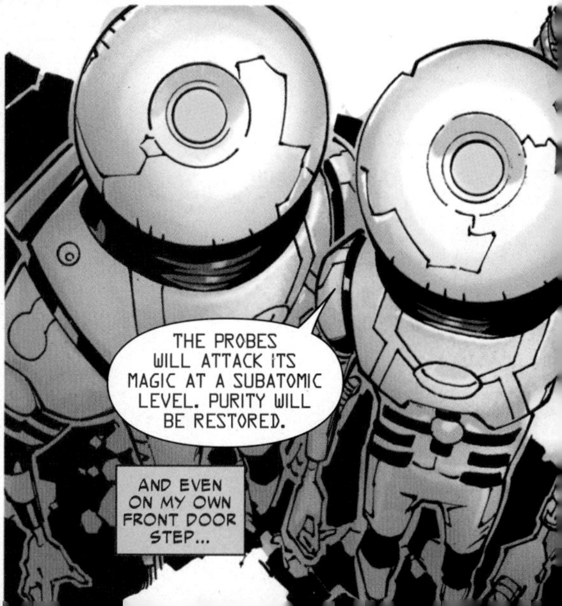
THE PROBES WILL ATTACK ITS MAGIC AT A SUBATOMIC LEVEL. PURITY WILL BE RESTORED.
AND EVEN ON MY OWN FRONT DOOR STEP...

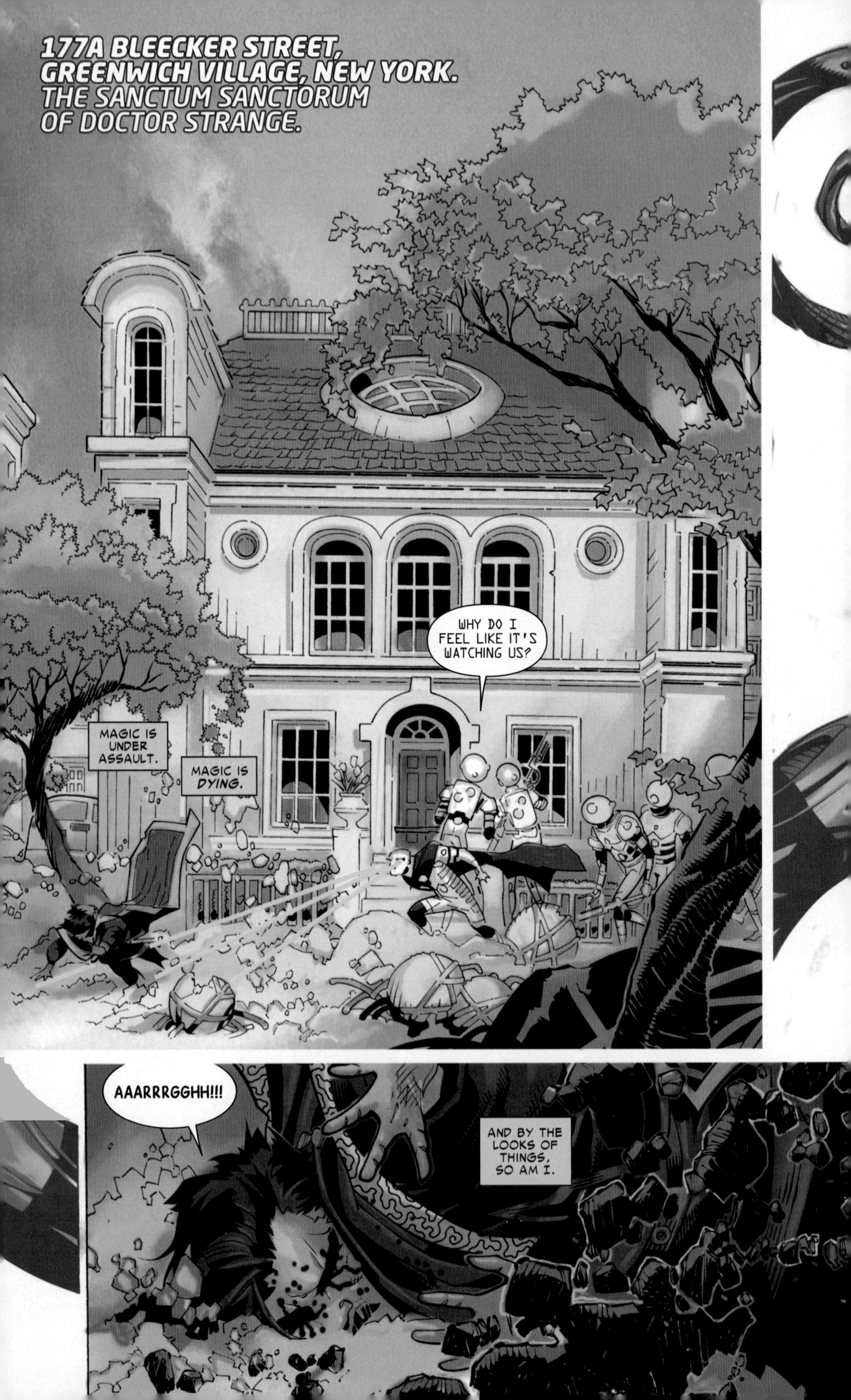
177A BLEECKER STREET, GREENWICH VILLAGE, NEW YORK. THE SANCTUM SANCTORUM OF DOCTOR STRANGE.
MAGIC IS UNDER ASSAULT.
MAGIC IS DYING.
WHY DO I FEEL LIKE IT'S WATCHING US?
AAARRRGGHH!!!
AND BY THE LOOKS OF THINGS, SO AM I.

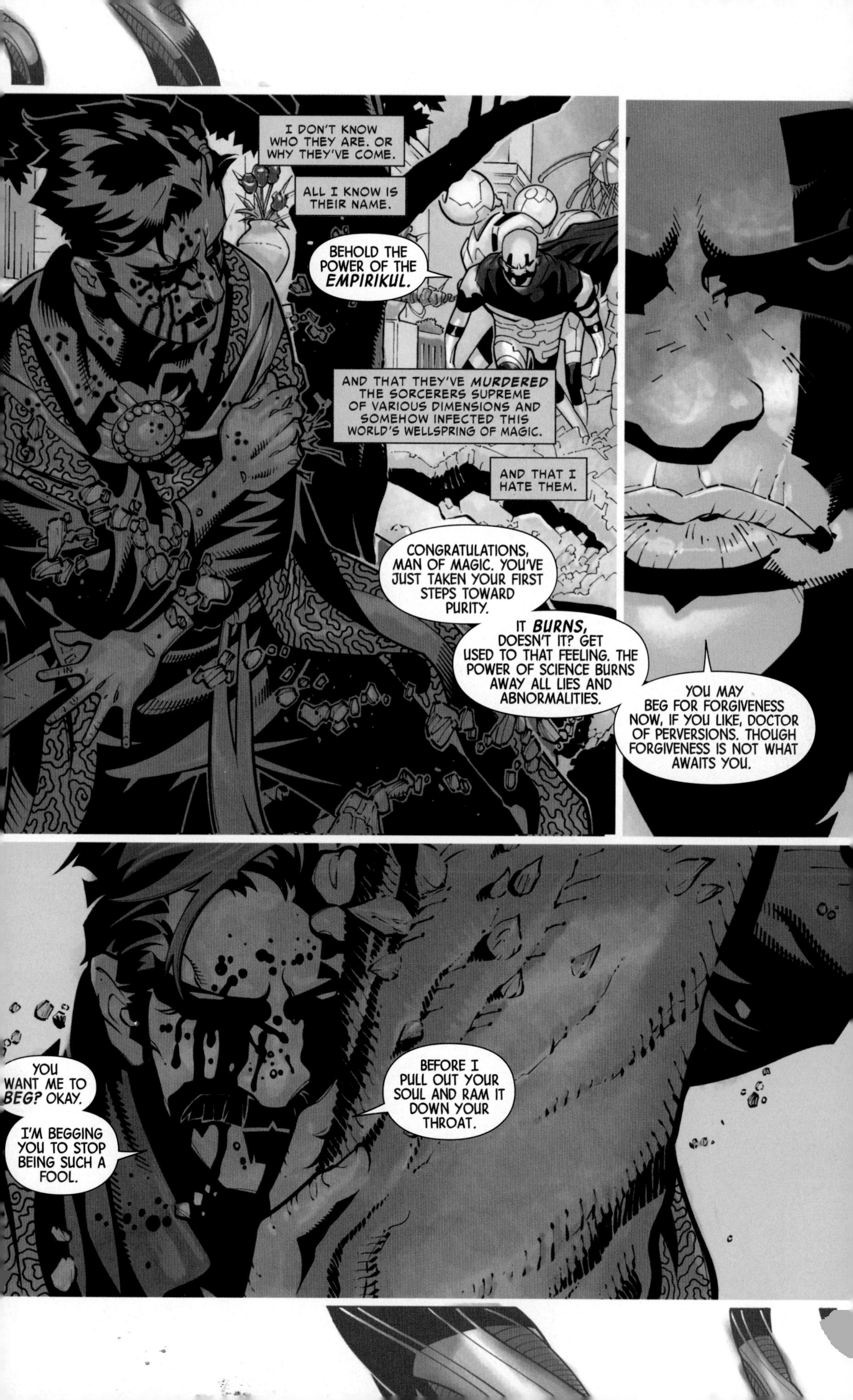
I DON'T KNOW WHO THEY ARE. OR WHY THEY'VE COME.
ALL I KNOW IS THEIR NAME.
BEHOLD THE POWER OF THE EMPIRIKUL.
AND THAT THEY'VE MURDERED THE SORCERERS SUPREME OF VARIOUS DIMENSIONS AND SOMEHOW INFECTED THIS WORLD'S WELLSPRING OF MAGIC.
AND THAT I HATE THEM.
CONGRATULATIONS, MAN OF MAGIC. YOU'VE JUST TAKEN YOUR FIRST STEPS TOWARD PURITY.
IT BURNS, DOESN'T IT? GET USED TO THAT FEELING. THE POWER OF SCIENCE BURNS AWAY ALL LIES AND ABNORMALITIES.
YOU MAY BEG FOR FORGIVENESS NOW, IF YOU LIKE, DOCTOR OF PERVERSIONS. THOUGH FORGIVENESS IS NOT WHAT AWAITS YOU.
BEFORE I PULL OUT YOUR SOUL AND RAM IT DOWN YOUR THROAT.
YOU WANT ME TO BEG? OKAY.
I'M BEGGING YOU TO STOP BEING SUCH A FOOL.

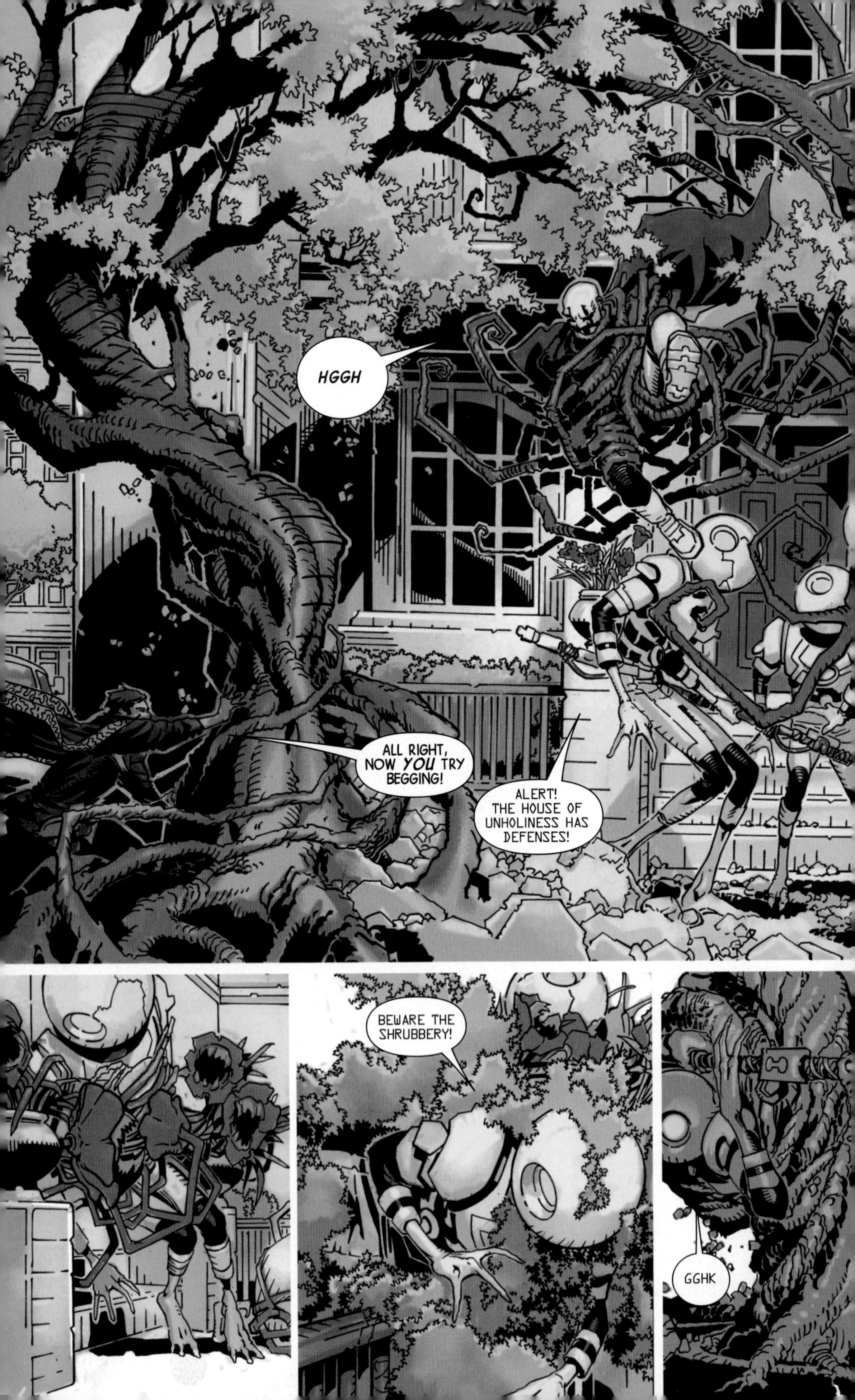
HGGH
ALL RIGHT, NOW YOU TRY BEGGING!
ALERT! THE HOUSE OF UNHOLINESS HAS DEFENSES!
BEWARE THE SHRUBBERY!
GGHK

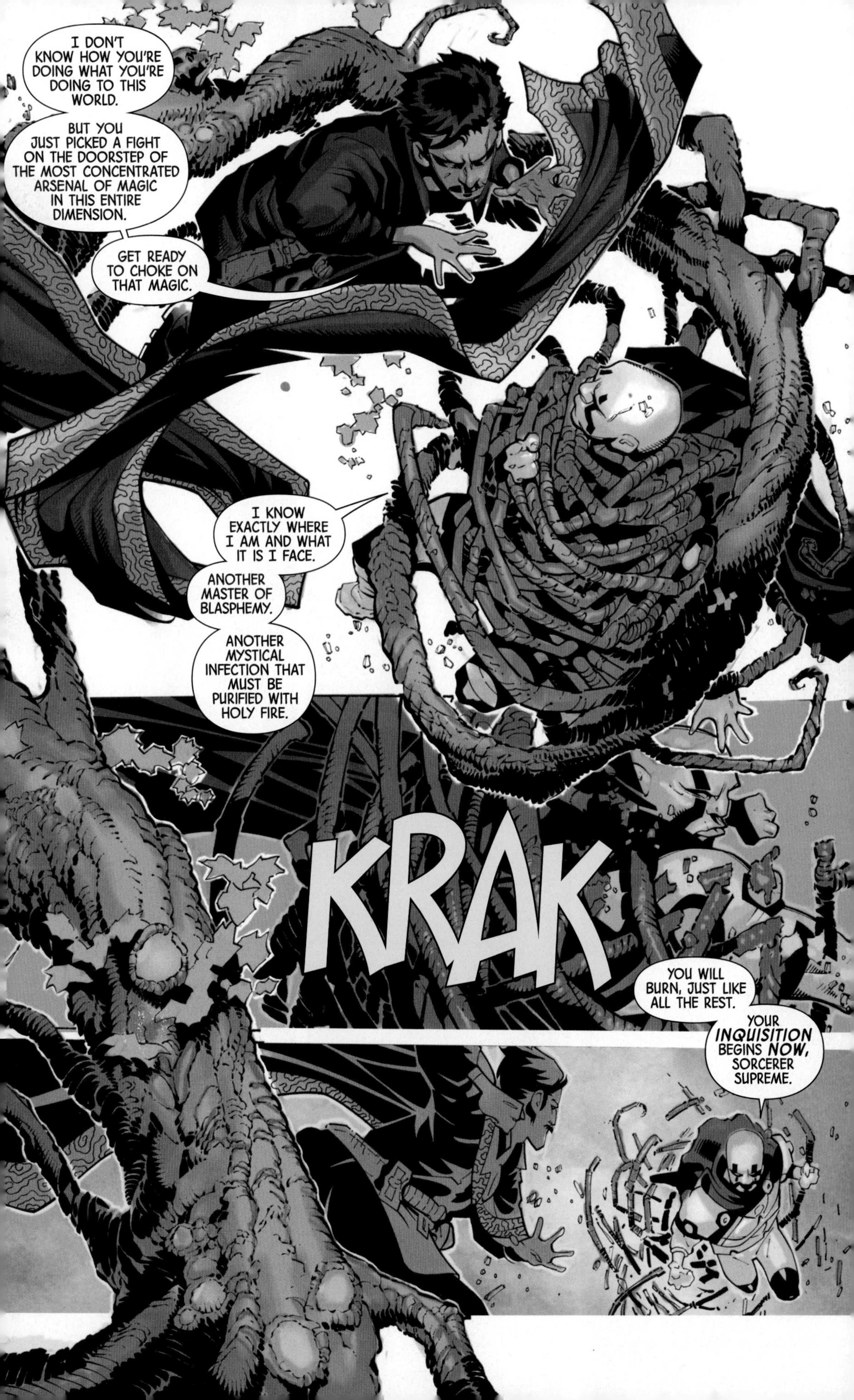
I DON'T KNOW HOW YOU'RE DOING WHAT YOU'RE DOING TO THIS WORLD.
BUT YOU JUST PICKED A FIGHT ON THE DOORSTEP OF THE MOST CONCENTRATED ARSENAL OF MAGIC IN THIS ENTIRE DIMENSION.
GET READY TO CHOKE ON THAT MAGIC.
I KNOW EXACTLY WHERE I AM AND WHAT IT IS I FACE.
ANOTHER MASTER OF BLASPHEMY.
ANOTHER MYSTICAL INFECTION THAT MUST BE PURIFIED WITH HOLY FIRE.
KRAK
YOU WILL BURN, JUST LIKE ALL THE REST.
YOUR *INQUISITION* BEGINS *NOW,* SORCERER SUPREME.

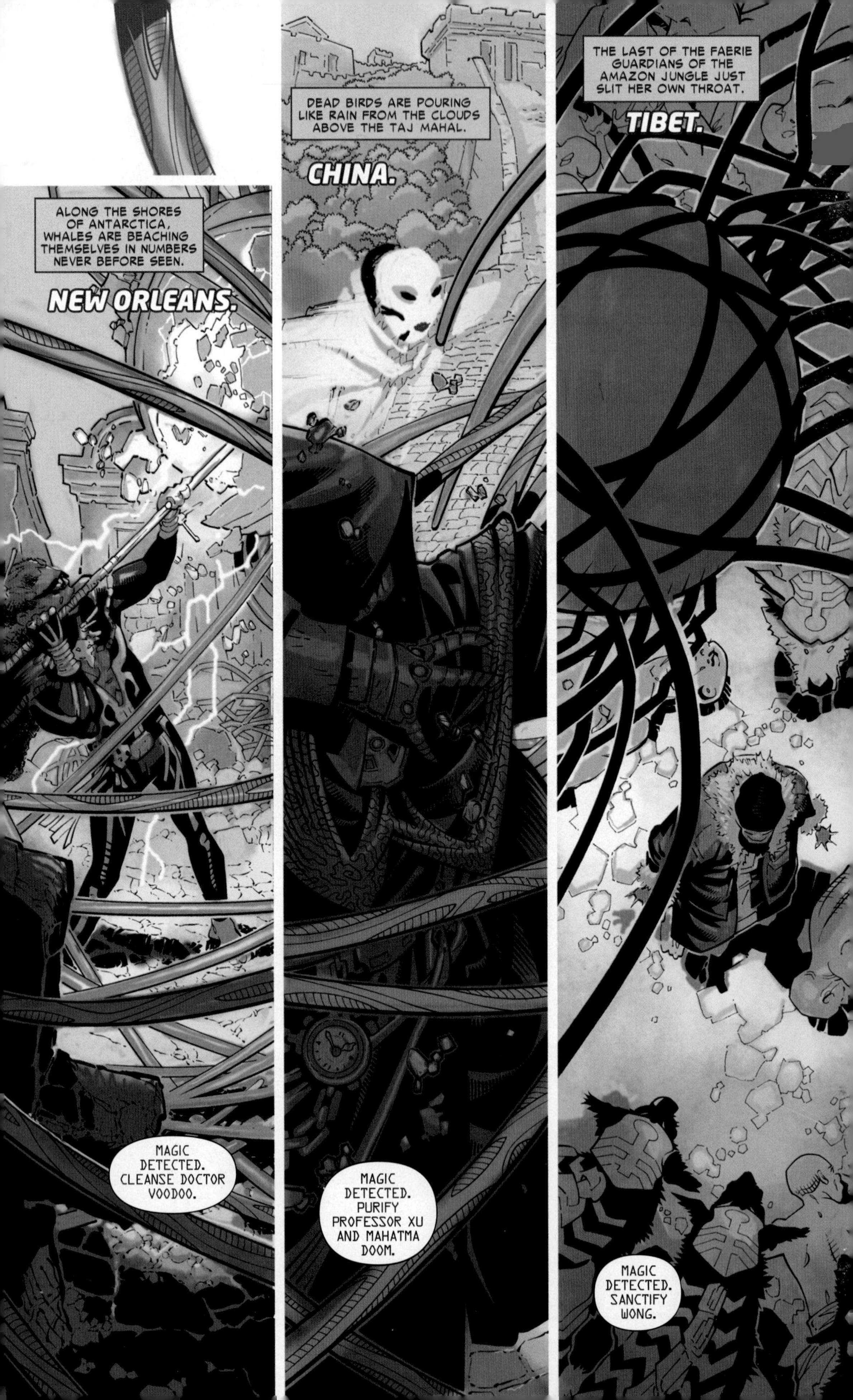
ALONG THE SHORES OF ANTARCTICA, WHALES ARE BEACHING THEMSELVES IN NUMBERS NEVER BEFORE SEEN.
NEW ORLEANS.
MAGIC DETECTED. CLEANSE DOCTOR VOODOO.
DEAD BIRDS ARE POURING LIKE RAIN FROM THE CLOUDS ABOVE THE TAJ MAHAL.
CHINA.
MAGIC DETECTED. PURIFY PROFESSOR XU AND MAHATMA DOOM.
THE LAST OF THE FAERIE GUARDIANS OF THE AMAZON JUNGLE JUST SLIT HER OWN THROAT.
TIBET.
MAGIC DETECTED. SANCTIFY WONG.

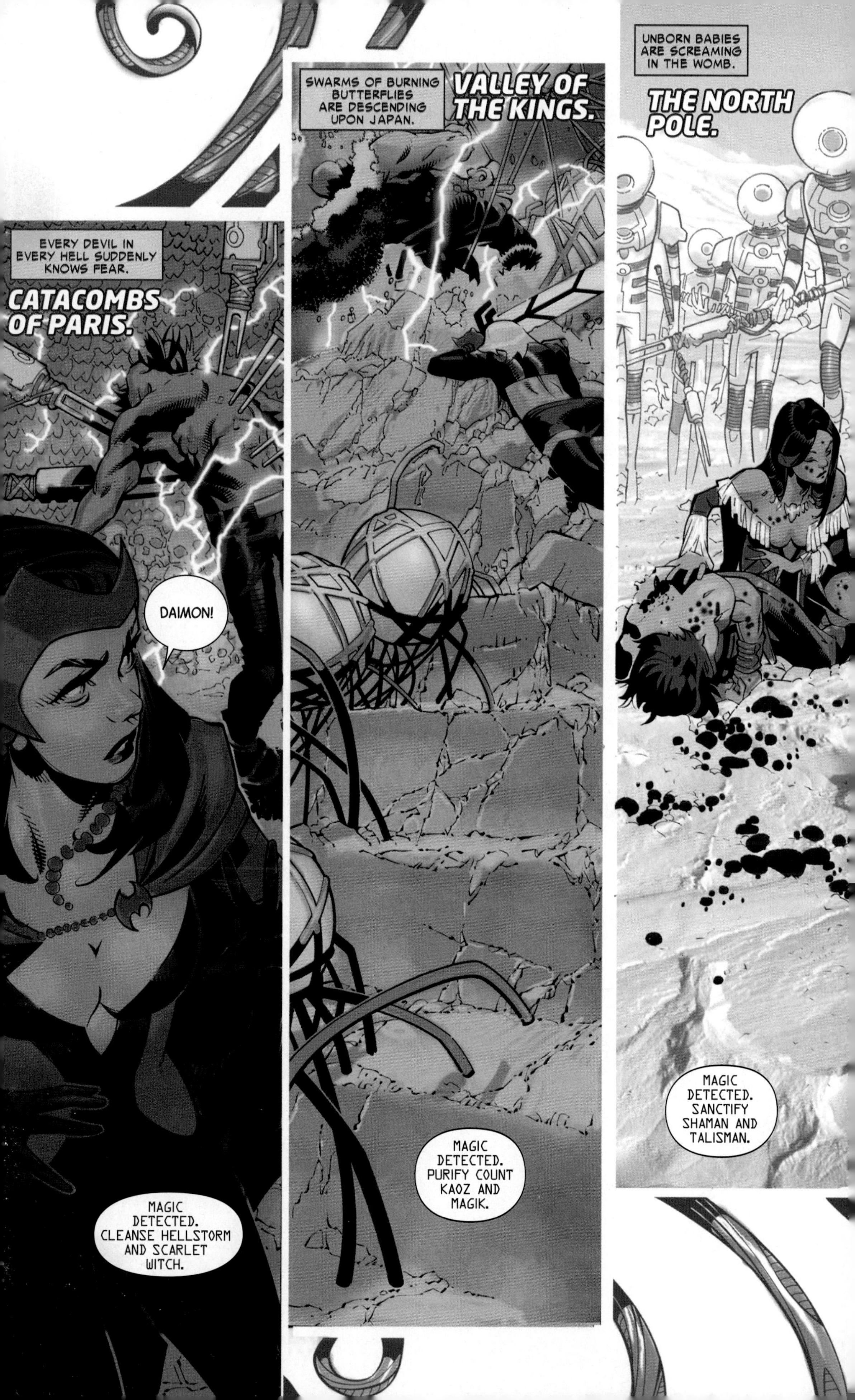
EVERY DEVIL IN EVERY HELL SUDDENLY KNOWS FEAR.
CATACOMBS OF PARIS.
DAIMON!
MAGIC DETECTED. CLEANSE HELLSTORM AND SCARLET WITCH.
SWARMS OF BURNING BUTTERFLIES ARE DESCENDING UPON JAPAN.
VALLEY OF THE KINGS.
MAGIC DETECTED. PURIFY COUNT KAOZ AND MAGIK.
UNBORN BABIES ARE SCREAMING IN THE WOMB.
THE NORTH POLE.
MAGIC DETECTED. SANCTIFY SHAMAN AND TALISMAN.

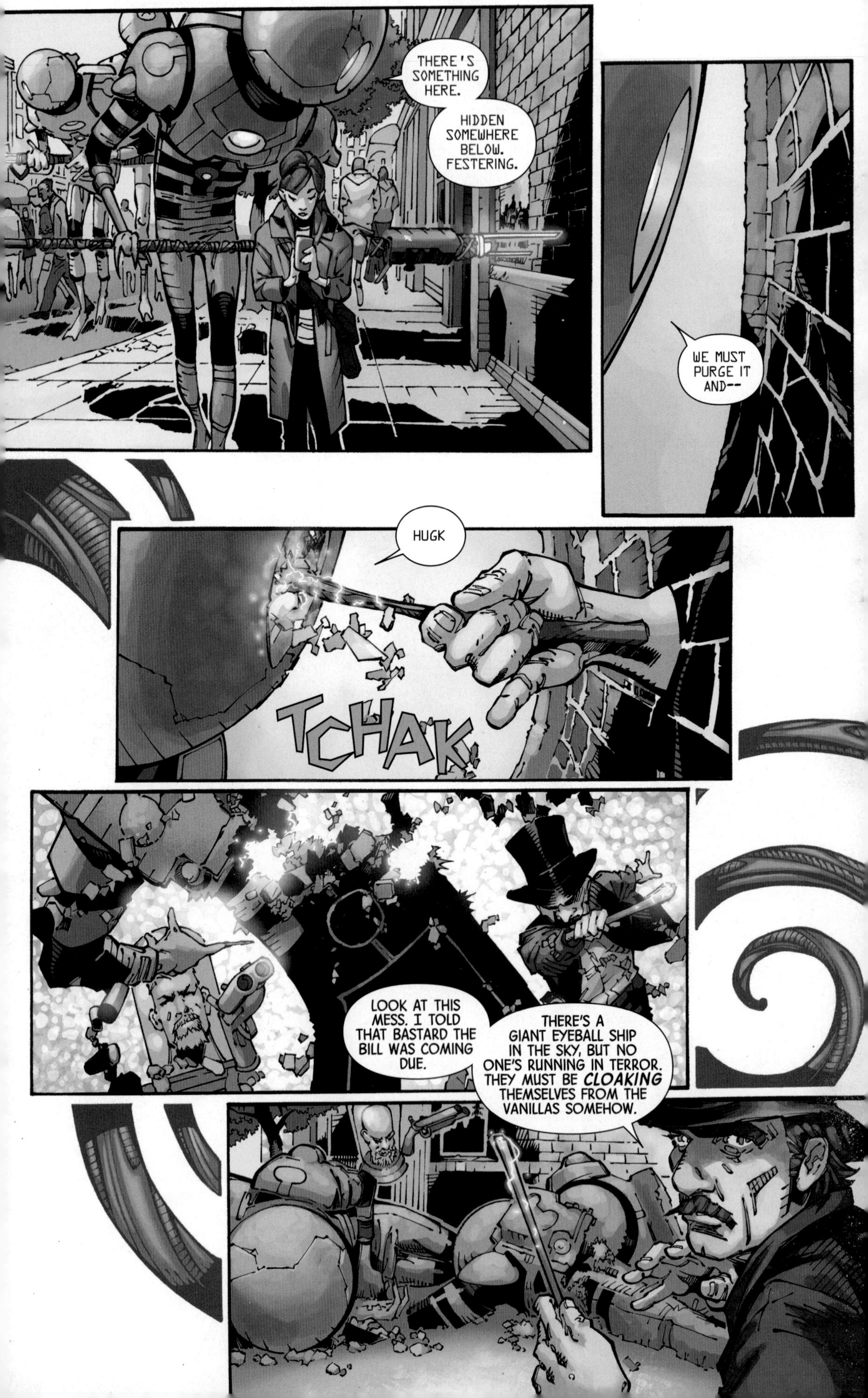
THERE'S SOMETHING HERE.
HIDDEN SOMEWHERE BELOW. FESTERING.
WE MUST PURGE IT AND--
HUGK
TCHAK
LOOK AT THIS MESS. I TOLD THAT BASTARD THE BILL WAS COMING DUE.
THERE'S A GIANT EYEBALL SHIP IN THE SKY, BUT NO ONE'S RUNNING IN TERROR. THEY MUST BE CLOAKING THEMSELVES FROM THE VANILLAS SOMEHOW.

YOU STAY HERE AND GUARD THE BAR, CHONDU.

WHAT? WHERE ARE *YOU* GOING, MONAKO?

TO DO WHAT I WAS BORN TO DO.

DIE WITH A WAND IN MY HAND.

GUGGH

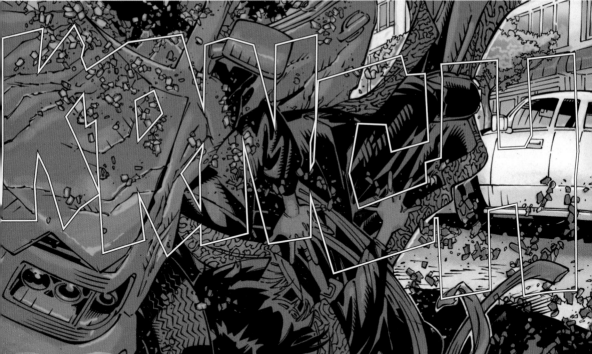

KKNGHH

BUTTERFLIES BURNING. BABIES CLINGING TO THEIR CORDS, REFUSING TO BE BORN...MAGIC IS GASPING FOR LIFE, AND I'M...

I'M THE ONLY DOCTOR WHO CAN SAVE IT.

HHHNNG

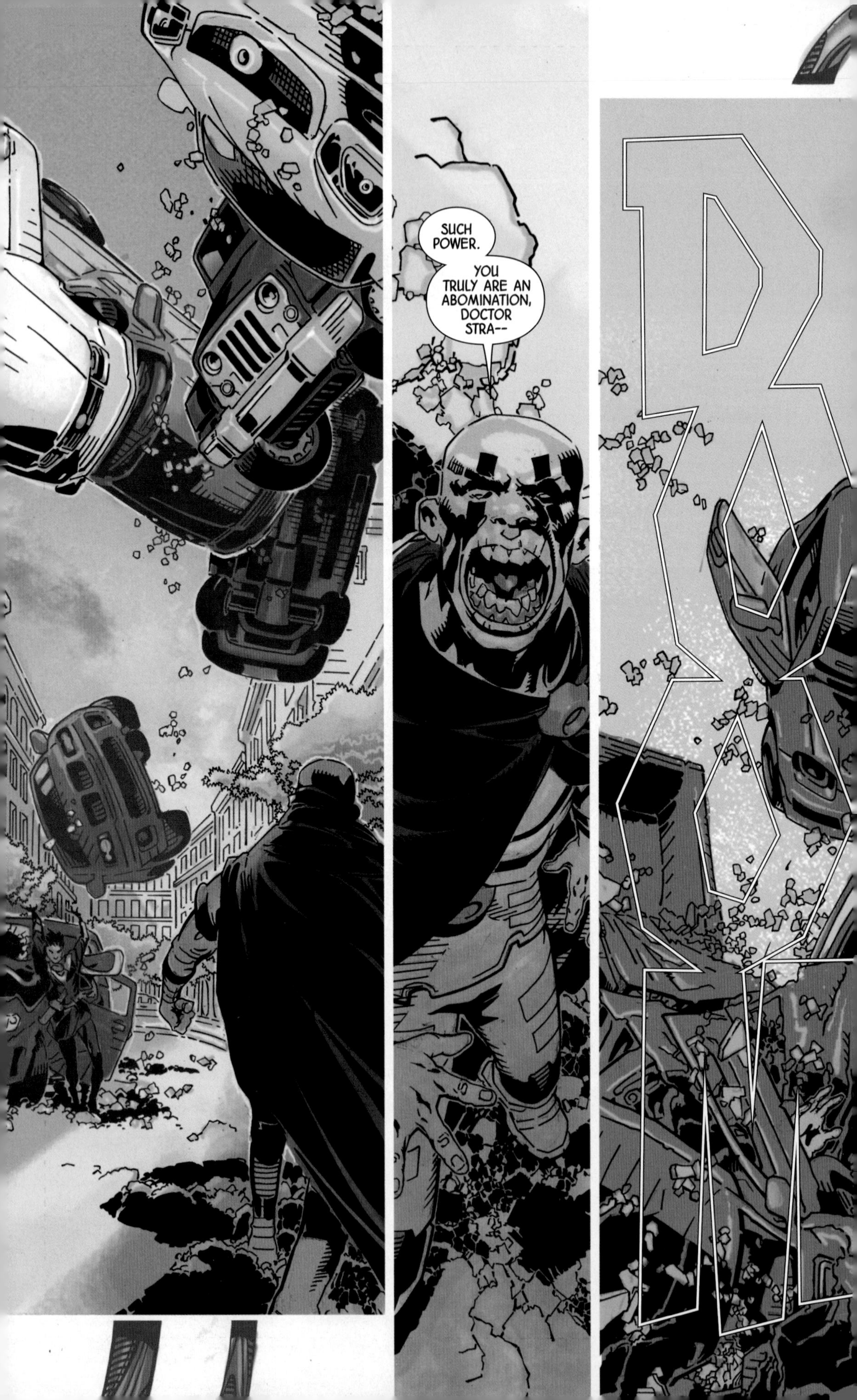
SUCH POWER.
YOU TRULY ARE AN ABOMINATION, DOCTOR STRA--

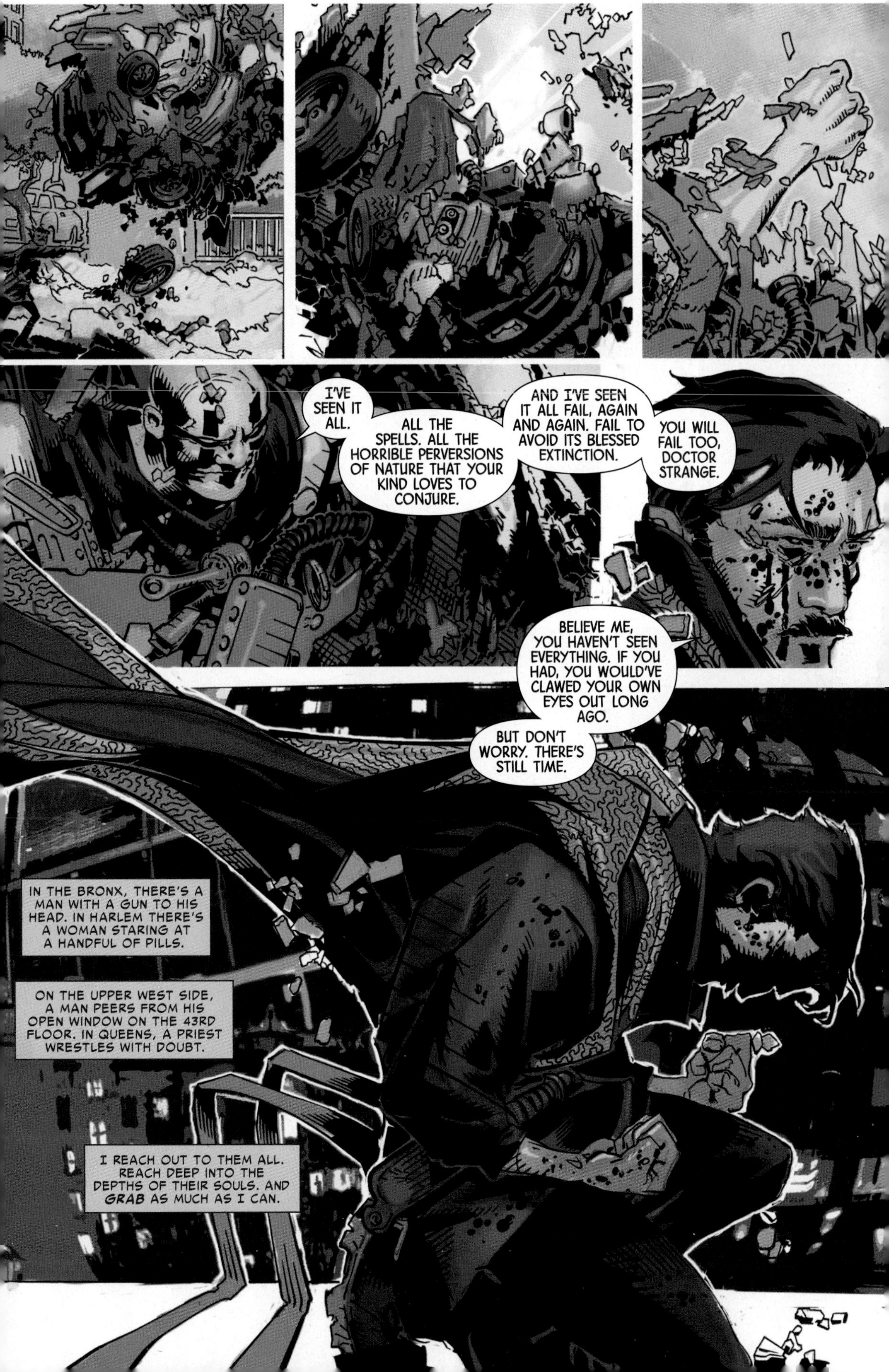
I'VE SEEN IT ALL.
ALL THE SPELLS. ALL THE HORRIBLE PERVERSIONS OF NATURE THAT YOUR KIND LOVES TO CONJURE.
AND I'VE SEEN IT ALL FAIL, AGAIN AND AGAIN. FAIL TO AVOID ITS BLESSED EXTINCTION.
YOU WILL FAIL TOO, DOCTOR STRANGE.
BELIEVE ME, YOU HAVEN'T SEEN EVERYTHING. IF YOU HAD, YOU WOULD'VE CLAWED YOUR OWN EYES OUT LONG AGO.
BUT DON'T WORRY. THERE'S STILL TIME.
IN THE BRONX, THERE'S A MAN WITH A GUN TO HIS HEAD. IN HARLEM THERE'S A WOMAN STARING AT A HANDFUL OF PILLS.
ON THE UPPER WEST SIDE, A MAN PEERS FROM HIS OPEN WINDOW ON THE 43RD FLOOR. IN QUEENS, A PRIEST WRESTLES WITH DOUBT.
I REACH OUT TO THEM ALL. REACH DEEP INTO THE DEPTHS OF THEIR SOULS. AND GRAB AS MUCH AS I CAN.

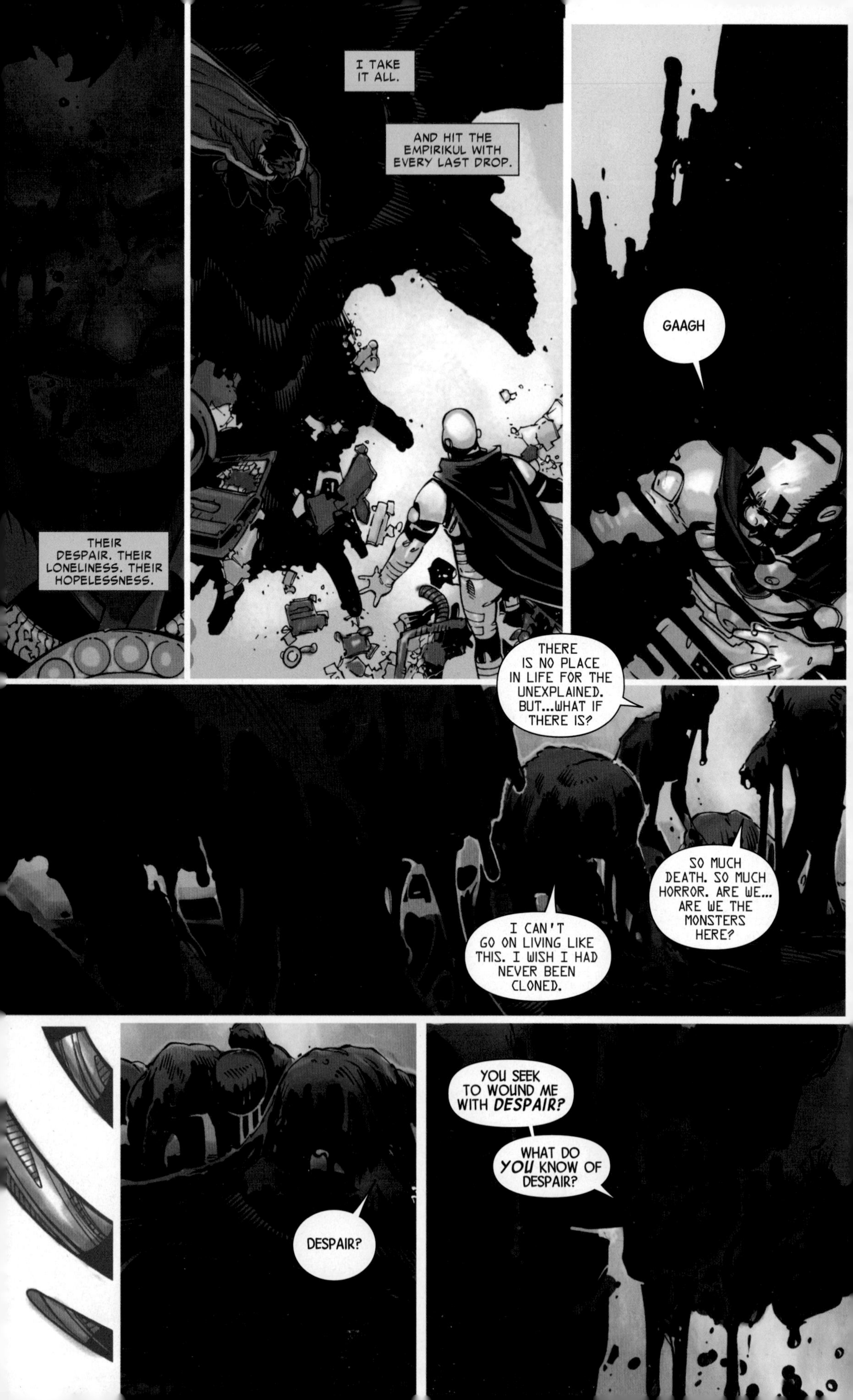
THEIR DESPAIR. THEIR LONELINESS. THEIR HOPELESSNESS.
I TAKE IT ALL.
AND HIT THE EMPIRIKUL WITH EVERY LAST DROP.
GAAGH
THERE IS NO PLACE IN LIFE FOR THE UNEXPLAINED. BUT...WHAT IF THERE IS?
SO MUCH DEATH. SO MUCH HORROR. ARE WE... ARE WE THE MONSTERS HERE?
I CAN'T GO ON LIVING LIKE THIS. I WISH I HAD NEVER BEEN CLONED.
DESPAIR?
YOU SEEK TO WOUND ME WITH *DESPAIR?*
WHAT DO *YOU* KNOW OF DESPAIR?

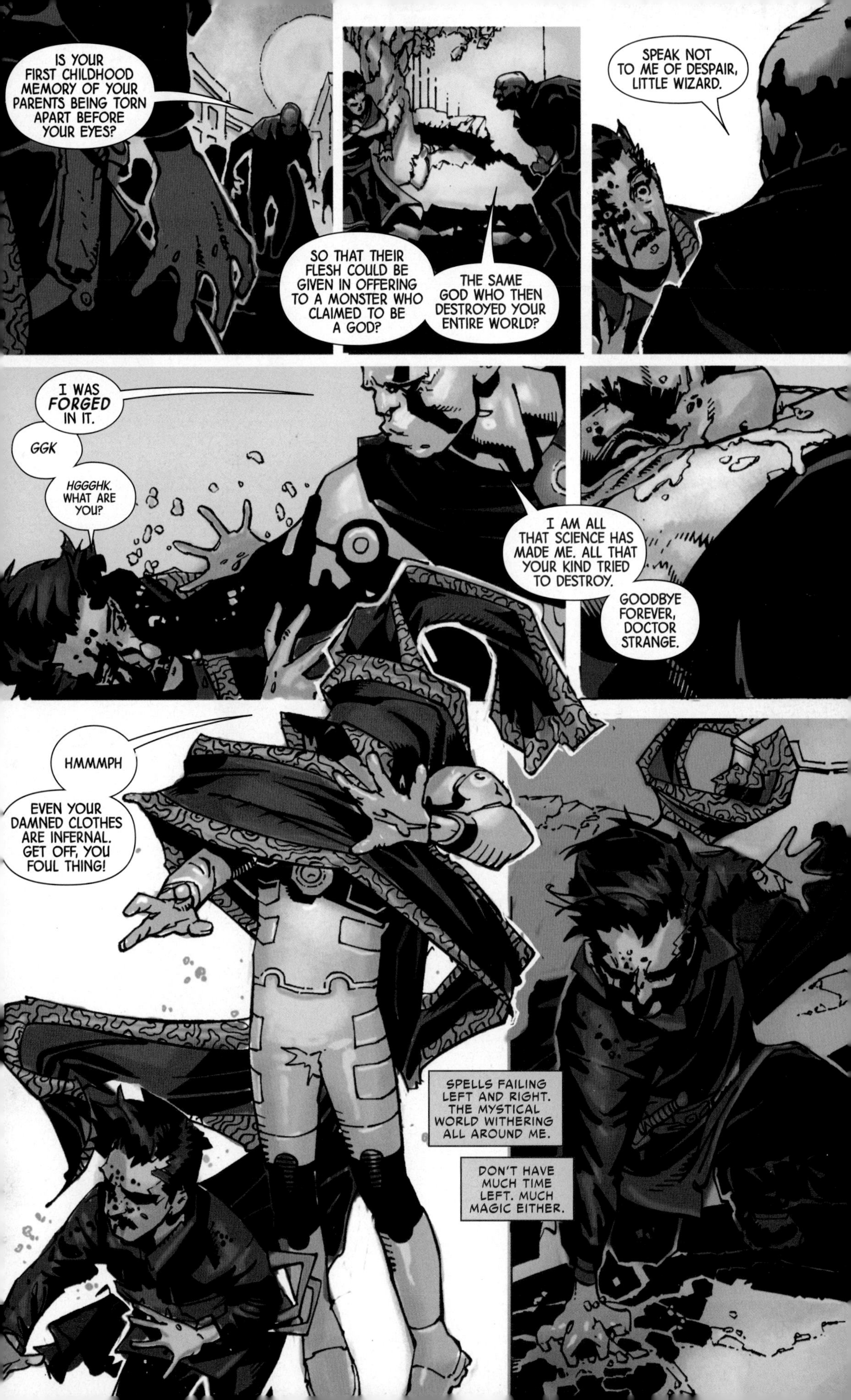
IS YOUR FIRST CHILDHOOD MEMORY OF YOUR PARENTS BEING TORN APART BEFORE YOUR EYES?
SO THAT THEIR FLESH COULD BE GIVEN IN OFFERING TO A MONSTER WHO CLAIMED TO BE A GOD?
THE SAME GOD WHO THEN DESTROYED YOUR ENTIRE WORLD?
SPEAK NOT TO ME OF DESPAIR, LITTLE WIZARD.
I WAS *FORGED* IN IT.
GGK
HGGGHK. WHAT ARE YOU?
I AM ALL THAT SCIENCE HAS MADE ME. ALL THAT YOUR KIND TRIED TO DESTROY.
GOODBYE FOREVER, DOCTOR STRANGE.
HMMMPH
EVEN YOUR DAMNED CLOTHES ARE INFERNAL. GET OFF, YOU FOUL THING!
SPELLS FAILING LEFT AND RIGHT. THE MYSTICAL WORLD WITHERING ALL AROUND ME.
DON'T HAVE MUCH TIME LEFT. MUCH MAGIC EITHER.

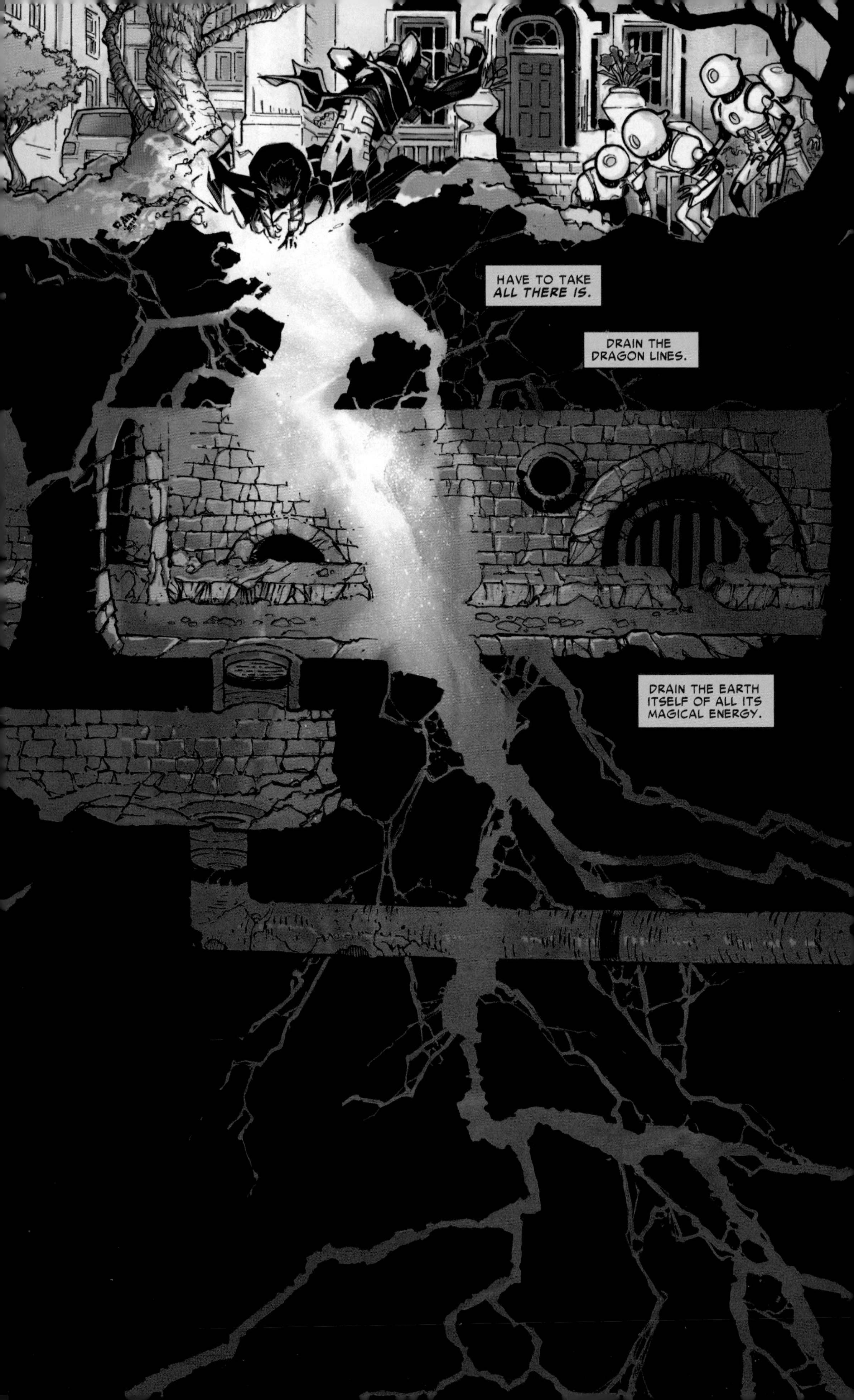
HAVE TO TAKE ALL THERE IS.
DRAIN THE DRAGON LINES.
DRAIN THE EARTH ITSELF OF ALL ITS MAGICAL ENERGY.

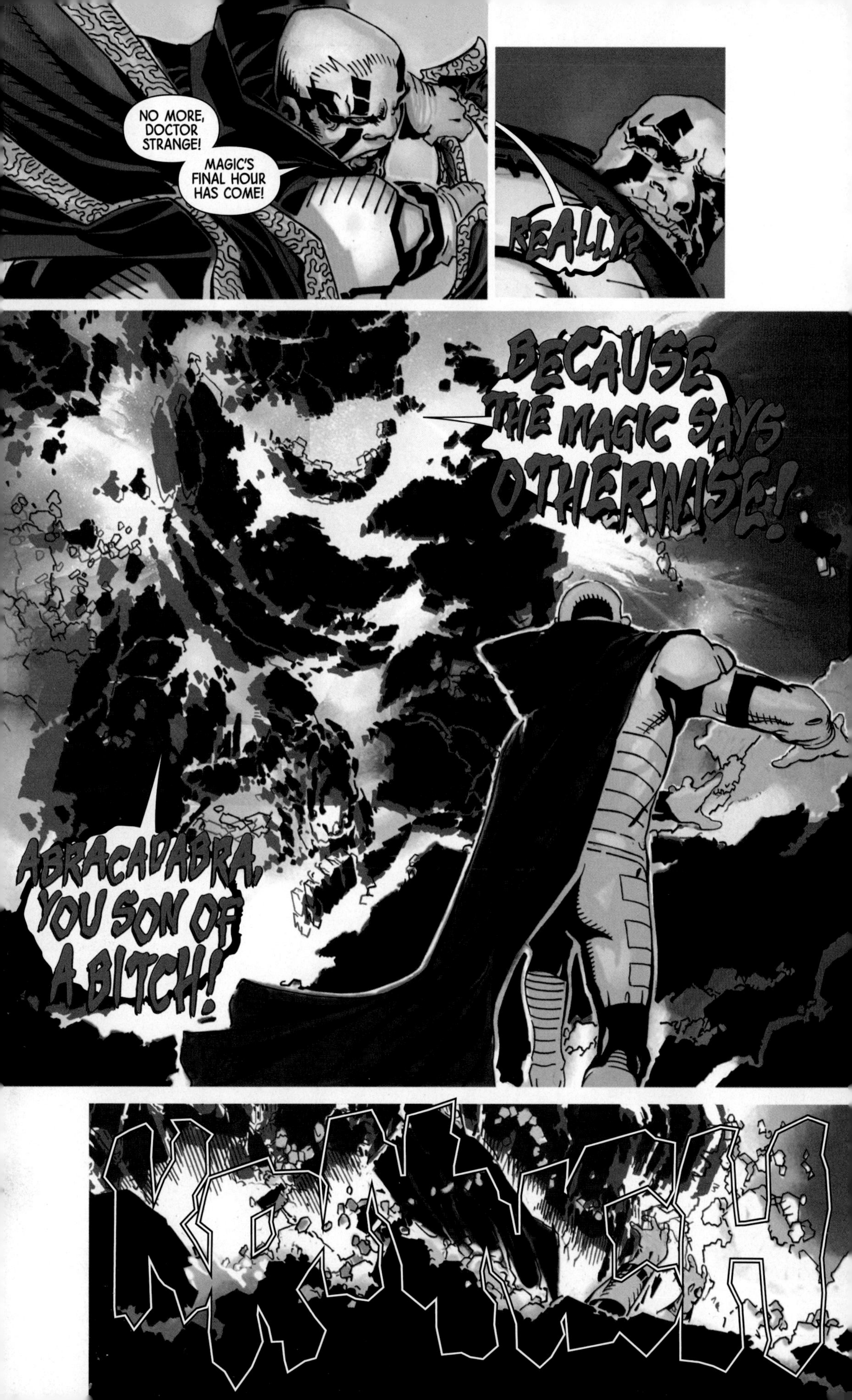
NO MORE, DOCTOR STRANGE!
MAGIC'S FINAL HOUR HAS COME!
REALLY?
BECAUSE THE MAGIC SAYS OTHERWISE!
ABRACADABRA, YOU SON OF A BITCH!

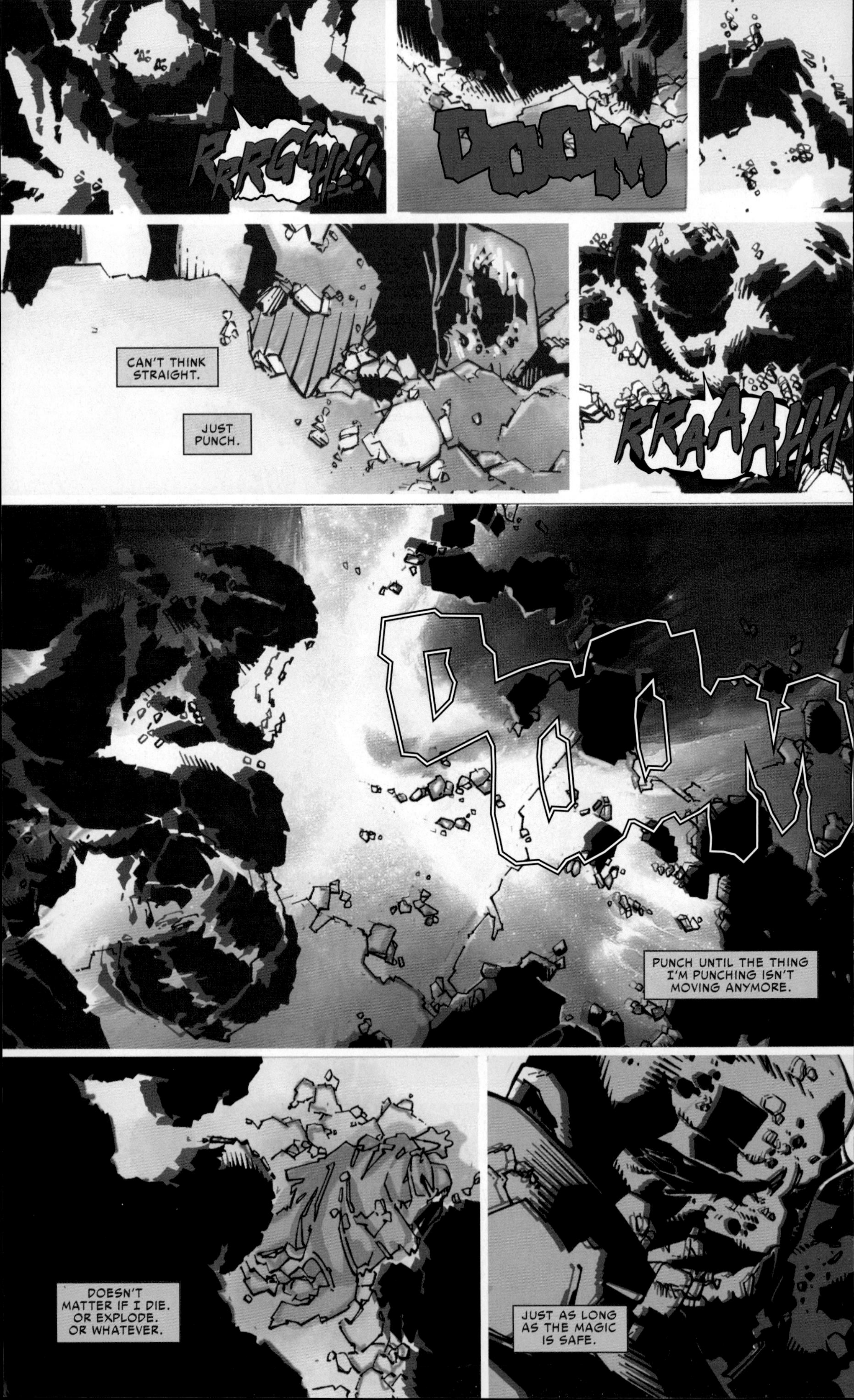
RRRGGH!!!
DOOM
CAN'T THINK STRAIGHT.
JUST PUNCH.
RRAAAHH
DOOM
PUNCH UNTIL THE THING I'M PUNCHING ISN'T MOVING ANYMORE.
DOESN'T MATTER IF I DIE. OR EXPLODE. OR WHATEVER.
JUST AS LONG AS THE MAGIC IS SAFE.

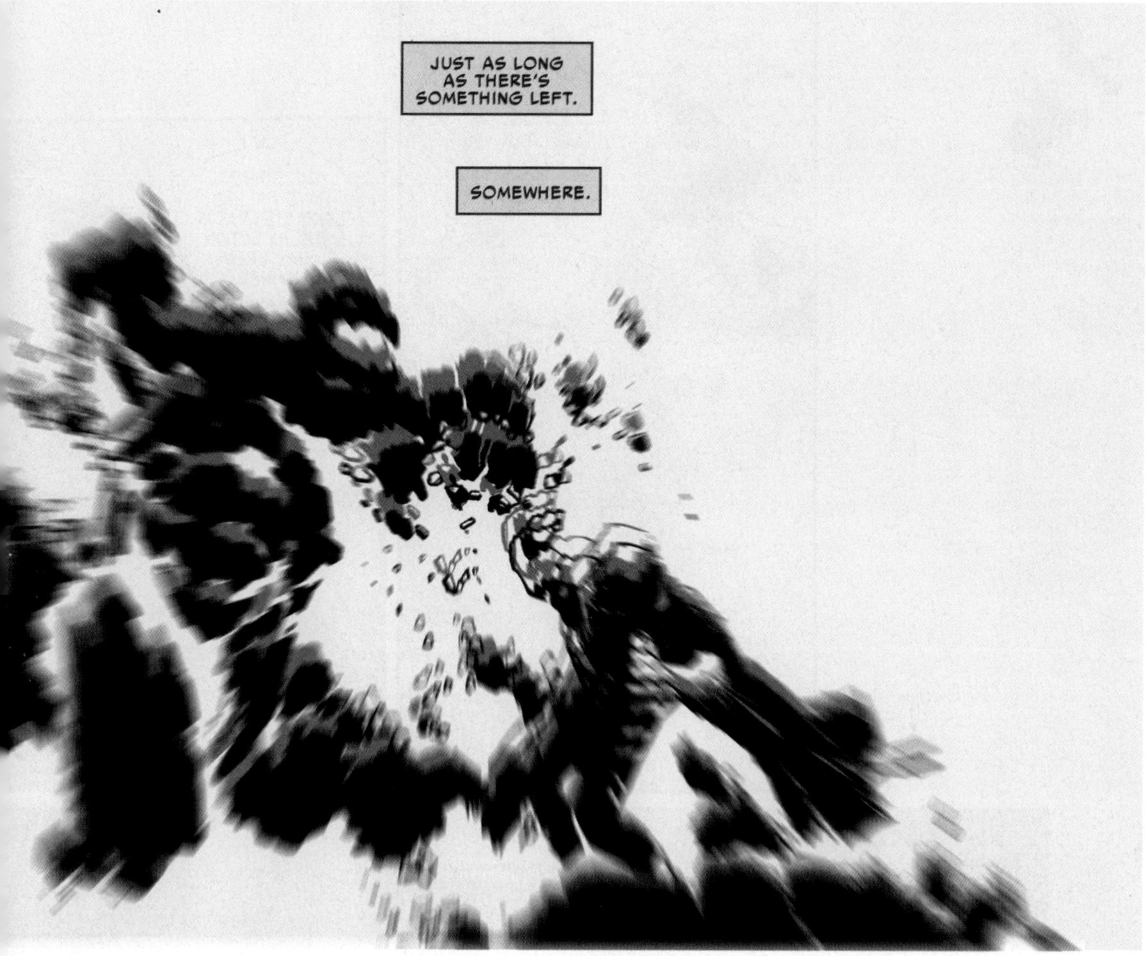
JUST AS LONG AS THERE'S SOMETHING LEFT.
SOMEWHERE.

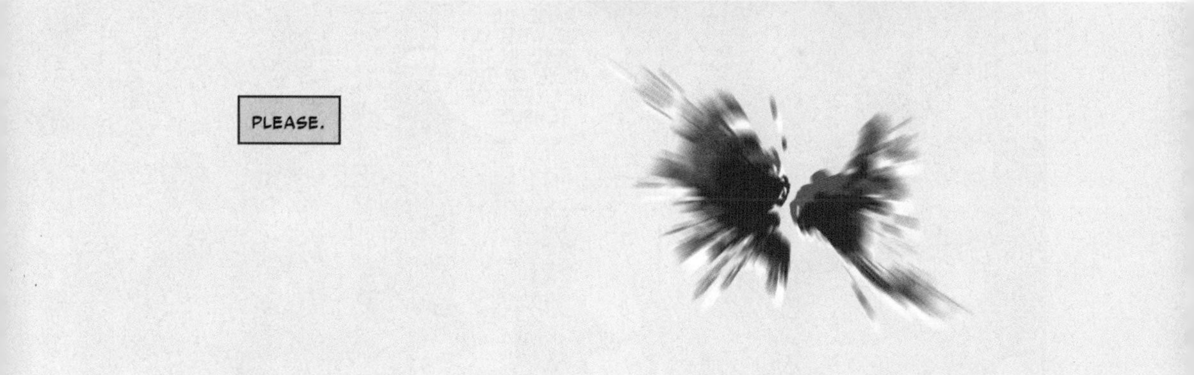
PLEASE.

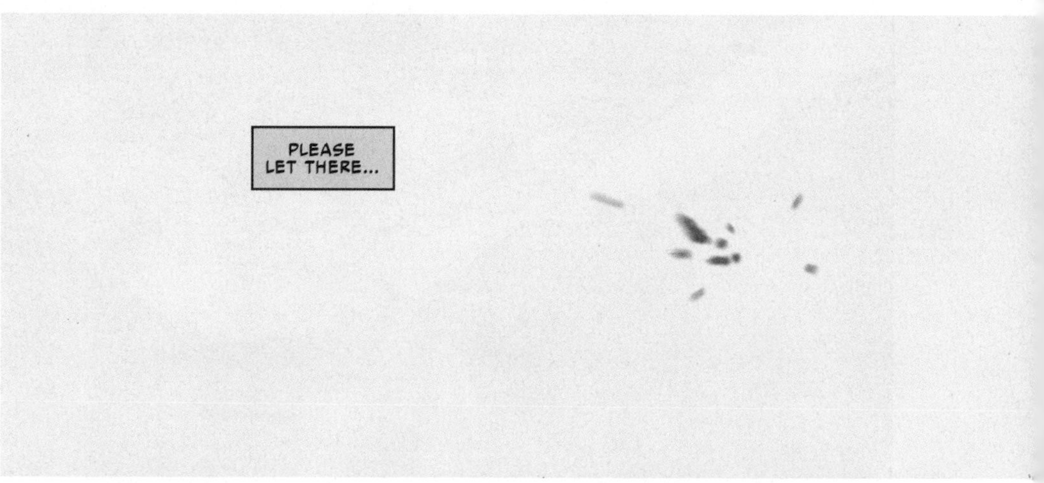
PLEASE LET THERE...

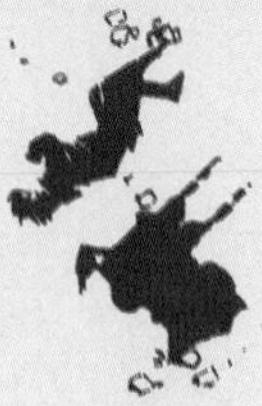

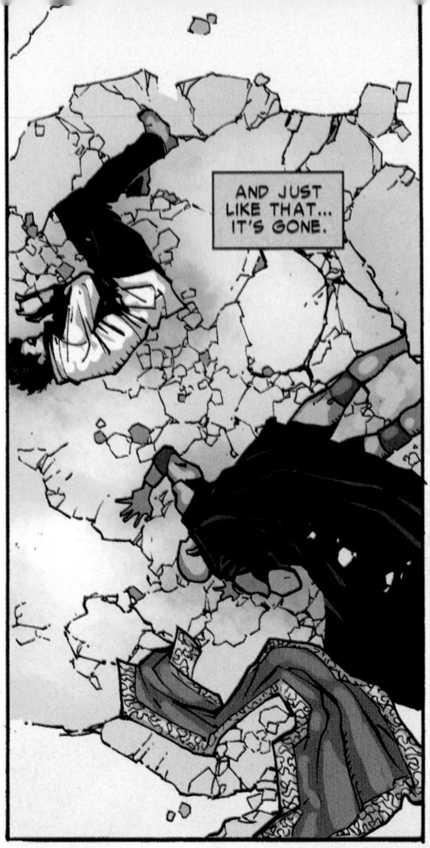
AND JUST LIKE THAT... IT'S GONE.

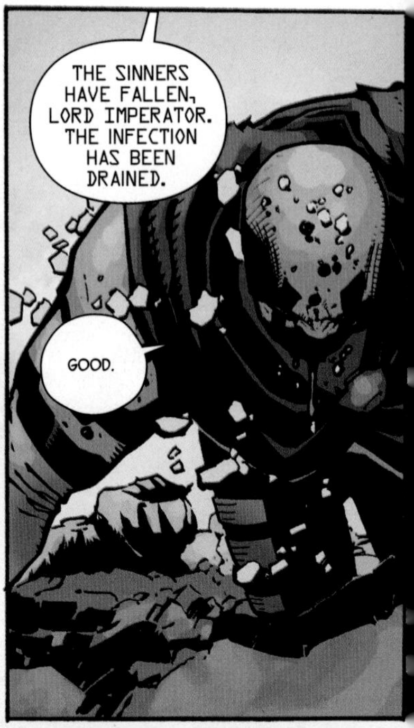
THE SINNERS HAVE FALLEN, LORD IMPERATOR. THE INFECTION HAS BEEN DRAINED.
GOOD.

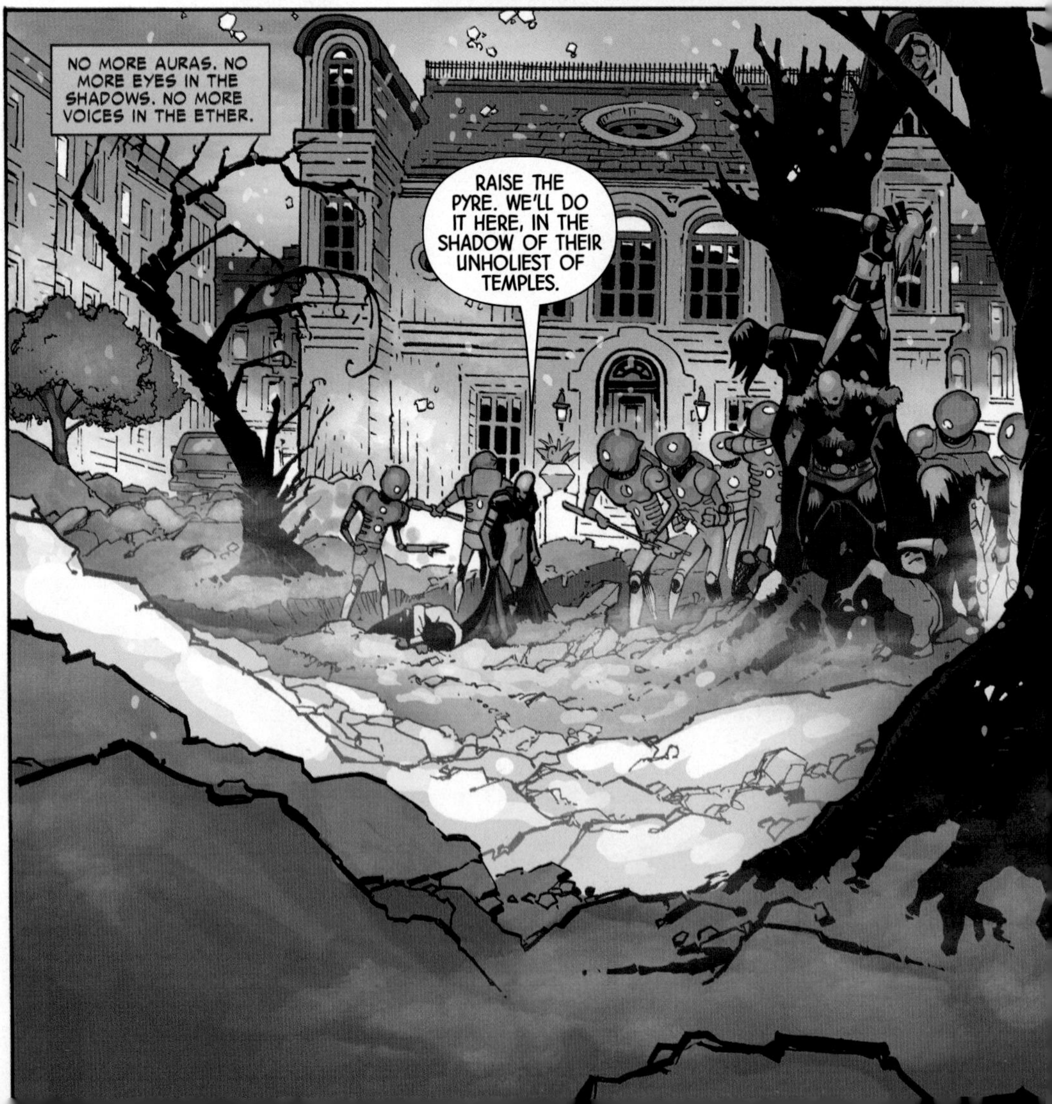
NO MORE AURAS. NO MORE EYES IN THE SHADOWS. NO MORE VOICES IN THE ETHER.
RAISE THE PYRE. WE'LL DO IT HERE, IN THE SHADOW OF THEIR UNHOLIEST OF TEMPLES.

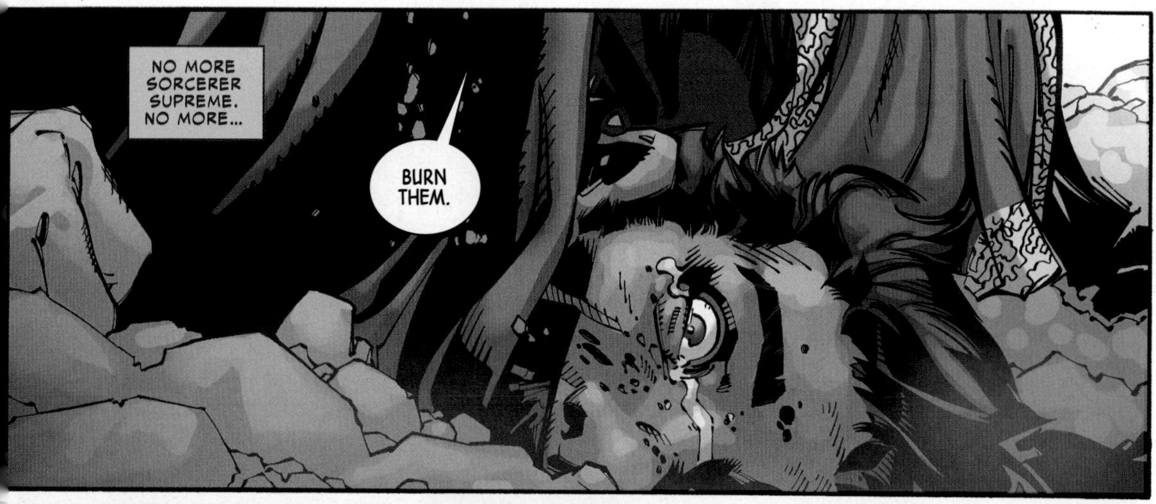
NO MORE SORCERER SUPREME. NO MORE...
BURN THEM.

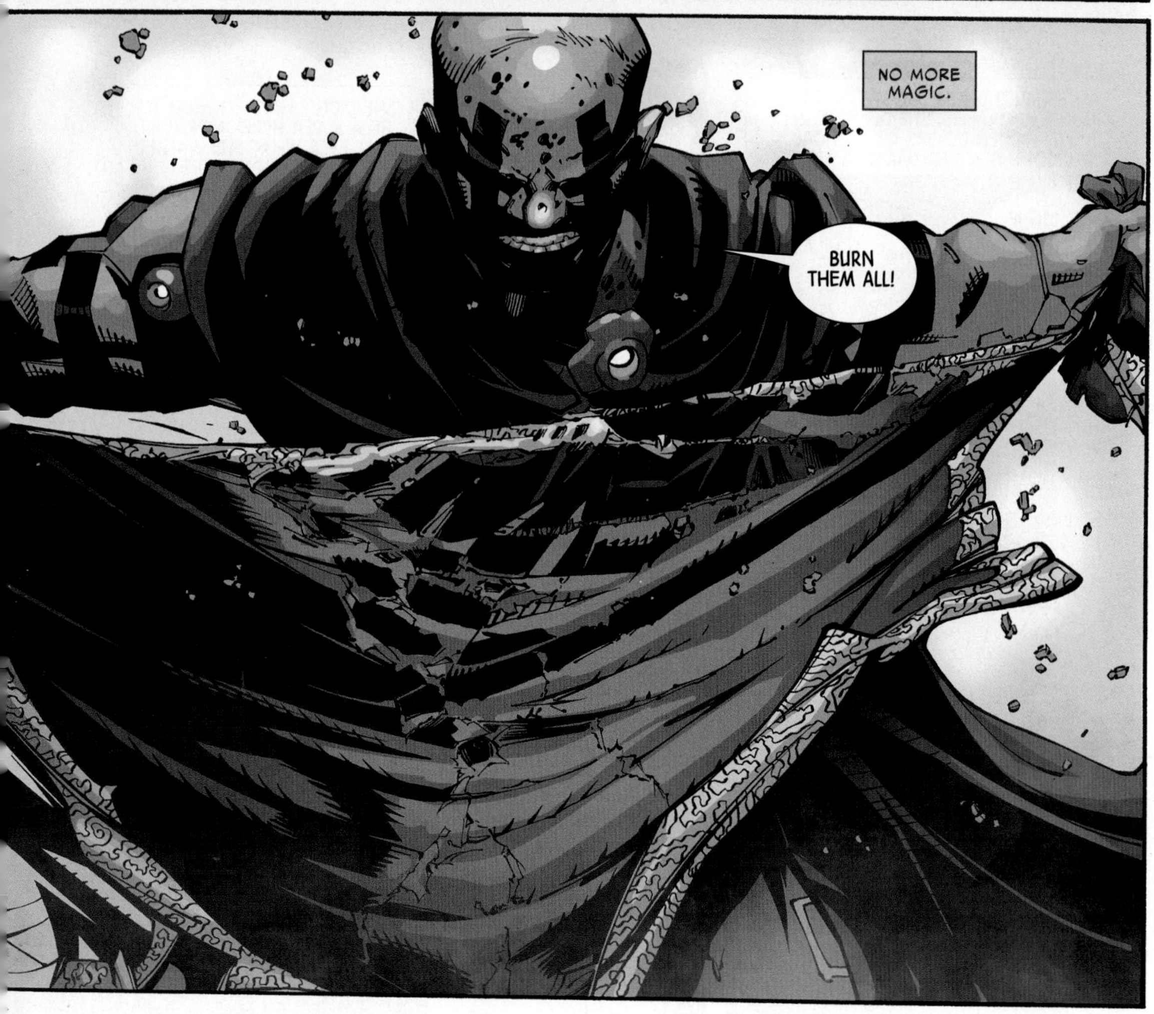
NO MORE MAGIC.
BURN THEM ALL!

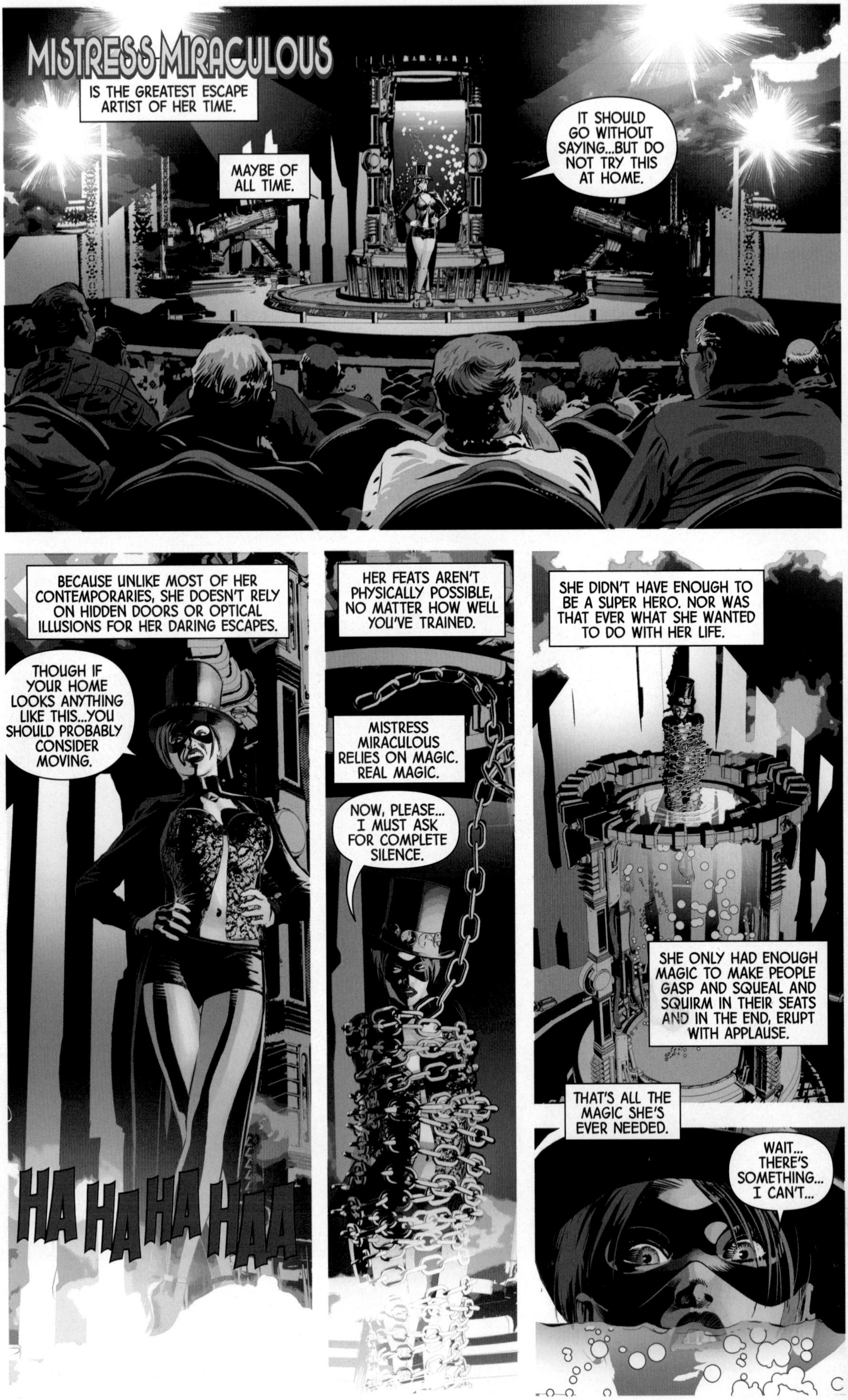
MISTRESS MIRACULOUS
IS THE GREATEST ESCAPE ARTIST OF HER TIME.
MAYBE OF ALL TIME.
IT SHOULD GO WITHOUT SAYING...BUT DO NOT TRY THIS AT HOME.
BECAUSE UNLIKE MOST OF HER CONTEMPORARIES, SHE DOESN'T RELY ON HIDDEN DOORS OR OPTICAL ILLUSIONS FOR HER DARING ESCAPES.
THOUGH IF YOUR HOME LOOKS ANYTHING LIKE THIS...YOU SHOULD PROBABLY CONSIDER MOVING.
HA HA HA HA HAA
HER FEATS AREN'T PHYSICALLY POSSIBLE, NO MATTER HOW WELL YOU'VE TRAINED.
MISTRESS MIRACULOUS RELIES ON MAGIC. REAL MAGIC.
NOW, PLEASE... I MUST ASK FOR COMPLETE SILENCE.
SHE DIDN'T HAVE ENOUGH TO BE A SUPER HERO. NOR WAS THAT EVER WHAT SHE WANTED TO DO WITH HER LIFE.
SHE ONLY HAD ENOUGH MAGIC TO MAKE PEOPLE GASP AND SQUEAL AND SQUIRM IN THEIR SEATS AND IN THE END, ERUPT WITH APPLAUSE.
THAT'S ALL THE MAGIC SHE'S EVER NEEDED.
WAIT... THERE'S SOMETHING... I CAN'T...

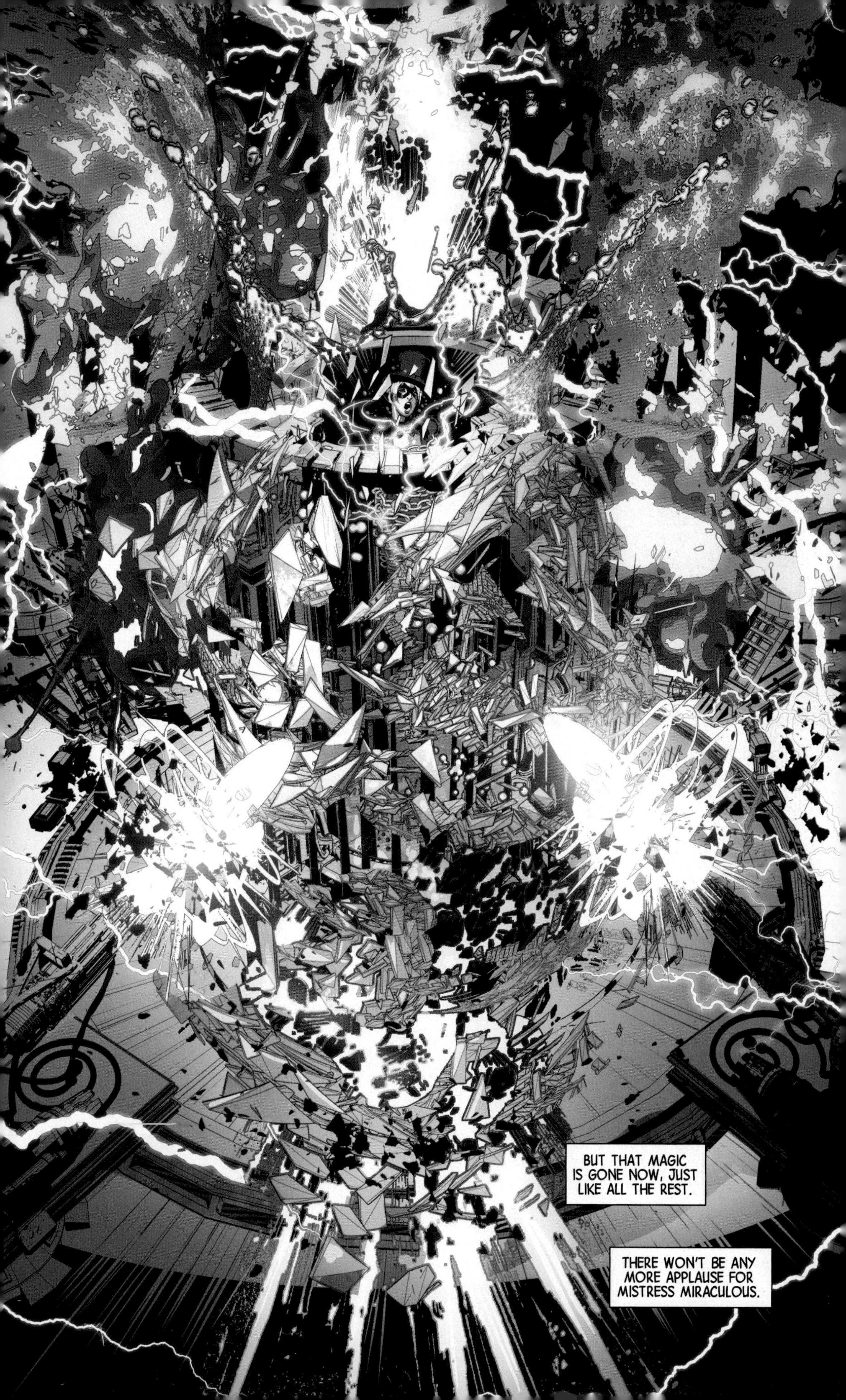
BUT THAT MAGIC IS GONE NOW, JUST LIKE ALL THE REST.
THERE WON'T BE ANY MORE APPLAUSE FOR MISTRESS MIRACULOUS.

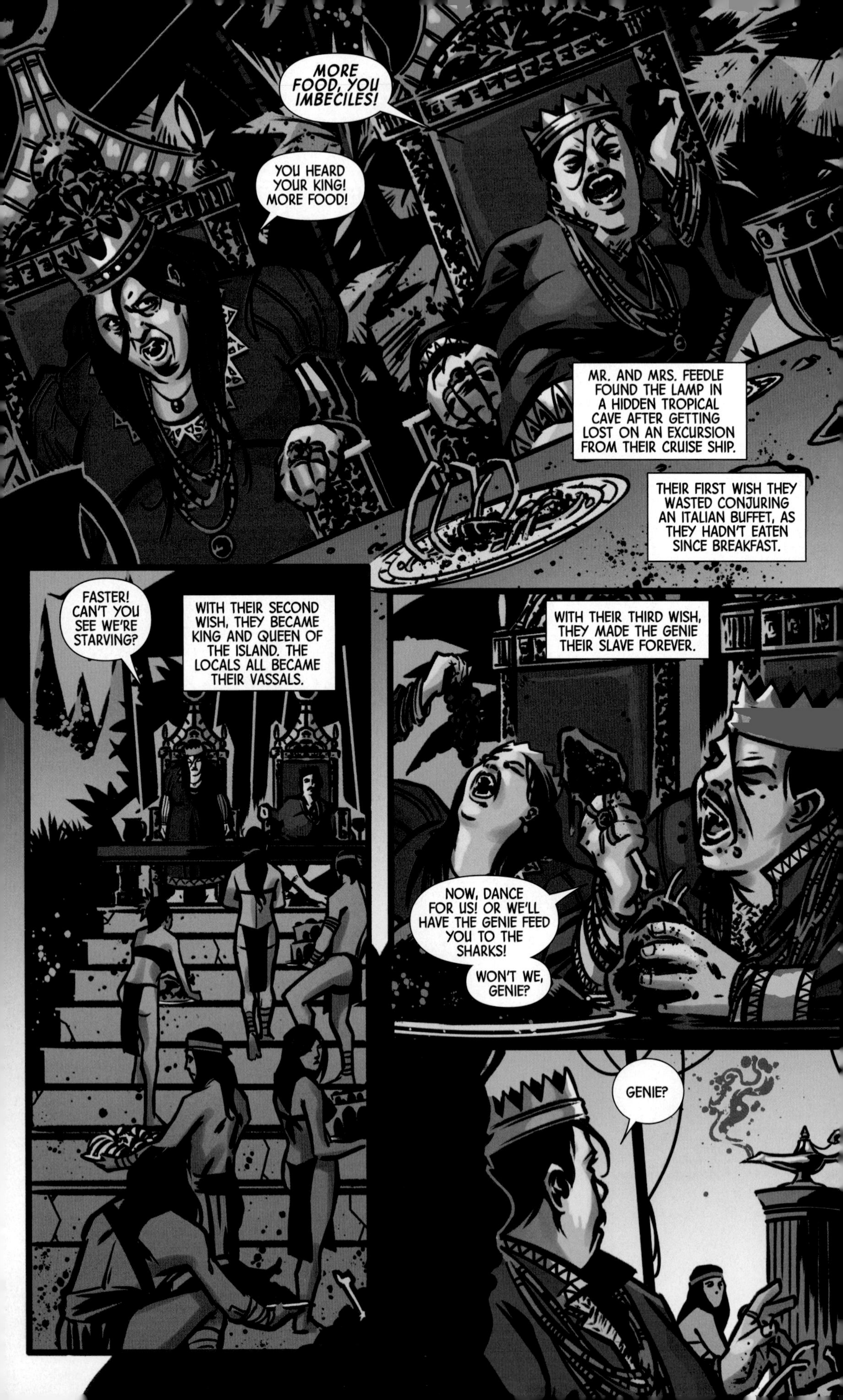
MORE FOOD, YOU IMBECILES!
YOU HEARD YOUR KING! MORE FOOD!
MR. AND MRS. FEEDLE FOUND THE LAMP IN A HIDDEN TROPICAL CAVE AFTER GETTING LOST ON AN EXCURSION FROM THEIR CRUISE SHIP.
THEIR FIRST WISH THEY WASTED CONJURING AN ITALIAN BUFFET, AS THEY HADN'T EATEN SINCE BREAKFAST.
FASTER! CAN'T YOU SEE WE'RE STARVING?
WITH THEIR SECOND WISH, THEY BECAME KING AND QUEEN OF THE ISLAND. THE LOCALS ALL BECAME THEIR VASSALS.
WITH THEIR THIRD WISH, THEY MADE THE GENIE THEIR SLAVE FOREVER.
NOW, DANCE FOR US! OR WE'LL HAVE THE GENIE FEED YOU TO THE SHARKS!
WON'T WE, GENIE?
GENIE?

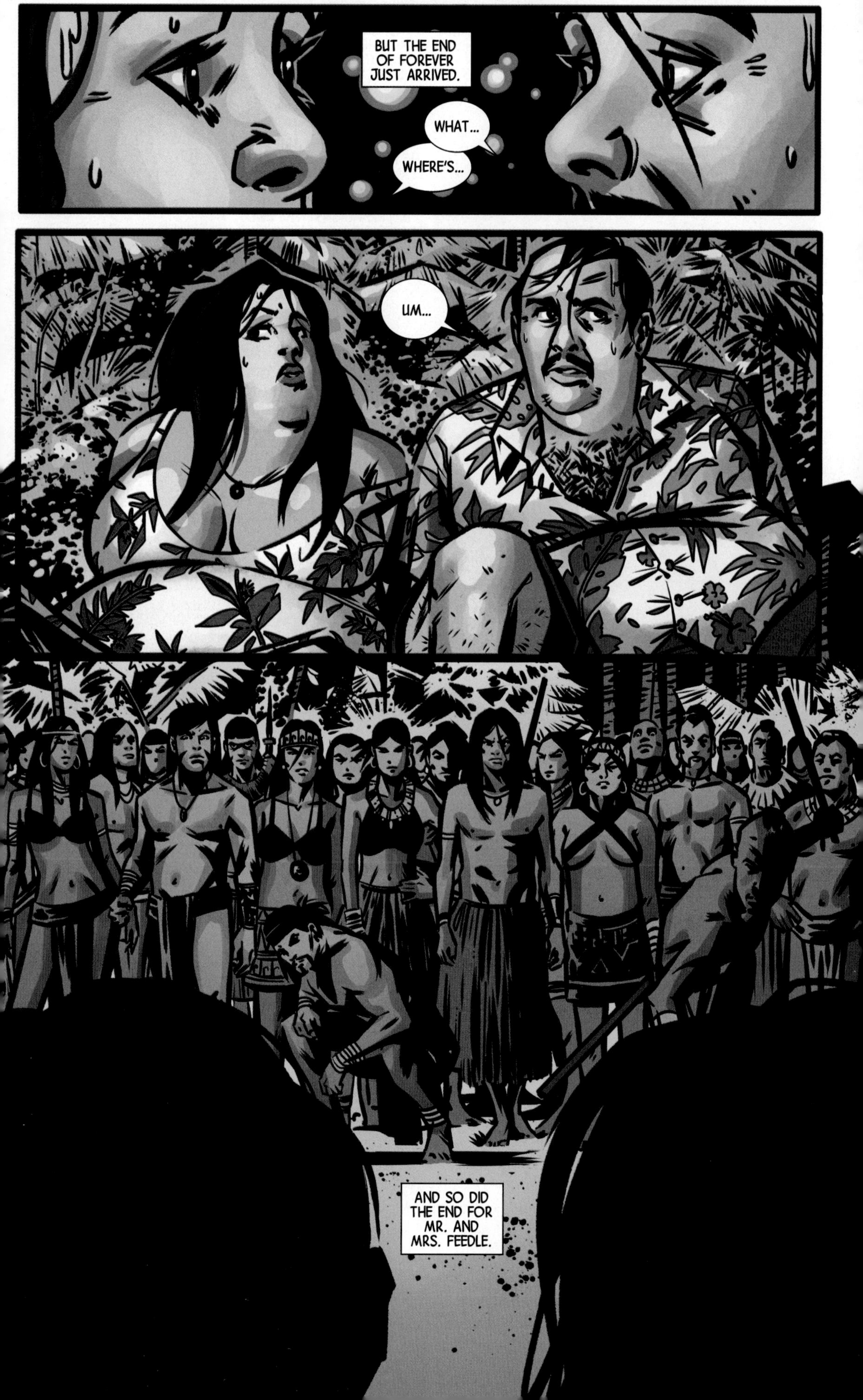
BUT THE END OF FOREVER JUST ARRIVED.
WHAT...
WHERE'S...
UM...
AND SO DID THE END FOR MR. AND MRS. FEEDLE.

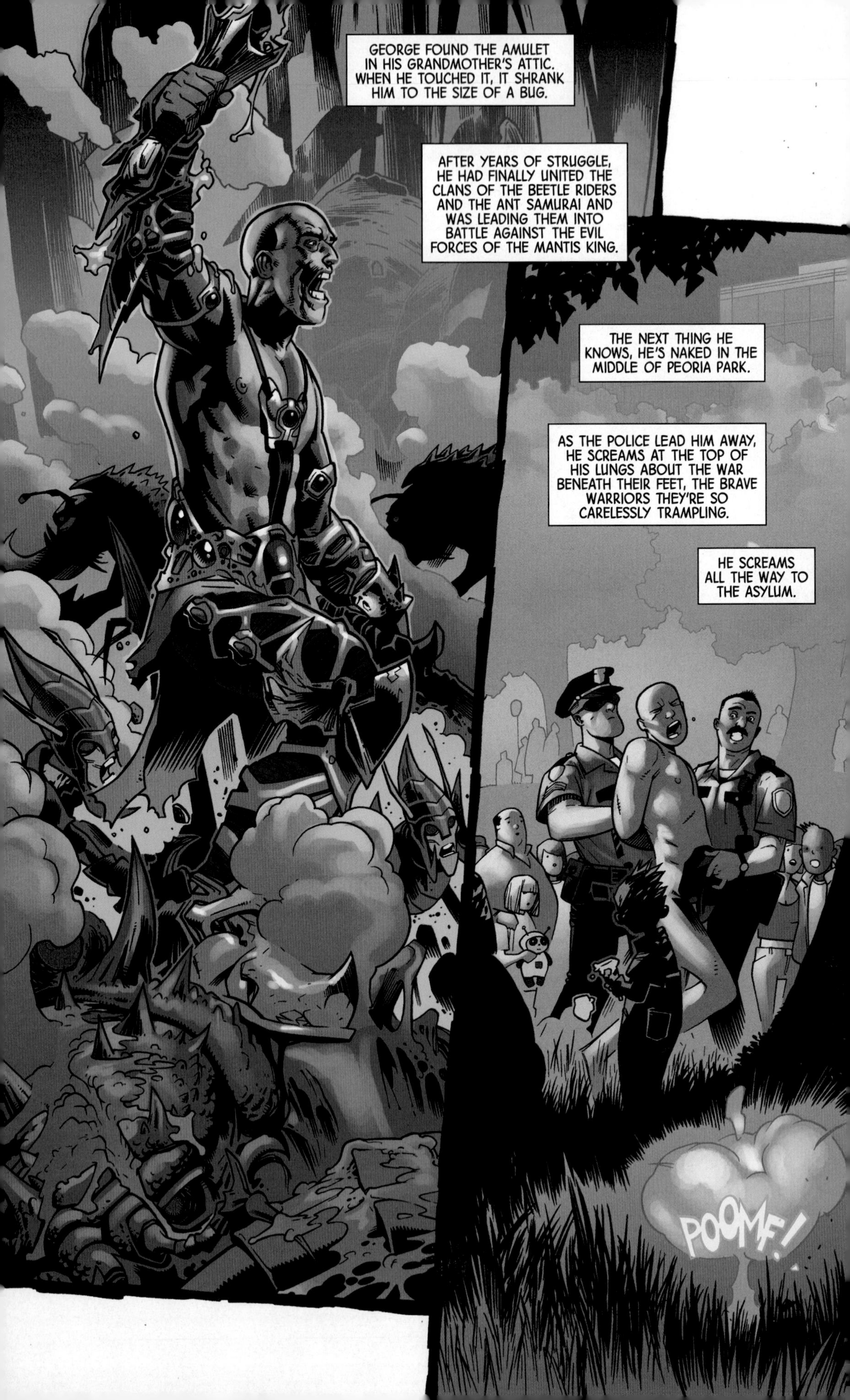
GEORGE FOUND THE AMULET IN HIS GRANDMOTHER'S ATTIC. WHEN HE TOUCHED IT, IT SHRANK HIM TO THE SIZE OF A BUG.
AFTER YEARS OF STRUGGLE, HE HAD FINALLY UNITED THE CLANS OF THE BEETLE RIDERS AND THE ANT SAMURAI AND WAS LEADING THEM INTO BATTLE AGAINST THE EVIL FORCES OF THE MANTIS KING.
THE NEXT THING HE KNOWS, HE'S NAKED IN THE MIDDLE OF PEORIA PARK.
AS THE POLICE LEAD HIM AWAY, HE SCREAMS AT THE TOP OF HIS LUNGS ABOUT THE WAR BENEATH THEIR FEET, THE BRAVE WARRIORS THEY'RE SO CARELESSLY TRAMPLING.
HE SCREAMS ALL THE WAY TO THE ASYLUM.
POOMF!

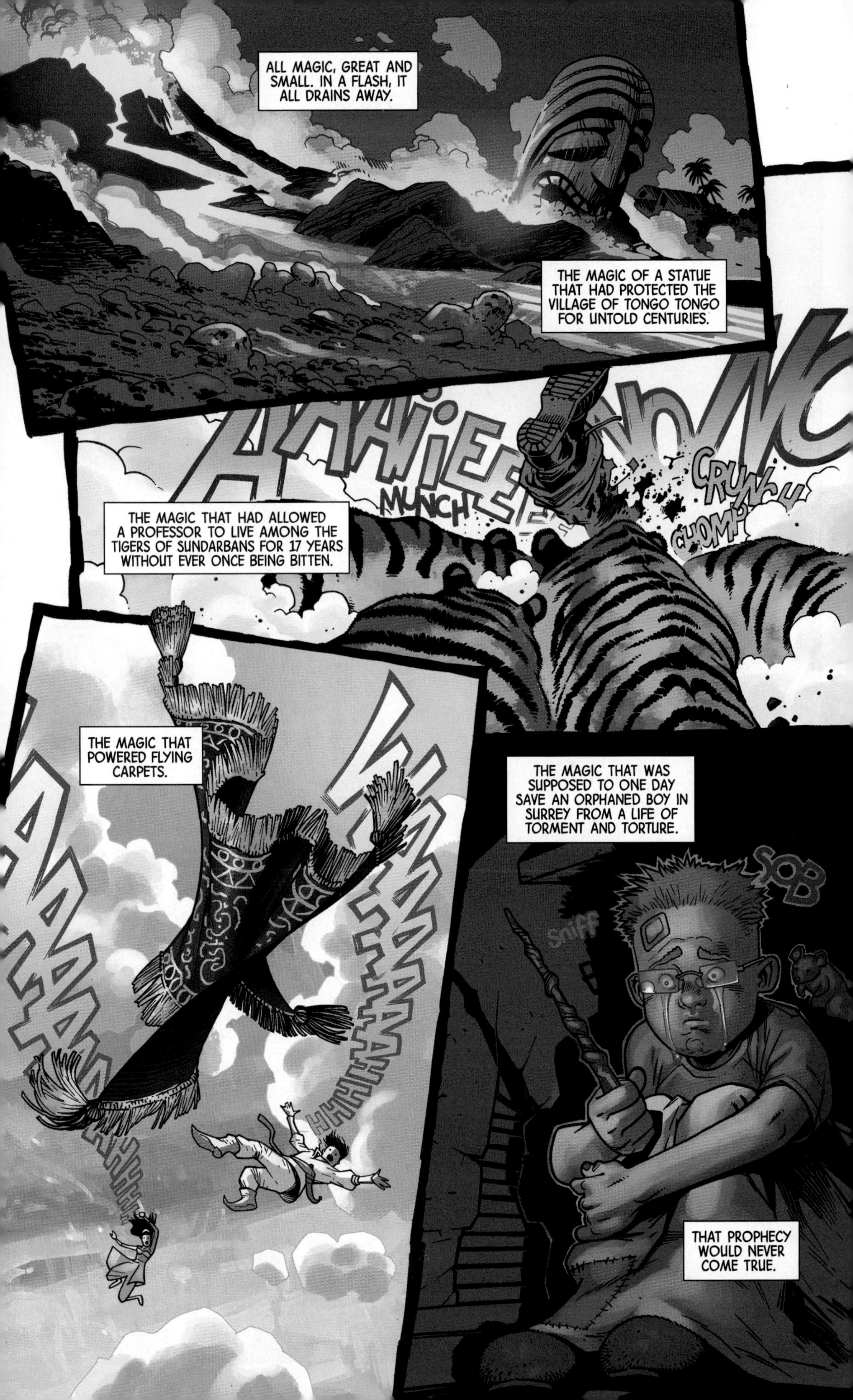
ALL MAGIC, GREAT AND SMALL. IN A FLASH, IT ALL DRAINS AWAY.
THE MAGIC OF A STATUE THAT HAD PROTECTED THE VILLAGE OF TONGO TONGO FOR UNTOLD CENTURIES.
THE MAGIC THAT HAD ALLOWED A PROFESSOR TO LIVE AMONG THE TIGERS OF SUNDARBANS FOR 17 YEARS WITHOUT EVER ONCE BEING BITTEN.
MUNCH
CRUNCH
CHOMP
THE MAGIC THAT POWERED FLYING CARPETS.
THE MAGIC THAT WAS SUPPOSED TO ONE DAY SAVE AN ORPHANED BOY IN SURREY FROM A LIFE OF TORMENT AND TORTURE.
SOB
Sniff
THAT PROPHECY WOULD NEVER COME TRUE.

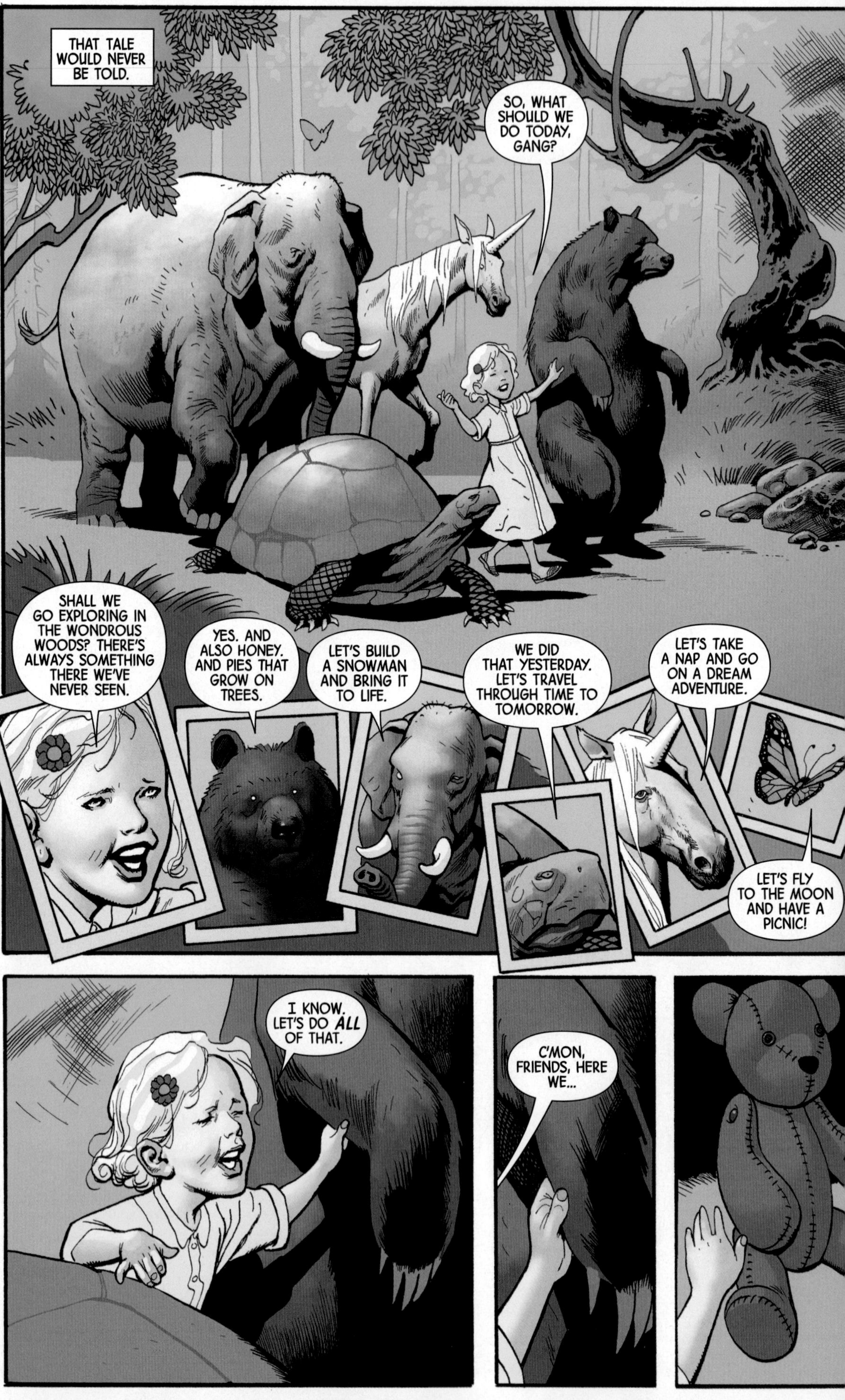

THAT TALE WOULD NEVER BE TOLD.
SO, WHAT SHOULD WE DO TODAY, GANG?
SHALL WE GO EXPLORING IN THE WONDROUS WOODS? THERE'S ALWAYS SOMETHING THERE WE'VE NEVER SEEN.
YES. AND ALSO HONEY. AND PIES THAT GROW ON TREES.
LET'S BUILD A SNOWMAN AND BRING IT TO LIFE.
WE DID THAT YESTERDAY. LET'S TRAVEL THROUGH TIME TO TOMORROW.
LET'S TAKE A NAP AND GO ON A DREAM ADVENTURE.
LET'S FLY TO THE MOON AND HAVE A PICNIC!
I KNOW. LET'S DO ALL OF THAT.
C'MON, FRIENDS, HERE WE...

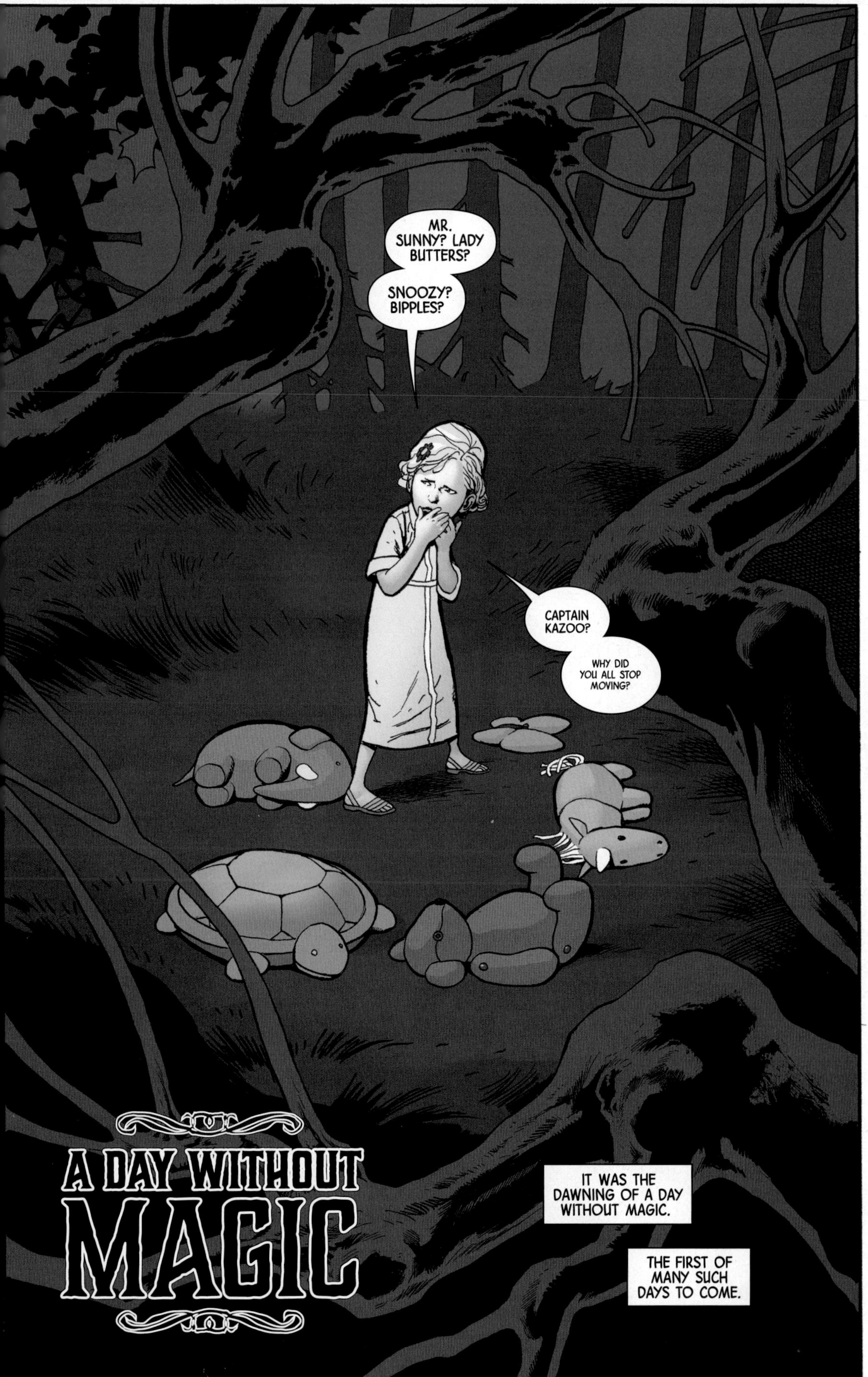
MR. SUNNY? LADY BUTTERS?
SNOOZY? BIPPLES?
CAPTAIN KAZOO?
WHY DID YOU ALL STOP MOVING?
A DAY WITHOUT MAGIC
IT WAS THE DAWNING OF A DAY WITHOUT MAGIC.
THE FIRST OF MANY SUCH DAYS TO COME.

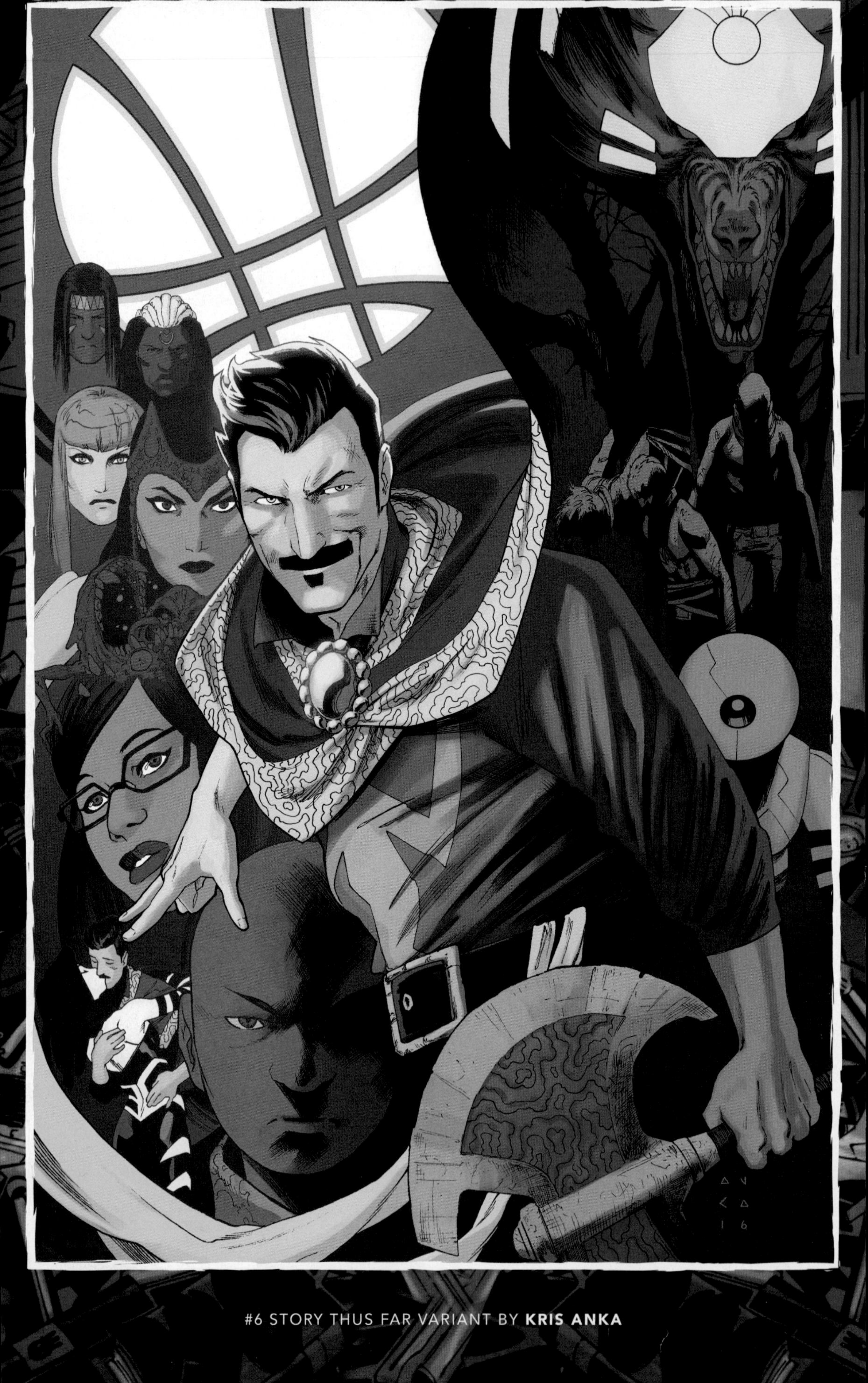

#6 STORY THUS FAR VARIANT BY **KRIS ANKA**

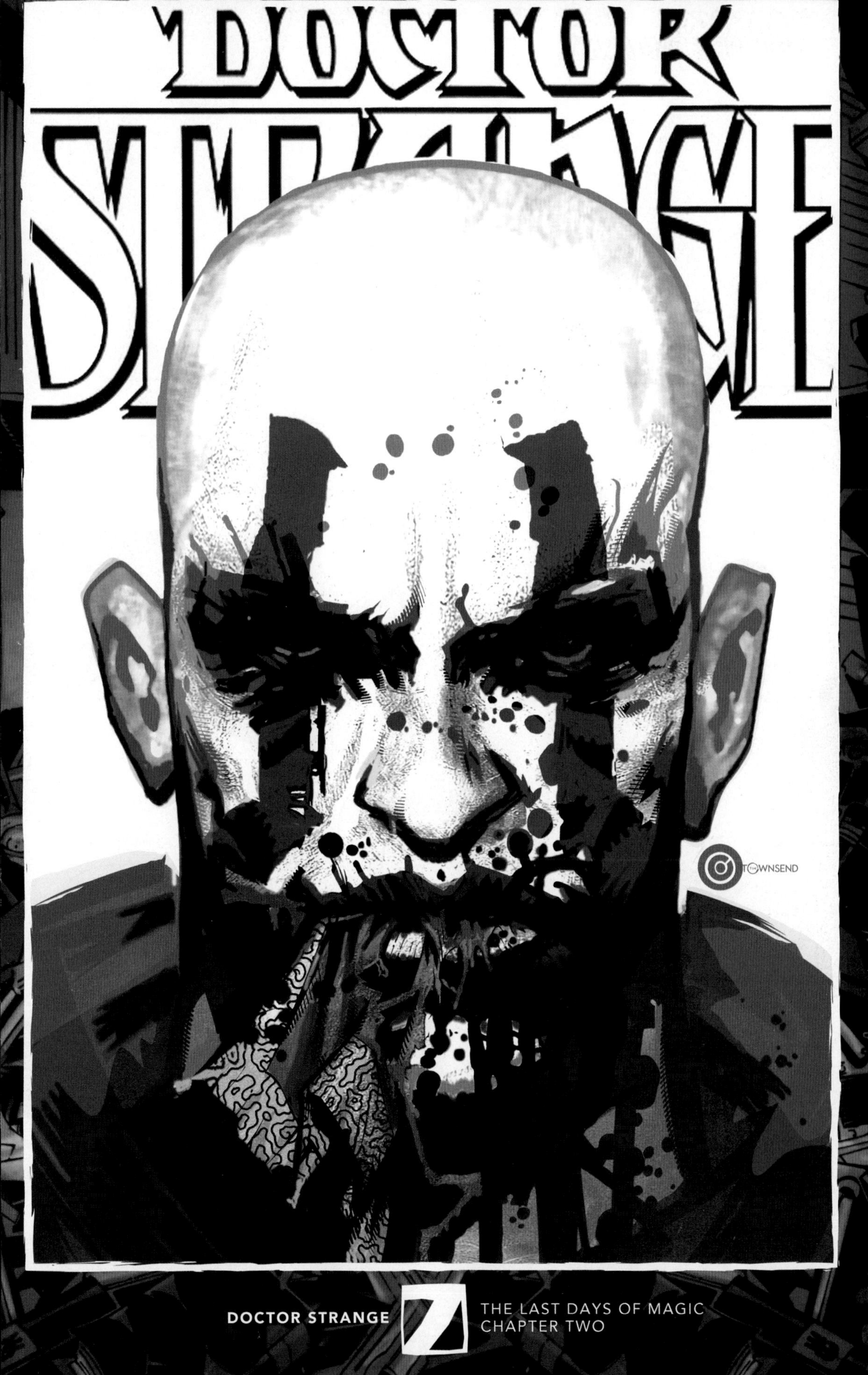
DOCTOR STRANGE
TOWNSEND
DOCTOR STRANGE
7
THE LAST DAYS OF MAGIC
CHAPTER TWO

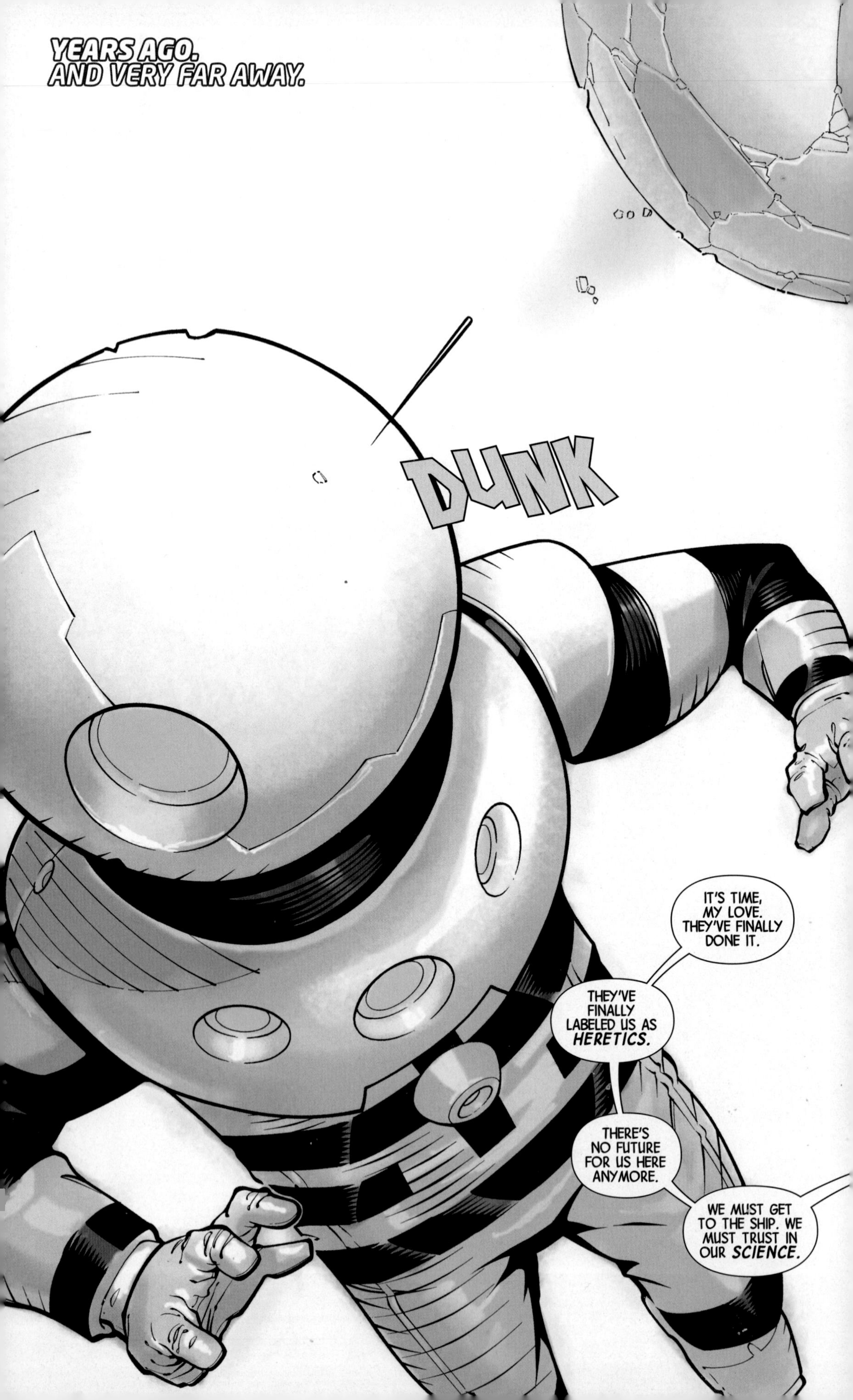
YEARS AGO.
AND VERY FAR AWAY.
DUNK
IT'S TIME, MY LOVE. THEY'VE FINALLY DONE IT.
THEY'VE FINALLY LABELED US AS *HERETICS.*
THERE'S NO FUTURE FOR US HERE ANYMORE.
WE MUST GET TO THE SHIP. WE MUST TRUST IN OUR *SCIENCE.*

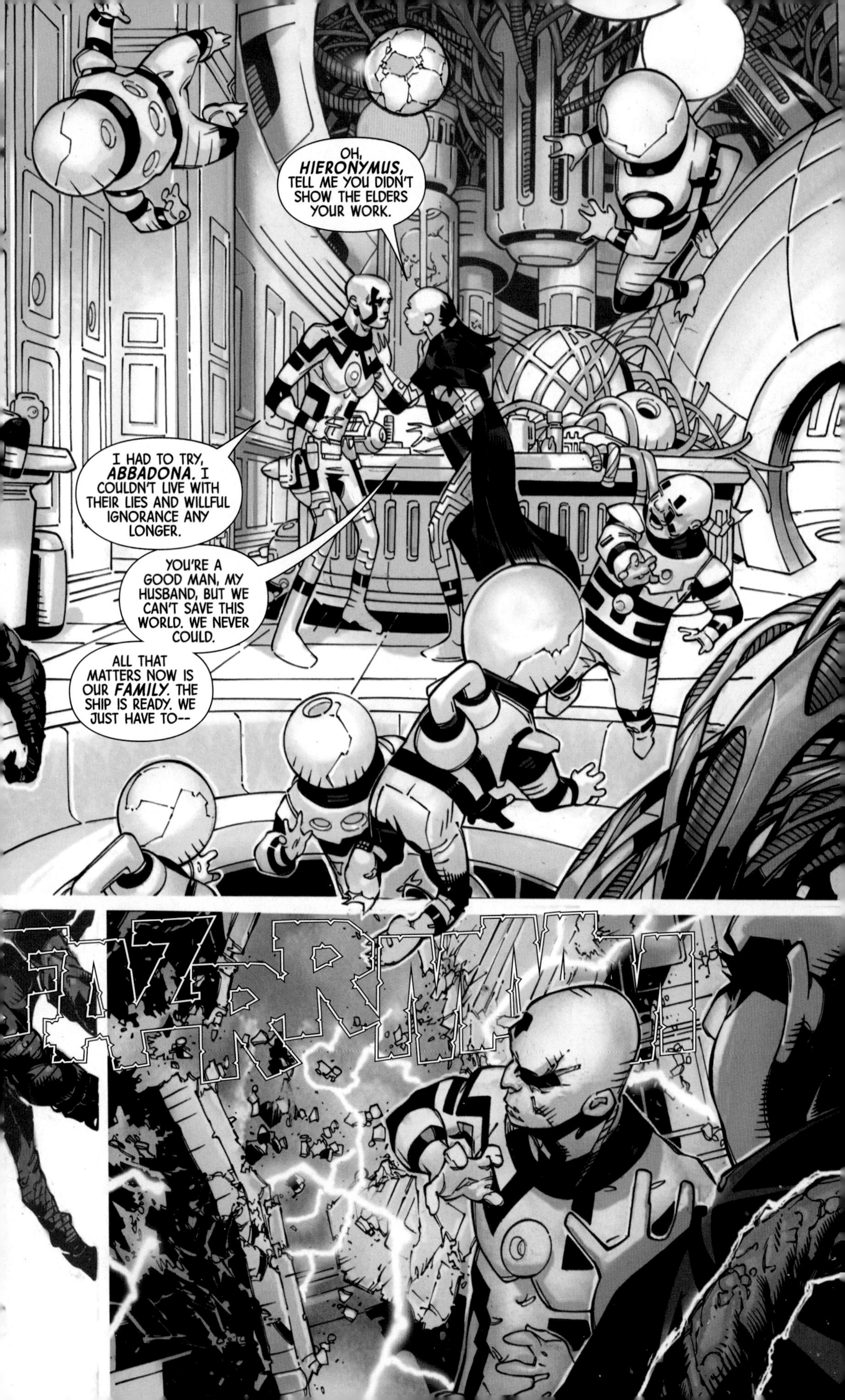
OH, HIERONYMUS, TELL ME YOU DIDN'T SHOW THE ELDERS YOUR WORK.
I HAD TO TRY, ABBADONA. I COULDN'T LIVE WITH THEIR LIES AND WILLFUL IGNORANCE ANY LONGER.
YOU'RE A GOOD MAN, MY HUSBAND, BUT WE CAN'T SAVE THIS WORLD. WE NEVER COULD.
ALL THAT MATTERS NOW IS OUR FAMILY. THE SHIP IS READY. WE JUST HAVE TO--

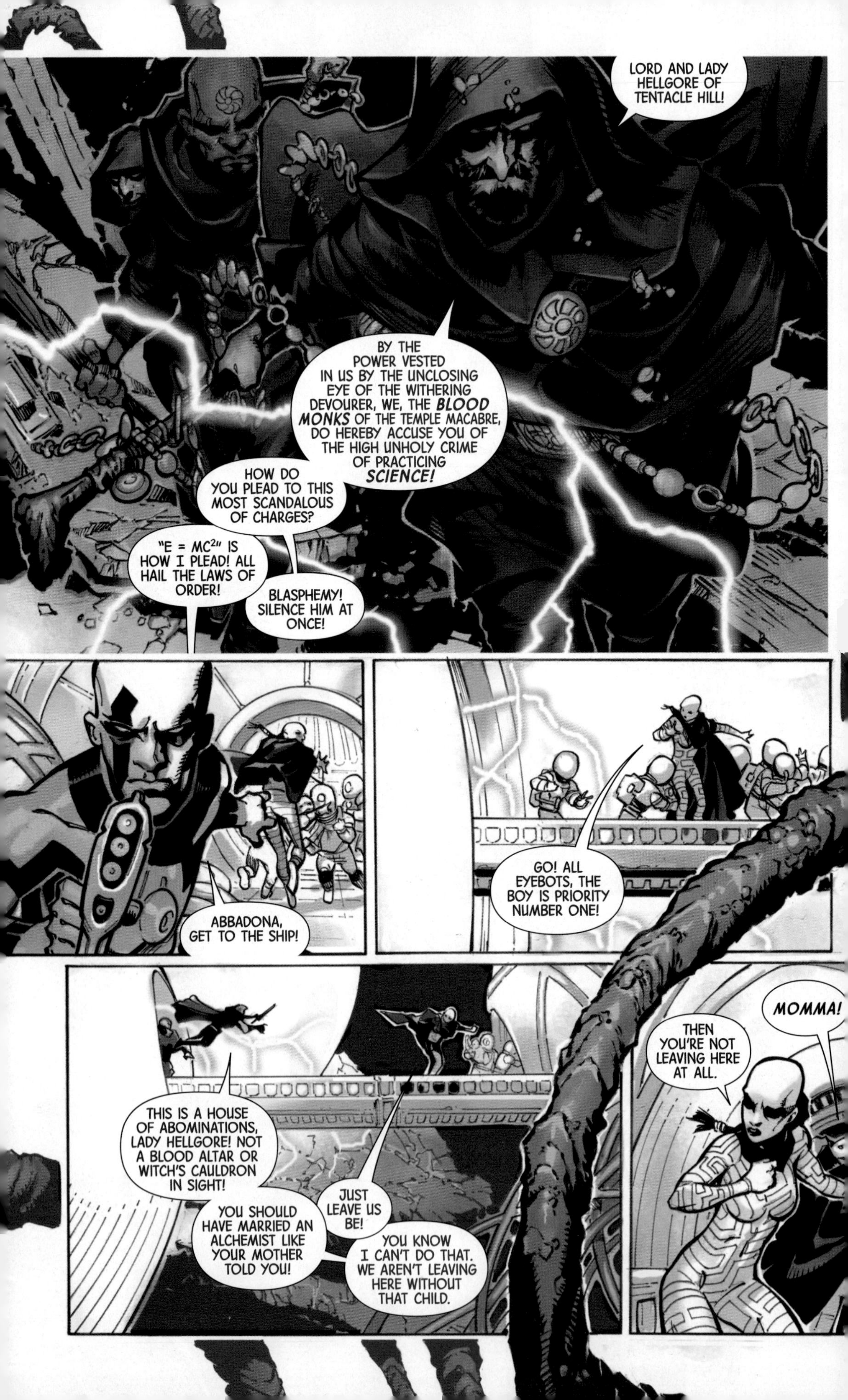
LORD AND LADY HELLGORE OF TENTACLE HILL!
BY THE POWER VESTED IN US BY THE UNCLOSING EYE OF THE WITHERING DEVOURER, WE, THE BLOOD MONKS OF THE TEMPLE MACABRE, DO HEREBY ACCUSE YOU OF THE HIGH UNHOLY CRIME OF PRACTICING SCIENCE!
HOW DO YOU PLEAD TO THIS MOST SCANDALOUS OF CHARGES?
"E = MC²" IS HOW I PLEAD! ALL HAIL THE LAWS OF ORDER!
BLASPHEMY! SILENCE HIM AT ONCE!
ABBADONA, GET TO THE SHIP!
GO! ALL EYEBOTS, THE BOY IS PRIORITY NUMBER ONE!
THIS IS A HOUSE OF ABOMINATIONS, LADY HELLGORE! NOT A BLOOD ALTAR OR WITCH'S CAULDRON IN SIGHT!
YOU SHOULD HAVE MARRIED AN ALCHEMIST LIKE YOUR MOTHER TOLD YOU!
JUST LEAVE US BE!
YOU KNOW I CAN'T DO THAT. WE AREN'T LEAVING HERE WITHOUT THAT CHILD.
THEN YOU'RE NOT LEAVING HERE AT ALL.
MOMMA!

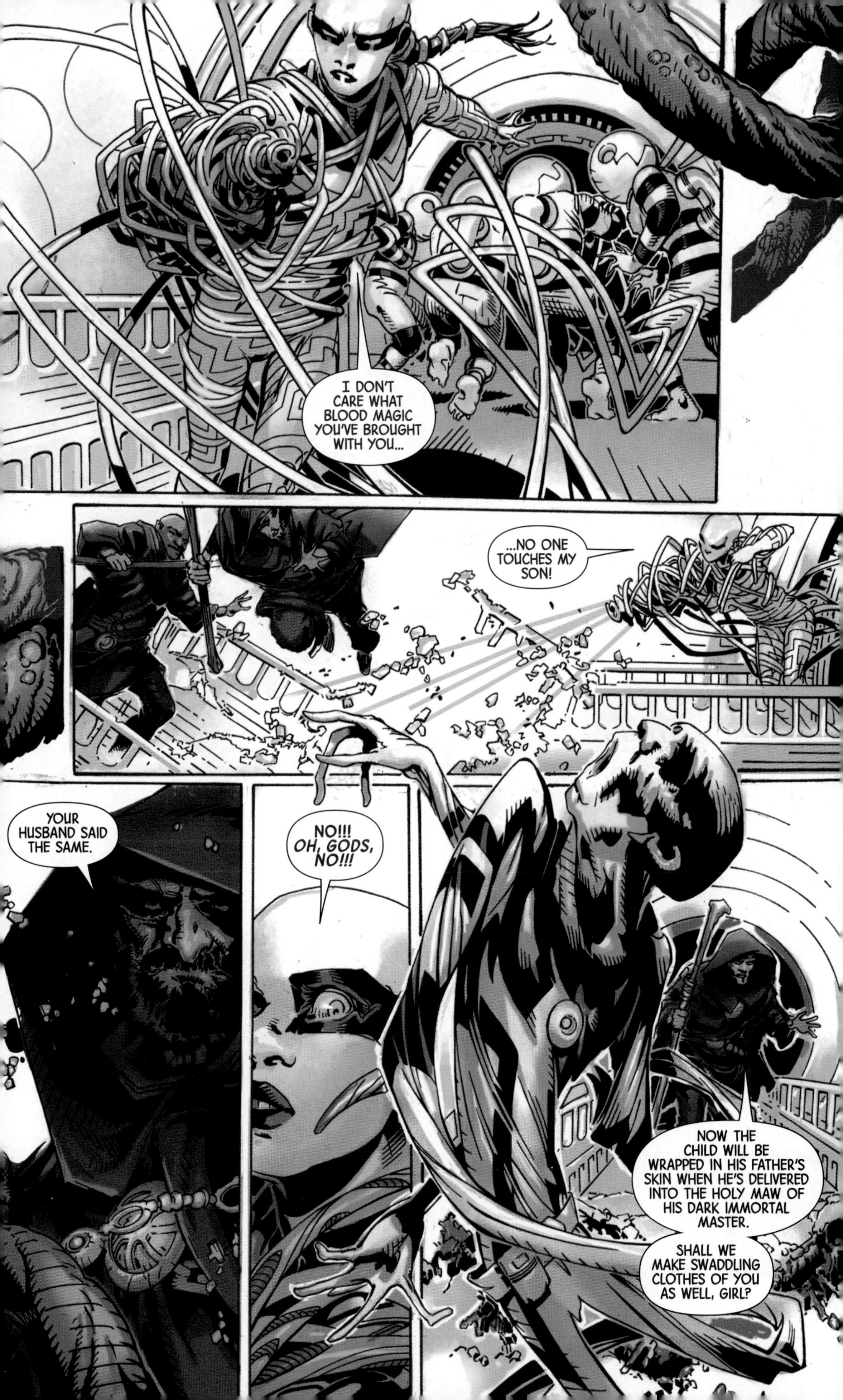

I DON'T CARE WHAT BLOOD MAGIC YOU'VE BROUGHT WITH YOU...
...NO ONE TOUCHES MY SON!
YOUR HUSBAND SAID THE SAME.
NO!!! *OH, GODS,* NO!!!
NOW THE CHILD WILL BE WRAPPED IN HIS FATHER'S SKIN WHEN HE'S DELIVERED INTO THE HOLY MAW OF HIS DARK IMMORTAL MASTER.
SHALL WE MAKE SWADDLING CLOTHES OF YOU AS WELL, GIRL?

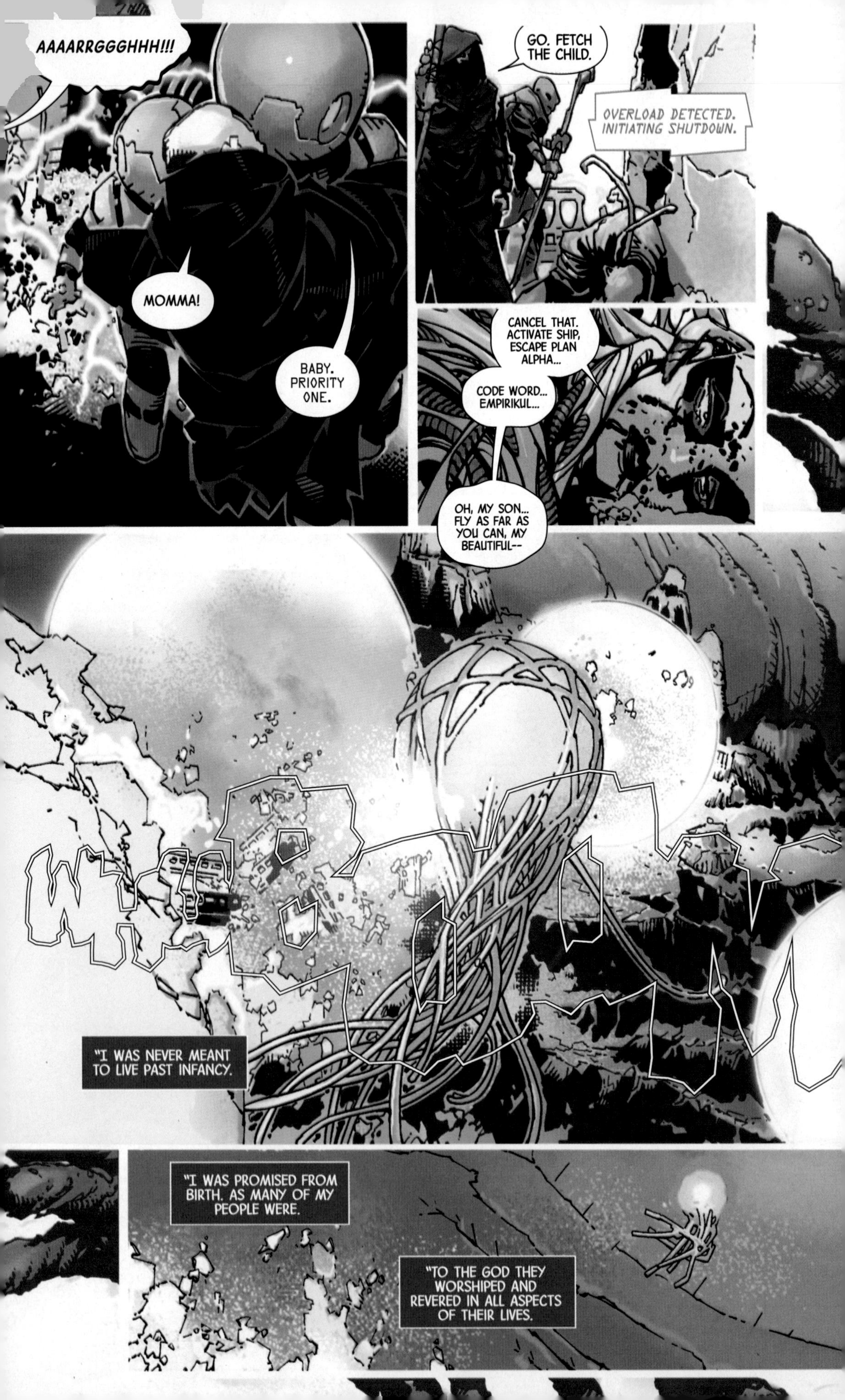
AAAARRGGGHHH!!!
MOMMA!
BABY. PRIORITY ONE.
GO. FETCH THE CHILD.
OVERLOAD DETECTED. INITIATING SHUTDOWN.
CANCEL THAT. ACTIVATE SHIP, ESCAPE PLAN ALPHA...
CODE WORD... EMPIRIKUL...
OH, MY SON... FLY AS FAR AS YOU CAN, MY BEAUTIFUL--
"I WAS NEVER MEANT TO LIVE PAST INFANCY.
"I WAS PROMISED FROM BIRTH. AS MANY OF MY PEOPLE WERE.
"TO THE GOD THEY WORSHIPED AND REVERED IN ALL ASPECTS OF THEIR LIVES.

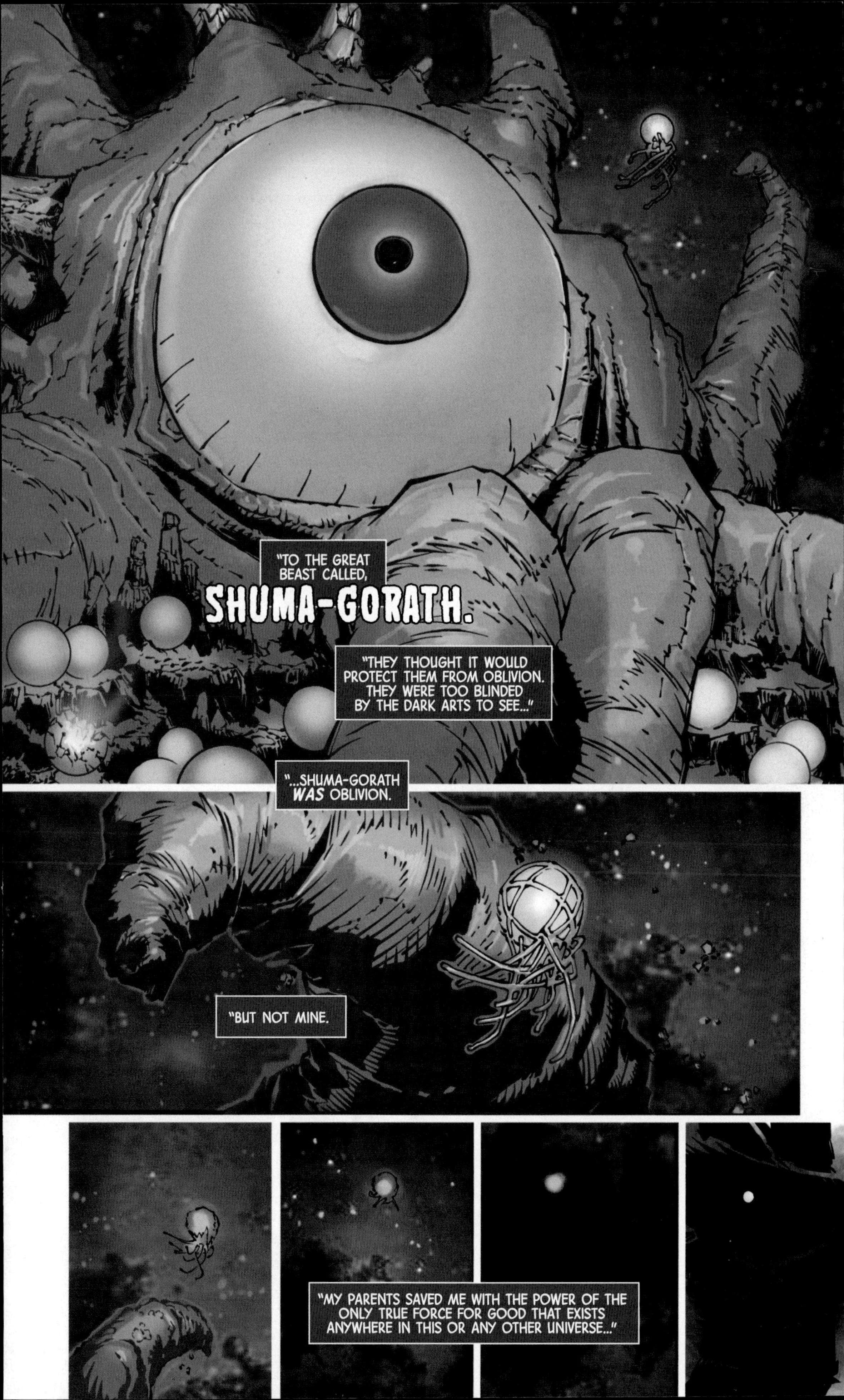
"TO THE GREAT BEAST CALLED,
SHUMA-GORATH.
"THEY THOUGHT IT WOULD PROTECT THEM FROM OBLIVION. THEY WERE TOO BLINDED BY THE DARK ARTS TO SEE..."
"...SHUMA-GORATH *WAS* OBLIVION.
"BUT NOT MINE.
"MY PARENTS SAVED ME WITH THE POWER OF THE ONLY TRUE FORCE FOR GOOD THAT EXISTS ANYWHERE IN THIS OR ANY OTHER UNIVERSE..."

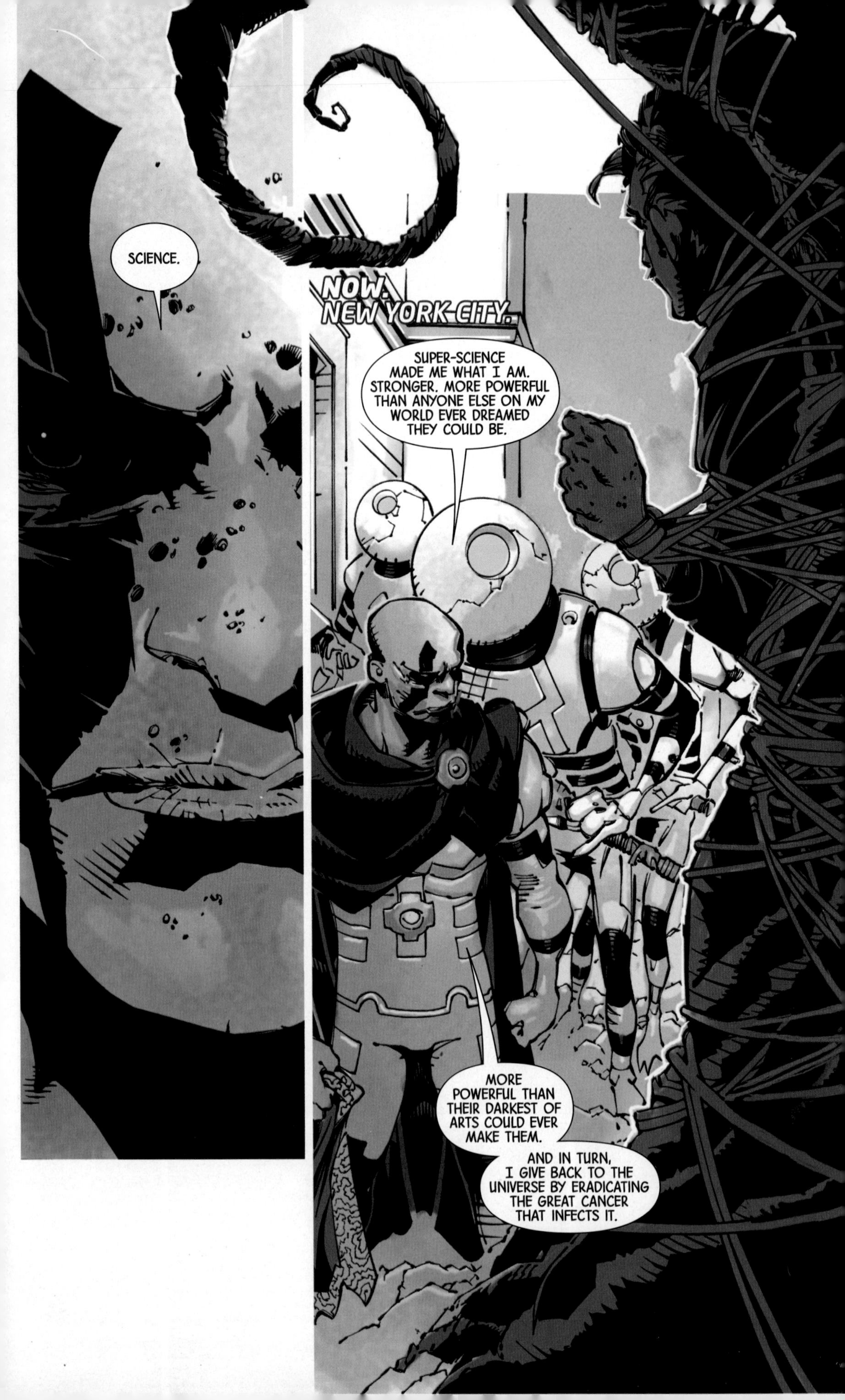
SCIENCE.
NOW.
NEW YORK CITY.
SUPER-SCIENCE MADE ME WHAT I AM. STRONGER. MORE POWERFUL THAN ANYONE ELSE ON MY WORLD EVER DREAMED THEY COULD BE.
MORE POWERFUL THAN THEIR DARKEST OF ARTS COULD EVER MAKE THEM.
AND IN TURN, I GIVE BACK TO THE UNIVERSE BY ERADICATING THE GREAT CANCER THAT INFECTS IT.

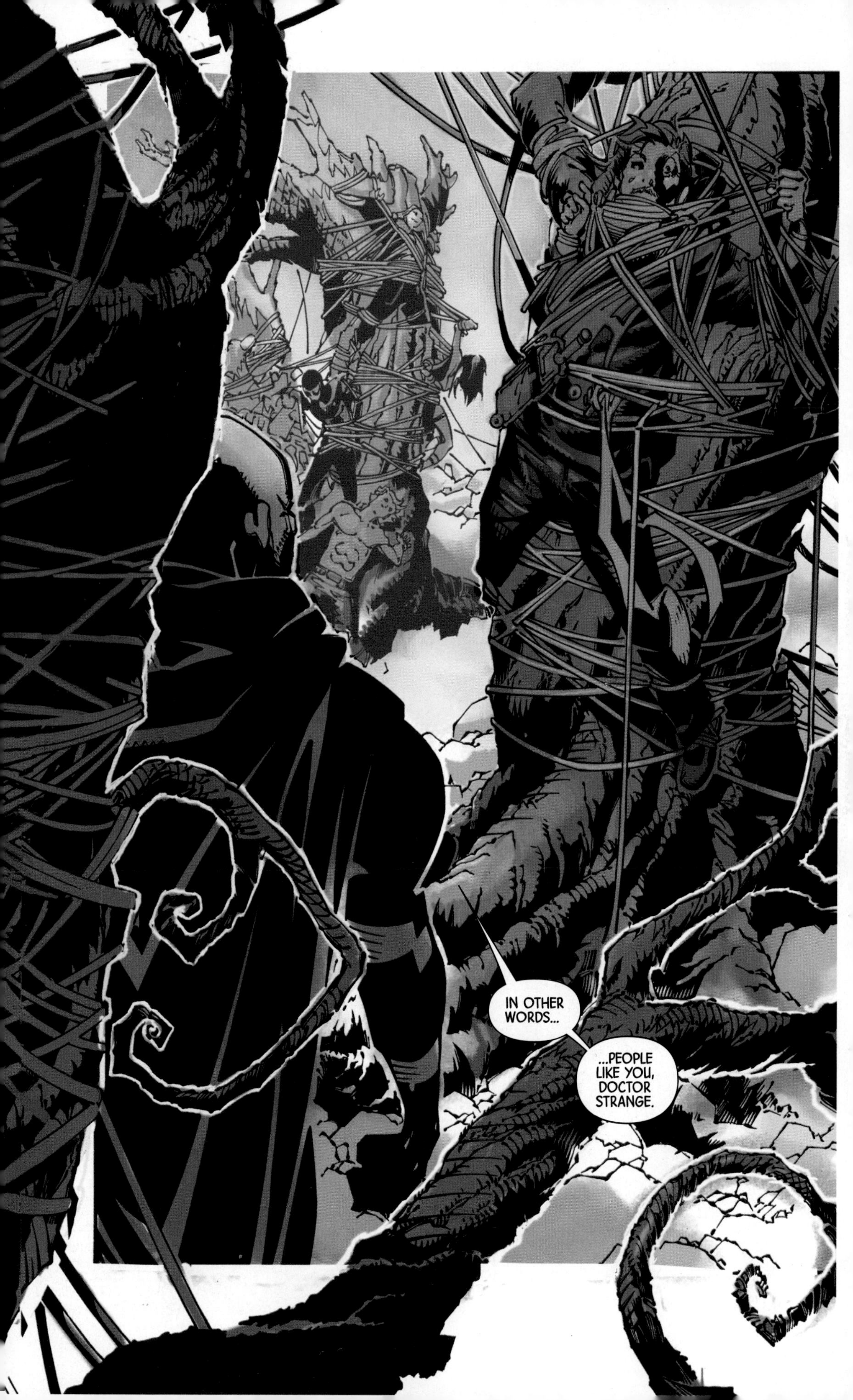
IN OTHER WORDS...
...PEOPLE LIKE YOU, DOCTOR STRANGE.

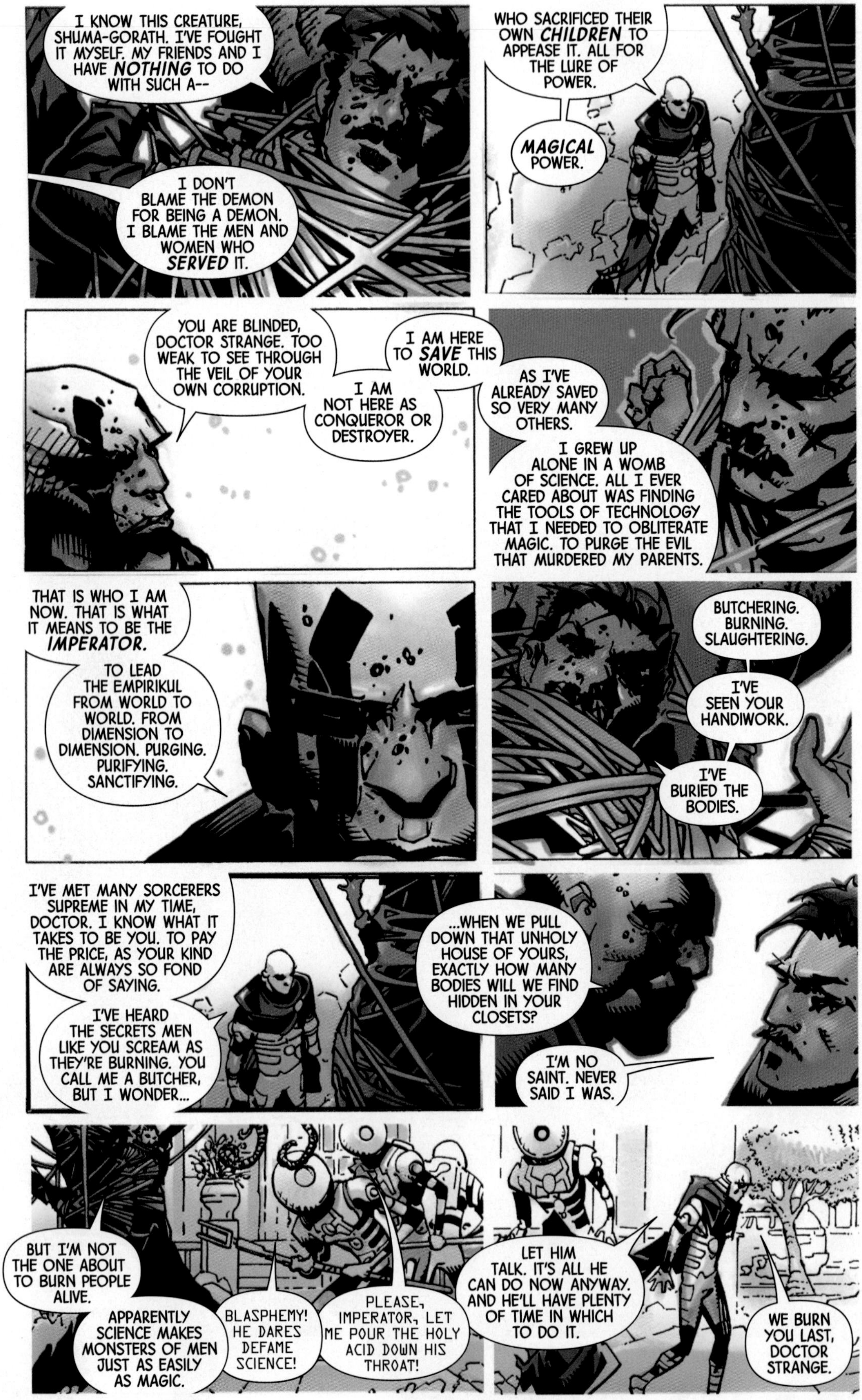
I KNOW THIS CREATURE, SHUMA-GORATH. I'VE FOUGHT IT MYSELF. MY FRIENDS AND I HAVE NOTHING TO DO WITH SUCH A--
I DON'T BLAME THE DEMON FOR BEING A DEMON. I BLAME THE MEN AND WOMEN WHO SERVED IT.
WHO SACRIFICED THEIR OWN CHILDREN TO APPEASE IT. ALL FOR THE LURE OF POWER.
MAGICAL POWER.
YOU ARE BLINDED, DOCTOR STRANGE. TOO WEAK TO SEE THROUGH THE VEIL OF YOUR OWN CORRUPTION.
I AM NOT HERE AS CONQUEROR OR DESTROYER.
I AM HERE TO SAVE THIS WORLD.
AS I'VE ALREADY SAVED SO VERY MANY OTHERS.
I GREW UP ALONE IN A WOMB OF SCIENCE. ALL I EVER CARED ABOUT WAS FINDING THE TOOLS OF TECHNOLOGY THAT I NEEDED TO OBLITERATE MAGIC. TO PURGE THE EVIL THAT MURDERED MY PARENTS.
THAT IS WHO I AM NOW. THAT IS WHAT IT MEANS TO BE THE IMPERATOR.
TO LEAD THE EMPIRIKUL FROM WORLD TO WORLD. FROM DIMENSION TO DIMENSION. PURGING. PURIFYING. SANCTIFYING.
BUTCHERING. BURNING. SLAUGHTERING.
I'VE SEEN YOUR HANDIWORK.
I'VE BURIED THE BODIES.
I'VE MET MANY SORCERERS SUPREME IN MY TIME, DOCTOR. I KNOW WHAT IT TAKES TO BE YOU. TO PAY THE PRICE, AS YOUR KIND ARE ALWAYS SO FOND OF SAYING.
I'VE HEARD THE SECRETS MEN LIKE YOU SCREAM AS THEY'RE BURNING. YOU CALL ME A BUTCHER, BUT I WONDER...
...WHEN WE PULL DOWN THAT UNHOLY HOUSE OF YOURS, EXACTLY HOW MANY BODIES WILL WE FIND HIDDEN IN YOUR CLOSETS?
I'M NO SAINT. NEVER SAID I WAS.
BUT I'M NOT THE ONE ABOUT TO BURN PEOPLE ALIVE.
APPARENTLY SCIENCE MAKES MONSTERS OF MEN JUST AS EASILY AS MAGIC.
BLASPHEMY! HE DARES DEFAME SCIENCE!
PLEASE, IMPERATOR, LET ME POUR THE HOLY ACID DOWN HIS THROAT!
LET HIM TALK. IT'S ALL HE CAN DO NOW ANYWAY. AND HE'LL HAVE PLENTY OF TIME IN WHICH TO DO IT.
WE BURN YOU LAST, DOCTOR STRANGE.

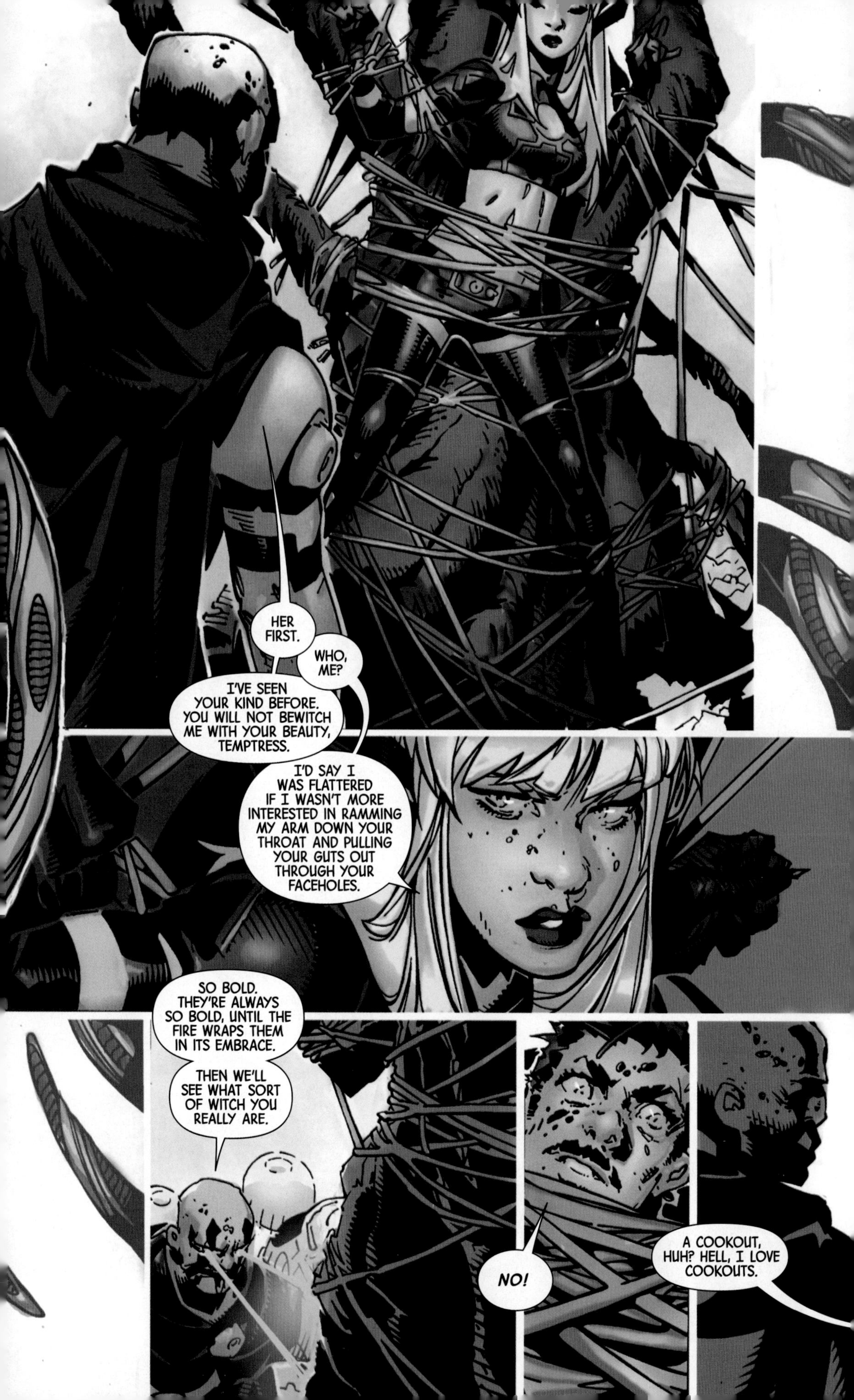
HER FIRST.
WHO, ME?
I'VE SEEN YOUR KIND BEFORE. YOU WILL NOT BEWITCH ME WITH YOUR BEAUTY, TEMPTRESS.
I'D SAY I WAS FLATTERED IF I WASN'T MORE INTERESTED IN RAMMING MY ARM DOWN YOUR THROAT AND PULLING YOUR GUTS OUT THROUGH YOUR FACEHOLES.
SO BOLD. THEY'RE ALWAYS SO BOLD, UNTIL THE FIRE WRAPS THEM IN ITS EMBRACE.
THEN WE'LL SEE WHAT SORT OF WITCH YOU REALLY ARE.
NO!
A COOKOUT, HUH? HELL, I LOVE COOKOUTS.

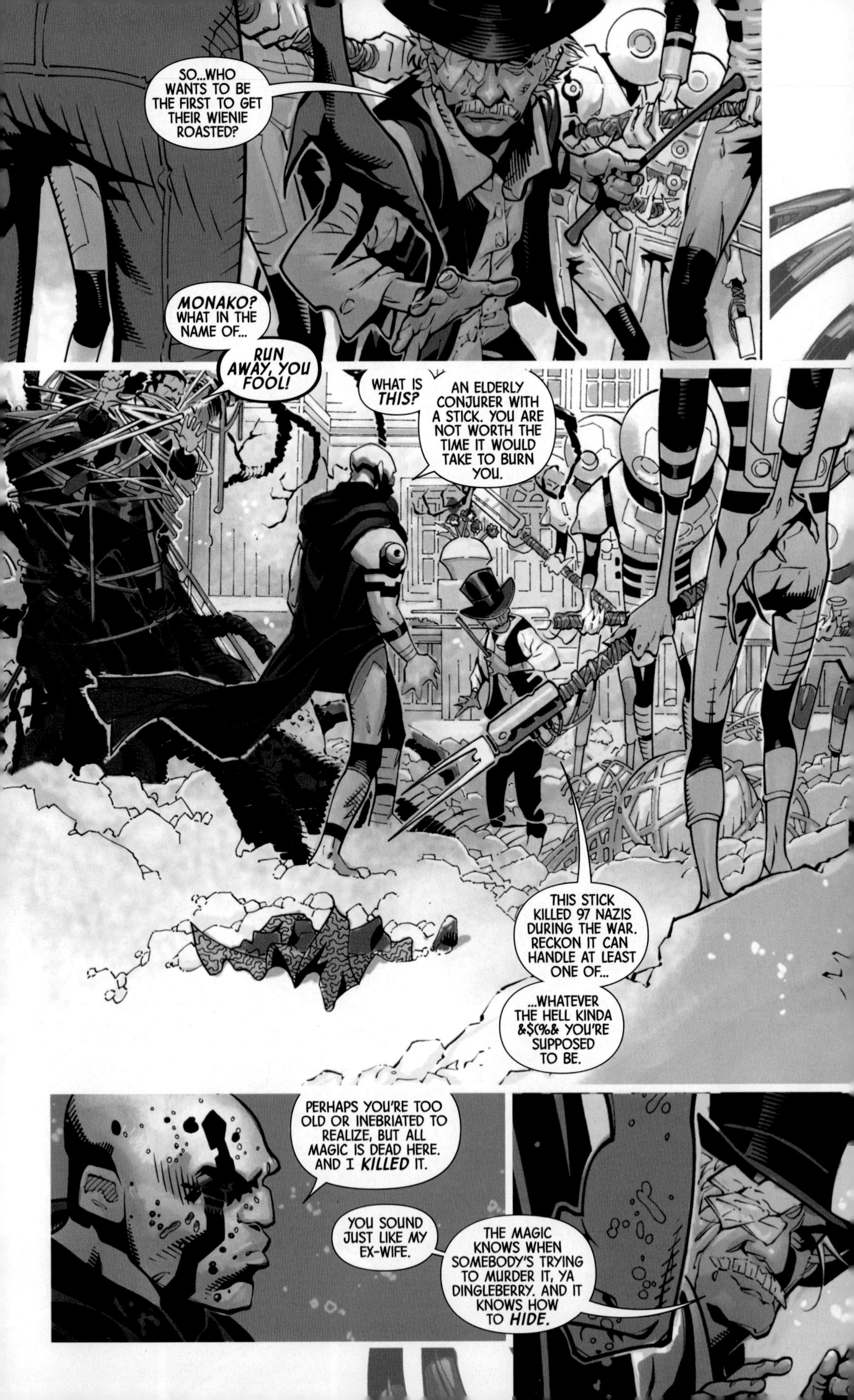
SO...WHO WANTS TO BE THE FIRST TO GET THEIR WIENIE ROASTED?
MONAKO? WHAT IN THE NAME OF...
RUN AWAY, YOU FOOL!
WHAT IS THIS?
AN ELDERLY CONJURER WITH A STICK. YOU ARE NOT WORTH THE TIME IT WOULD TAKE TO BURN YOU.
THIS STICK KILLED 97 NAZIS DURING THE WAR. RECKON IT CAN HANDLE AT LEAST ONE OF...
...WHATEVER THE HELL KINDA &$(%& YOU'RE SUPPOSED TO BE.
PERHAPS YOU'RE TOO OLD OR INEBRIATED TO REALIZE, BUT ALL MAGIC IS DEAD HERE. AND I KILLED IT.
YOU SOUND JUST LIKE MY EX-WIFE.
THE MAGIC KNOWS WHEN SOMEBODY'S TRYING TO MURDER IT, YA DINGLEBERRY. AND IT KNOWS HOW TO HIDE.

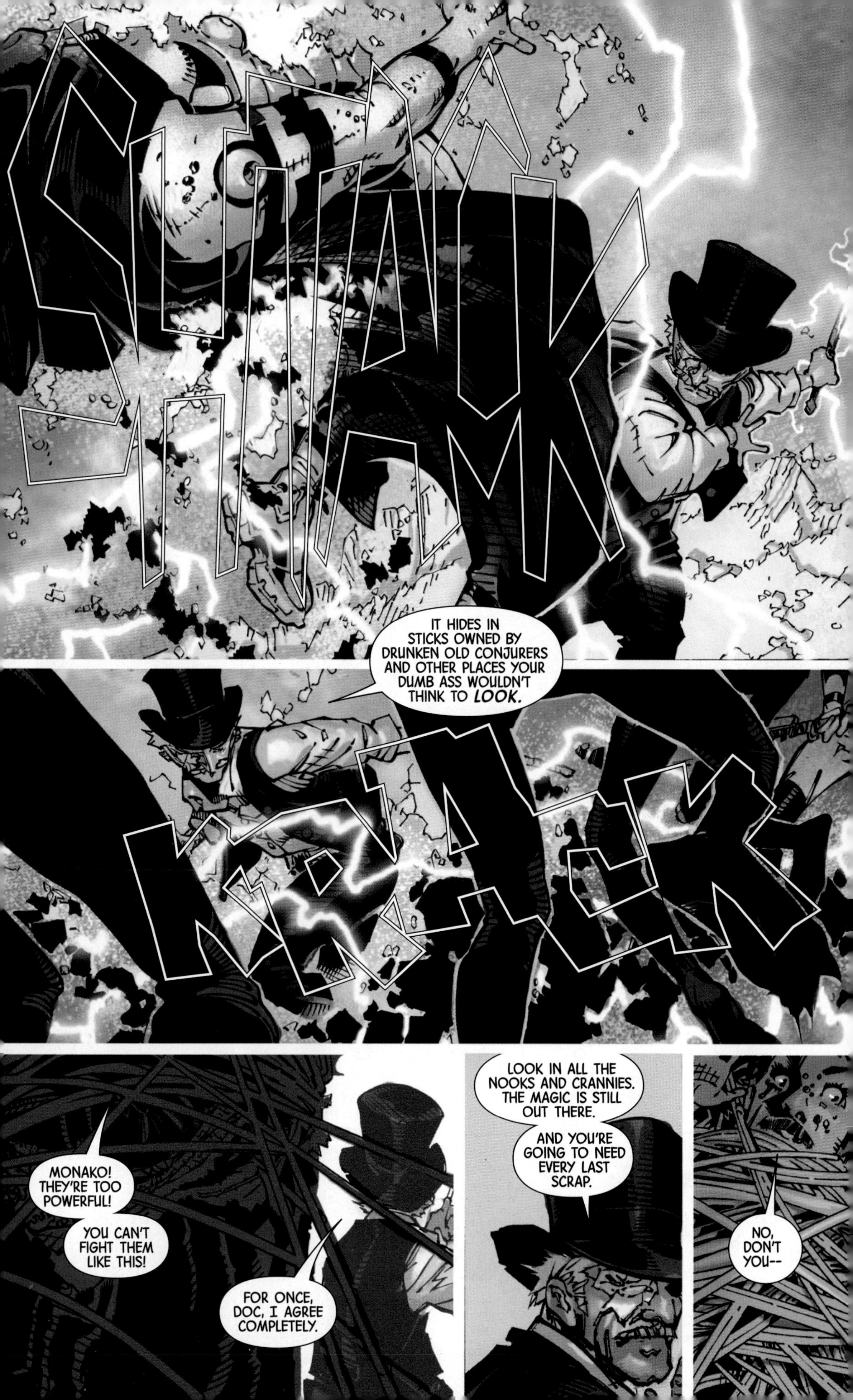
IT HIDES IN STICKS OWNED BY DRUNKEN OLD CONJURERS AND OTHER PLACES YOUR DUMB ASS WOULDN'T THINK TO *LOOK.*
MONAKO! THEY'RE TOO POWERFUL!
YOU CAN'T FIGHT THEM LIKE THIS!
FOR ONCE, DOC, I AGREE COMPLETELY.
LOOK IN ALL THE NOOKS AND CRANNIES. THE MAGIC IS STILL OUT THERE.
AND YOU'RE GOING TO NEED EVERY LAST SCRAP.
NO, DON'T YOU--

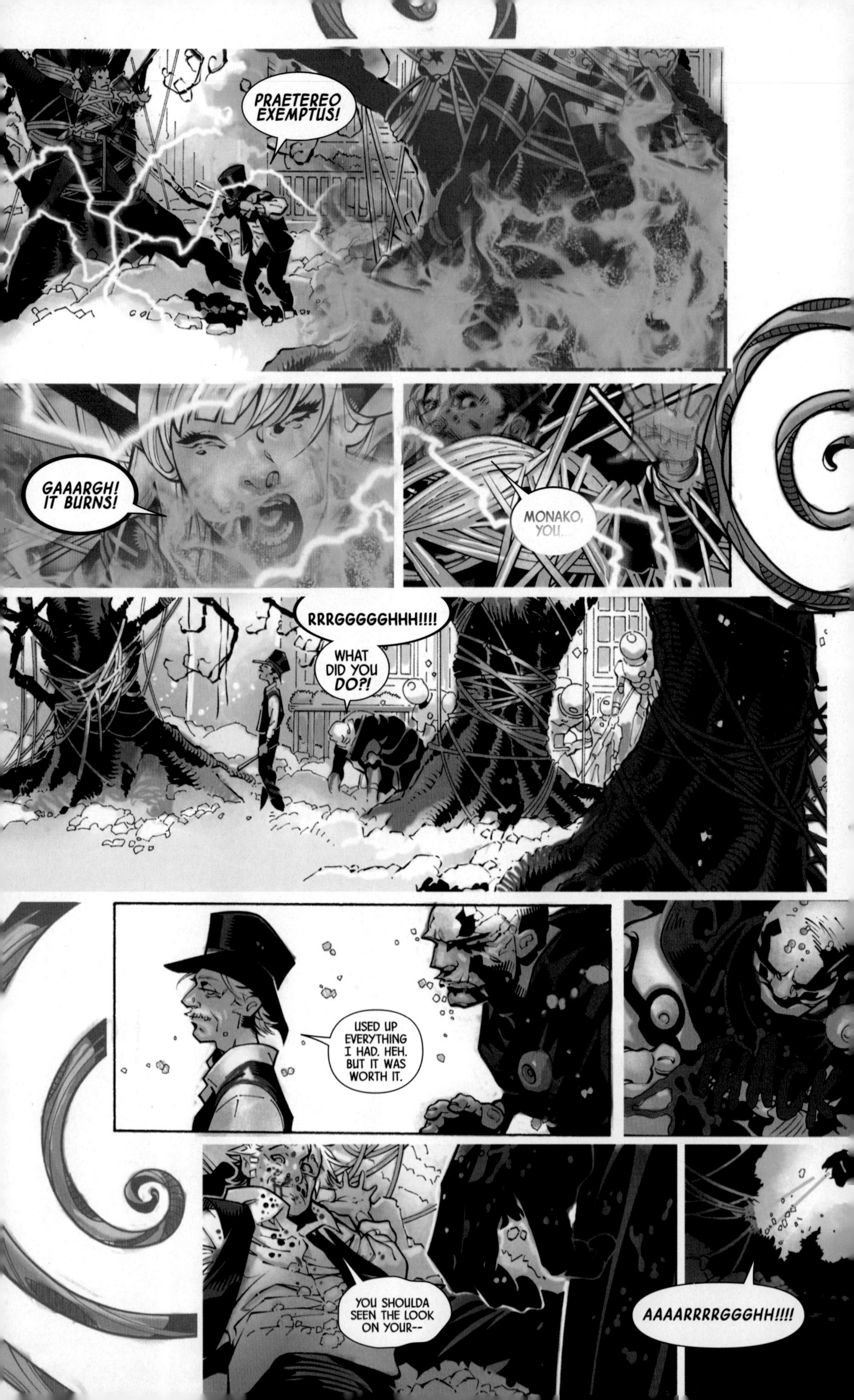
PRAETEREO EXEMPTUS!
GAAARGH! IT BURNS!
MONAKO, YOU...
RRRGGGGGHH!!!!
WHAT DID YOU DO?!
USED UP EVERYTHING I HAD. HEH. BUT IT WAS WORTH IT.
THACK
YOU SHOULDA SEEN THE LOOK ON YOUR--
AAAARRRRGGGH!!!!

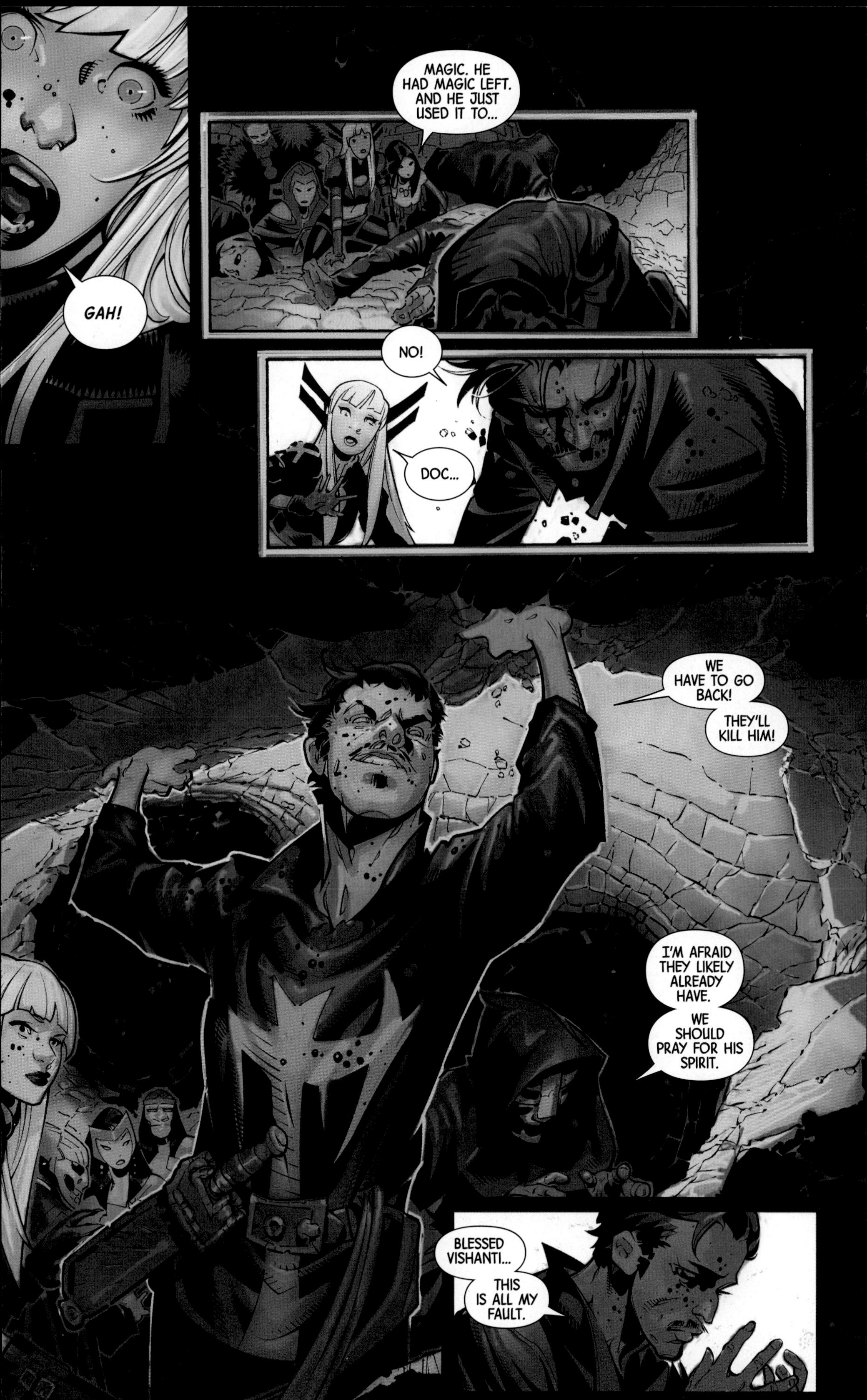
GAH!
MAGIC. HE HAD MAGIC LEFT. AND HE JUST USED IT TO...
NO!
DOC...
WE HAVE TO GO BACK!
THEY'LL KILL HIM!
I'M AFRAID THEY LIKELY ALREADY HAVE.
WE SHOULD PRAY FOR HIS SPIRIT.
BLESSED VISHANTI...
THIS IS ALL MY FAULT.

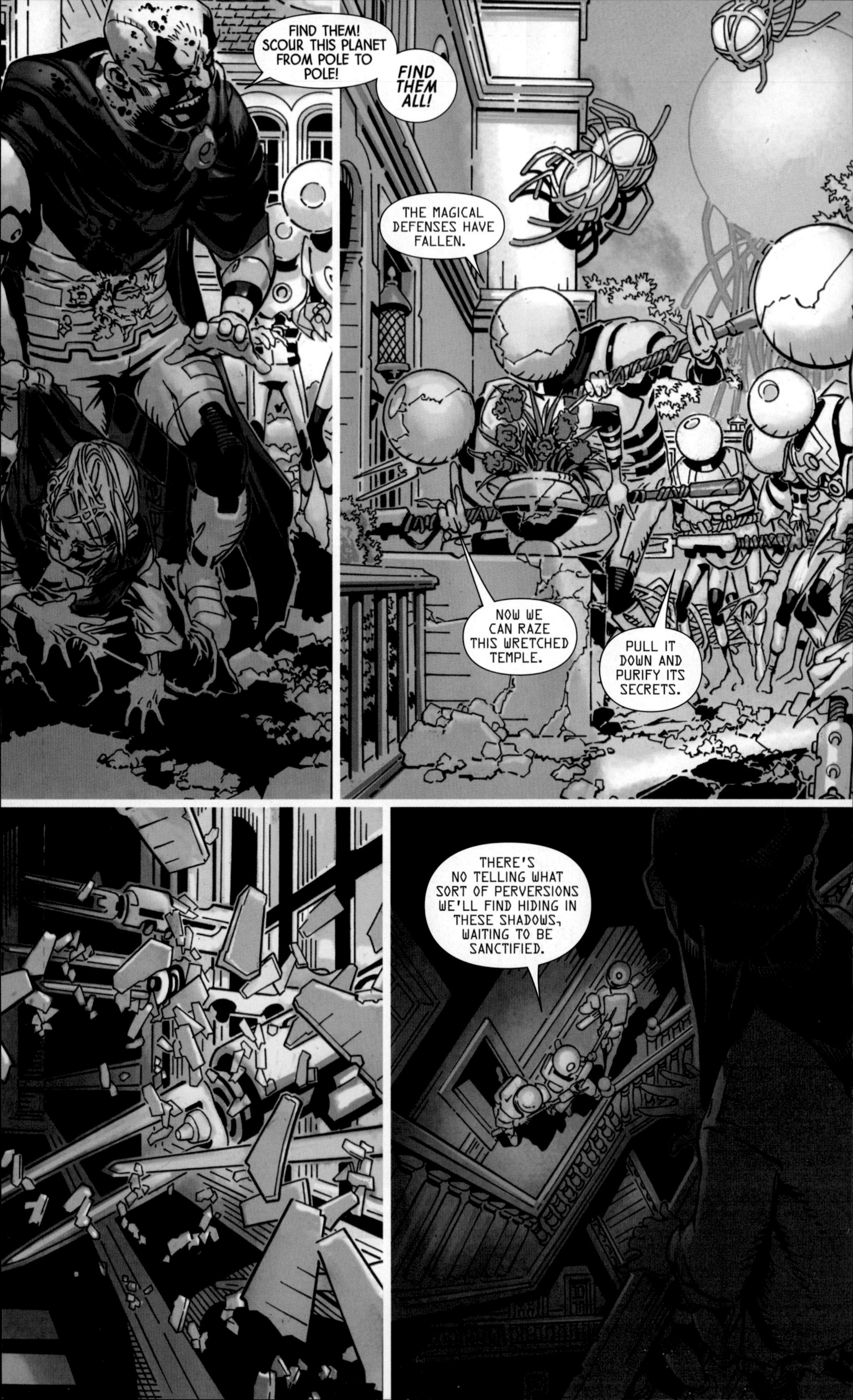
FIND THEM! SCOUR THIS PLANET FROM POLE TO POLE!
FIND THEM ALL!
THE MAGICAL DEFENSES HAVE FALLEN.
NOW WE CAN RAZE THIS WRETCHED TEMPLE.
PULL IT DOWN AND PURIFY ITS SECRETS.
THERE'S NO TELLING WHAT SORT OF PERVERSIONS WE'LL FIND HIDING IN THESE SHADOWS, WAITING TO BE SANCTIFIED.

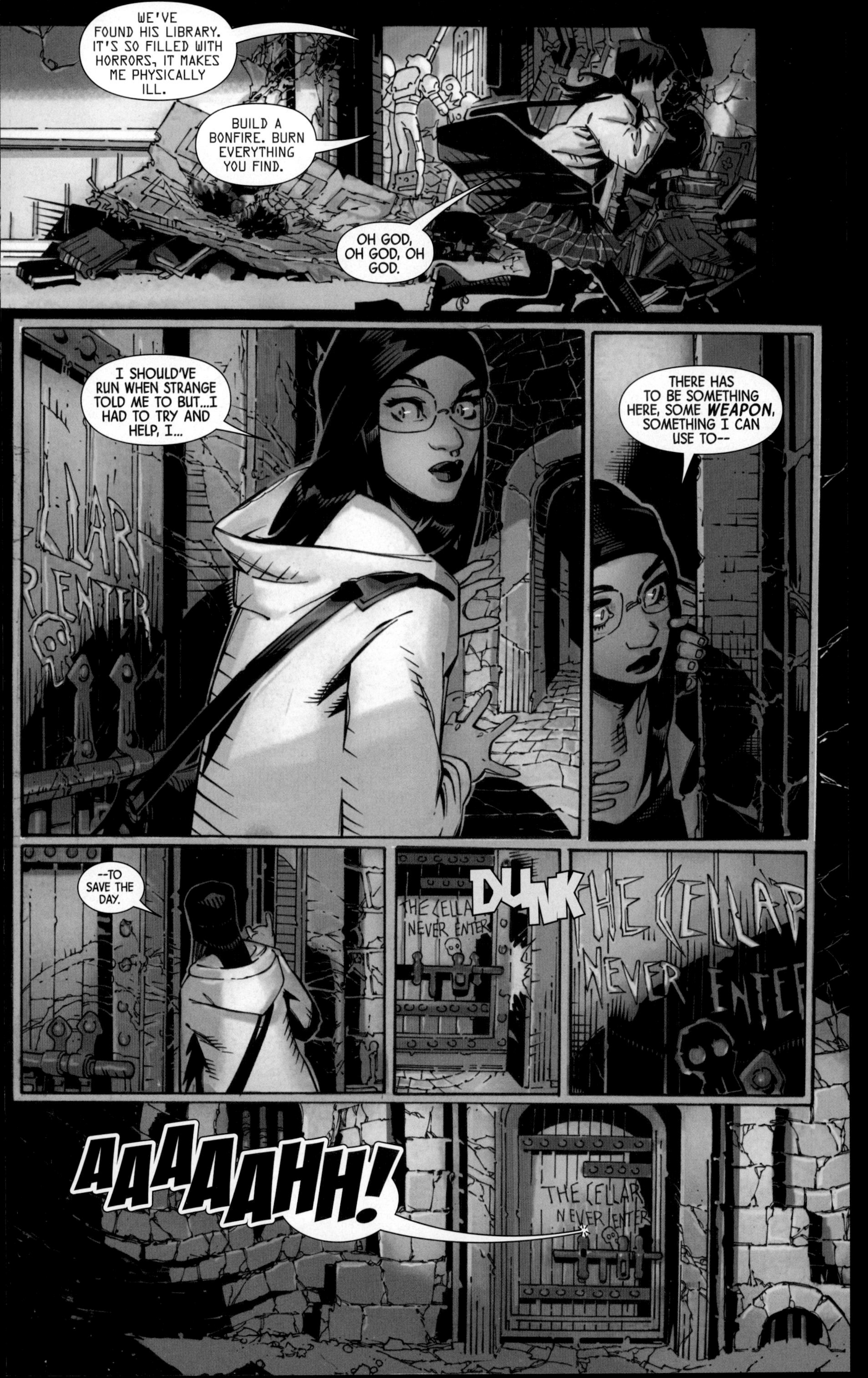
WE'VE FOUND HIS LIBRARY. IT'S SO FILLED WITH HORRORS, IT MAKES ME PHYSICALLY ILL.
BUILD A BONFIRE. BURN EVERYTHING YOU FIND.
OH GOD, OH GOD, OH GOD.
I SHOULD'VE RUN WHEN STRANGE TOLD ME TO BUT...I HAD TO TRY AND HELP, I...
THERE HAS TO BE SOMETHING HERE, SOME WEAPON, SOMETHING I CAN USE TO--
--TO SAVE THE DAY.
THE CELLAR NEVER ENTER
DUNK
THE CELLAR NEVER ENTER
AAAAAHH!
THE CELLAR NEVER ENTER

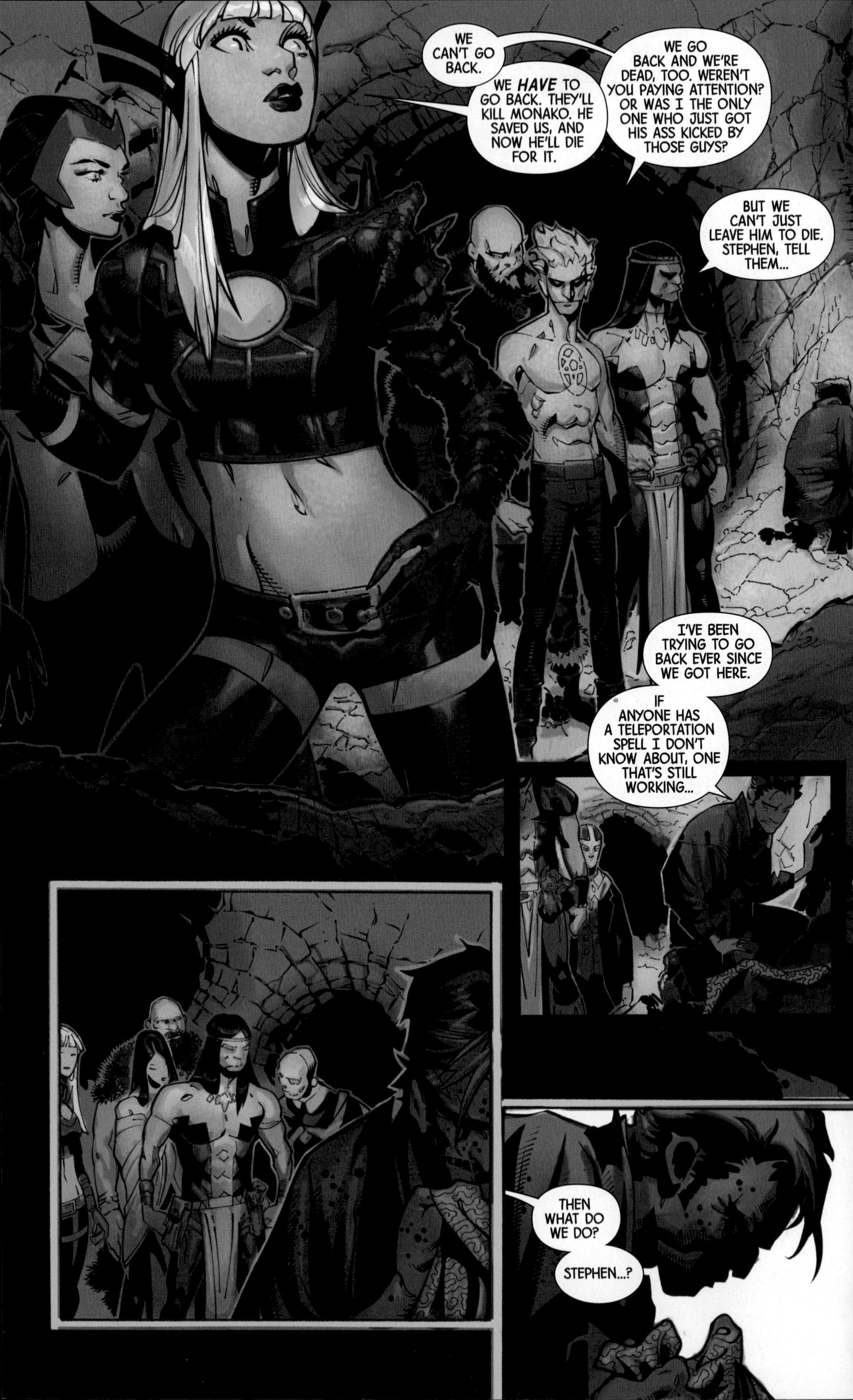

WE CAN'T GO BACK.
WE *HAVE* TO GO BACK. THEY'LL KILL MONAKO. HE SAVED US, AND NOW HE'LL DIE FOR IT.
WE GO BACK AND WE'RE DEAD, TOO. WEREN'T YOU PAYING ATTENTION? OR WAS I THE ONLY ONE WHO JUST GOT HIS ASS KICKED BY THOSE GUYS?
BUT WE CAN'T JUST LEAVE HIM TO DIE. STEPHEN, TELL THEM...
I'VE BEEN TRYING TO GO BACK EVER SINCE WE GOT HERE.
IF ANYONE HAS A TELEPORTATION SPELL I DON'T KNOW ABOUT, ONE THAT'S STILL WORKING...
THEN WHAT DO WE DO?
STEPHEN...?

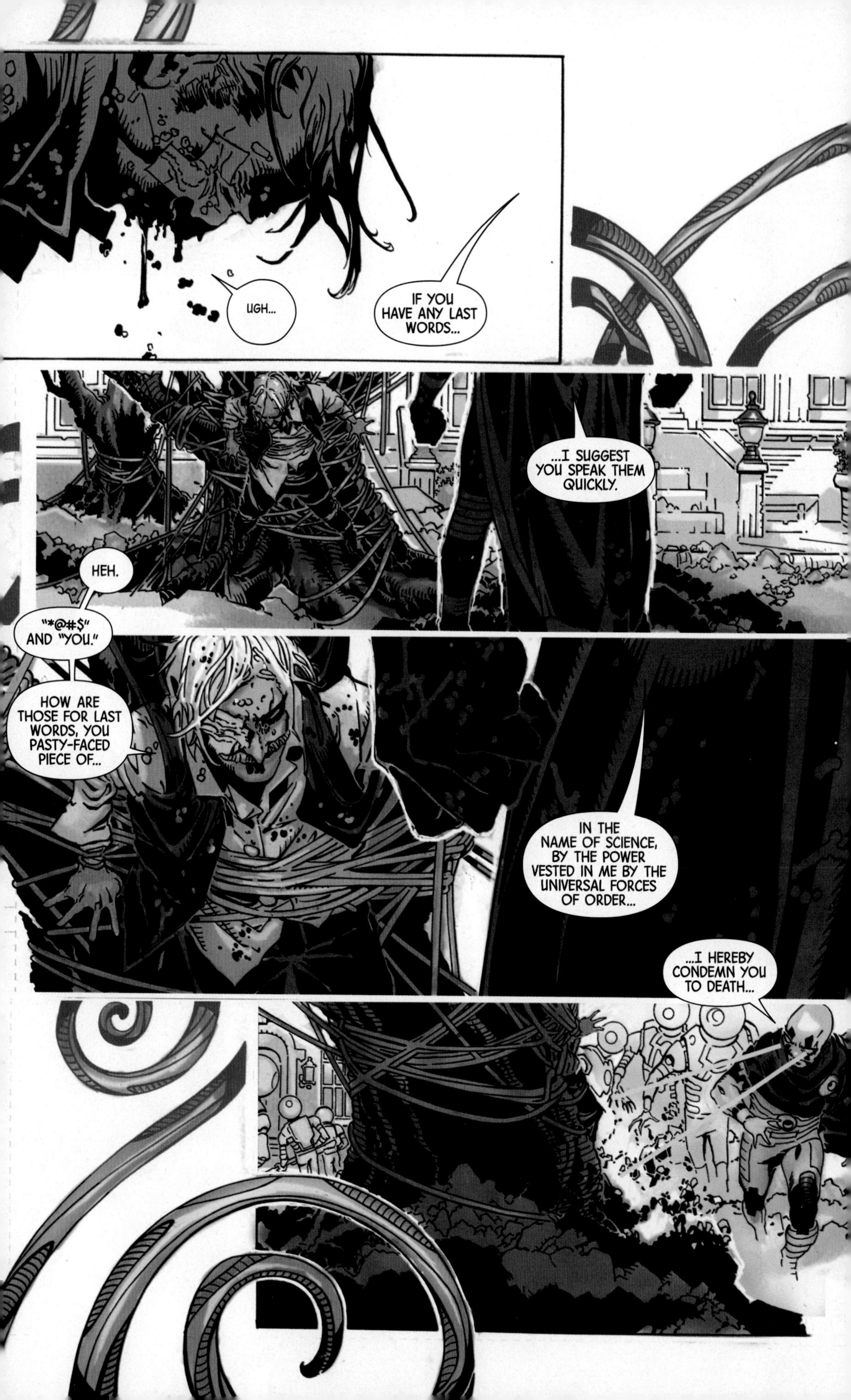
UGH...
IF YOU HAVE ANY LAST WORDS...
...I SUGGEST YOU SPEAK THEM QUICKLY.
HEH.
"*@#$" AND "YOU."
HOW ARE THOSE FOR LAST WORDS, YOU PASTY-FACED PIECE OF...
IN THE NAME OF SCIENCE, BY THE POWER VESTED IN ME BY THE UNIVERSAL FORCES OF ORDER...
...I HEREBY CONDEMN YOU TO DEATH...

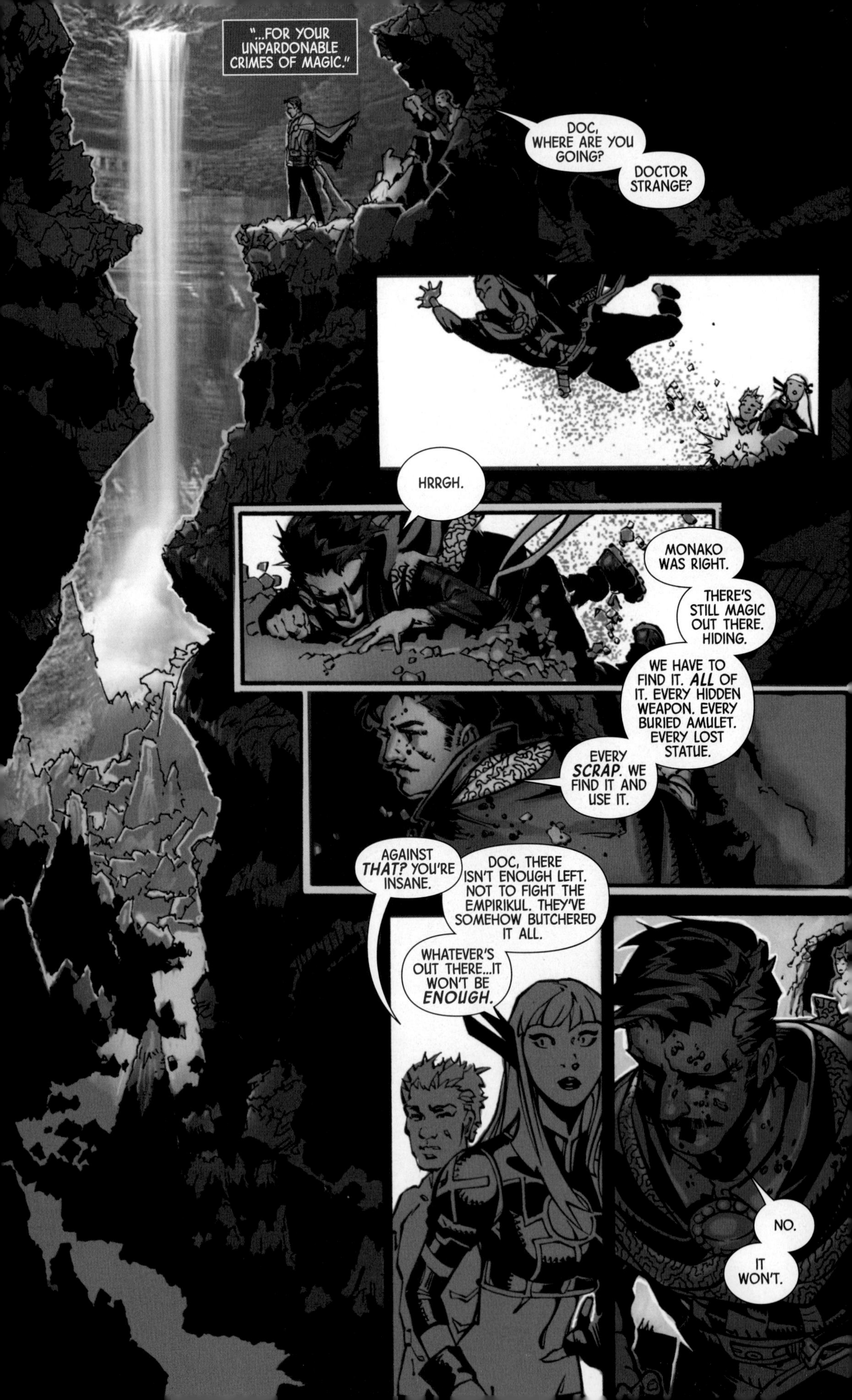
"...FOR YOUR UNPARDONABLE CRIMES OF MAGIC."
DOC, WHERE ARE YOU GOING?
DOCTOR STRANGE?
HRRGH.
MONAKO WAS RIGHT.
THERE'S STILL MAGIC OUT THERE. HIDING.
WE HAVE TO FIND IT. ALL OF IT. EVERY HIDDEN WEAPON. EVERY BURIED AMULET. EVERY LOST STATUE.
EVERY SCRAP. WE FIND IT AND USE IT.
AGAINST THAT? YOU'RE INSANE.
DOC, THERE ISN'T ENOUGH LEFT. NOT TO FIGHT THE EMPIRIKUL. THEY'VE SOMEHOW BUTCHERED IT ALL.
WHATEVER'S OUT THERE...IT WON'T BE ENOUGH.
NO.
IT WON'T.

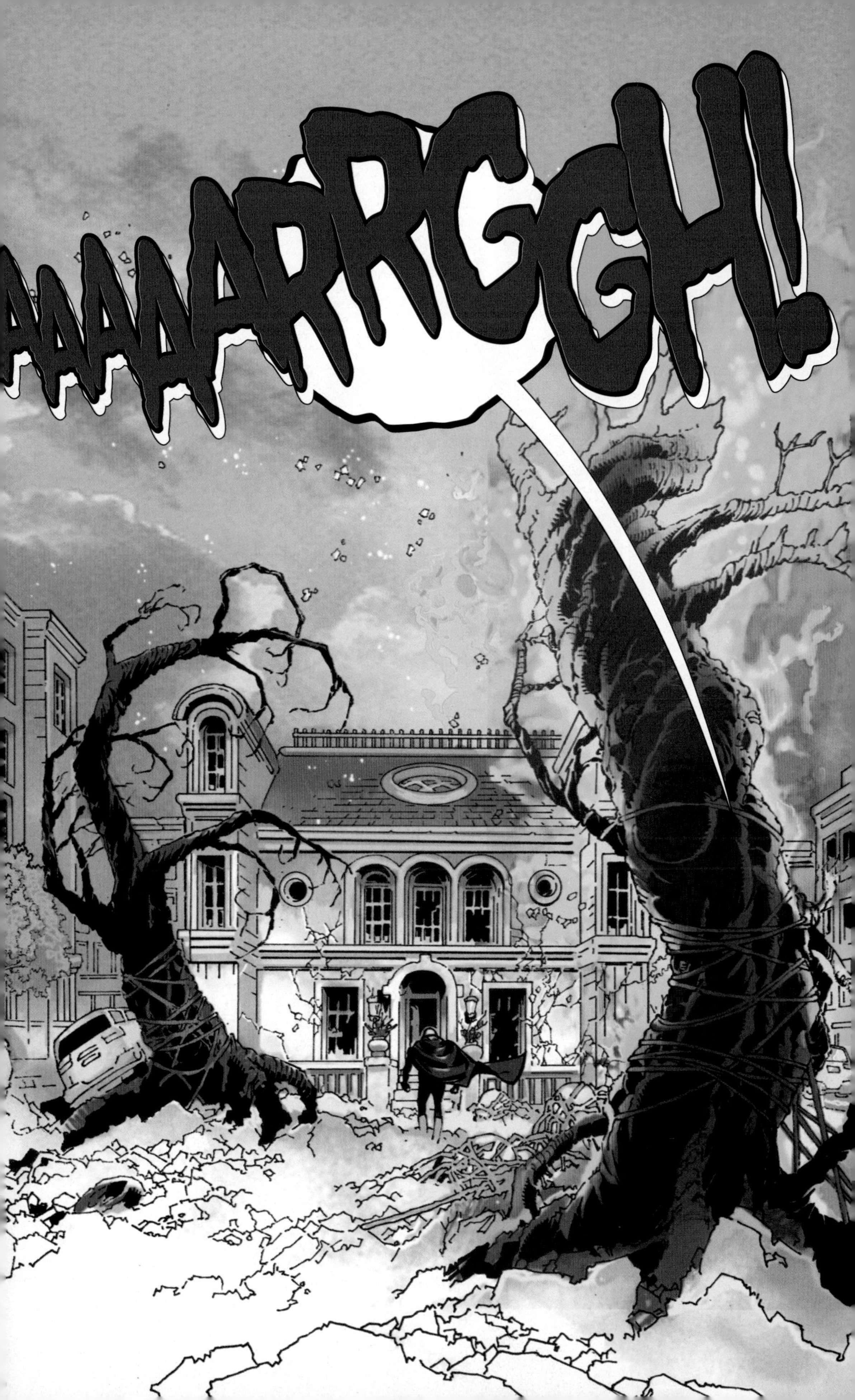
AAAAARRGGH!

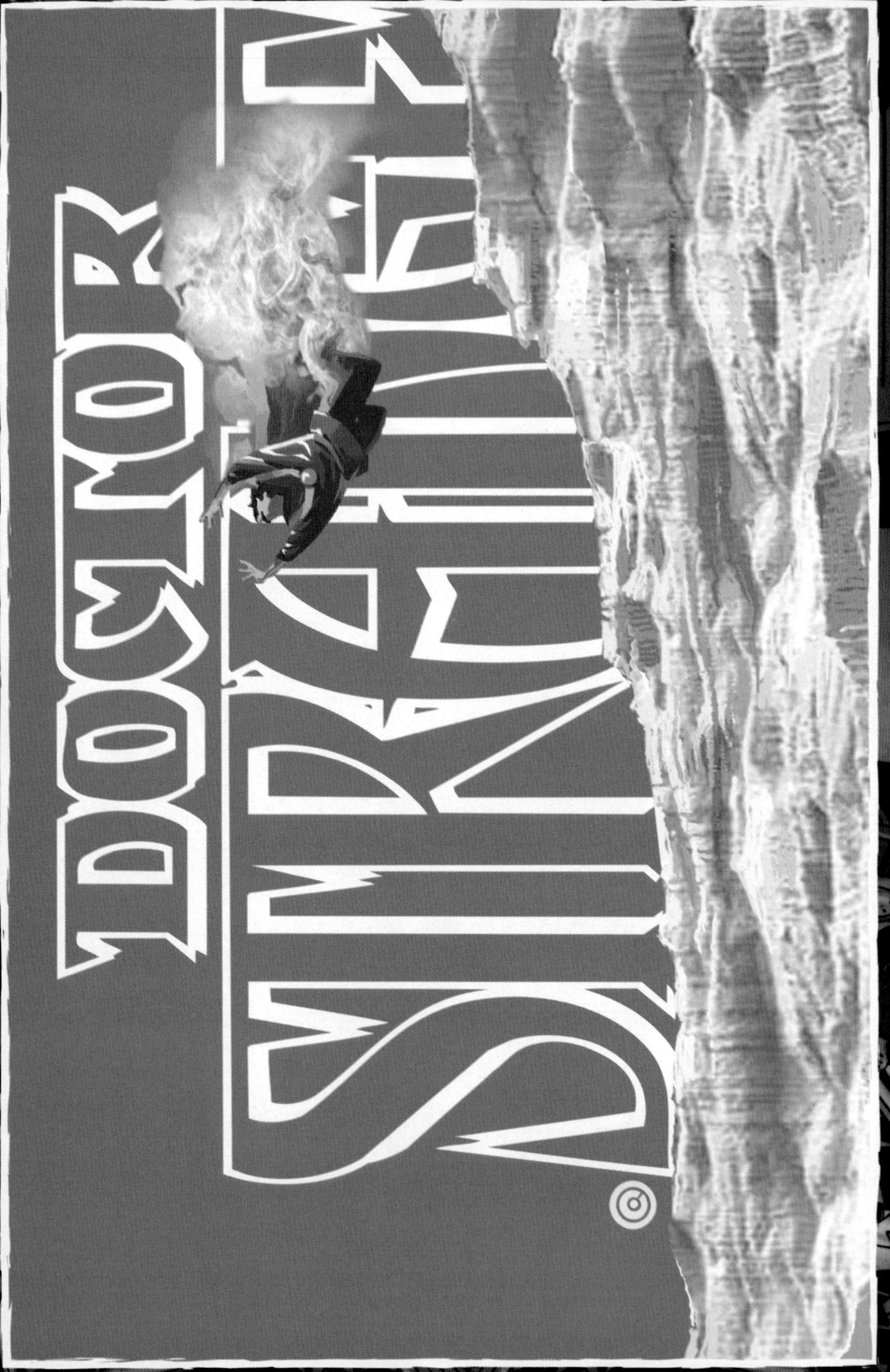
DOCTOR
STRANGE

DOCTOR STRANGE

THE LAST DAYS OF MAGIC
CHAPTER THREE

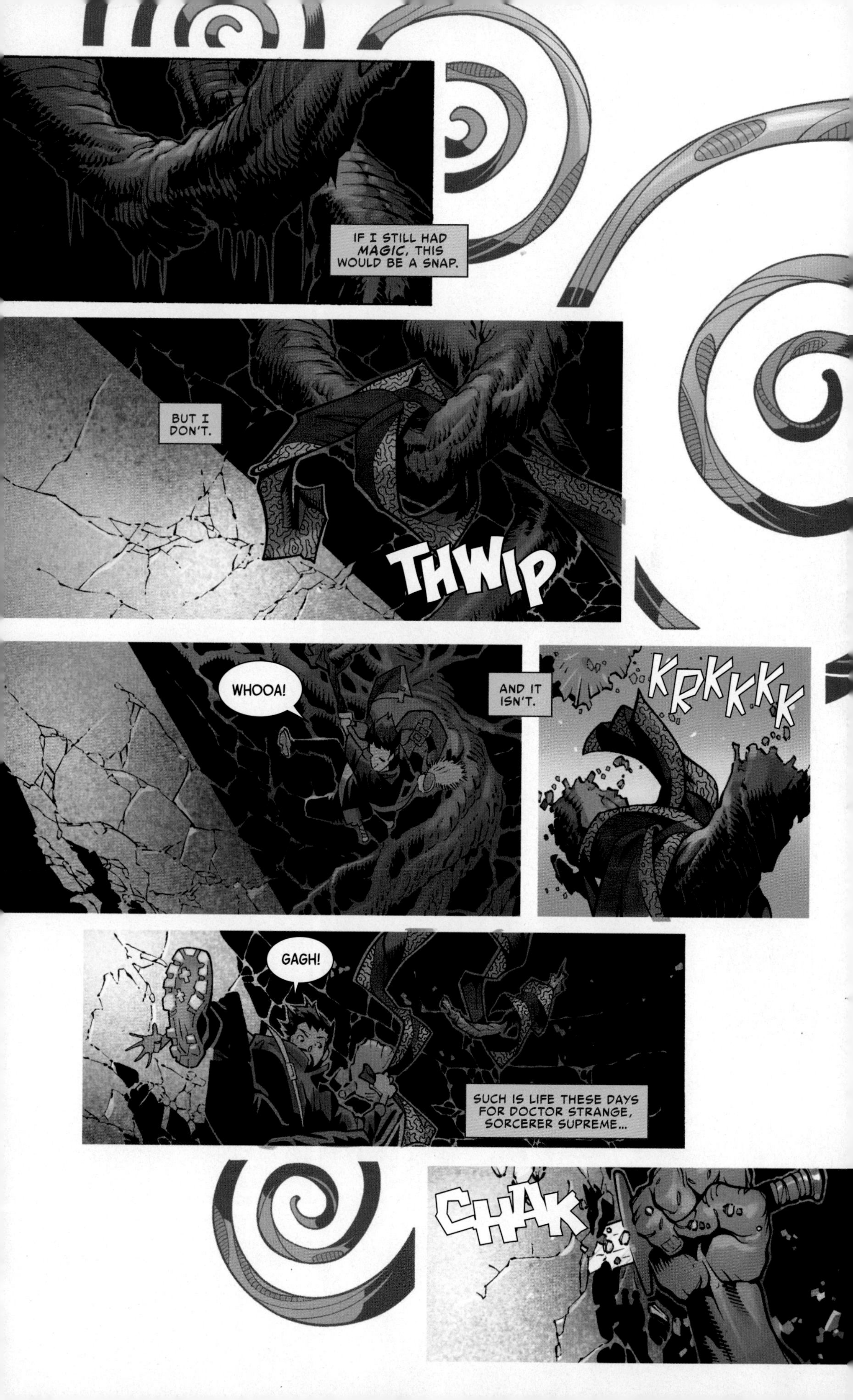
IF I STILL HAD MAGIC, THIS WOULD BE A SNAP.
BUT I DON'T.
THWIP
WHOOA!
AND IT ISN'T.
KRKKKK
GAGH!
SUCH IS LIFE THESE DAYS FOR DOCTOR STRANGE, SORCERER SUPREME...
CHAK

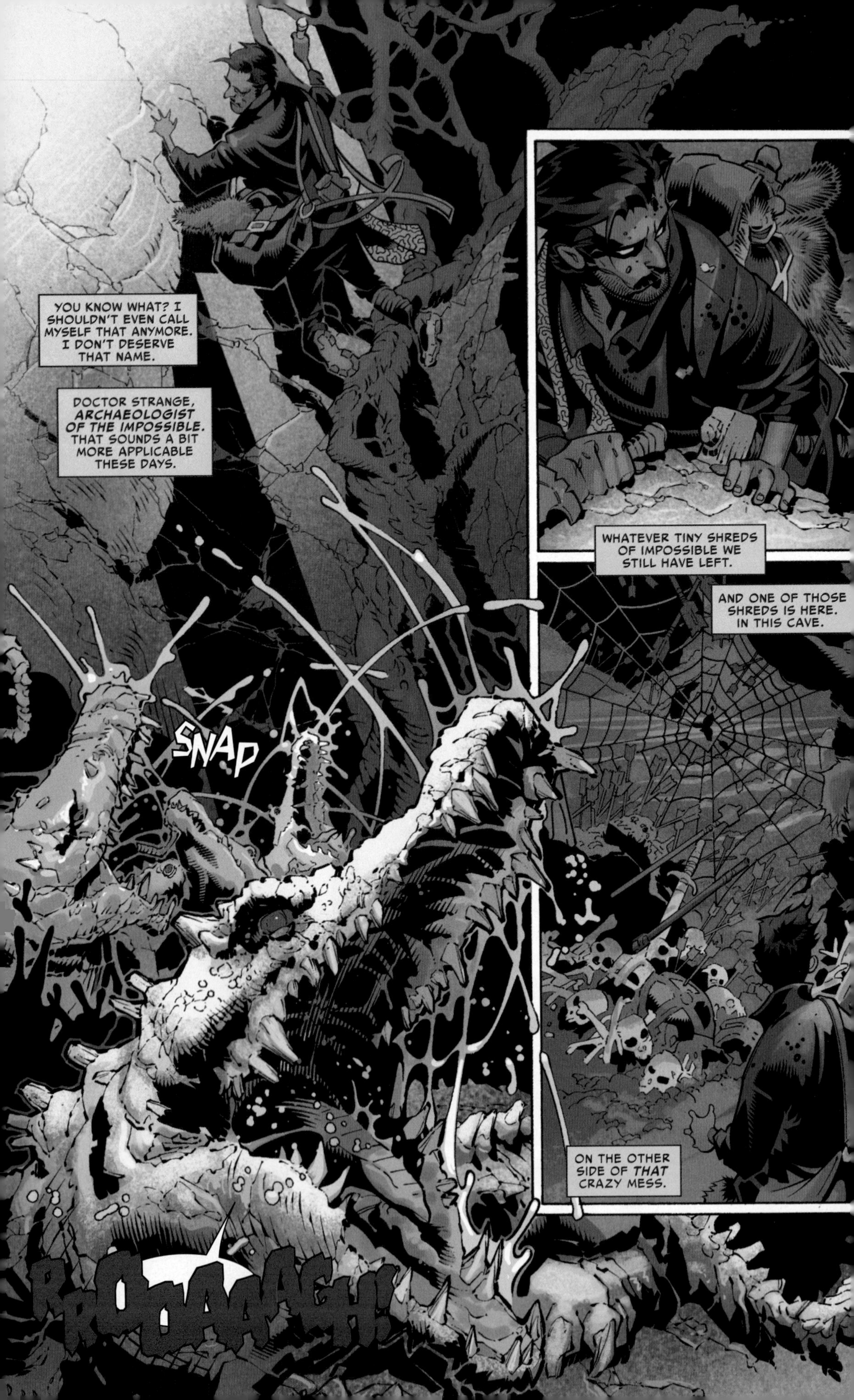
YOU KNOW WHAT? I SHOULDN'T EVEN CALL MYSELF THAT ANYMORE. I DON'T DESERVE THAT NAME.
DOCTOR STRANGE, *ARCHAEOLOGIST OF THE IMPOSSIBLE.* THAT SOUNDS A BIT MORE APPLICABLE THESE DAYS.
WHATEVER TINY SHREDS OF IMPOSSIBLE WE STILL HAVE LEFT.
AND ONE OF THOSE SHREDS IS HERE. IN THIS CAVE.
SNAP
ON THE OTHER SIDE OF *THAT* CRAZY MESS.
RROAAACH!

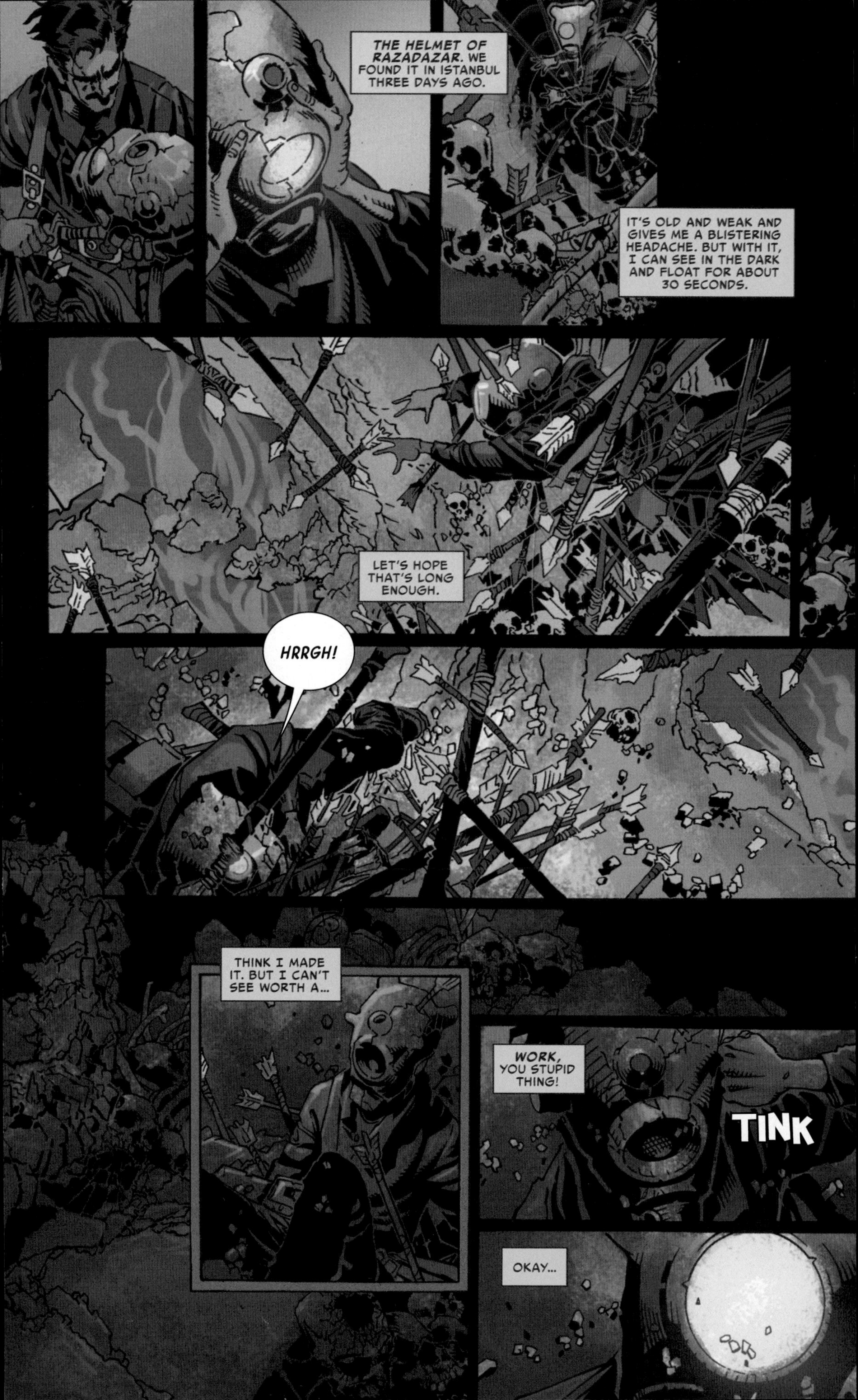
THE HELMET OF RAZADAZAR. WE FOUND IT IN ISTANBUL THREE DAYS AGO.
IT'S OLD AND WEAK AND GIVES ME A BLISTERING HEADACHE. BUT WITH IT, I CAN SEE IN THE DARK AND FLOAT FOR ABOUT 30 SECONDS.
LET'S HOPE THAT'S LONG ENOUGH.
HRRGH!
THINK I MADE IT. BUT I CAN'T SEE WORTH A...
WORK, YOU STUPID THING!
TINK
OKAY...

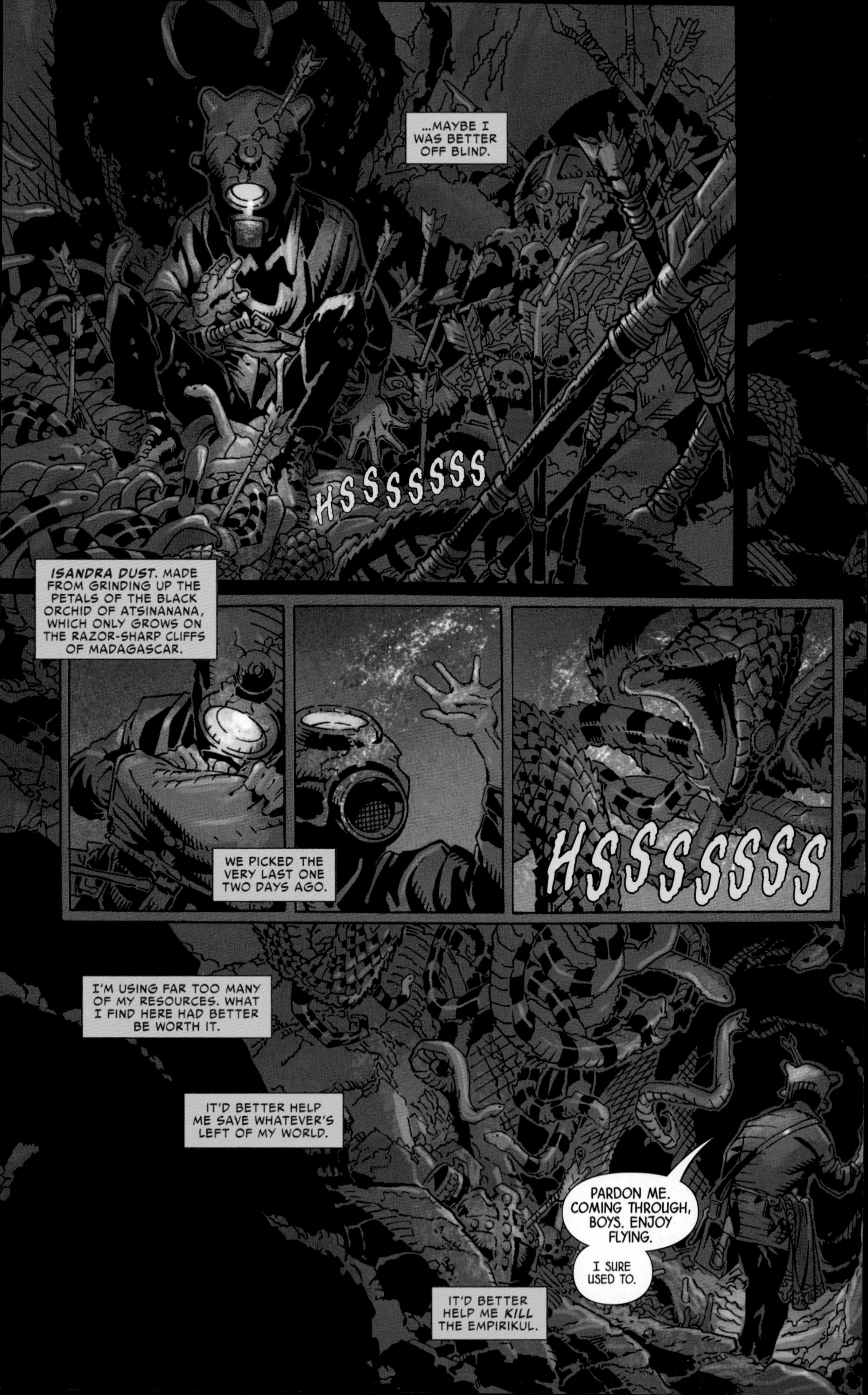
...MAYBE I WAS BETTER OFF BLIND.
HSSSSSSS
ISANDRA DUST. MADE FROM GRINDING UP THE PETALS OF THE BLACK ORCHID OF ATSINANANA, WHICH ONLY GROWS ON THE RAZOR-SHARP CLIFFS OF MADAGASCAR.
WE PICKED THE VERY LAST ONE TWO DAYS AGO.
HSSSSSSS
I'M USING FAR TOO MANY OF MY RESOURCES. WHAT I FIND HERE HAD BETTER BE WORTH IT.
IT'D BETTER HELP ME SAVE WHATEVER'S LEFT OF MY WORLD.
PARDON ME. COMING THROUGH, BOYS. ENJOY FLYING.
I SURE USED TO.
IT'D BETTER HELP ME ***KILL*** THE EMPIRIKUL.

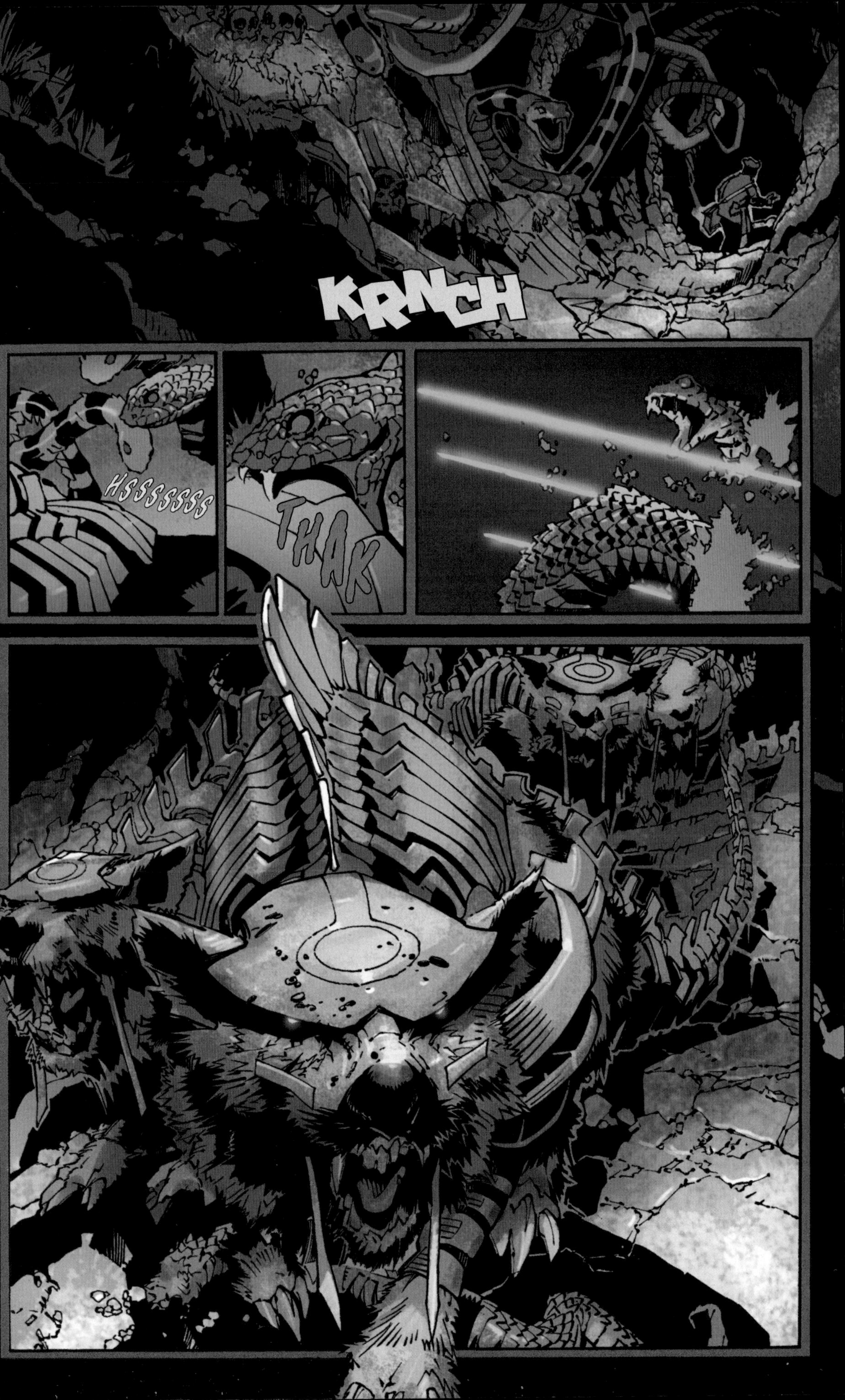
KRNCH
HSSSSSSS
THAK

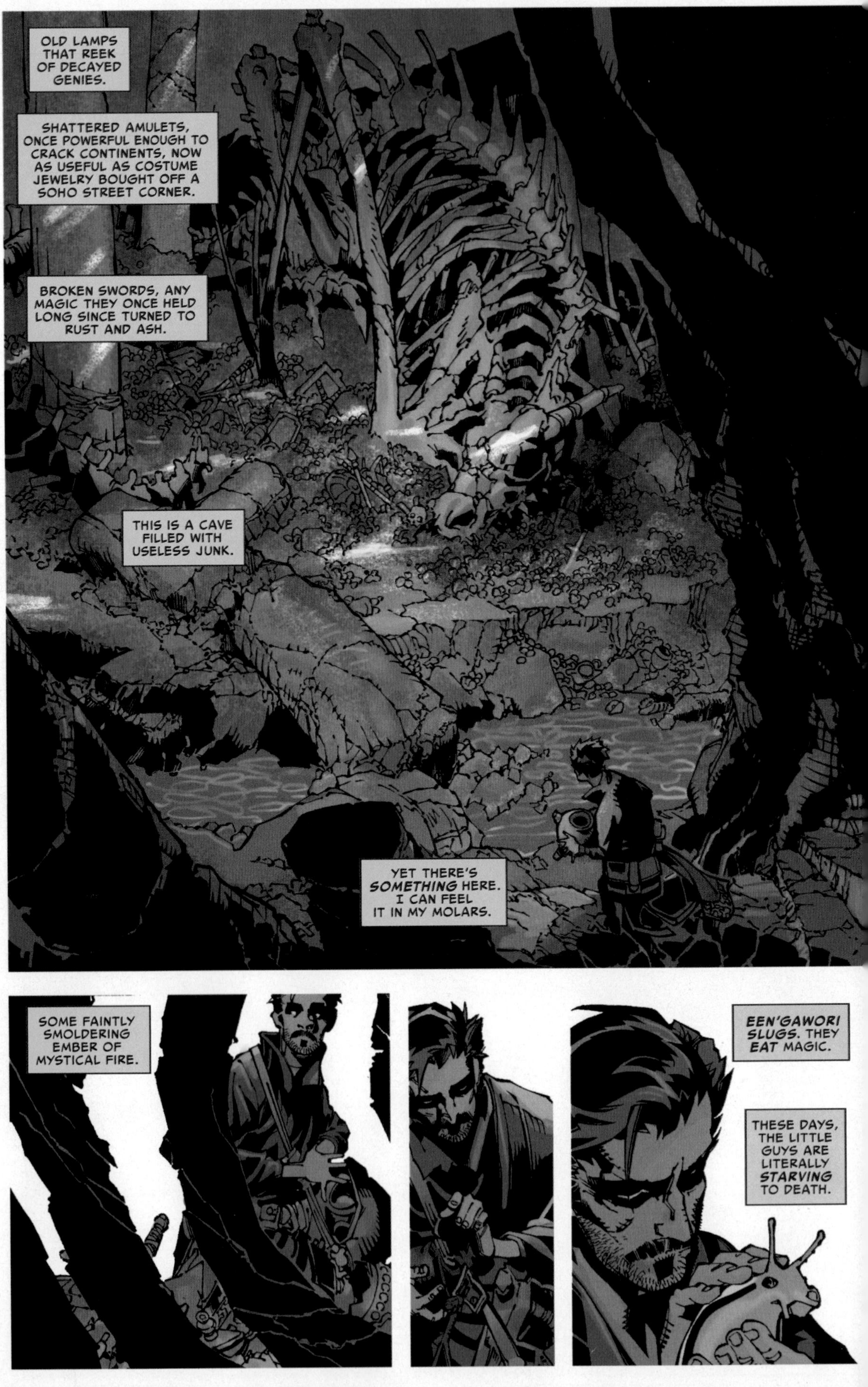
OLD LAMPS THAT REEK OF DECAYED GENIES.
SHATTERED AMULETS, ONCE POWERFUL ENOUGH TO CRACK CONTINENTS, NOW AS USEFUL AS COSTUME JEWELRY BOUGHT OFF A SOHO STREET CORNER.
BROKEN SWORDS, ANY MAGIC THEY ONCE HELD LONG SINCE TURNED TO RUST AND ASH.
THIS IS A CAVE FILLED WITH USELESS JUNK.
YET THERE'S *SOMETHING* HERE. I CAN FEEL IT IN MY MOLARS.
SOME FAINTLY SMOLDERING EMBER OF MYSTICAL FIRE.
EEN'GAWORI SLUGS. THEY *EAT* MAGIC.
THESE DAYS, THE LITTLE GUYS ARE LITERALLY *STARVING* TO DEATH.

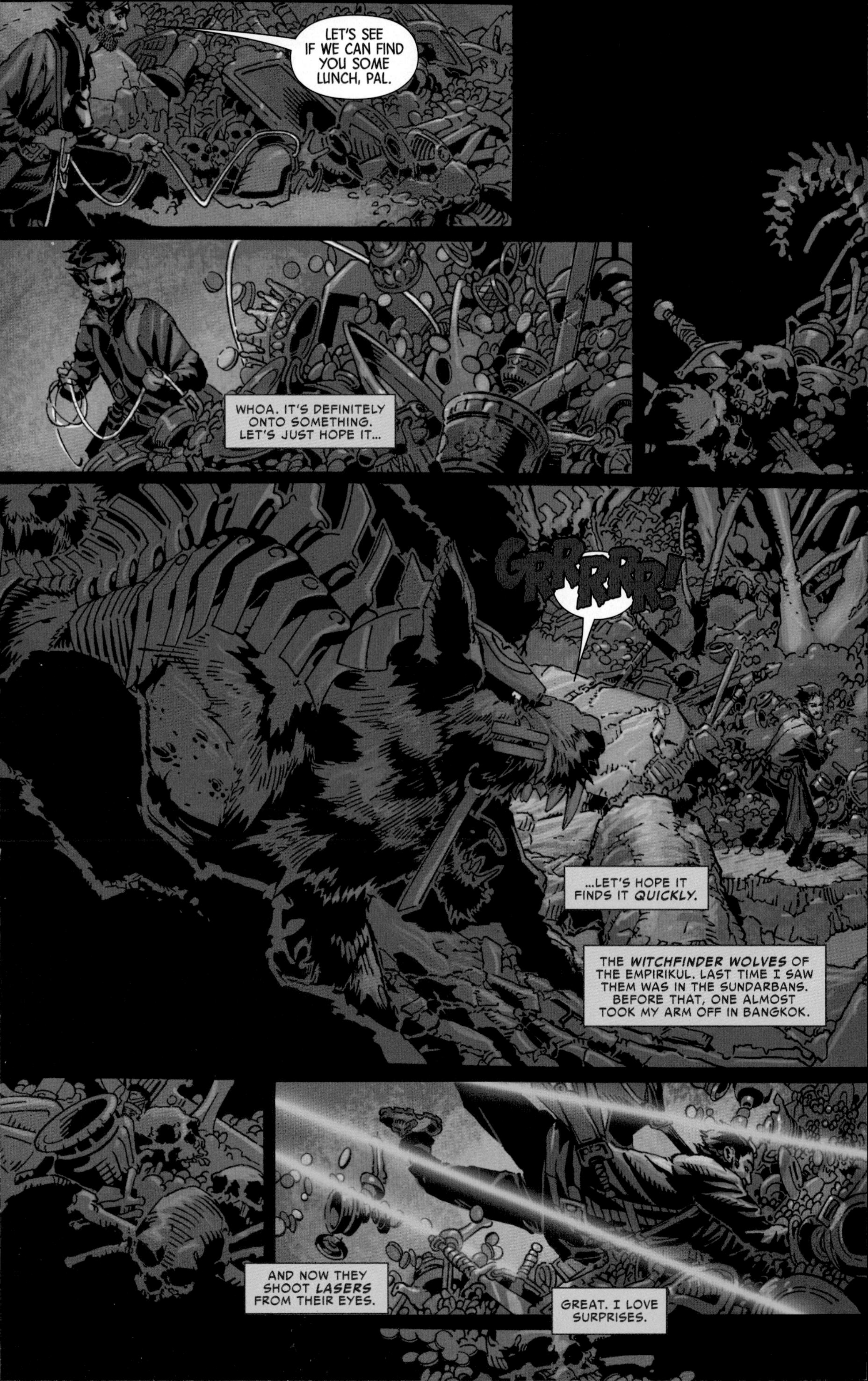
LET'S SEE IF WE CAN FIND YOU SOME LUNCH, PAL.
WHOA. IT'S DEFINITELY ONTO SOMETHING. LET'S JUST HOPE IT...
GRRRRR!
...LET'S HOPE IT FINDS IT QUICKLY.
THE WITCHFINDER WOLVES OF THE EMPIRIKUL. LAST TIME I SAW THEM WAS IN THE SUNDARBANS. BEFORE THAT, ONE ALMOST TOOK MY ARM OFF IN BANGKOK.
AND NOW THEY SHOOT LASERS FROM THEIR EYES.
GREAT. I LOVE SURPRISES.

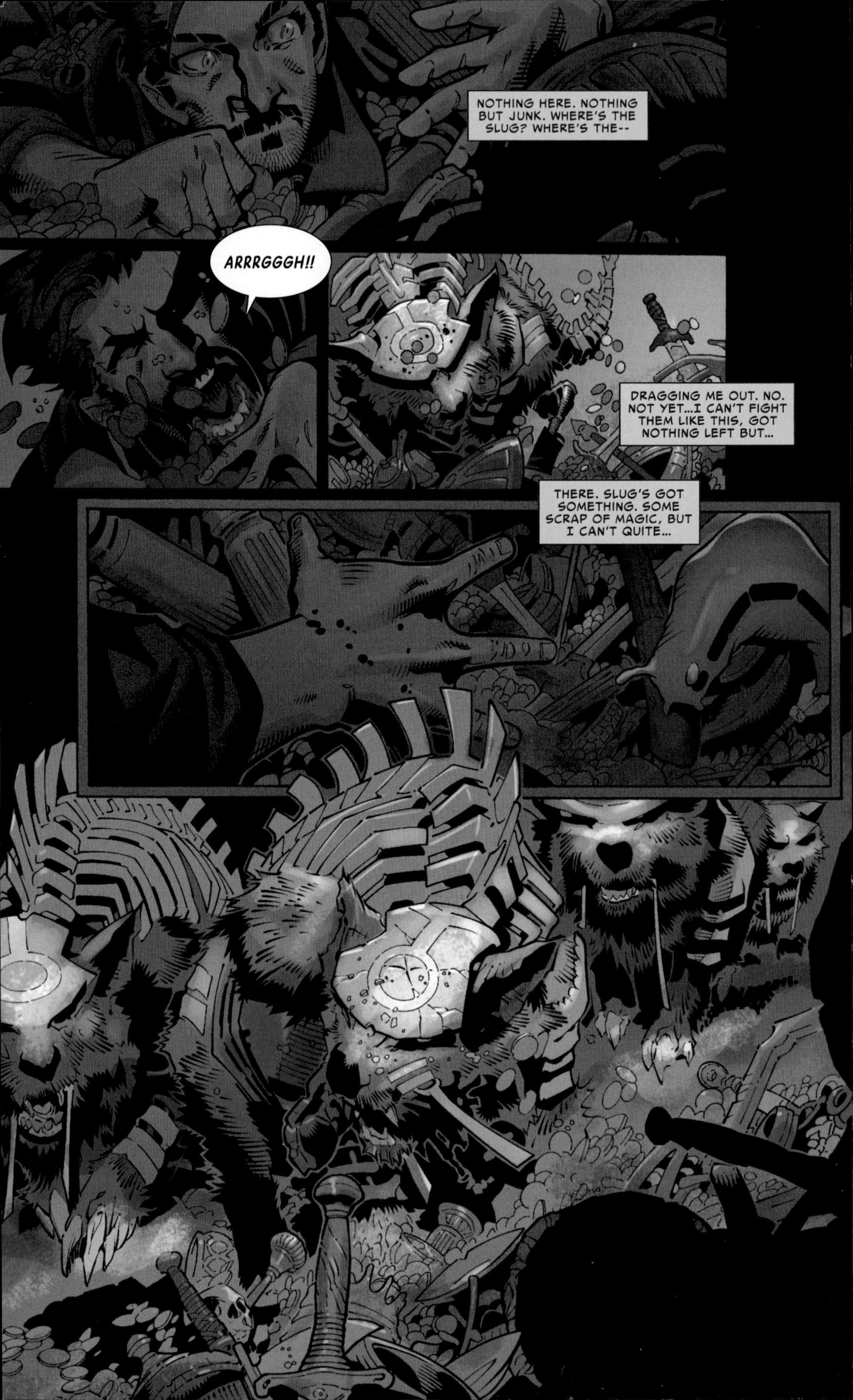
NOTHING HERE. NOTHING BUT JUNK. WHERE'S THE SLUG? WHERE'S THE--
ARRRGGGH!!
DRAGGING ME OUT. NO. NOT YET...I CAN'T FIGHT THEM LIKE THIS, GOT NOTHING LEFT BUT...
THERE. SLUG'S GOT SOMETHING. SOME SCRAP OF MAGIC, BUT I CAN'T QUITE...

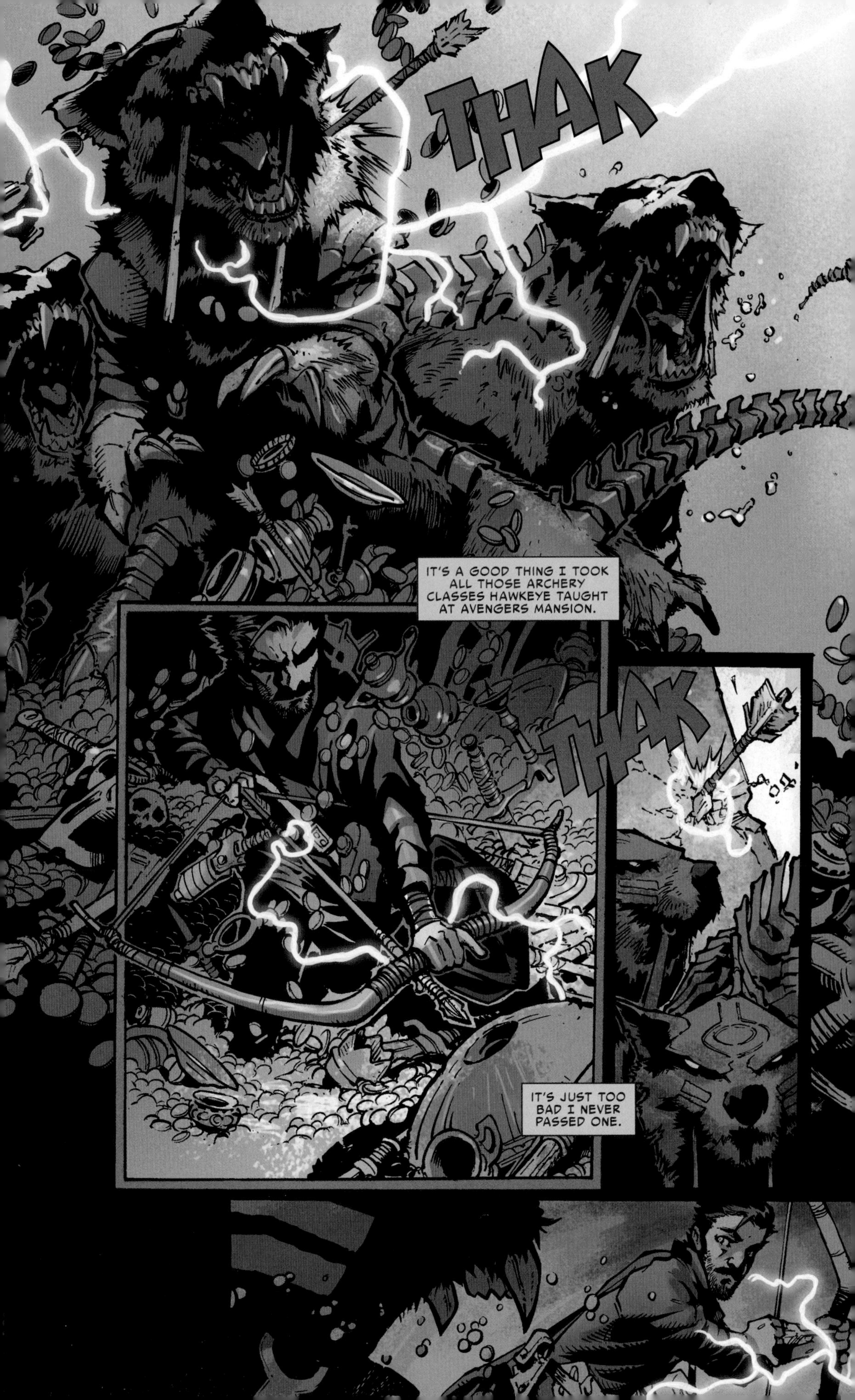
THAK
IT'S A GOOD THING I TOOK ALL THOSE ARCHERY CLASSES HAWKEYE TAUGHT AT AVENGERS MANSION.
IT'S JUST TOO BAD I NEVER PASSED ONE.
THAK

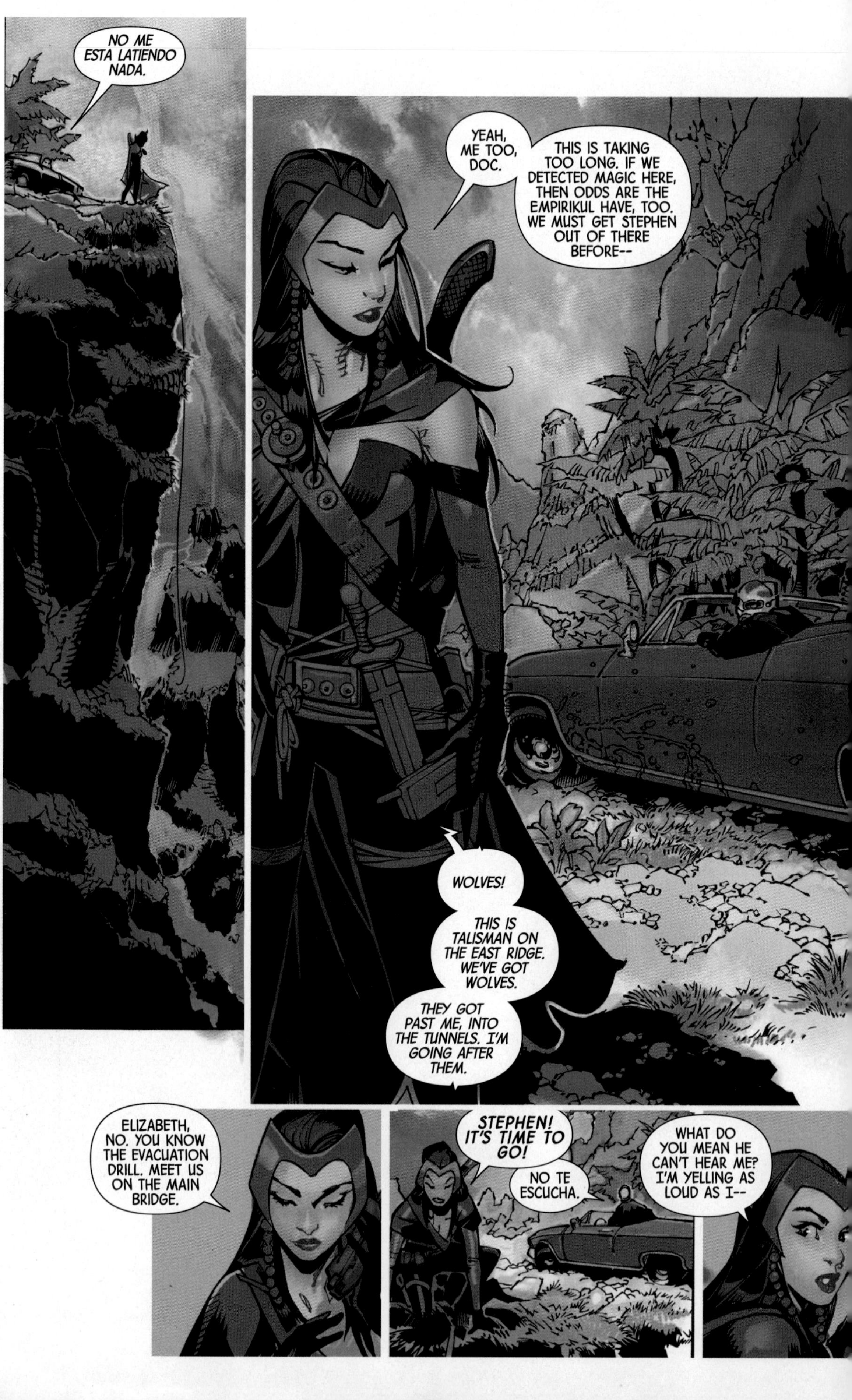
NO ME ESTA LATIENDO NADA.
YEAH, ME TOO, DOC.
THIS IS TAKING TOO LONG. IF WE DETECTED MAGIC HERE, THEN ODDS ARE THE EMPIRIKUL HAVE, TOO. WE MUST GET STEPHEN OUT OF THERE BEFORE--
WOLVES!
THIS IS TALISMAN ON THE EAST RIDGE. WE'VE GOT WOLVES.
THEY GOT PAST ME, INTO THE TUNNELS. I'M GOING AFTER THEM.
ELIZABETH, NO. YOU KNOW THE EVACUATION DRILL. MEET US ON THE MAIN BRIDGE.
STEPHEN! IT'S TIME TO GO!
NO TE ESCUCHA.
WHAT DO YOU MEAN HE CAN'T HEAR ME? I'M YELLING AS LOUD AS I--

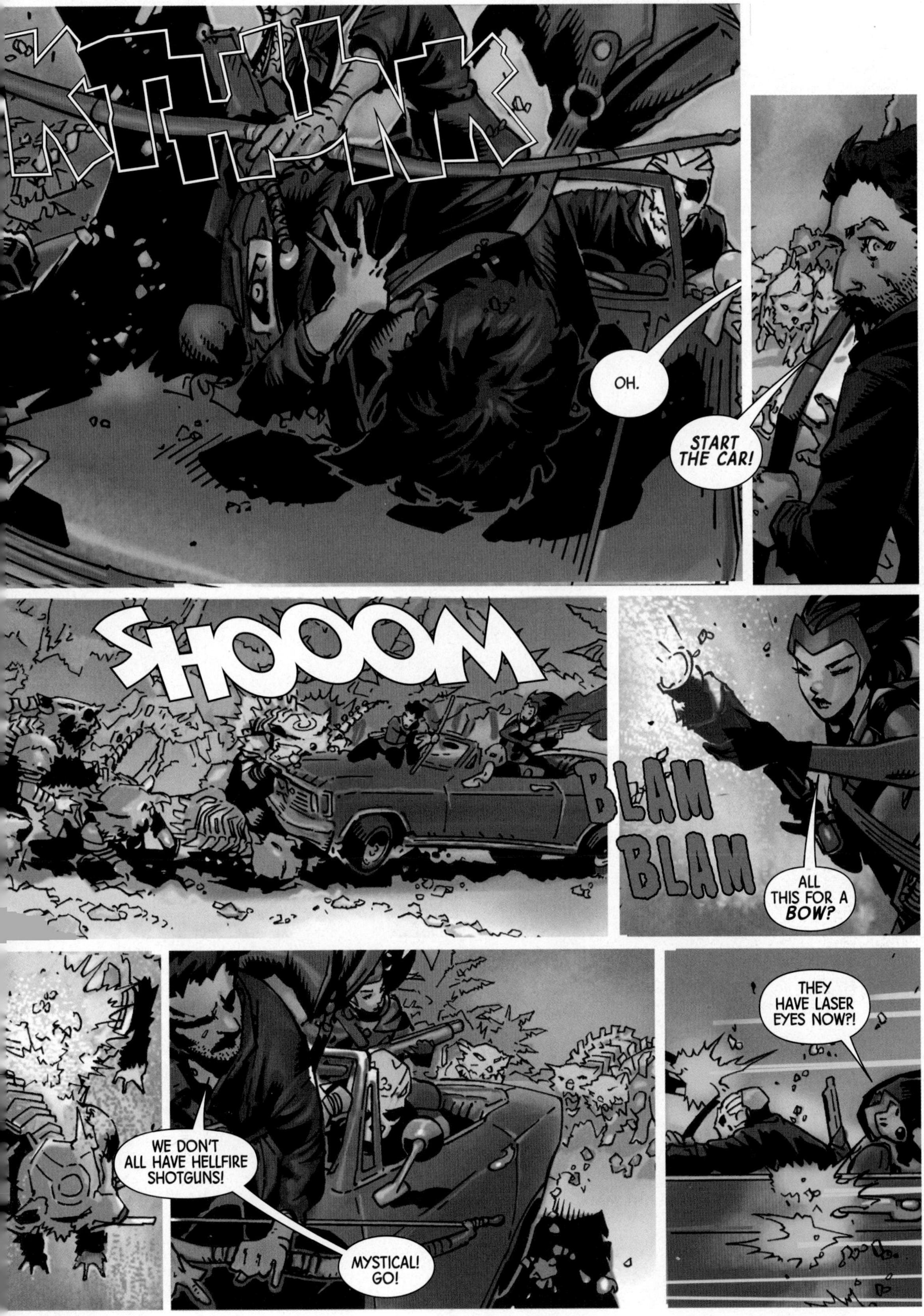
KTHUNK
OH.
START THE CAR!
SHOOOM
BLAM
BLAM
ALL THIS FOR A BOW?
WE DON'T ALL HAVE HELLFIRE SHOTGUNS!
MYSTICAL! GO!
THEY HAVE LASER EYES NOW?!

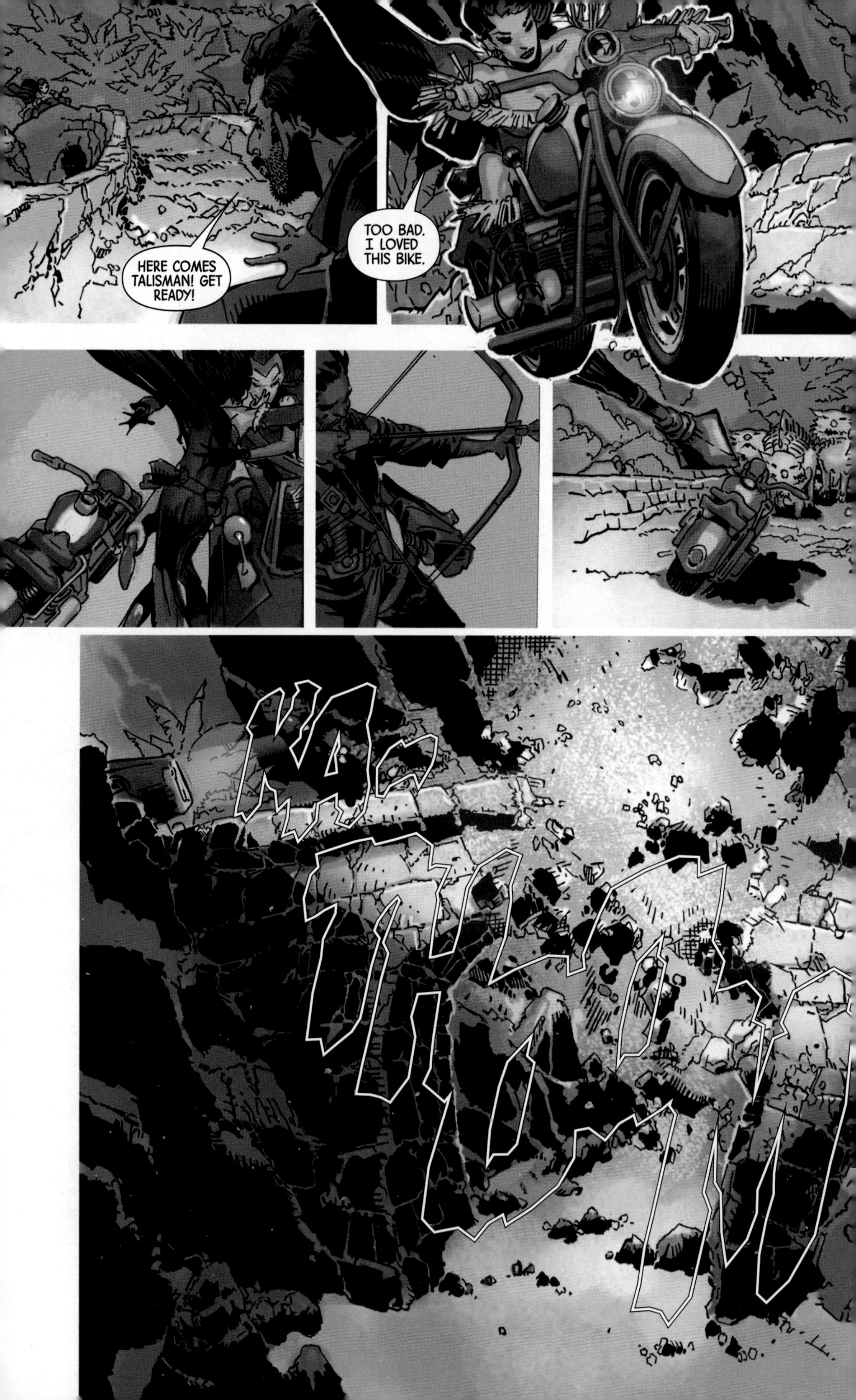
HERE COMES TALISMAN! GET READY!
TOO BAD. I LOVED THIS BIKE.

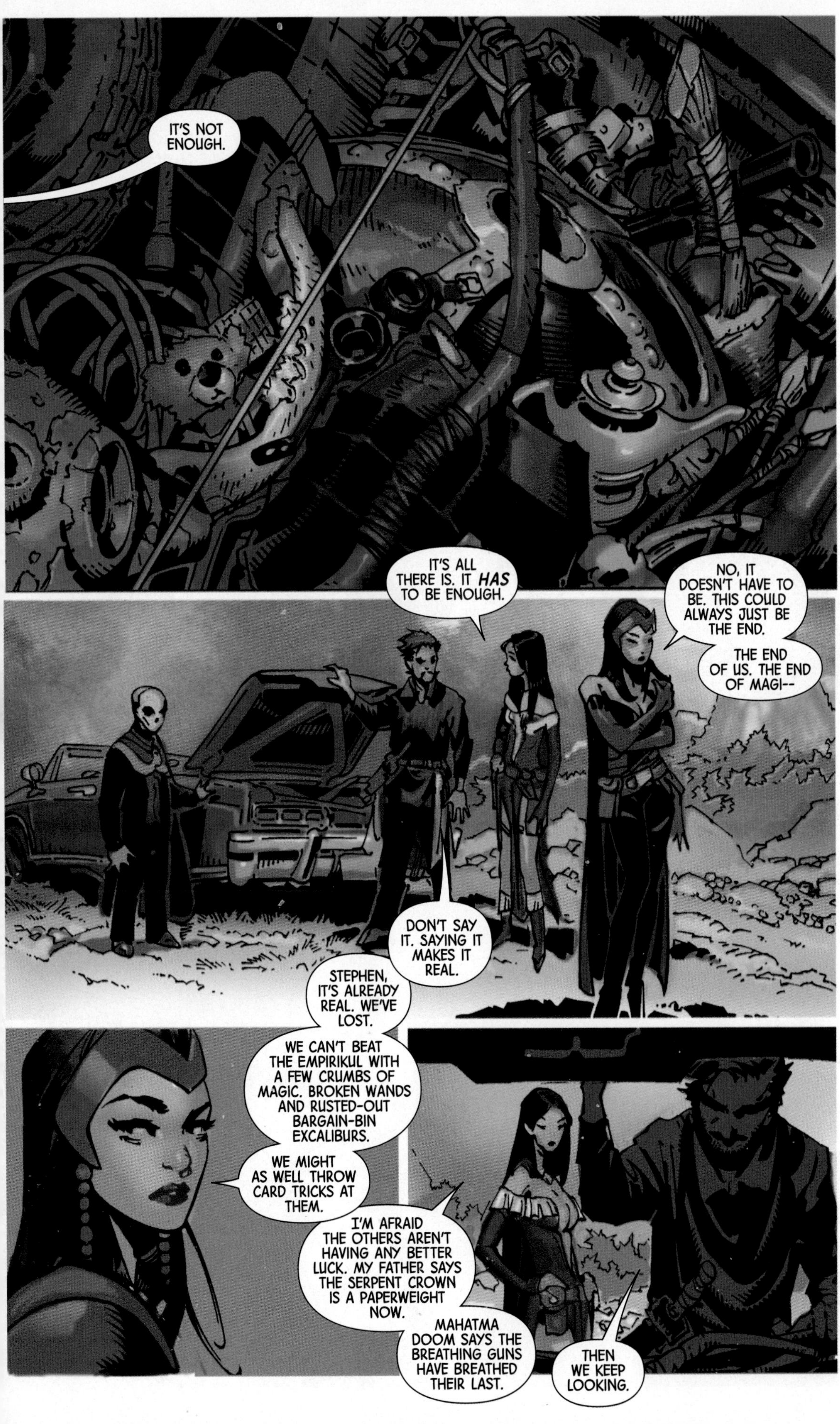

IT'S NOT ENOUGH.
IT'S ALL THERE IS. IT *HAS* TO BE ENOUGH.
NO, IT DOESN'T HAVE TO BE. THIS COULD ALWAYS JUST BE THE END.
THE END OF US. THE END OF MAGI--
DON'T SAY IT. SAYING IT MAKES IT REAL.
STEPHEN, IT'S ALREADY REAL. WE'VE LOST.
WE CAN'T BEAT THE EMPIRIKUL WITH A FEW CRUMBS OF MAGIC. BROKEN WANDS AND RUSTED-OUT BARGAIN-BIN EXCALIBURS.
WE MIGHT AS WELL THROW CARD TRICKS AT THEM.
I'M AFRAID THE OTHERS AREN'T HAVING ANY BETTER LUCK. MY FATHER SAYS THE SERPENT CROWN IS A PAPERWEIGHT NOW.
MAHATMA DOOM SAYS THE BREATHING GUNS HAVE BREATHED THEIR LAST.
THEN WE KEEP LOOKING.

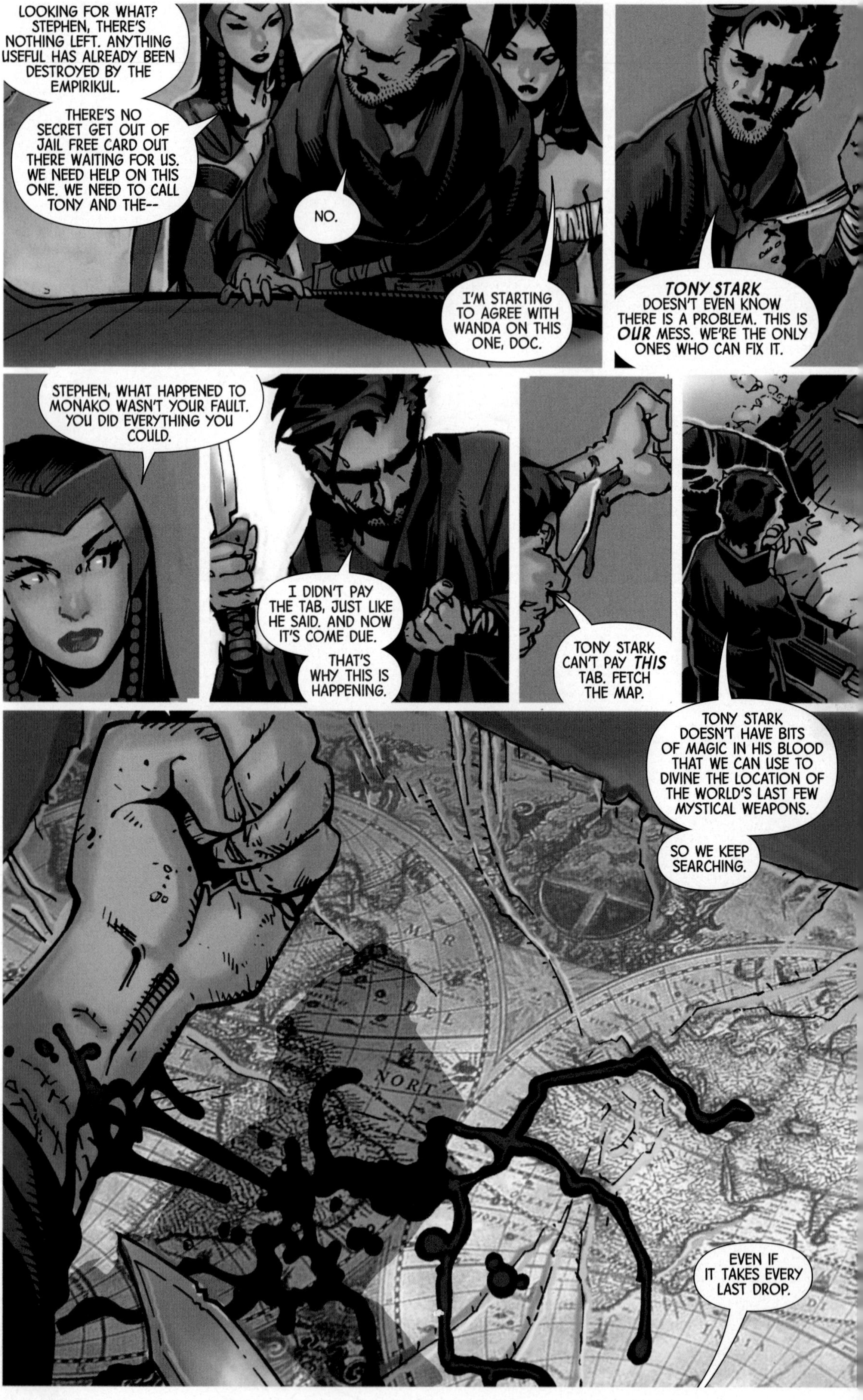
LOOKING FOR WHAT? STEPHEN, THERE'S NOTHING LEFT. ANYTHING USEFUL HAS ALREADY BEEN DESTROYED BY THE EMPIRIKUL.
THERE'S NO SECRET GET OUT OF JAIL FREE CARD OUT THERE WAITING FOR US. WE NEED HELP ON THIS ONE. WE NEED TO CALL TONY AND THE--
NO.
I'M STARTING TO AGREE WITH WANDA ON THIS ONE, DOC.
TONY STARK DOESN'T EVEN KNOW THERE IS A PROBLEM. THIS IS *OUR* MESS. WE'RE THE ONLY ONES WHO CAN FIX IT.
STEPHEN, WHAT HAPPENED TO MONAKO WASN'T YOUR FAULT. YOU DID EVERYTHING YOU COULD.
I DIDN'T PAY THE TAB, JUST LIKE HE SAID. AND NOW IT'S COME DUE.
THAT'S WHY THIS IS HAPPENING.
TONY STARK CAN'T PAY *THIS* TAB. FETCH THE MAP.
TONY STARK DOESN'T HAVE BITS OF MAGIC IN HIS BLOOD THAT WE CAN USE TO DIVINE THE LOCATION OF THE WORLD'S LAST FEW MYSTICAL WEAPONS.
SO WE KEEP SEARCHING.
EVEN IF IT TAKES EVERY LAST DROP.

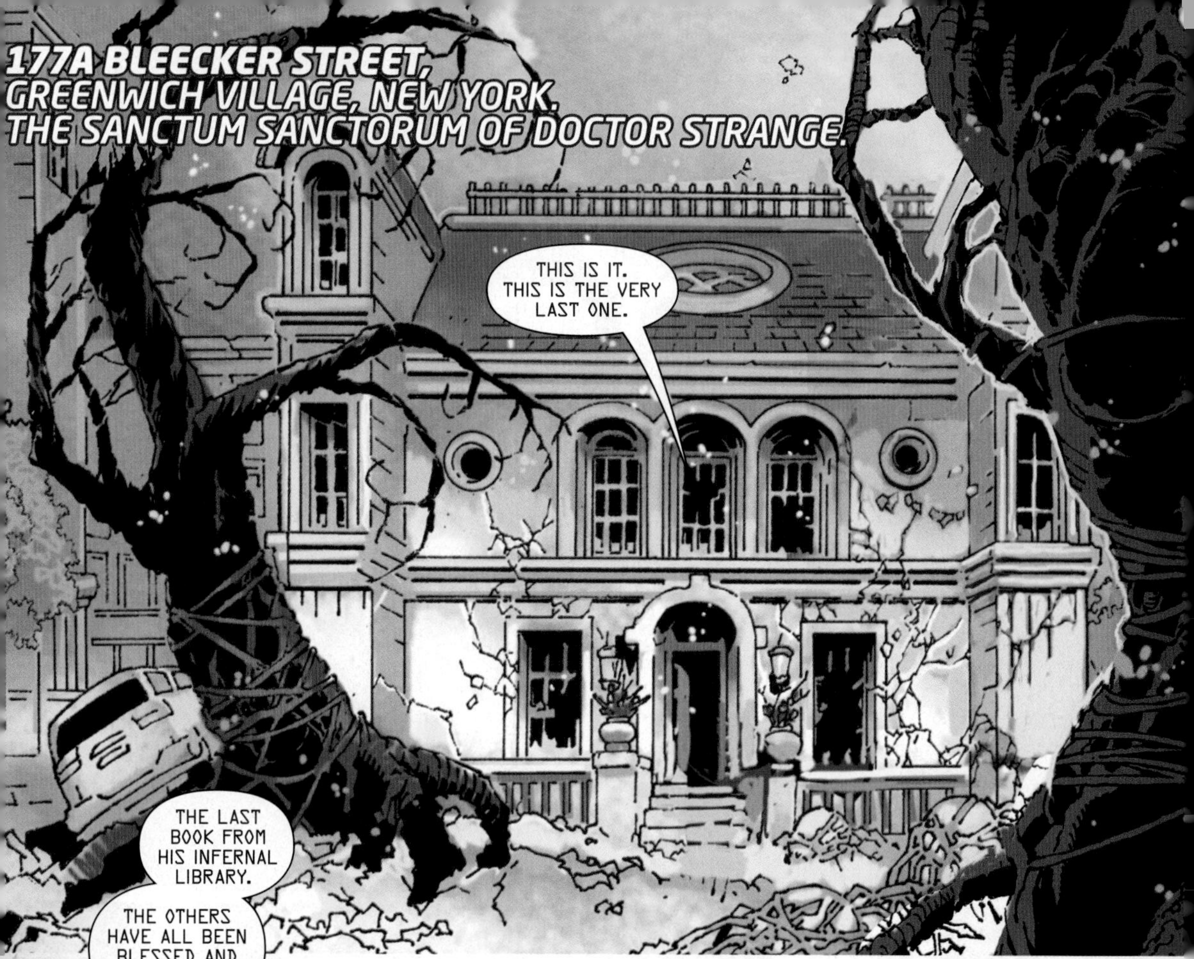
177A BLEECKER STREET,
GREENWICH VILLAGE, NEW YORK.
THE SANCTUM SANCTORUM OF DOCTOR STRANGE.
THIS IS IT. THIS IS THE VERY LAST ONE.
THE LAST BOOK FROM HIS INFERNAL LIBRARY.

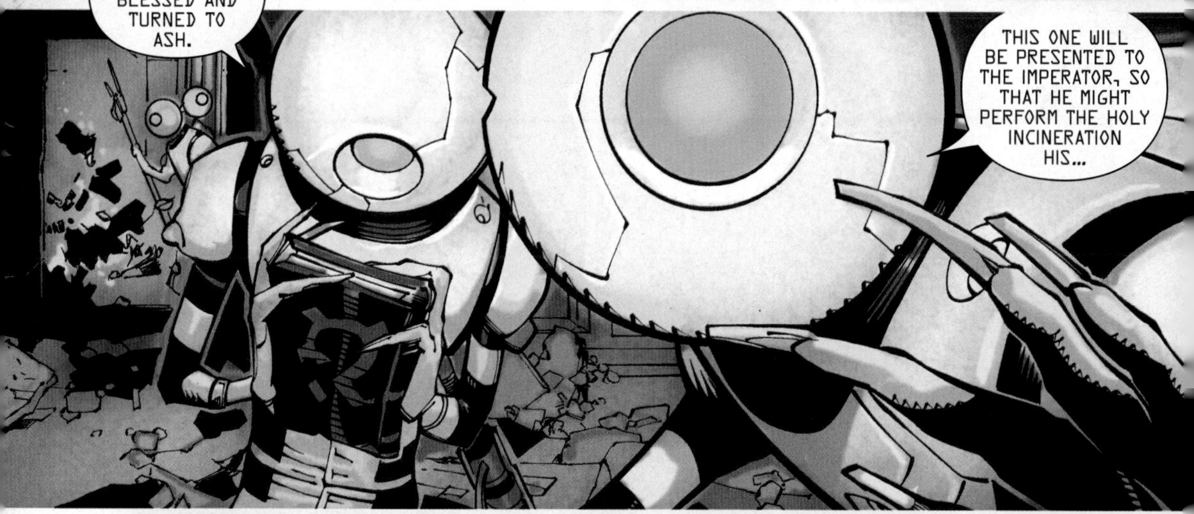
THE OTHERS HAVE ALL BEEN BLESSED AND TURNED TO ASH.
THIS ONE WILL BE PRESENTED TO THE IMPERATOR, SO THAT HE MIGHT PERFORM THE HOLY INCINERATION HIS...

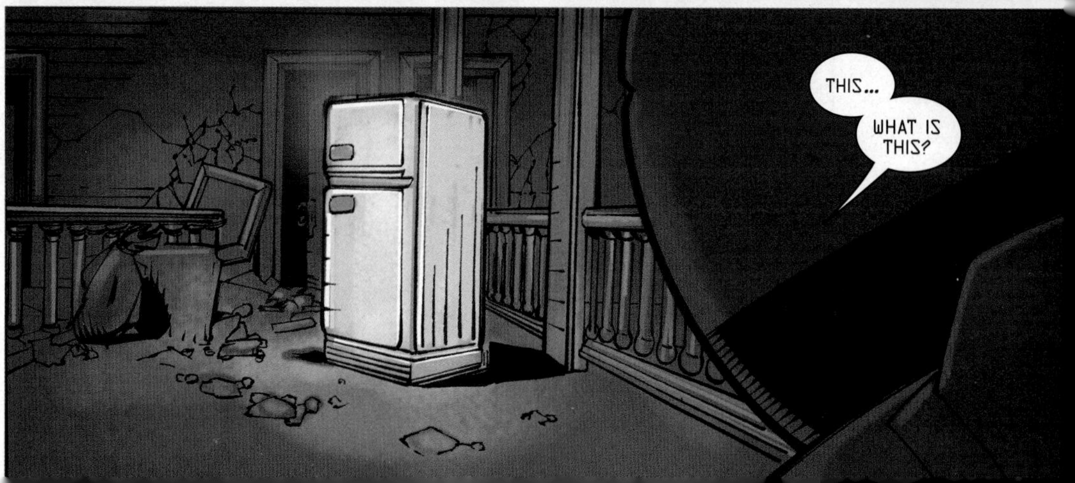
THIS...
WHAT IS THIS?

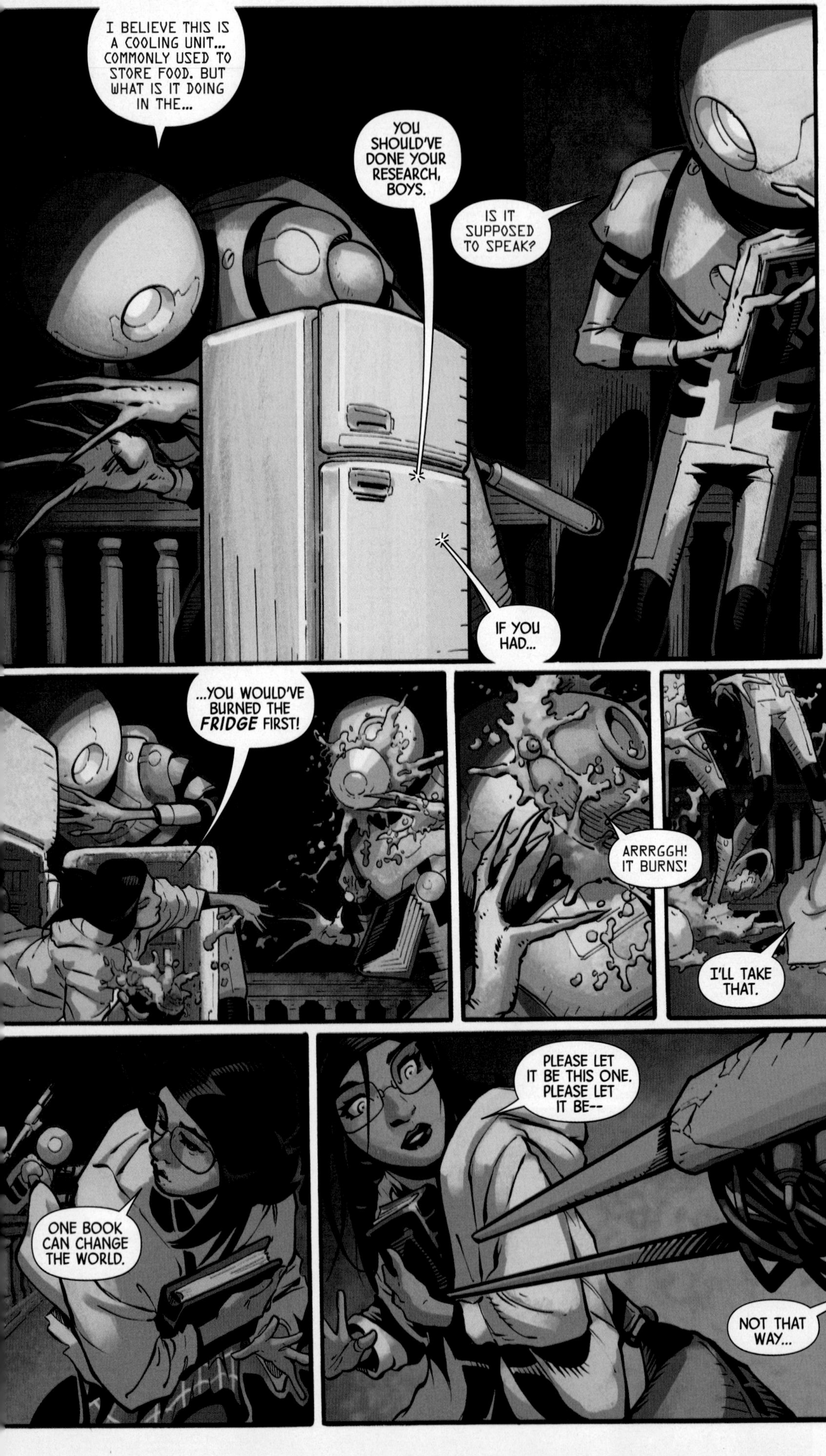
I BELIEVE THIS IS A COOLING UNIT... COMMONLY USED TO STORE FOOD. BUT WHAT IS IT DOING IN THE...
YOU SHOULD'VE DONE YOUR RESEARCH, BOYS.
IS IT SUPPOSED TO SPEAK?
IF YOU HAD...
...YOU WOULD'VE BURNED THE FRIDGE FIRST!
ARRRGGH! IT BURNS!
I'LL TAKE THAT.
ONE BOOK CAN CHANGE THE WORLD.
PLEASE LET IT BE THIS ONE. PLEASE LET IT BE--
NOT THAT WAY...

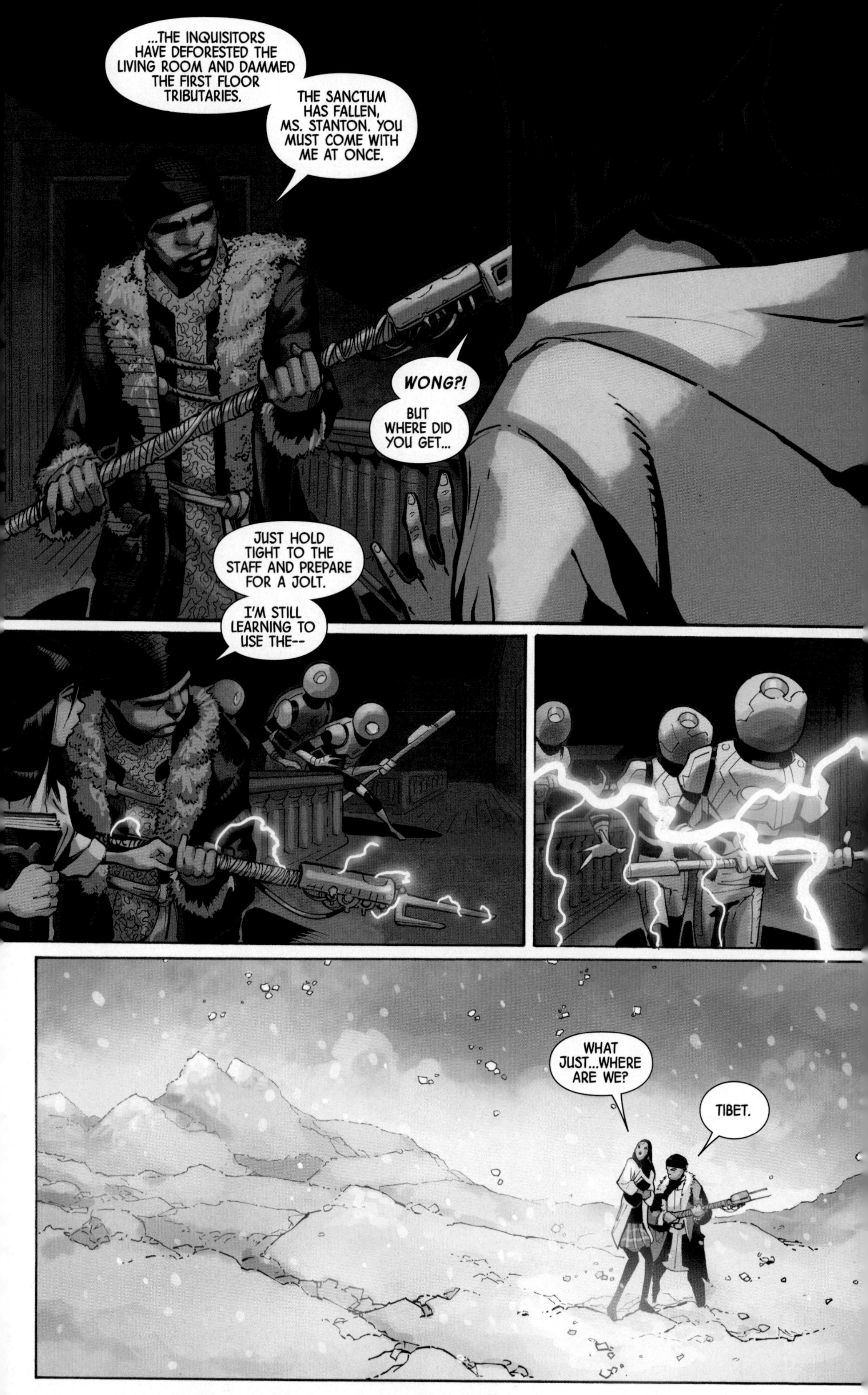
...THE INQUISITORS HAVE DEFORESTED THE LIVING ROOM AND DAMMED THE FIRST FLOOR TRIBUTARIES.
THE SANCTUM HAS FALLEN, MS. STANTON. YOU MUST COME WITH ME AT ONCE.
WONG?!
BUT WHERE DID YOU GET...
JUST HOLD TIGHT TO THE STAFF AND PREPARE FOR A JOLT.
I'M STILL LEARNING TO USE THE--
WHAT JUST...WHERE ARE WE?
TIBET.

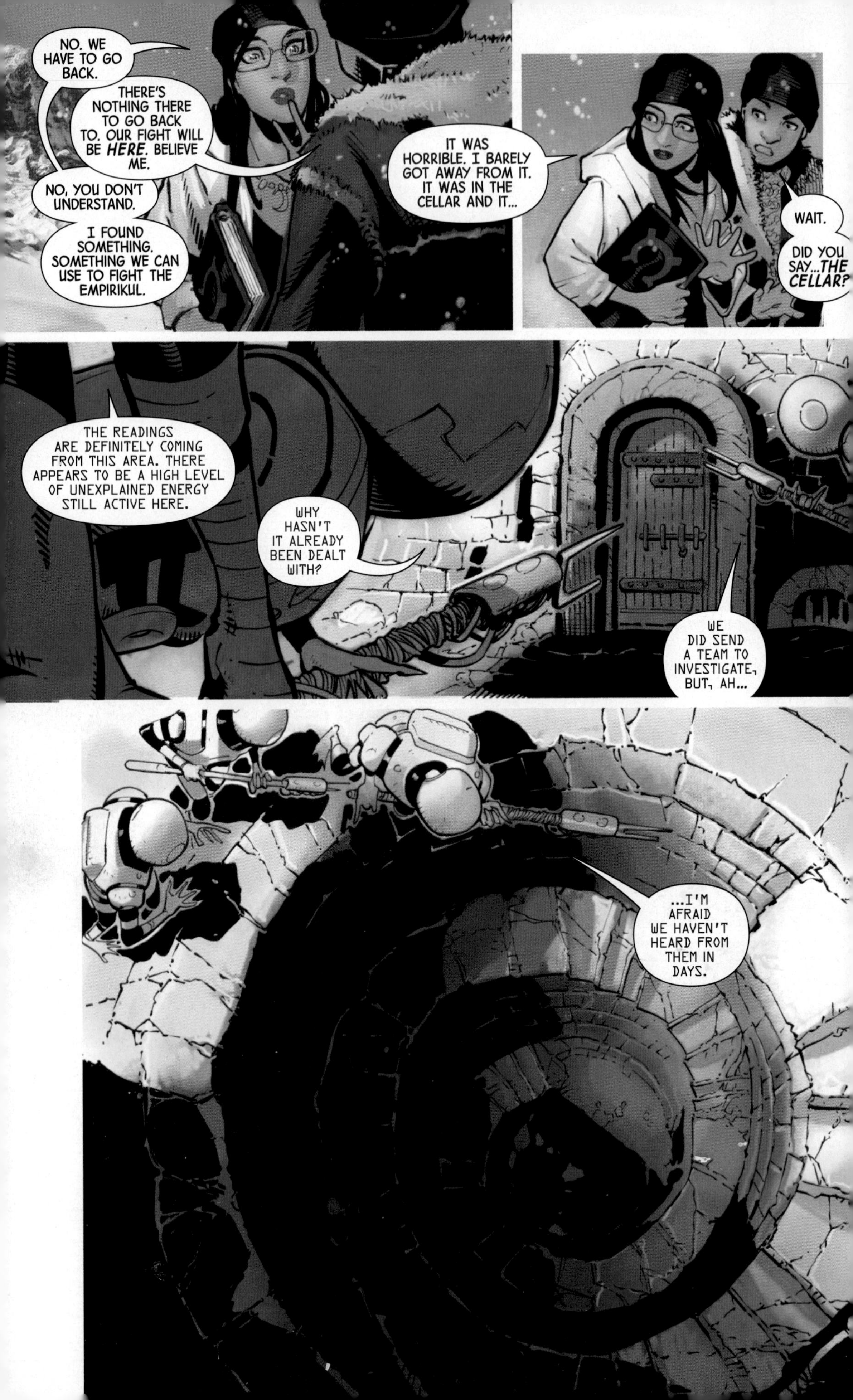
NO. WE HAVE TO GO BACK.
THERE'S NOTHING THERE TO GO BACK TO. OUR FIGHT WILL BE **HERE**. BELIEVE ME.
NO, YOU DON'T UNDERSTAND.
I FOUND SOMETHING. SOMETHING WE CAN USE TO FIGHT THE EMPIRIKUL.
IT WAS HORRIBLE. I BARELY GOT AWAY FROM IT. IT WAS IN THE CELLAR AND IT...
WAIT.
DID YOU SAY...**THE CELLAR?**
THE READINGS ARE DEFINITELY COMING FROM THIS AREA. THERE APPEARS TO BE A HIGH LEVEL OF UNEXPLAINED ENERGY STILL ACTIVE HERE.
WHY HASN'T IT ALREADY BEEN DEALT WITH?
WE DID SEND A TEAM TO INVESTIGATE, BUT, AH...
...I'M AFRAID WE HAVEN'T HEARD FROM THEM IN DAYS.

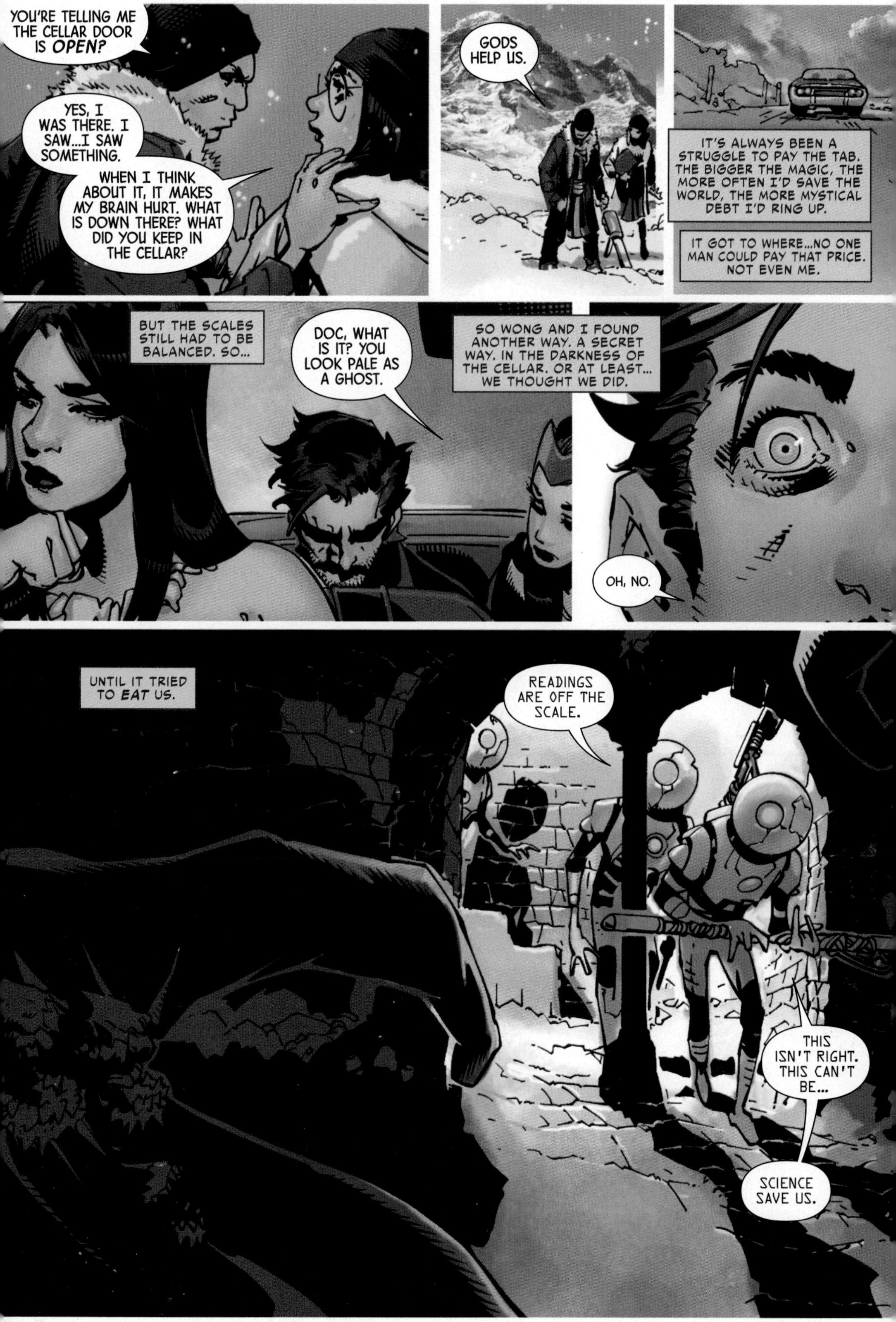
YOU'RE TELLING ME THE CELLAR DOOR IS *OPEN?*
YES, I WAS THERE. I SAW...I SAW SOMETHING.
WHEN I THINK ABOUT IT, IT MAKES MY BRAIN HURT. WHAT IS DOWN THERE? WHAT DID YOU KEEP IN THE CELLAR?
GODS HELP US.
IT'S ALWAYS BEEN A STRUGGLE TO PAY THE TAB. THE BIGGER THE MAGIC, THE MORE OFTEN I'D SAVE THE WORLD, THE MORE MYSTICAL DEBT I'D RING UP.
IT GOT TO WHERE...NO ONE MAN COULD PAY THAT PRICE. NOT EVEN ME.
BUT THE SCALES STILL HAD TO BE BALANCED. SO...
DOC, WHAT IS IT? YOU LOOK PALE AS A GHOST.
SO WONG AND I FOUND ANOTHER WAY. A SECRET WAY. IN THE DARKNESS OF THE CELLAR. OR AT LEAST... WE THOUGHT WE DID.
OH, NO.
UNTIL IT TRIED TO *EAT* US.
READINGS ARE OFF THE SCALE.
THIS ISN'T RIGHT. THIS CAN'T BE...
SCIENCE SAVE US.

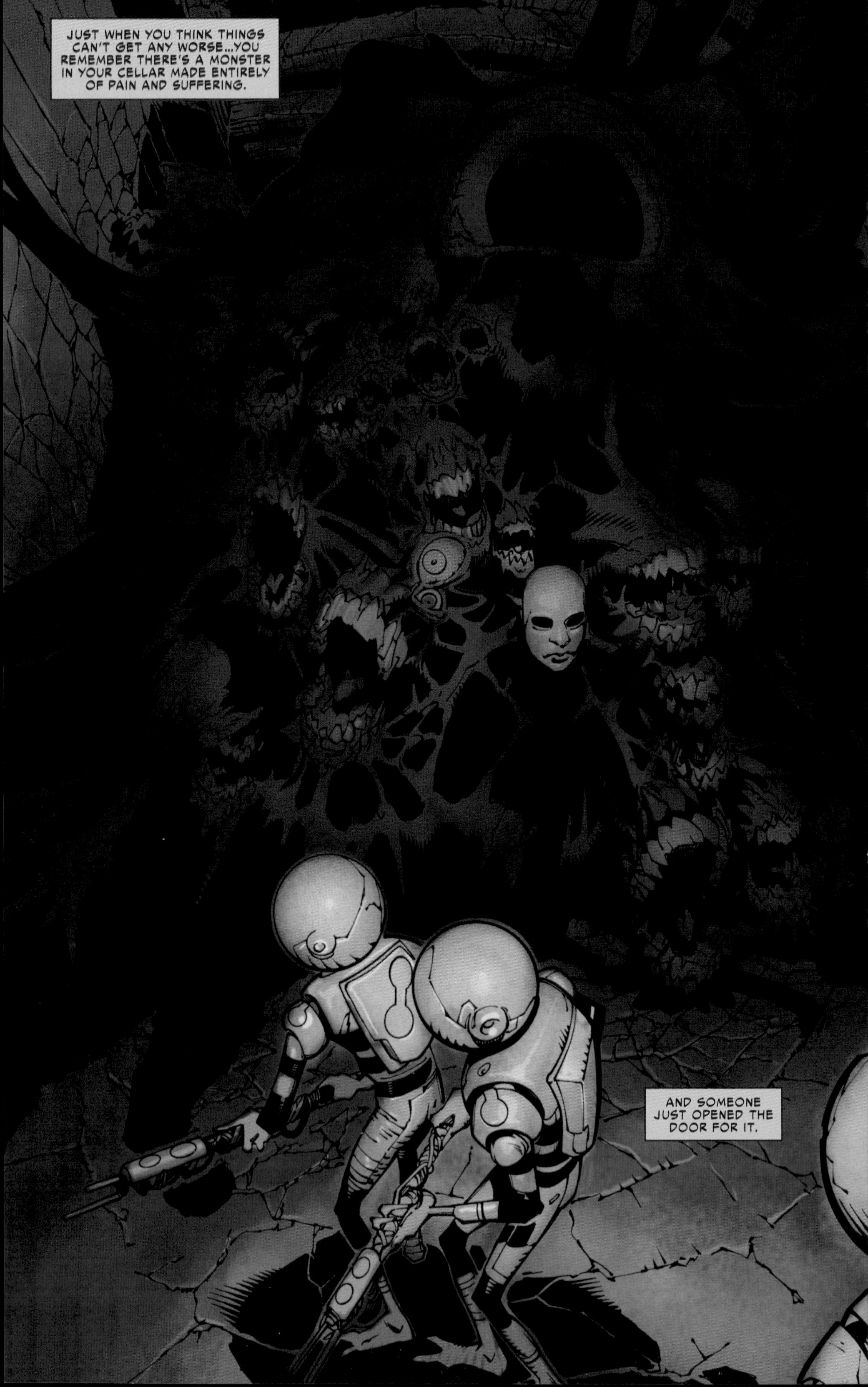
JUST WHEN YOU THINK THINGS CAN'T GET ANY WORSE...YOU REMEMBER THERE'S A MONSTER IN YOUR CELLAR MADE ENTIRELY OF PAIN AND SUFFERING.
AND SOMEONE JUST OPENED THE DOOR FOR IT.

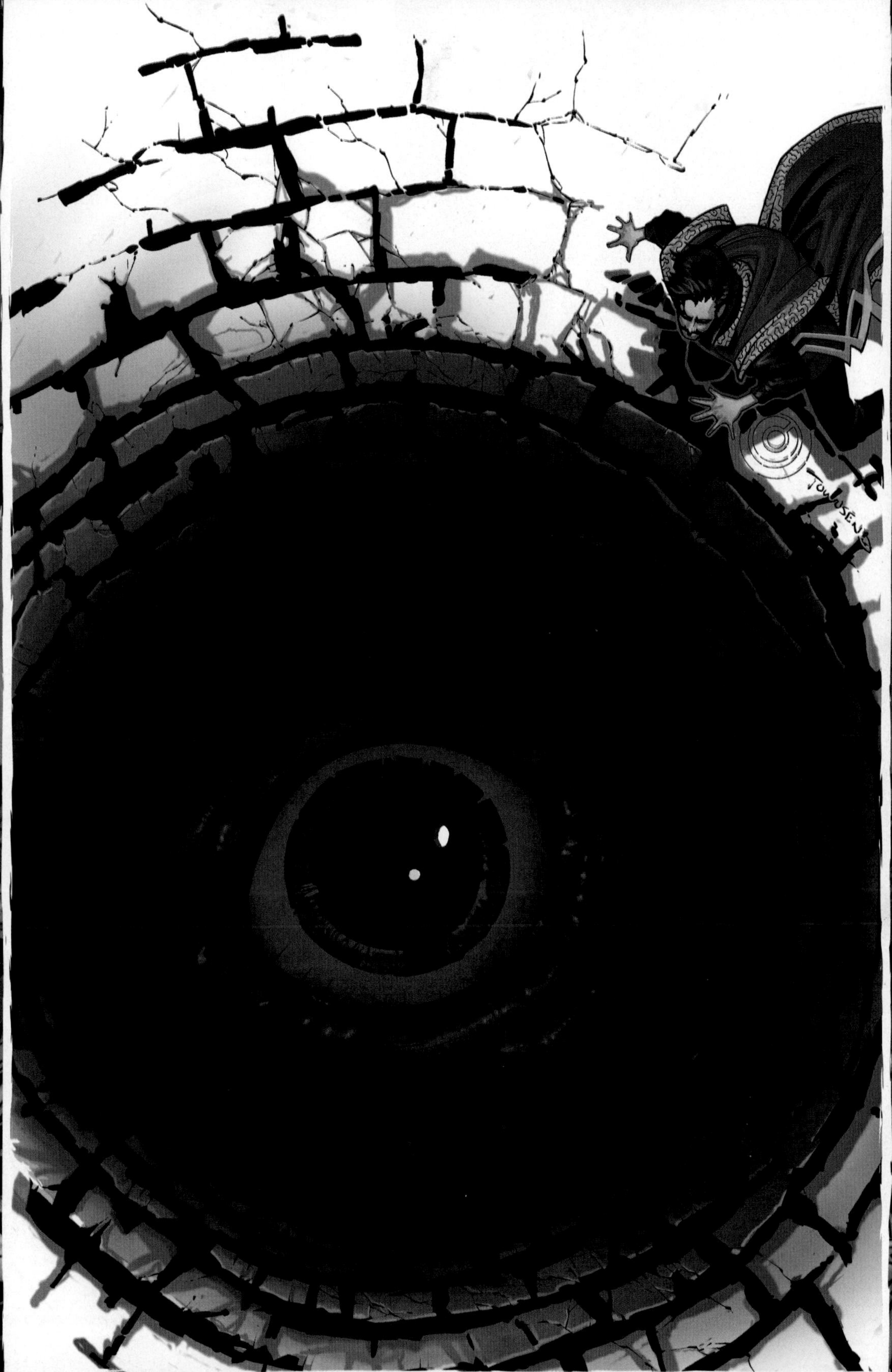
TOWNSEND

DOCTOR STRANGE 9 THE LAST DAYS OF MAGIC CHAPTER FOUR

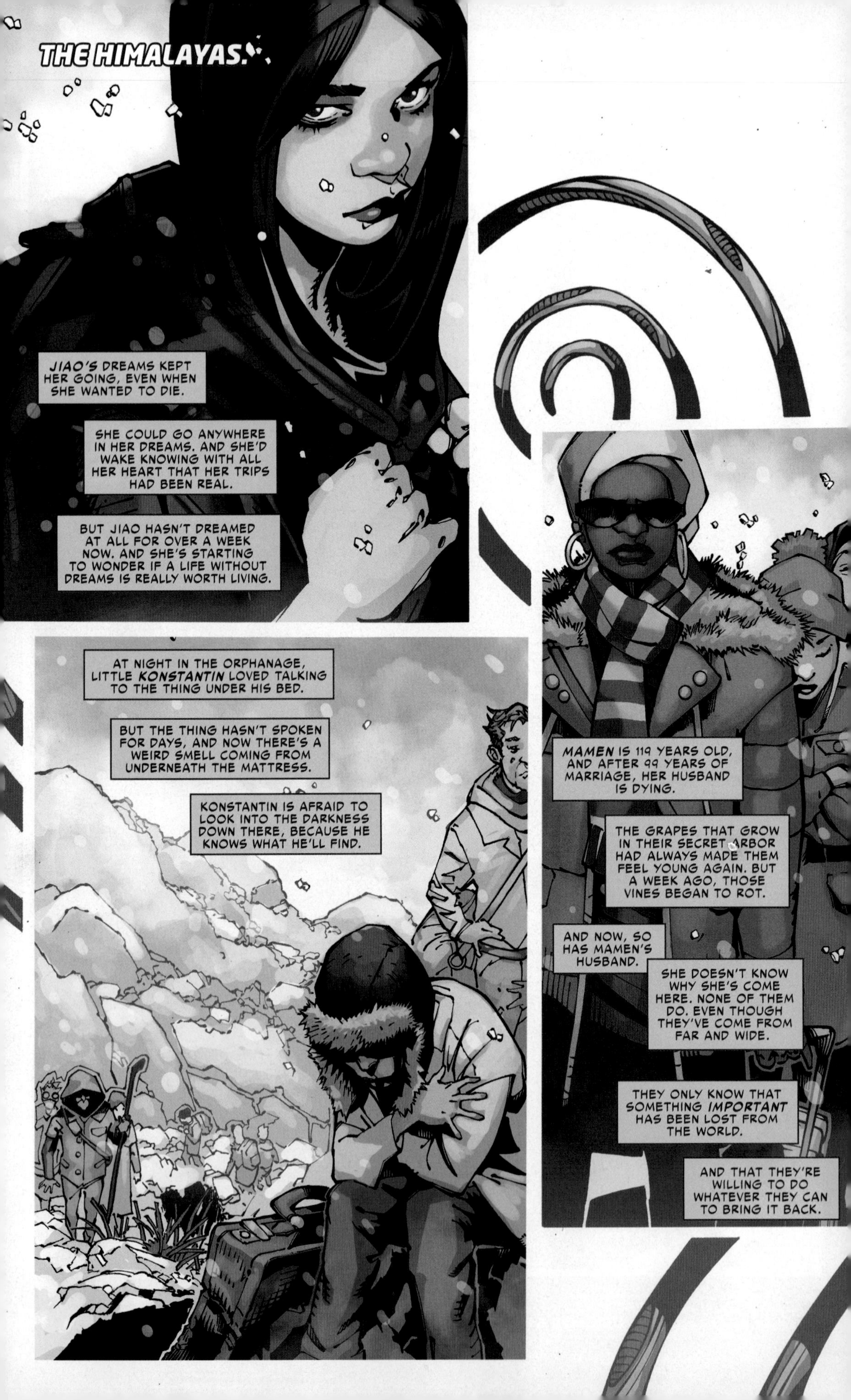
THE HIMALAYAS.
JIAO'S DREAMS KEPT HER GOING, EVEN WHEN SHE WANTED TO DIE.
SHE COULD GO ANYWHERE IN HER DREAMS. AND SHE'D WAKE KNOWING WITH ALL HER HEART THAT HER TRIPS HAD BEEN REAL.
BUT JIAO HASN'T DREAMED AT ALL FOR OVER A WEEK NOW. AND SHE'S STARTING TO WONDER IF A LIFE WITHOUT DREAMS IS REALLY WORTH LIVING.
MAMEN IS 119 YEARS OLD, AND AFTER 99 YEARS OF MARRIAGE, HER HUSBAND IS DYING.
THE GRAPES THAT GROW IN THEIR SECRET ARBOR HAD ALWAYS MADE THEM FEEL YOUNG AGAIN. BUT A WEEK AGO, THOSE VINES BEGAN TO ROT.
AND NOW, SO HAS MAMEN'S HUSBAND.
SHE DOESN'T KNOW WHY SHE'S COME HERE. NONE OF THEM DO. EVEN THOUGH THEY'VE COME FROM FAR AND WIDE.
THEY ONLY KNOW THAT SOMETHING IMPORTANT HAS BEEN LOST FROM THE WORLD.
AND THAT THEY'RE WILLING TO DO WHATEVER THEY CAN TO BRING IT BACK.
AT NIGHT IN THE ORPHANAGE, LITTLE KONSTANTIN LOVED TALKING TO THE THING UNDER HIS BED.
BUT THE THING HASN'T SPOKEN FOR DAYS, AND NOW THERE'S A WEIRD SMELL COMING FROM UNDERNEATH THE MATTRESS.
KONSTANTIN IS AFRAID TO LOOK INTO THE DARKNESS DOWN THERE, BECAUSE HE KNOWS WHAT HE'LL FIND.

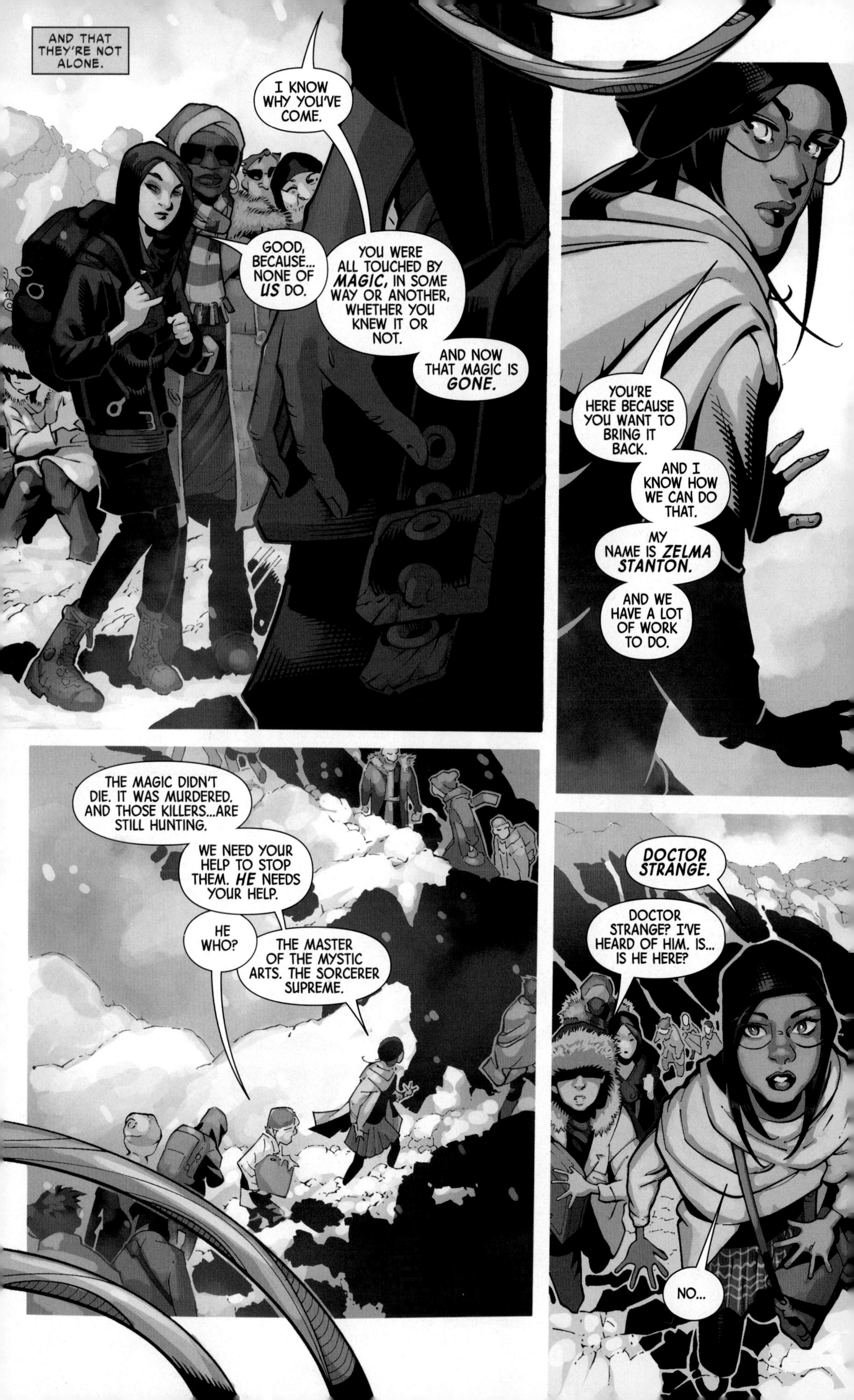
AND THAT THEY'RE NOT ALONE.
I KNOW WHY YOU'VE COME.
GOOD, BECAUSE... NONE OF US DO.
YOU WERE ALL TOUCHED BY MAGIC, IN SOME WAY OR ANOTHER, WHETHER YOU KNEW IT OR NOT.
AND NOW THAT MAGIC IS GONE.
YOU'RE HERE BECAUSE YOU WANT TO BRING IT BACK.
AND I KNOW HOW WE CAN DO THAT.
MY NAME IS ZELMA STANTON.
AND WE HAVE A LOT OF WORK TO DO.
THE MAGIC DIDN'T DIE. IT WAS MURDERED. AND THOSE KILLERS...ARE STILL HUNTING.
WE NEED YOUR HELP TO STOP THEM. HE NEEDS YOUR HELP.
HE WHO?
THE MASTER OF THE MYSTIC ARTS. THE SORCERER SUPREME.
DOCTOR STRANGE.
DOCTOR STRANGE? I'VE HEARD OF HIM. IS... IS HE HERE?
NO...

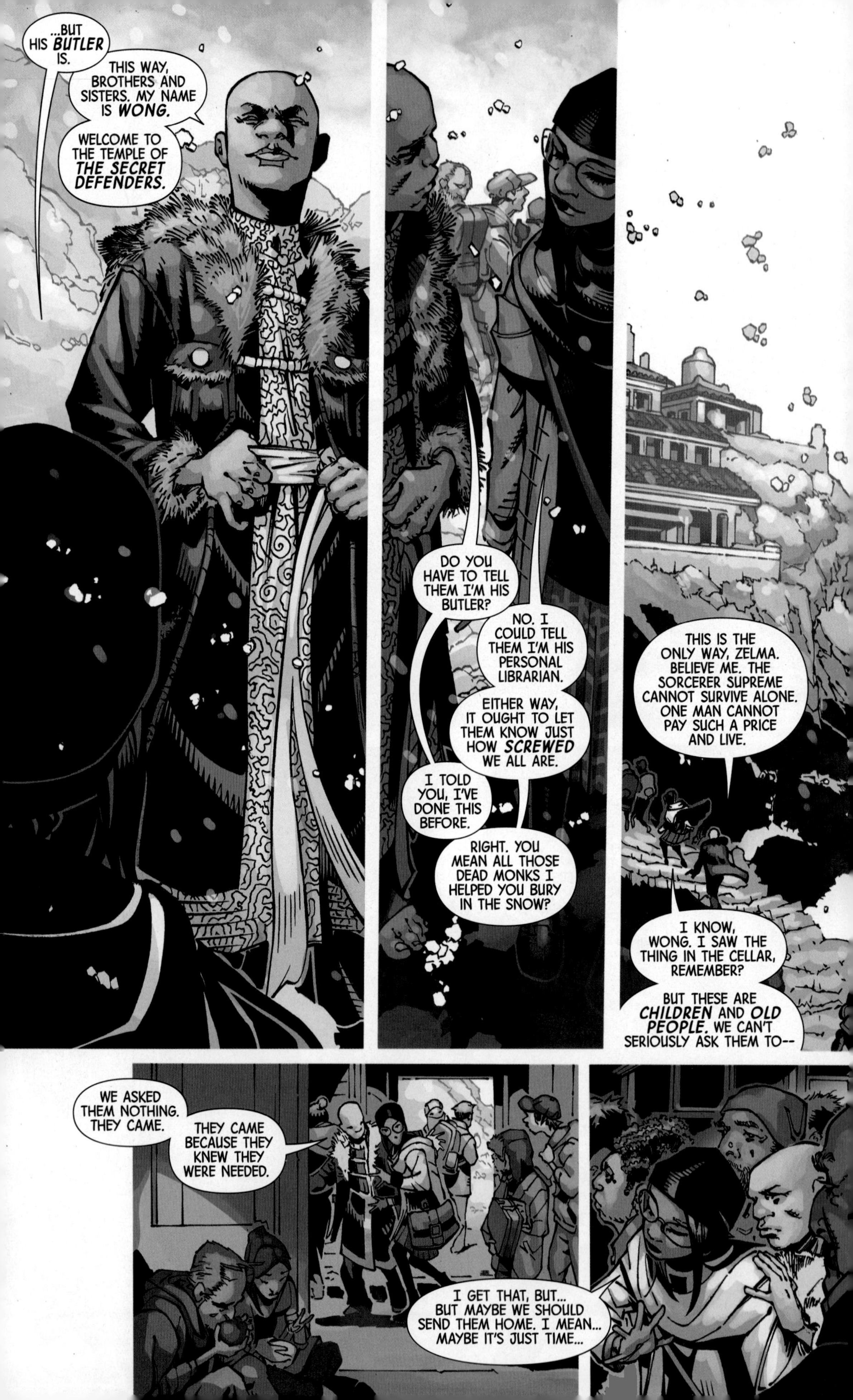
...BUT HIS BUTLER IS.
THIS WAY, BROTHERS AND SISTERS. MY NAME IS WONG.
WELCOME TO THE TEMPLE OF THE SECRET DEFENDERS.
DO YOU HAVE TO TELL THEM I'M HIS BUTLER?
NO. I COULD TELL THEM I'M HIS PERSONAL LIBRARIAN.
EITHER WAY, IT OUGHT TO LET THEM KNOW JUST HOW SCREWED WE ALL ARE.
I TOLD YOU, I'VE DONE THIS BEFORE.
RIGHT. YOU MEAN ALL THOSE DEAD MONKS I HELPED YOU BURY IN THE SNOW?
THIS IS THE ONLY WAY, ZELMA. BELIEVE ME. THE SORCERER SUPREME CANNOT SURVIVE ALONE. ONE MAN CANNOT PAY SUCH A PRICE AND LIVE.
I KNOW, WONG. I SAW THE THING IN THE CELLAR, REMEMBER?
BUT THESE ARE CHILDREN AND OLD PEOPLE. WE CAN'T SERIOUSLY ASK THEM TO--
WE ASKED THEM NOTHING. THEY CAME.
THEY CAME BECAUSE THEY KNEW THEY WERE NEEDED.
I GET THAT, BUT... BUT MAYBE WE SHOULD SEND THEM HOME. I MEAN... MAYBE IT'S JUST TIME...

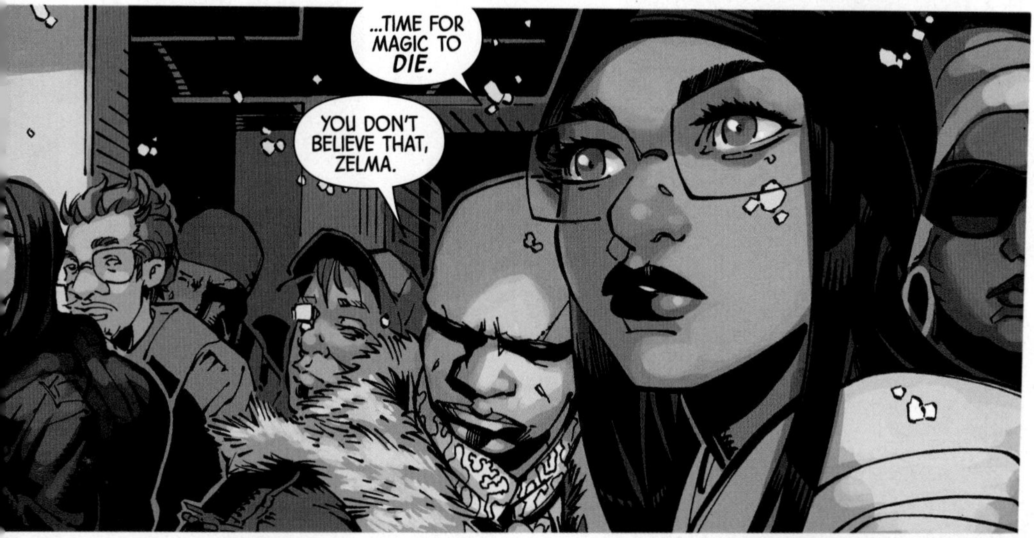
...TIME FOR MAGIC TO DIE.
YOU DON'T BELIEVE THAT, ZELMA.

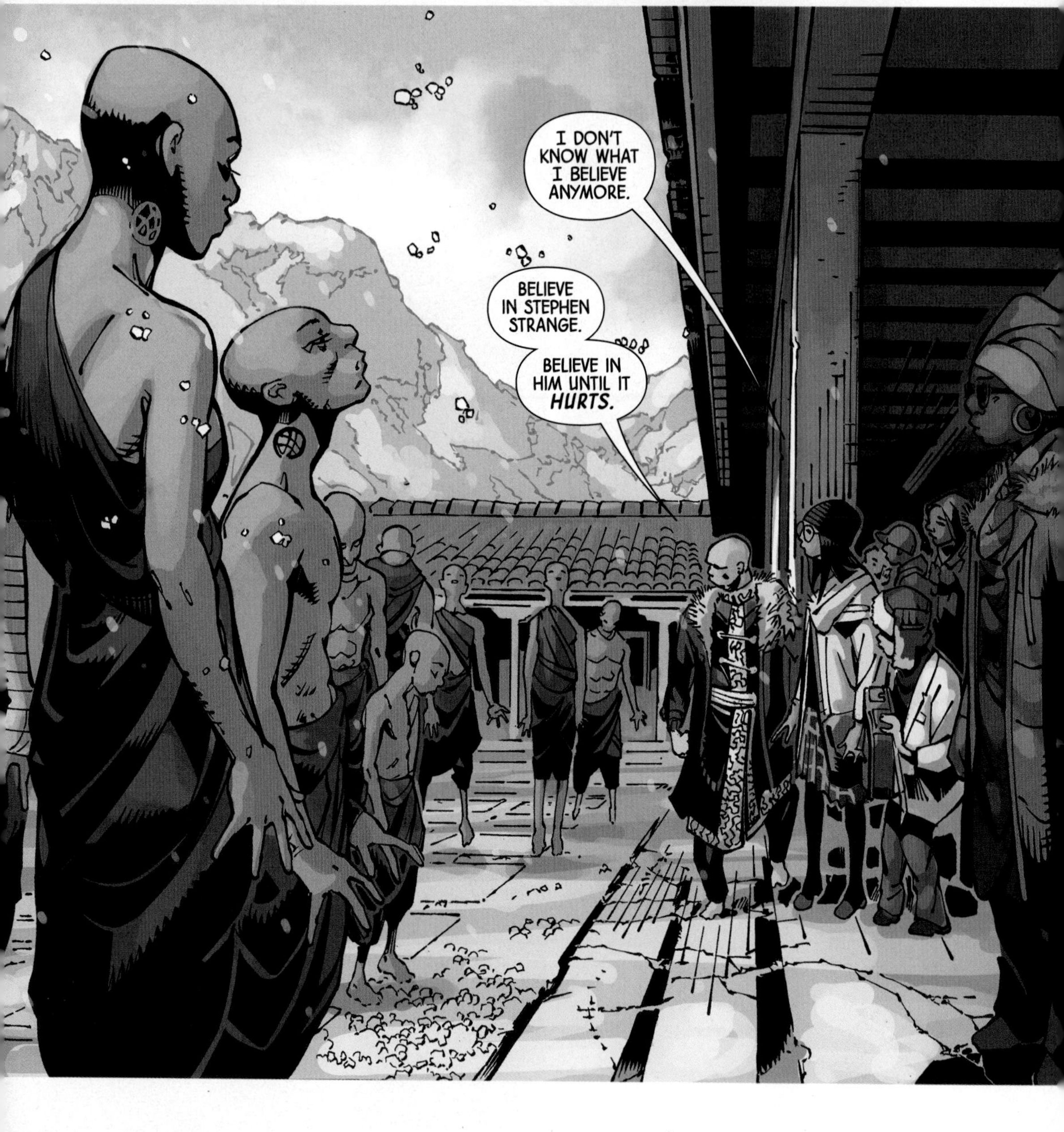
I DON'T KNOW WHAT I BELIEVE ANYMORE.
BELIEVE IN STEPHEN STRANGE.
BELIEVE IN HIM UNTIL IT HURTS.

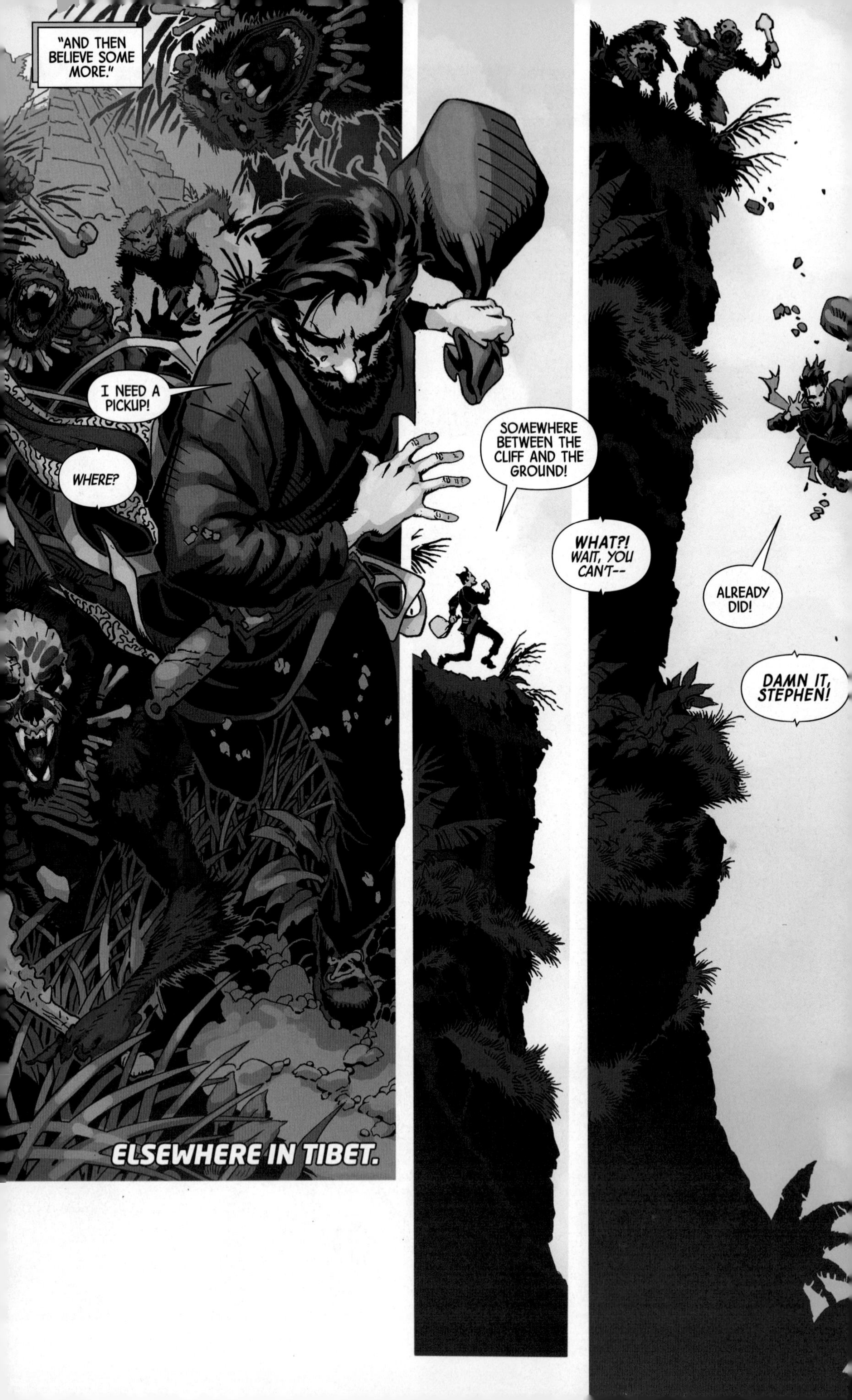
"AND THEN BELIEVE SOME MORE."
I NEED A PICKUP!
WHERE?
ELSEWHERE IN TIBET.
SOMEWHERE BETWEEN THE CLIFF AND THE GROUND!
WHAT?! WAIT, YOU CAN'T--
ALREADY DID!
DAMN IT, STEPHEN!

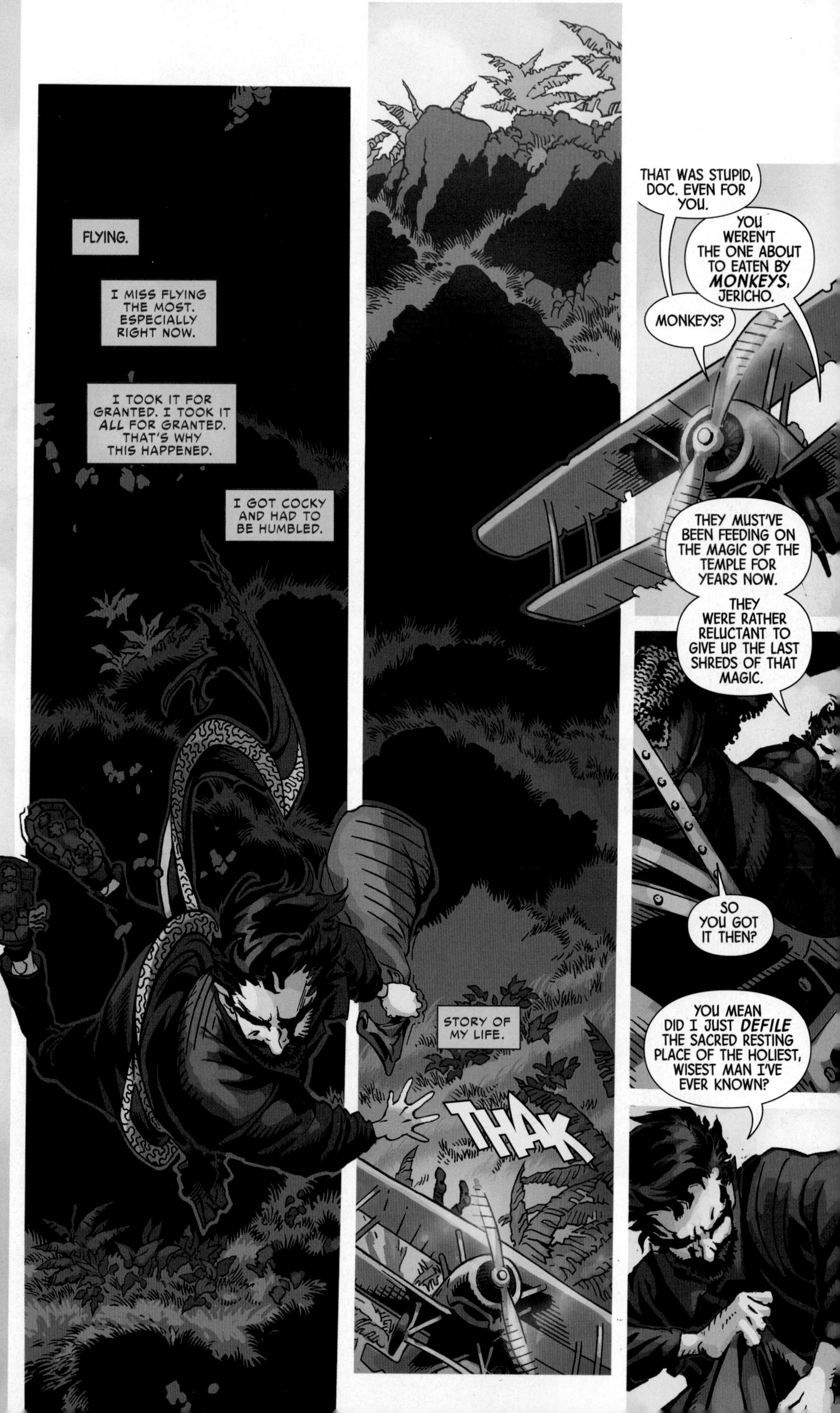
FLYING.
I MISS FLYING THE MOST. ESPECIALLY RIGHT NOW.
I TOOK IT FOR GRANTED. I TOOK IT ALL FOR GRANTED. THAT'S WHY THIS HAPPENED.
I GOT COCKY AND HAD TO BE HUMBLED.
STORY OF MY LIFE.
THAK
THAT WAS STUPID, DOC. EVEN FOR YOU.
YOU WEREN'T THE ONE ABOUT TO EATEN BY MONKEYS, JERICHO.
MONKEYS?
THEY MUST'VE BEEN FEEDING ON THE MAGIC OF THE TEMPLE FOR YEARS NOW.
THEY WERE RATHER RELUCTANT TO GIVE UP THE LAST SHREDS OF THAT MAGIC.
SO YOU GOT IT THEN?
YOU MEAN DID I JUST DEFILE THE SACRED RESTING PLACE OF THE HOLIEST, WISEST MAN I'VE EVER KNOWN?

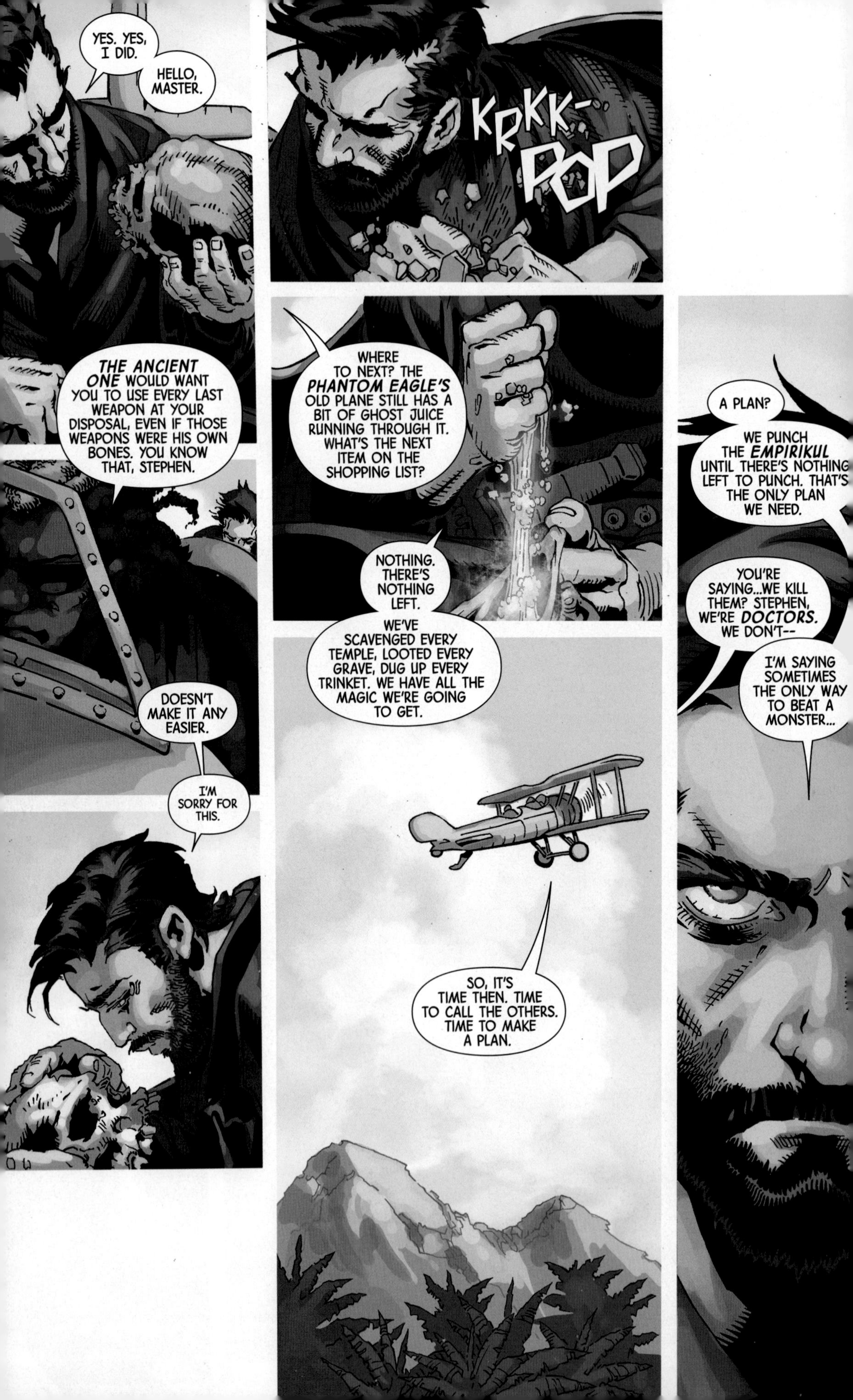
YES. YES, I DID.
HELLO, MASTER.
KRKK-POP
THE ANCIENT ONE WOULD WANT YOU TO USE EVERY LAST WEAPON AT YOUR DISPOSAL, EVEN IF THOSE WEAPONS WERE HIS OWN BONES. YOU KNOW THAT, STEPHEN.
DOESN'T MAKE IT ANY EASIER.
I'M SORRY FOR THIS.
WHERE TO NEXT? THE PHANTOM EAGLE'S OLD PLANE STILL HAS A BIT OF GHOST JUICE RUNNING THROUGH IT. WHAT'S THE NEXT ITEM ON THE SHOPPING LIST?
NOTHING. THERE'S NOTHING LEFT.
WE'VE SCAVENGED EVERY TEMPLE, LOOTED EVERY GRAVE, DUG UP EVERY TRINKET. WE HAVE ALL THE MAGIC WE'RE GOING TO GET.
SO, IT'S TIME THEN. TIME TO CALL THE OTHERS. TIME TO MAKE A PLAN.
A PLAN?
WE PUNCH THE EMPIRIKUL UNTIL THERE'S NOTHING LEFT TO PUNCH. THAT'S THE ONLY PLAN WE NEED.
YOU'RE SAYING...WE KILL THEM? STEPHEN, WE'RE DOCTORS. WE DON'T--
I'M SAYING SOMETIMES THE ONLY WAY TO BEAT A MONSTER...

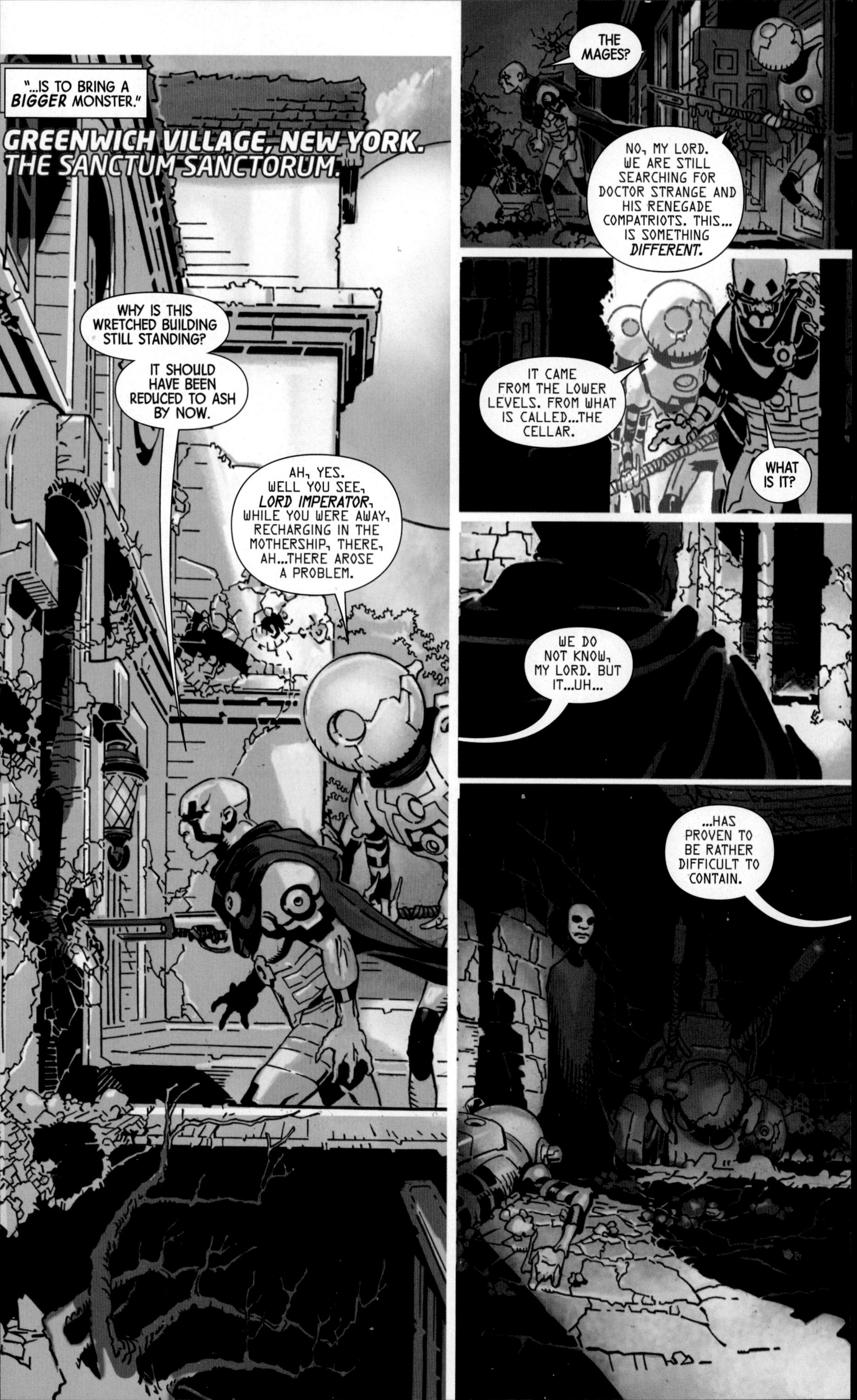

"...IS TO BRING A BIGGER MONSTER."
GREENWICH VILLAGE, NEW YORK. THE SANCTUM SANCTORUM.
WHY IS THIS WRETCHED BUILDING STILL STANDING?
IT SHOULD HAVE BEEN REDUCED TO ASH BY NOW.
AH, YES. WELL YOU SEE, LORD IMPERATOR, WHILE YOU WERE AWAY, RECHARGING IN THE MOTHERSHIP, THERE, AH...THERE AROSE A PROBLEM.
THE MAGES?
NO, MY LORD. WE ARE STILL SEARCHING FOR DOCTOR STRANGE AND HIS RENEGADE COMPATRIOTS. THIS... IS SOMETHING DIFFERENT.
IT CAME FROM THE LOWER LEVELS. FROM WHAT IS CALLED...THE CELLAR.
WHAT IS IT?
WE DO NOT KNOW, MY LORD. BUT IT...UH...
...HAS PROVEN TO BE RATHER DIFFICULT TO CONTAIN.

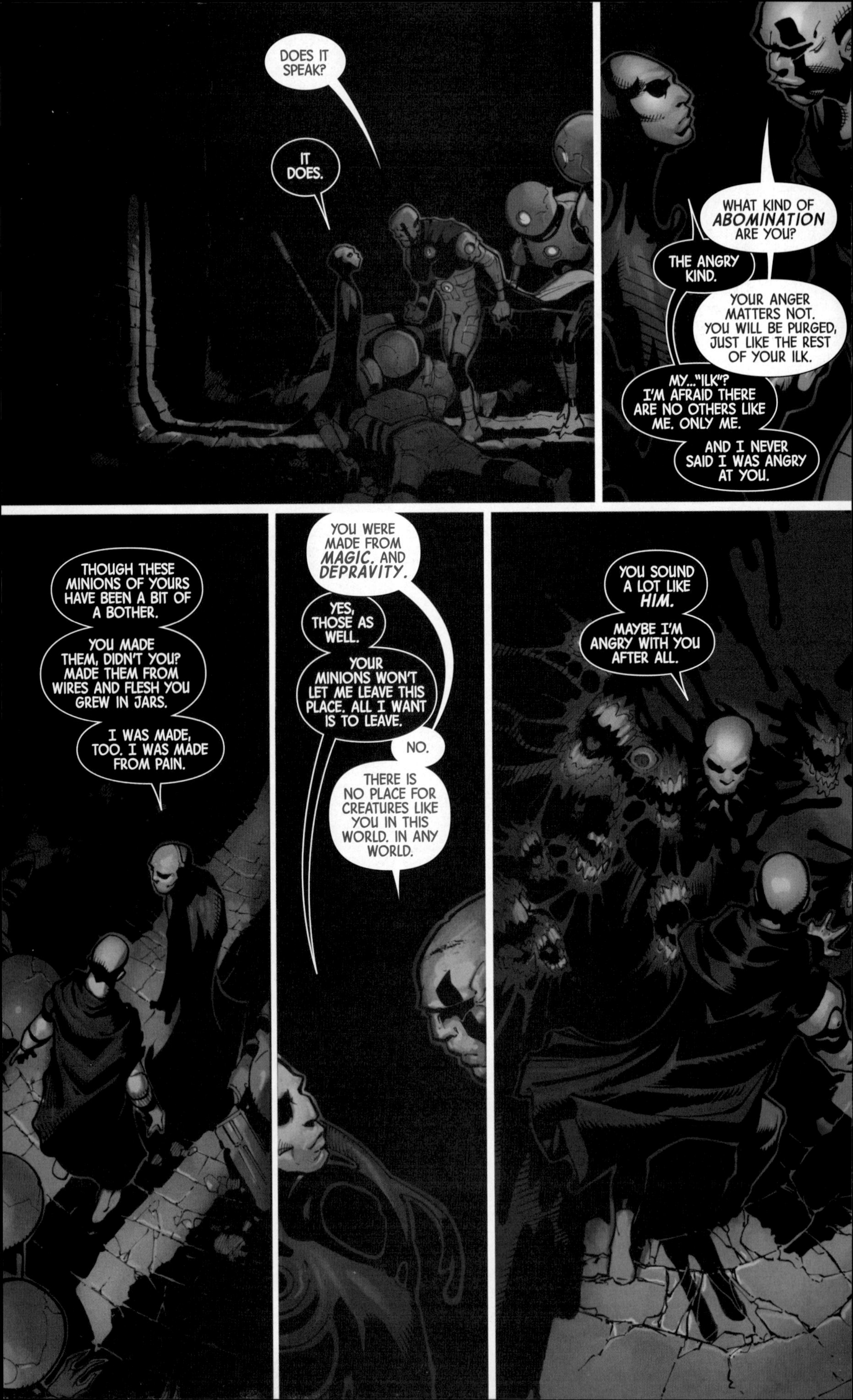
DOES IT SPEAK?
IT DOES.
WHAT KIND OF *ABOMINATION* ARE YOU?
THE ANGRY KIND.
YOUR ANGER MATTERS NOT. YOU WILL BE PURGED, JUST LIKE THE REST OF YOUR ILK.
MY..."ILK"? I'M AFRAID THERE ARE NO OTHERS LIKE ME. ONLY ME.
AND I NEVER SAID I WAS ANGRY AT YOU.
THOUGH THESE MINIONS OF YOURS HAVE BEEN A BIT OF A BOTHER.
YOU MADE THEM, DIDN'T YOU? MADE THEM FROM WIRES AND FLESH YOU GREW IN JARS.
I WAS MADE, TOO. I WAS MADE FROM PAIN.
YOU WERE MADE FROM *MAGIC.* AND *DEPRAVITY.*
YES, THOSE AS WELL.
YOUR MINIONS WON'T LET ME LEAVE THIS PLACE. ALL I WANT IS TO LEAVE.
NO.
THERE IS NO PLACE FOR CREATURES LIKE YOU IN THIS WORLD. IN ANY WORLD.
YOU SOUND A LOT LIKE *HIM.*
MAYBE I'M ANGRY WITH YOU AFTER ALL.

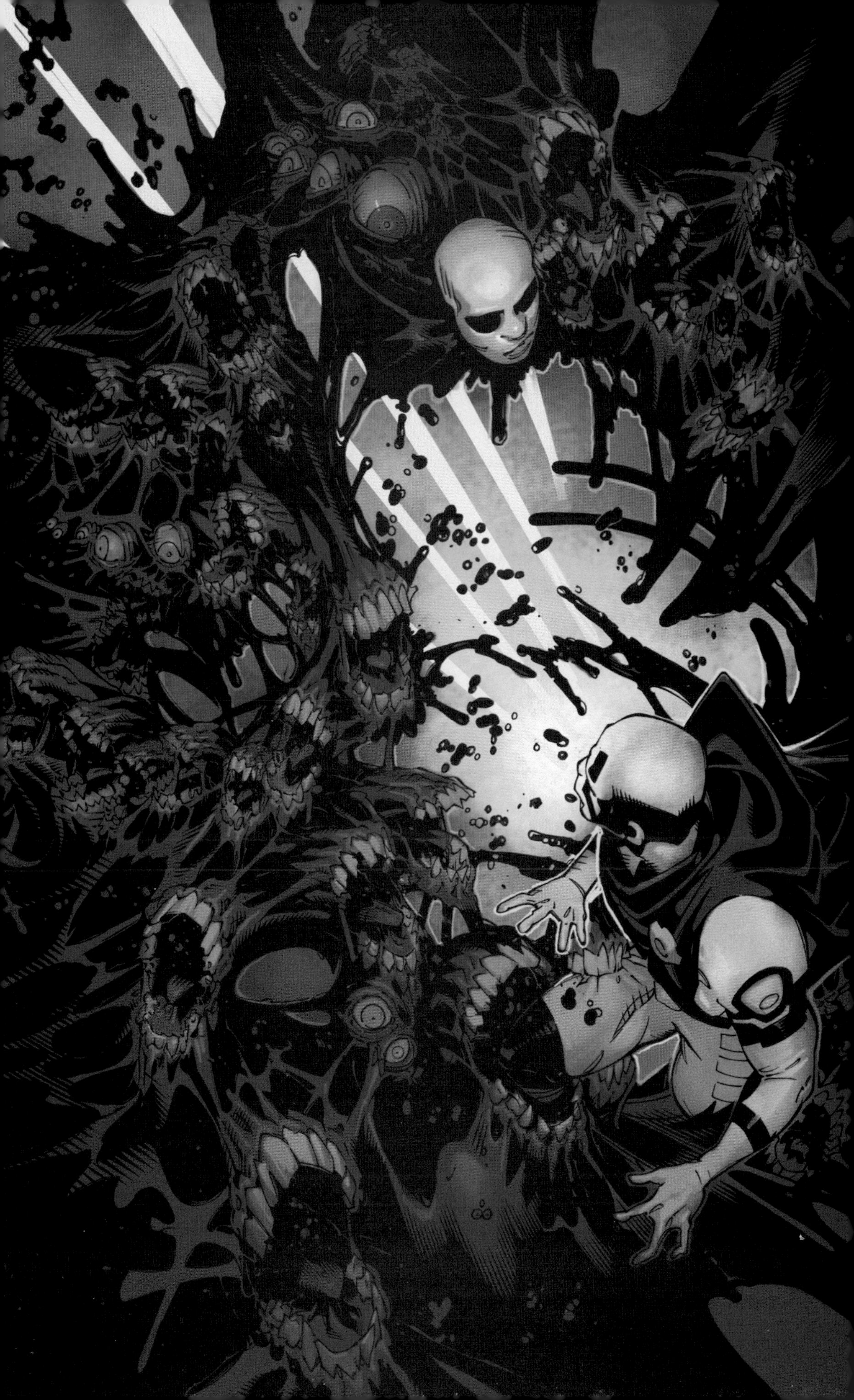

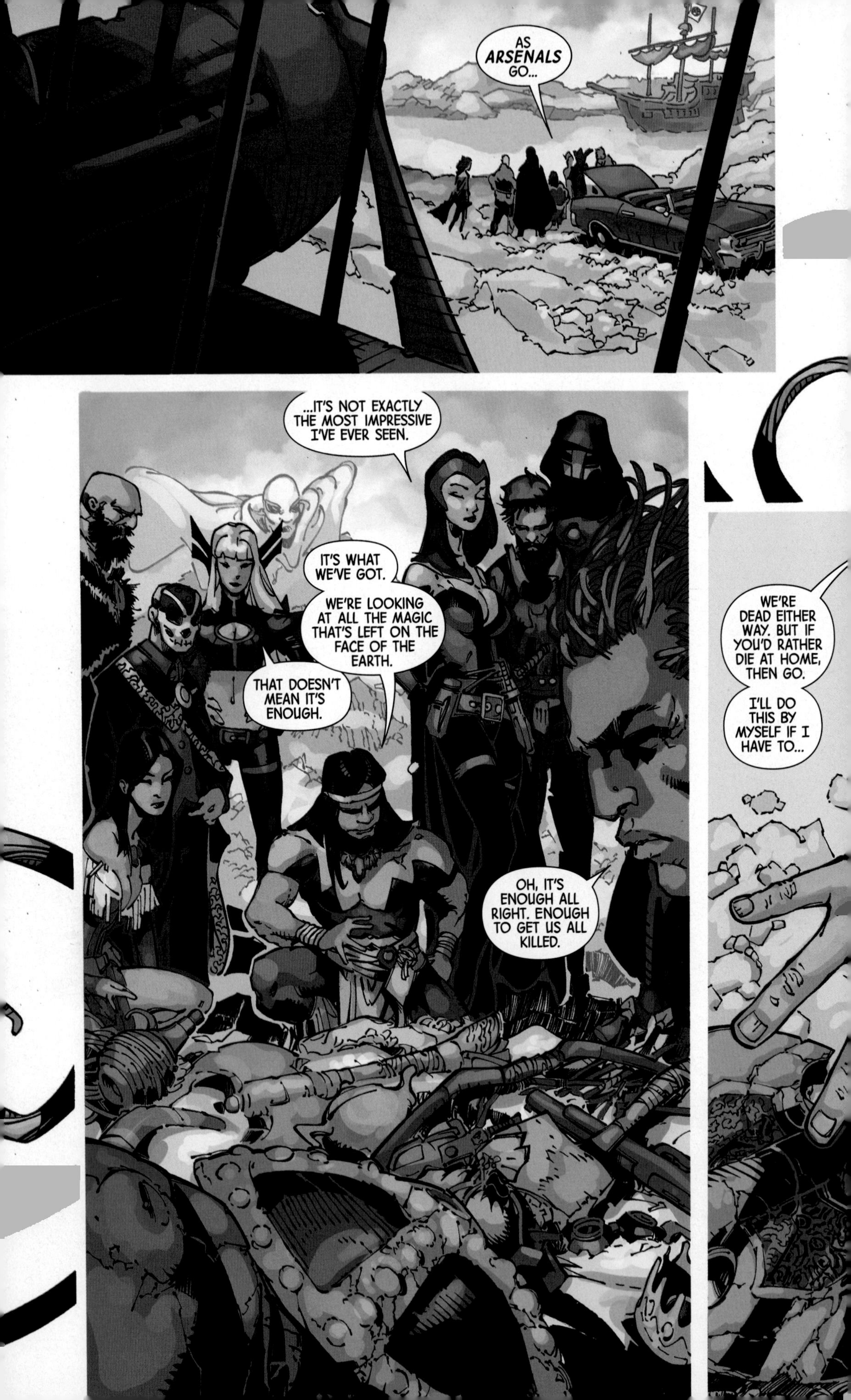
AS ARSENALS GO...
...IT'S NOT EXACTLY THE MOST IMPRESSIVE I'VE EVER SEEN.
IT'S WHAT WE'VE GOT.
WE'RE LOOKING AT ALL THE MAGIC THAT'S LEFT ON THE FACE OF THE EARTH.
THAT DOESN'T MEAN IT'S ENOUGH.
OH, IT'S ENOUGH ALL RIGHT. ENOUGH TO GET US ALL KILLED.
WE'RE DEAD EITHER WAY. BUT IF YOU'D RATHER DIE AT HOME, THEN GO.
I'LL DO THIS BY MYSELF IF I HAVE TO...

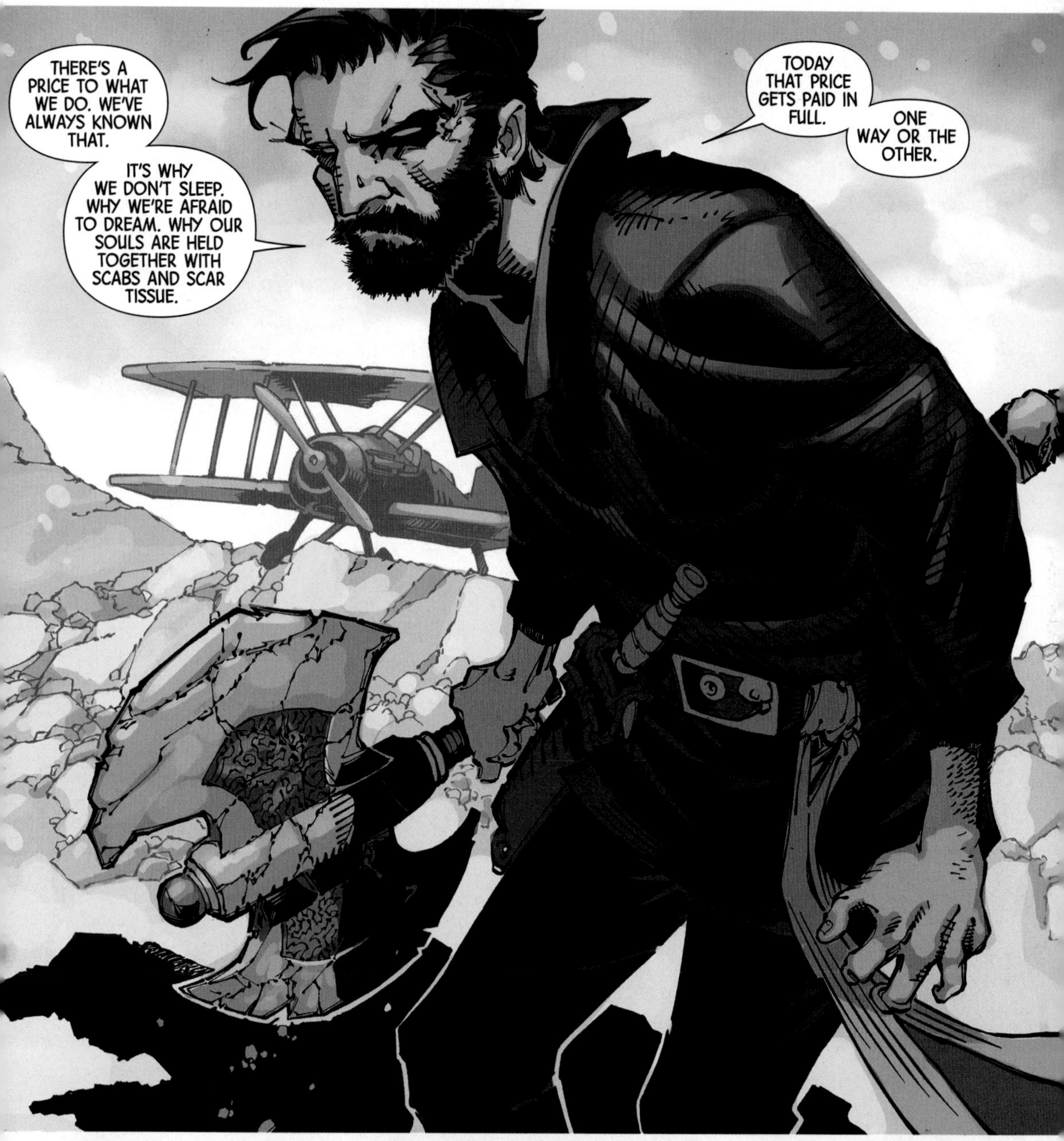
THERE'S A PRICE TO WHAT WE DO. WE'VE ALWAYS KNOWN THAT.
IT'S WHY WE DON'T SLEEP. WHY WE'RE AFRAID TO DREAM. WHY OUR SOULS ARE HELD TOGETHER WITH SCABS AND SCAR TISSUE.
TODAY THAT PRICE GETS PAID IN FULL.
ONE WAY OR THE OTHER.

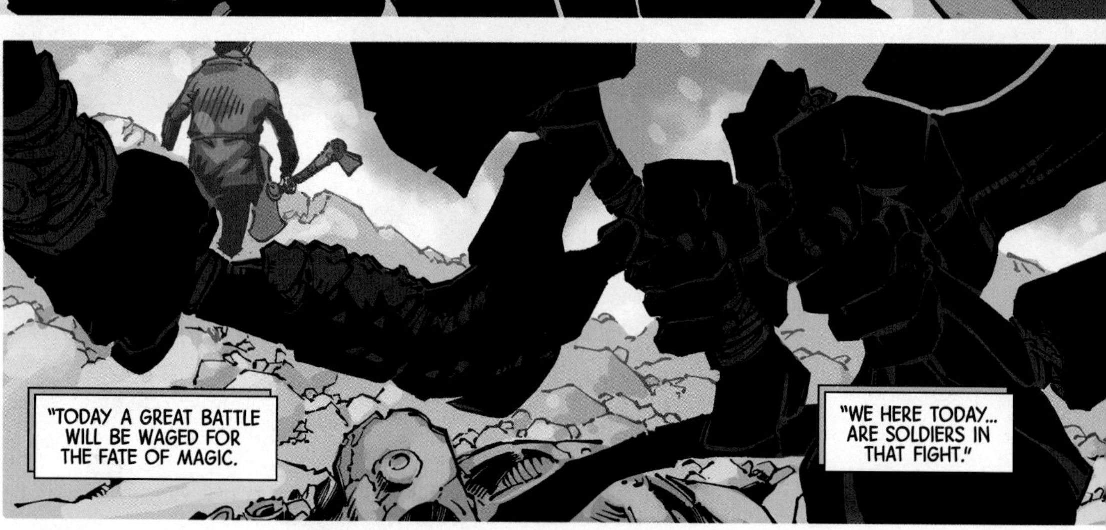
"TODAY A GREAT BATTLE WILL BE WAGED FOR THE FATE OF MAGIC.
"WE HERE TODAY... ARE SOLDIERS IN THAT FIGHT."

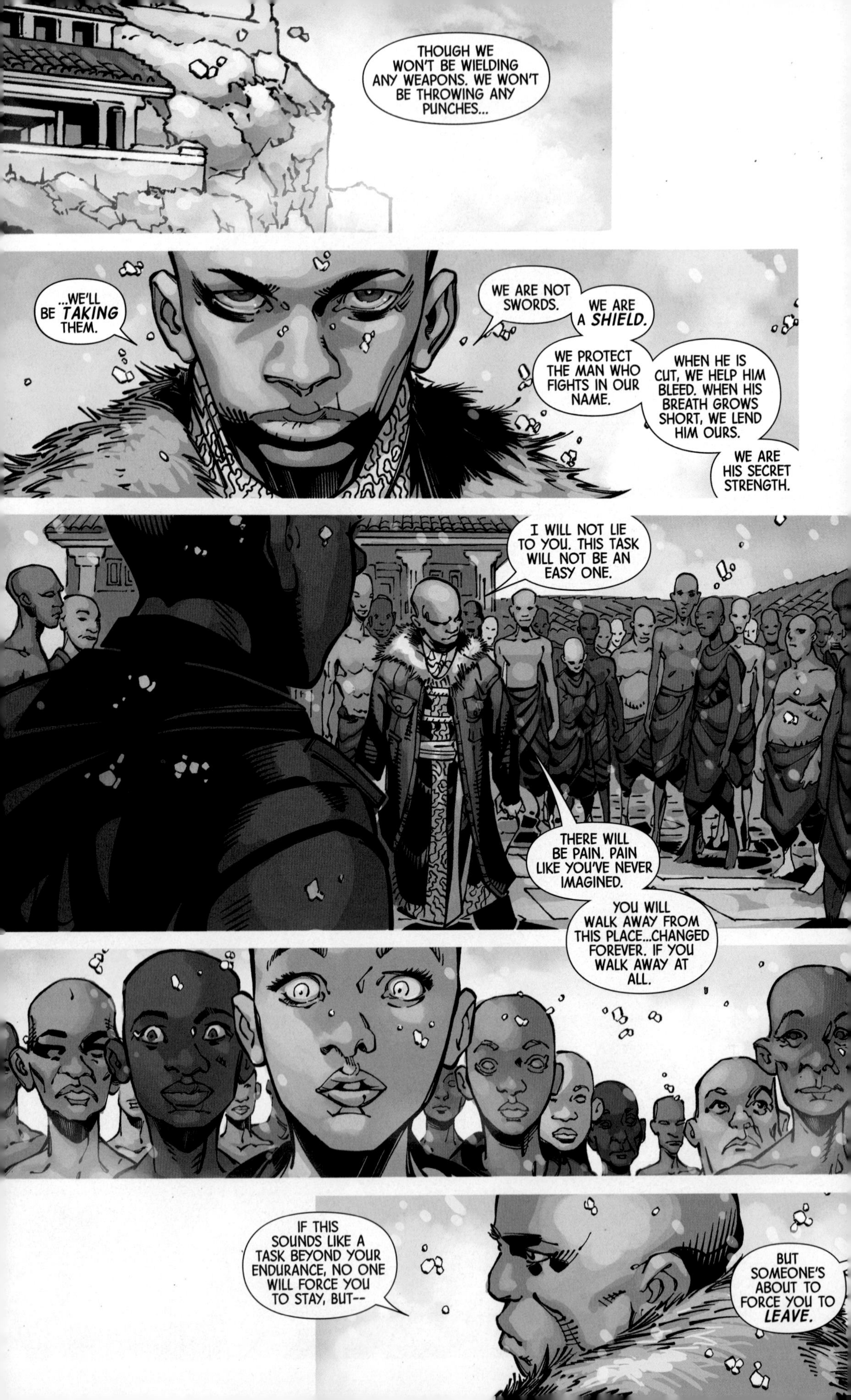
THOUGH WE WON'T BE WIELDING ANY WEAPONS. WE WON'T BE THROWING ANY PUNCHES...
...WE'LL BE TAKING THEM.
WE ARE NOT SWORDS.
WE ARE A SHIELD.
WE PROTECT THE MAN WHO FIGHTS IN OUR NAME.
WHEN HE IS CUT, WE HELP HIM BLEED. WHEN HIS BREATH GROWS SHORT, WE LEND HIM OURS.
WE ARE HIS SECRET STRENGTH.
I WILL NOT LIE TO YOU. THIS TASK WILL NOT BE AN EASY ONE.
THERE WILL BE PAIN. PAIN LIKE YOU'VE NEVER IMAGINED.
YOU WILL WALK AWAY FROM THIS PLACE...CHANGED FOREVER. IF YOU WALK AWAY AT ALL.
IF THIS SOUNDS LIKE A TASK BEYOND YOUR ENDURANCE, NO ONE WILL FORCE YOU TO STAY, BUT--
BUT SOMEONE'S ABOUT TO FORCE YOU TO LEAVE.

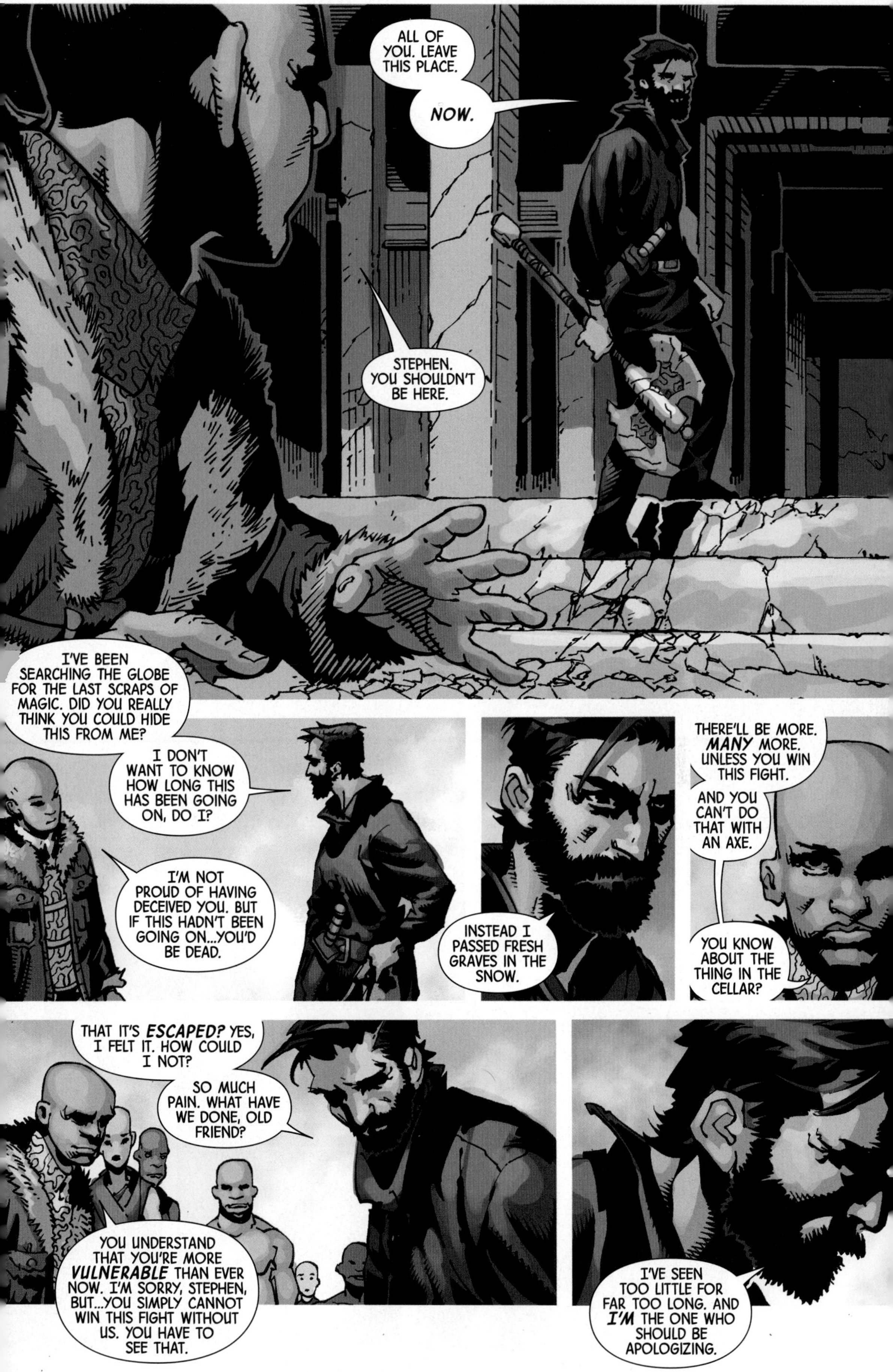
ALL OF YOU. LEAVE THIS PLACE.
NOW.
STEPHEN. YOU SHOULDN'T BE HERE.
I'VE BEEN SEARCHING THE GLOBE FOR THE LAST SCRAPS OF MAGIC. DID YOU REALLY THINK YOU COULD HIDE THIS FROM ME?
I DON'T WANT TO KNOW HOW LONG THIS HAS BEEN GOING ON, DO I?
I'M NOT PROUD OF HAVING DECEIVED YOU. BUT IF THIS HADN'T BEEN GOING ON...YOU'D BE DEAD.
INSTEAD I PASSED FRESH GRAVES IN THE SNOW.
THERE'LL BE MORE. MANY MORE. UNLESS YOU WIN THIS FIGHT.
AND YOU CAN'T DO THAT WITH AN AXE.
YOU KNOW ABOUT THE THING IN THE CELLAR?
THAT IT'S ESCAPED? YES, I FELT IT. HOW COULD I NOT?
SO MUCH PAIN. WHAT HAVE WE DONE, OLD FRIEND?
YOU UNDERSTAND THAT YOU'RE MORE VULNERABLE THAN EVER NOW. I'M SORRY, STEPHEN, BUT...YOU SIMPLY CANNOT WIN THIS FIGHT WITHOUT US. YOU HAVE TO SEE THAT.
I'VE SEEN TOO LITTLE FOR FAR TOO LONG. AND I'M THE ONE WHO SHOULD BE APOLOGIZING.

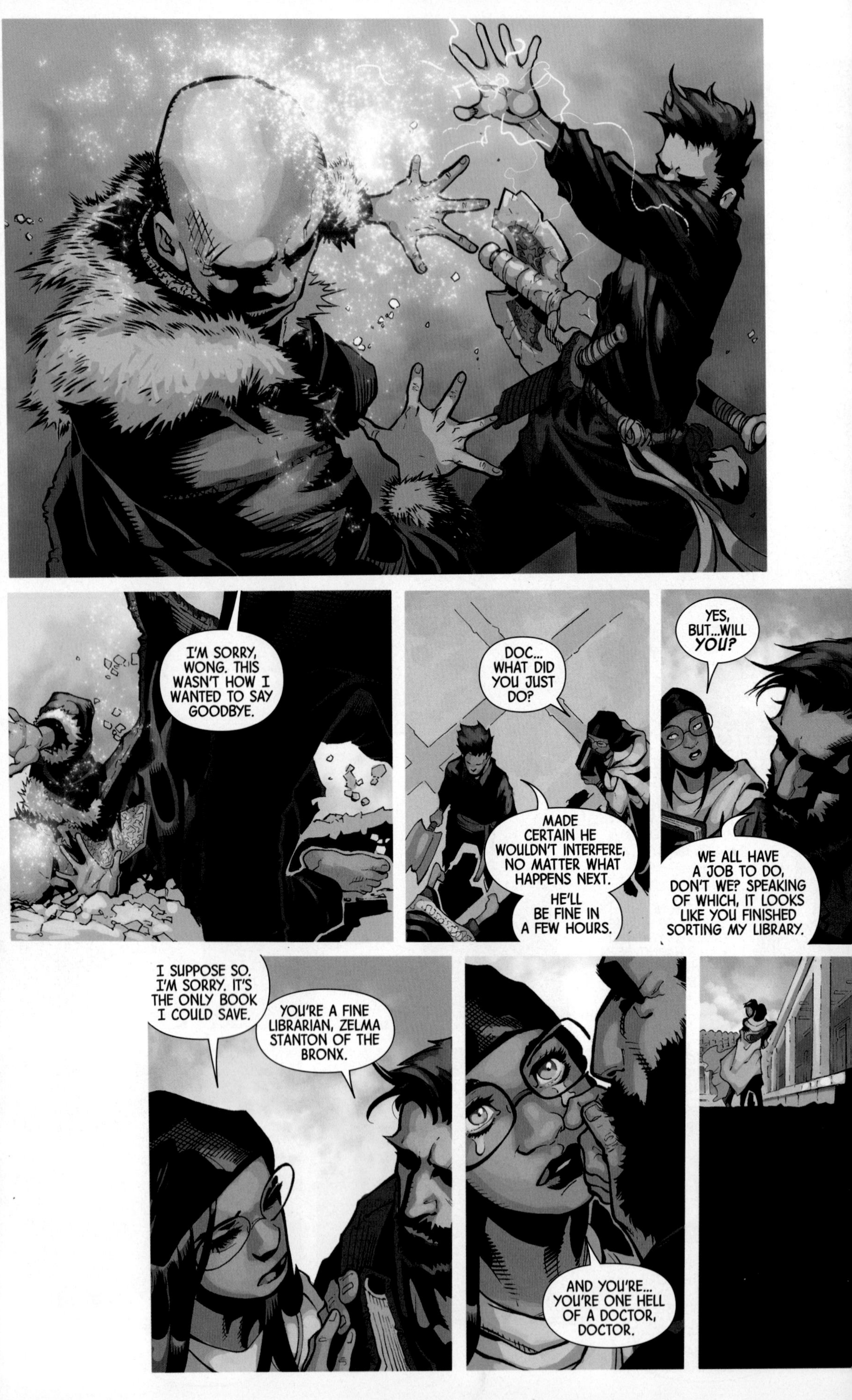
I'M SORRY, WONG. THIS WASN'T HOW I WANTED TO SAY GOODBYE.
DOC... WHAT DID YOU JUST DO?
MADE CERTAIN HE WOULDN'T INTERFERE, NO MATTER WHAT HAPPENS NEXT.
HE'LL BE FINE IN A FEW HOURS.
YES, BUT...WILL *YOU?*
WE ALL HAVE A JOB TO DO, DON'T WE? SPEAKING OF WHICH, IT LOOKS LIKE YOU FINISHED SORTING MY LIBRARY.
I SUPPOSE SO. I'M SORRY. IT'S THE ONLY BOOK I COULD SAVE.
YOU'RE A FINE LIBRARIAN, ZELMA STANTON OF THE BRONX.
AND YOU'RE... YOU'RE ONE HELL OF A DOCTOR, DOCTOR.

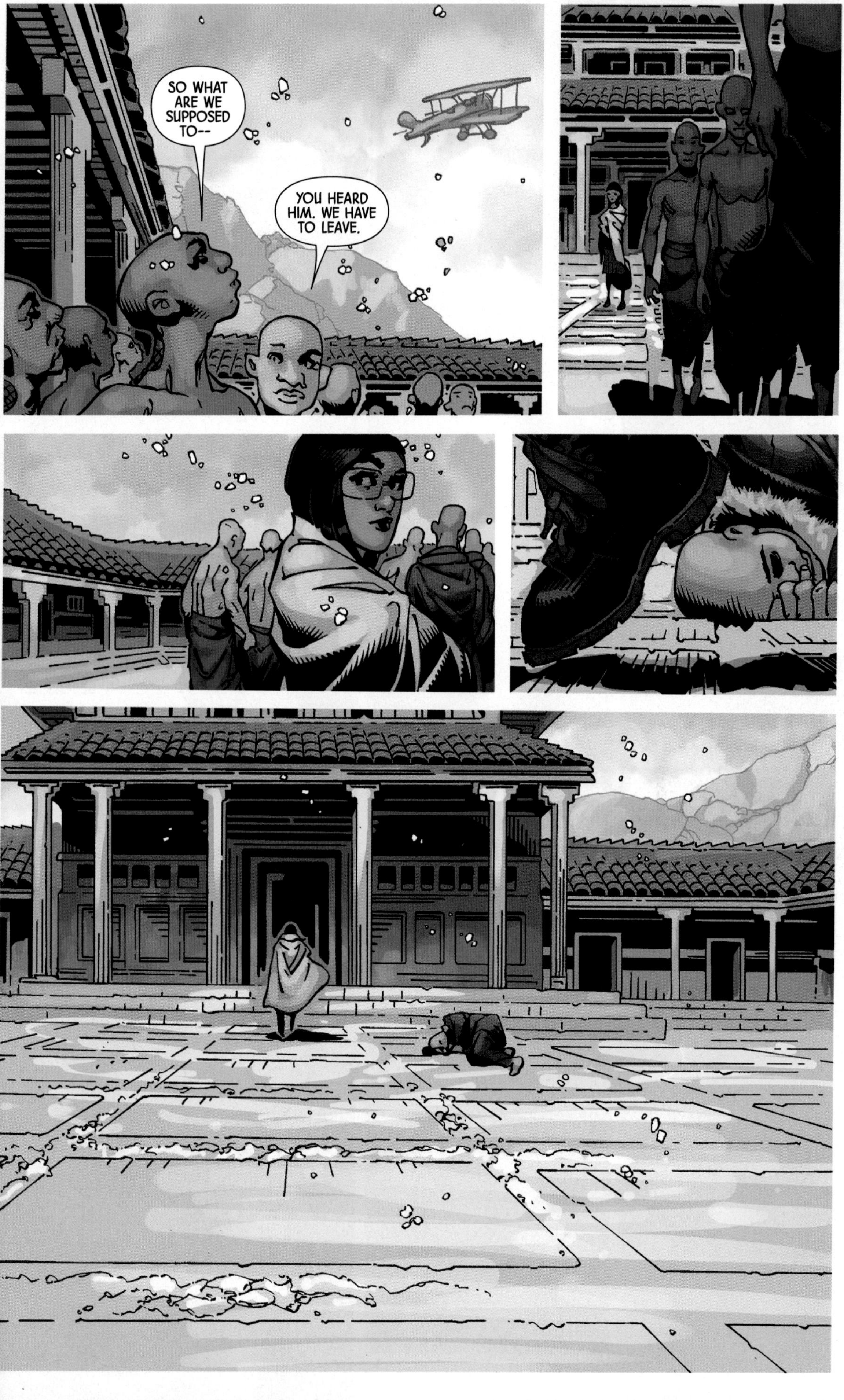
SO WHAT ARE WE SUPPOSED TO--
YOU HEARD HIM. WE HAVE TO LEAVE.

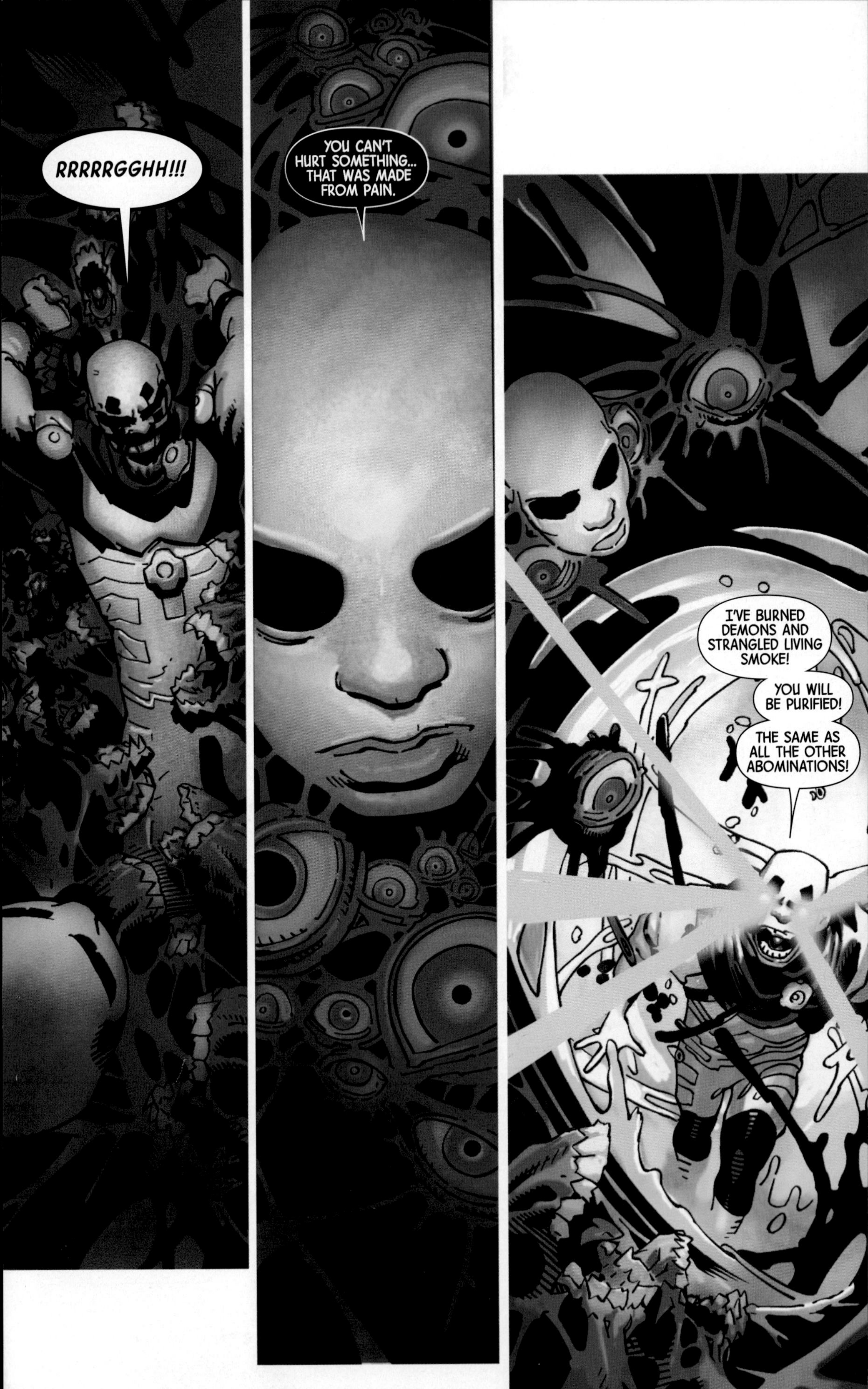
RRRRRGGHH!!!
YOU CAN'T HURT SOMETHING... THAT WAS MADE FROM PAIN.
I'VE BURNED DEMONS AND STRANGLED LIVING SMOKE!
YOU WILL BE PURIFIED!
THE SAME AS ALL THE OTHER ABOMINATIONS!

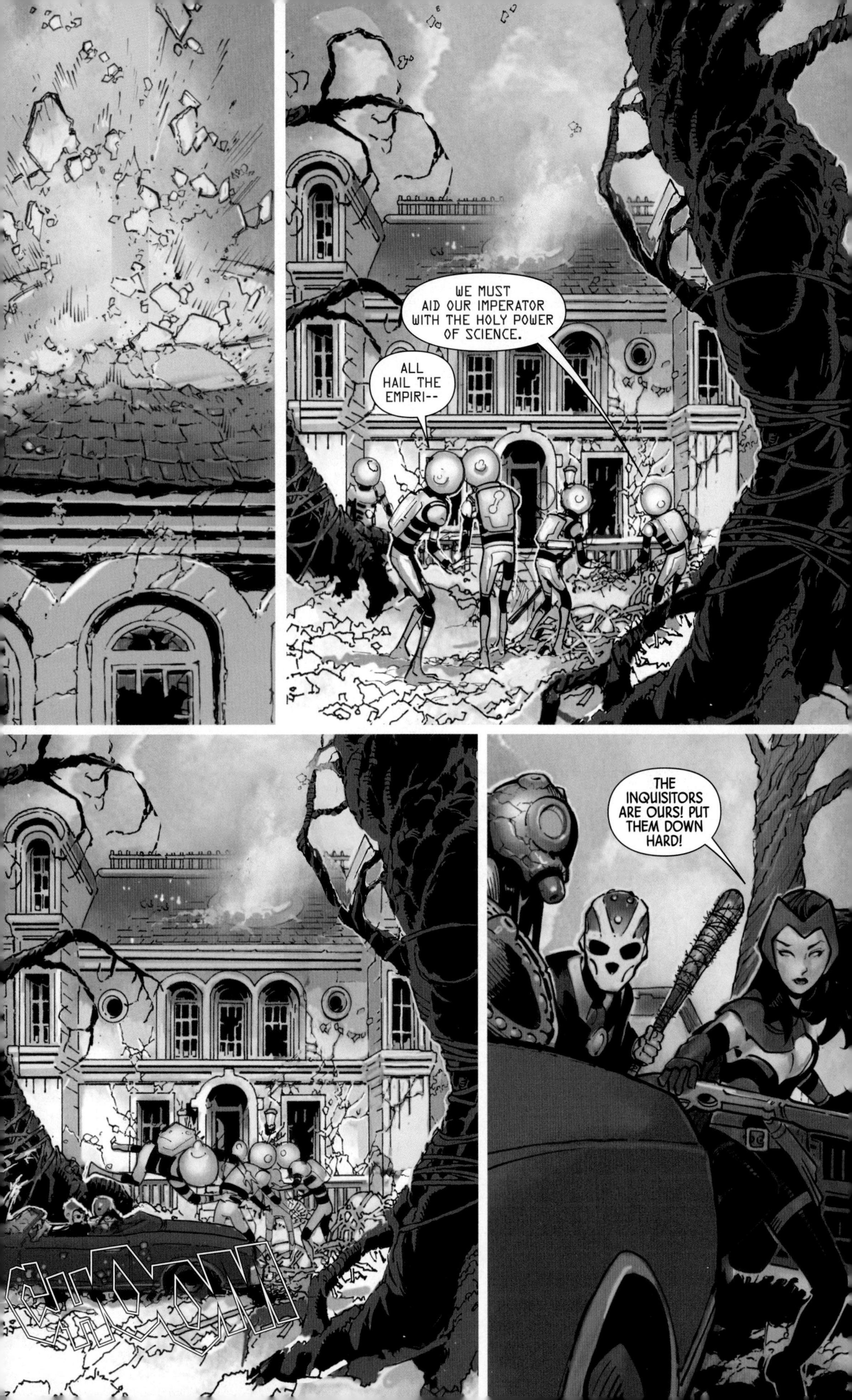
WE MUST AID OUR IMPERATOR WITH THE HOLY POWER OF SCIENCE.
ALL HAIL THE EMPIRI--
THE INQUISITORS ARE OURS! PUT THEM DOWN HARD!

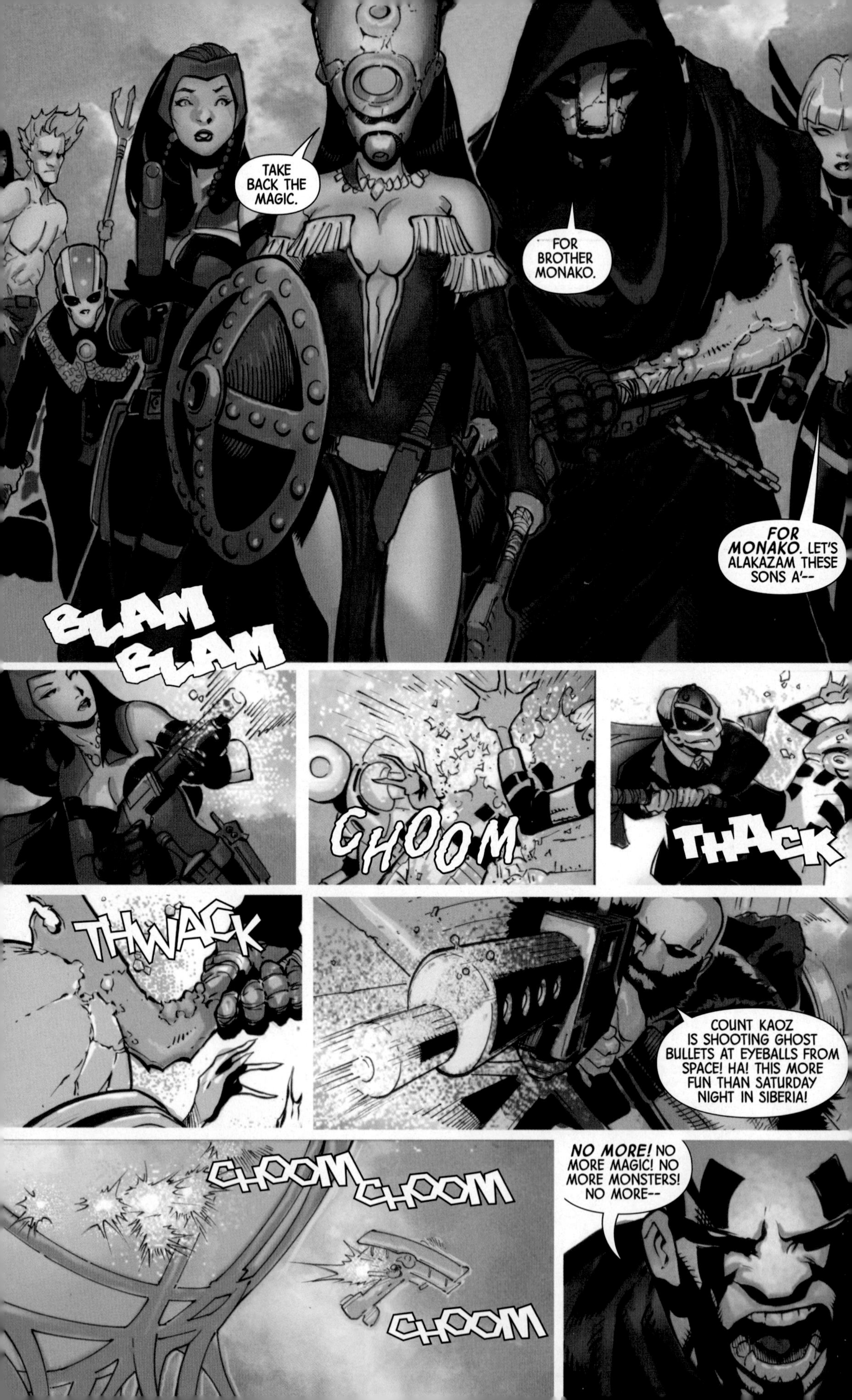
TAKE BACK THE MAGIC.
FOR BROTHER MONAKO.
FOR MONAKO. LET'S ALAKAZAM THESE SONS A'--
BLAM BLAM
CHOOM
THACK
THWACK
COUNT KAOZ IS SHOOTING GHOST BULLETS AT EYEBALLS FROM SPACE! HA! THIS MORE FUN THAN SATURDAY NIGHT IN SIBERIA!
CHOOM CHOOM
CHOOM
NO MORE! NO MORE MAGIC! NO MORE MONSTERS! NO MORE--

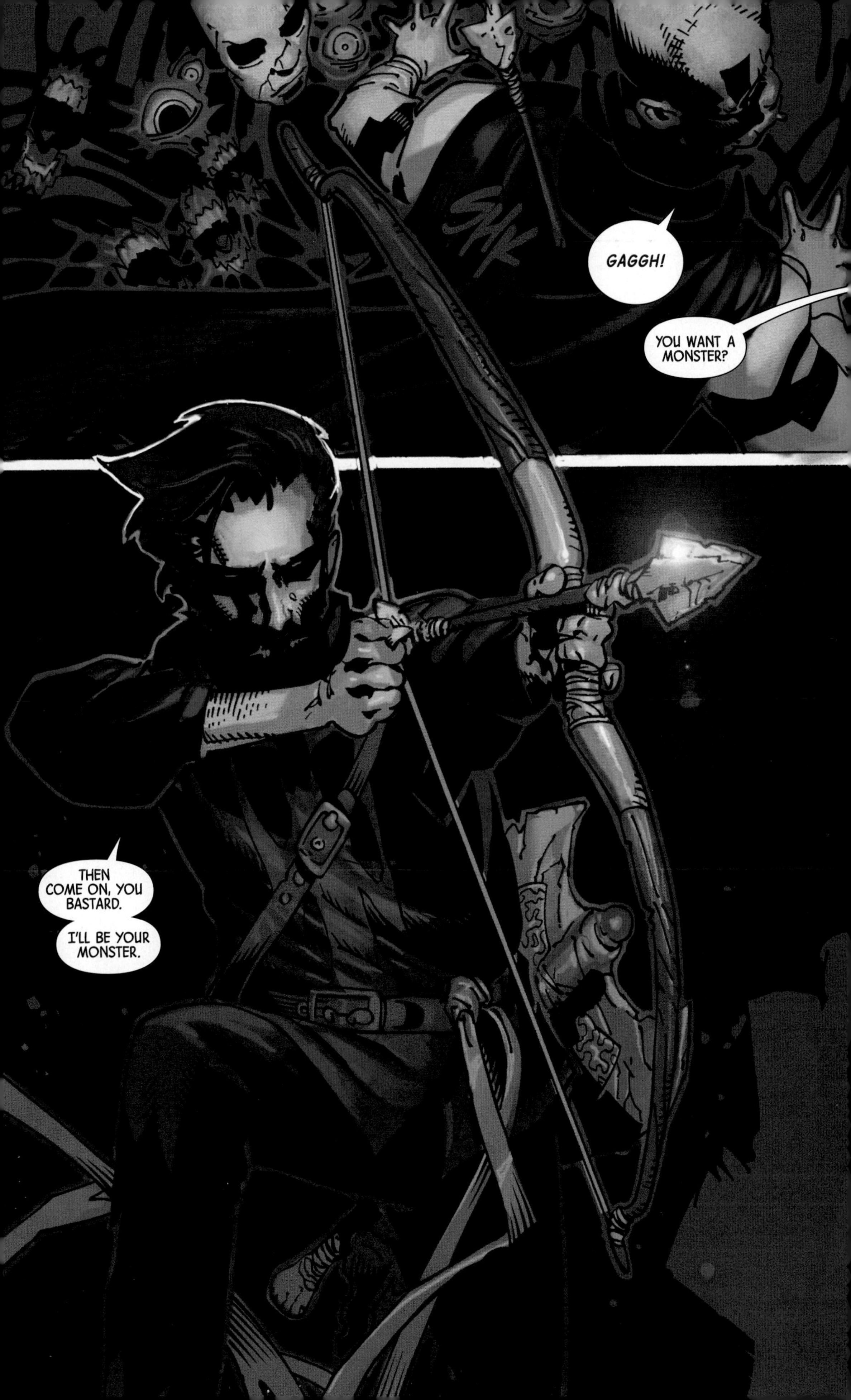
SNK
GAGGH!
YOU WANT A MONSTER?
THEN COME ON, YOU BASTARD.
I'LL BE YOUR MONSTER.

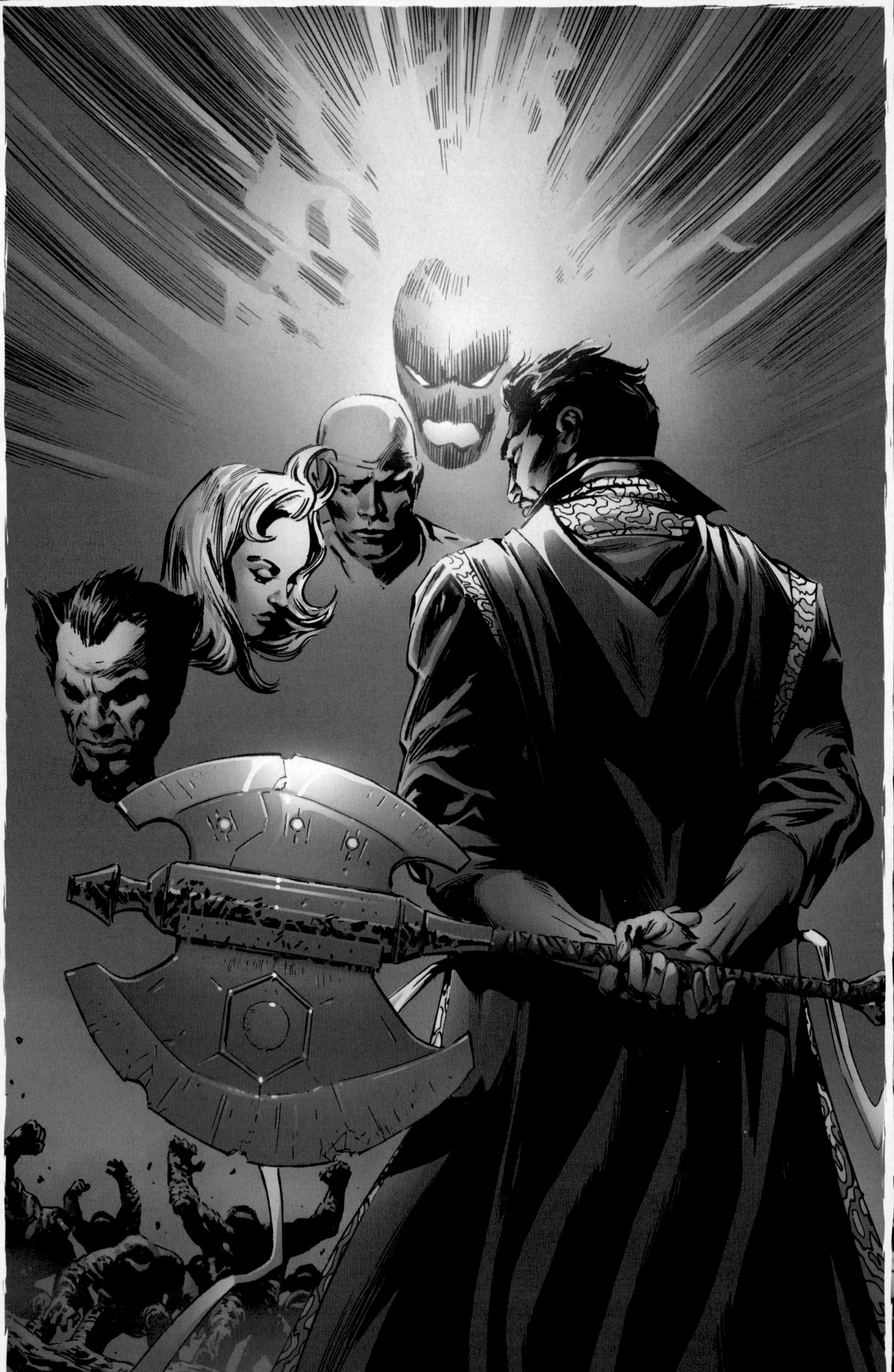

#6 CLASSIC VARIANT BY **BUTCH GUICE** & **FRANK D'ARMATA**

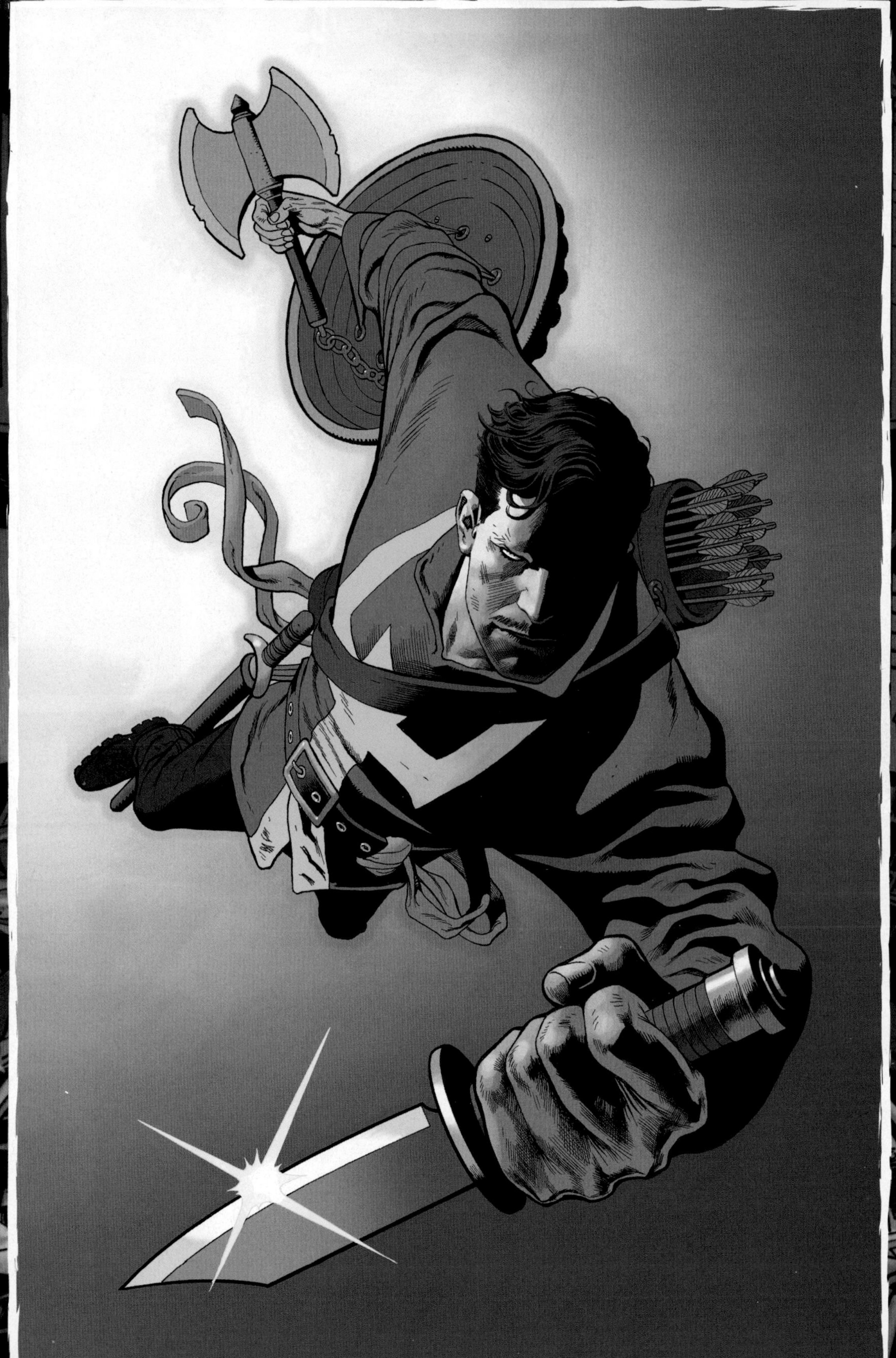

DOCTOR STRANGE 10 THE LAST DAYS OF MAGIC CONCLUSION

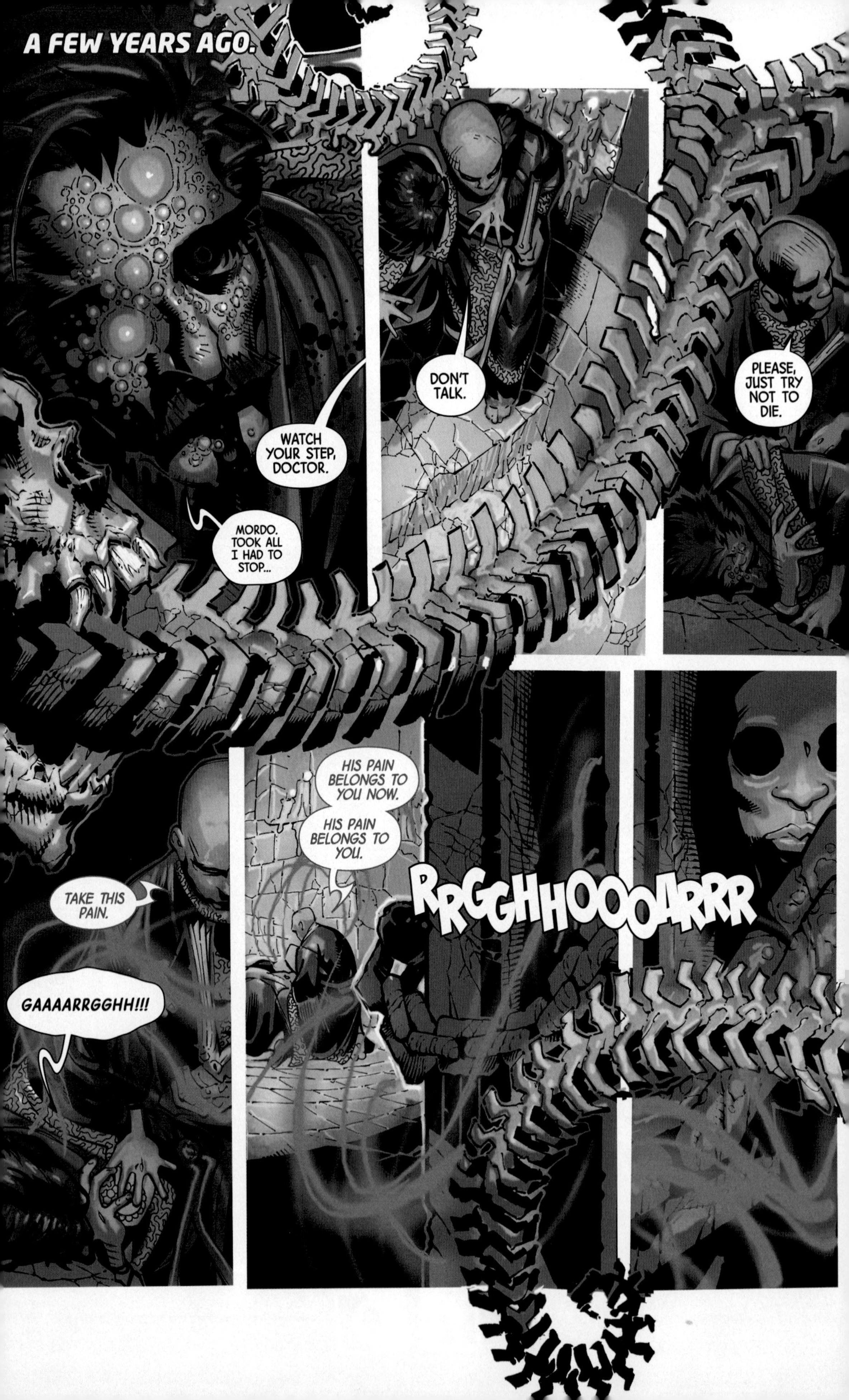
A FEW YEARS AGO.
WATCH YOUR STEP, DOCTOR.
MORDO. TOOK ALL I HAD TO STOP...
DON'T TALK.
PLEASE, JUST TRY NOT TO DIE.
TAKE THIS PAIN.
GAAAARRGGHH!!!
HIS PAIN BELONGS TO YOU NOW.
HIS PAIN BELONGS TO YOU.
RRGGHHOOOOARRR

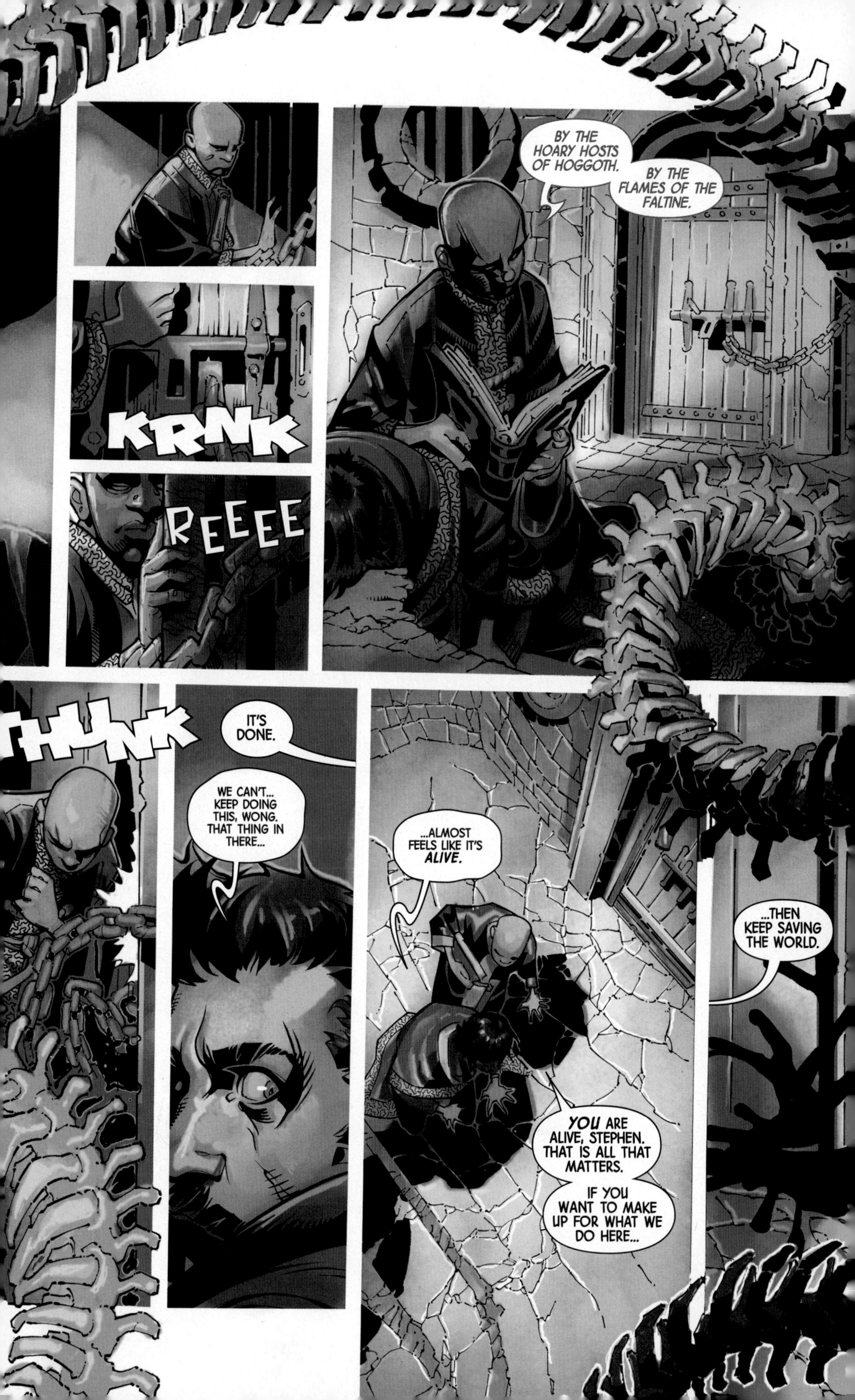
KRNK
REEEE
BY THE HOARY HOSTS OF HOGGOTH.
BY THE FLAMES OF THE FALTINE.
THUNK
IT'S DONE.
WE CAN'T... KEEP DOING THIS, WONG. THAT THING IN THERE...
...ALMOST FEELS LIKE IT'S ALIVE.
YOU ARE ALIVE, STEPHEN. THAT IS ALL THAT MATTERS.
IF YOU WANT TO MAKE UP FOR WHAT WE DO HERE...
...THEN KEEP SAVING THE WORLD.

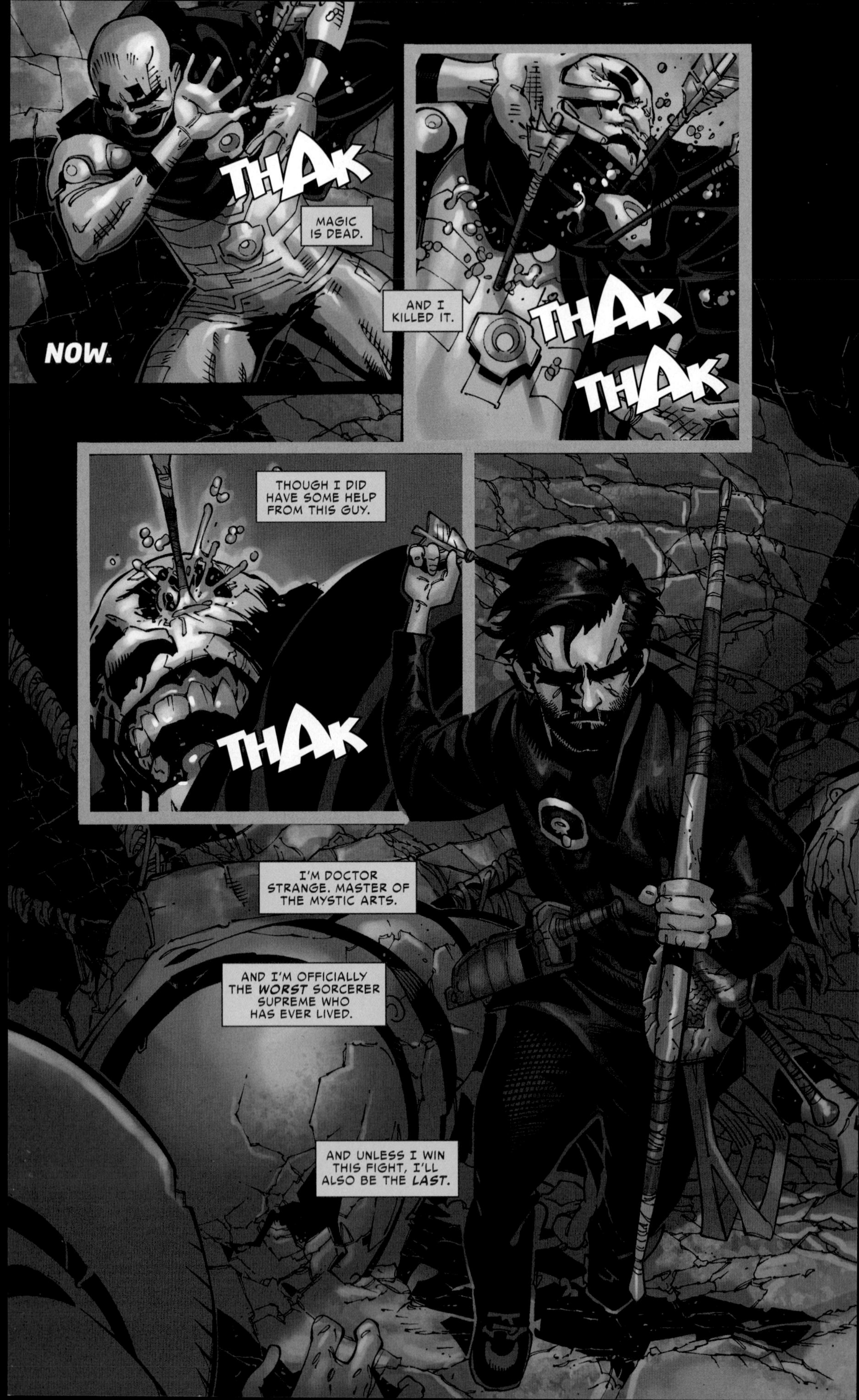
THAK
MAGIC IS DEAD.
NOW.
AND I KILLED IT.
THAK
THAK
THOUGH I DID HAVE SOME HELP FROM THIS GUY.
THAK
I'M DOCTOR STRANGE. MASTER OF THE MYSTIC ARTS.
AND I'M OFFICIALLY THE WORST SORCERER SUPREME WHO HAS EVER LIVED.
AND UNLESS I WIN THIS FIGHT, I'LL ALSO BE THE LAST.

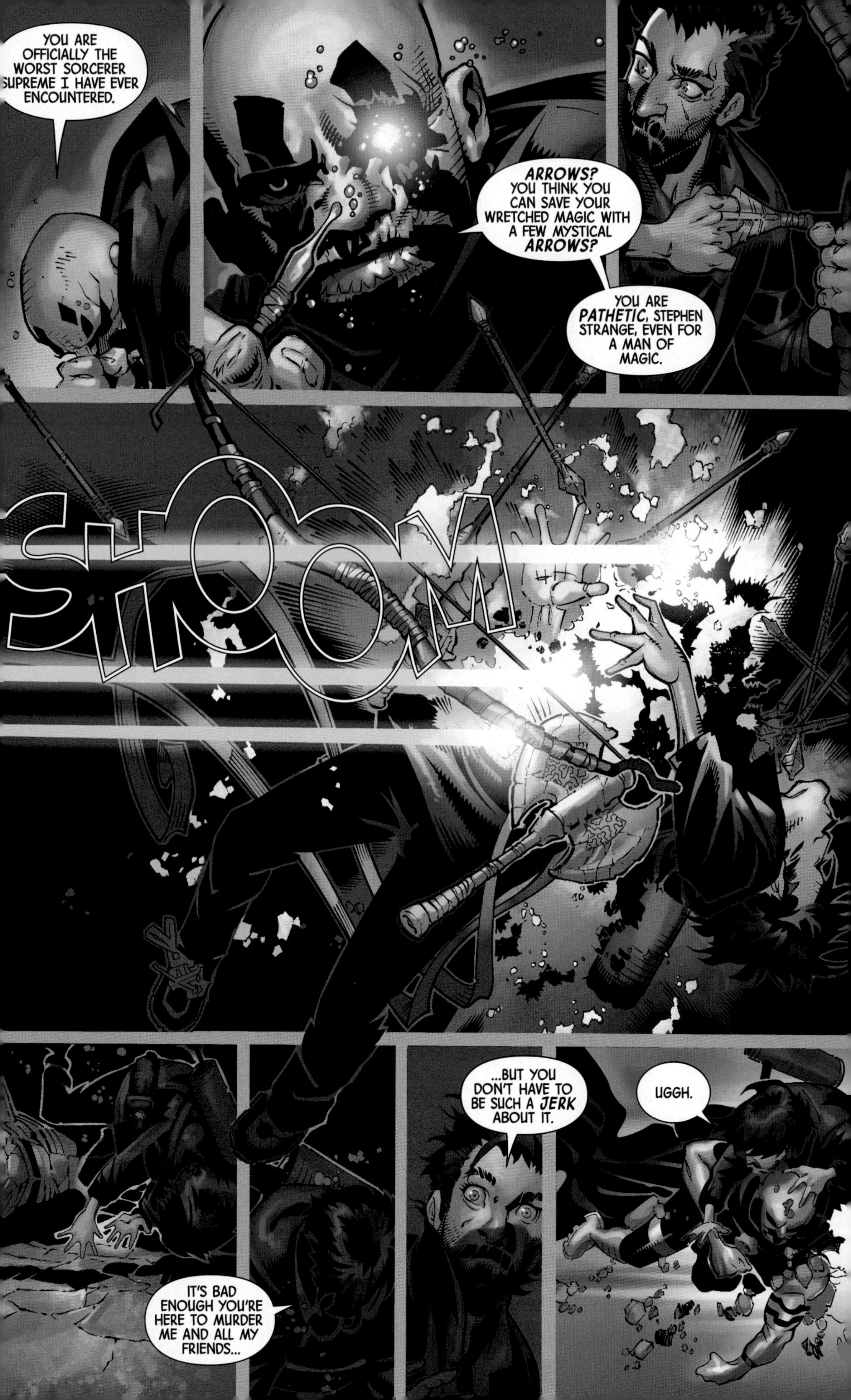
YOU ARE OFFICIALLY THE WORST SORCERER SUPREME I HAVE EVER ENCOUNTERED.
ARROWS? YOU THINK YOU CAN SAVE YOUR WRETCHED MAGIC WITH A FEW MYSTICAL ARROWS?
YOU ARE PATHETIC, STEPHEN STRANGE, EVEN FOR A MAN OF MAGIC.
SHOOM
IT'S BAD ENOUGH YOU'RE HERE TO MURDER ME AND ALL MY FRIENDS...
...BUT YOU DON'T HAVE TO BE SUCH A JERK ABOUT IT.
UGGH.

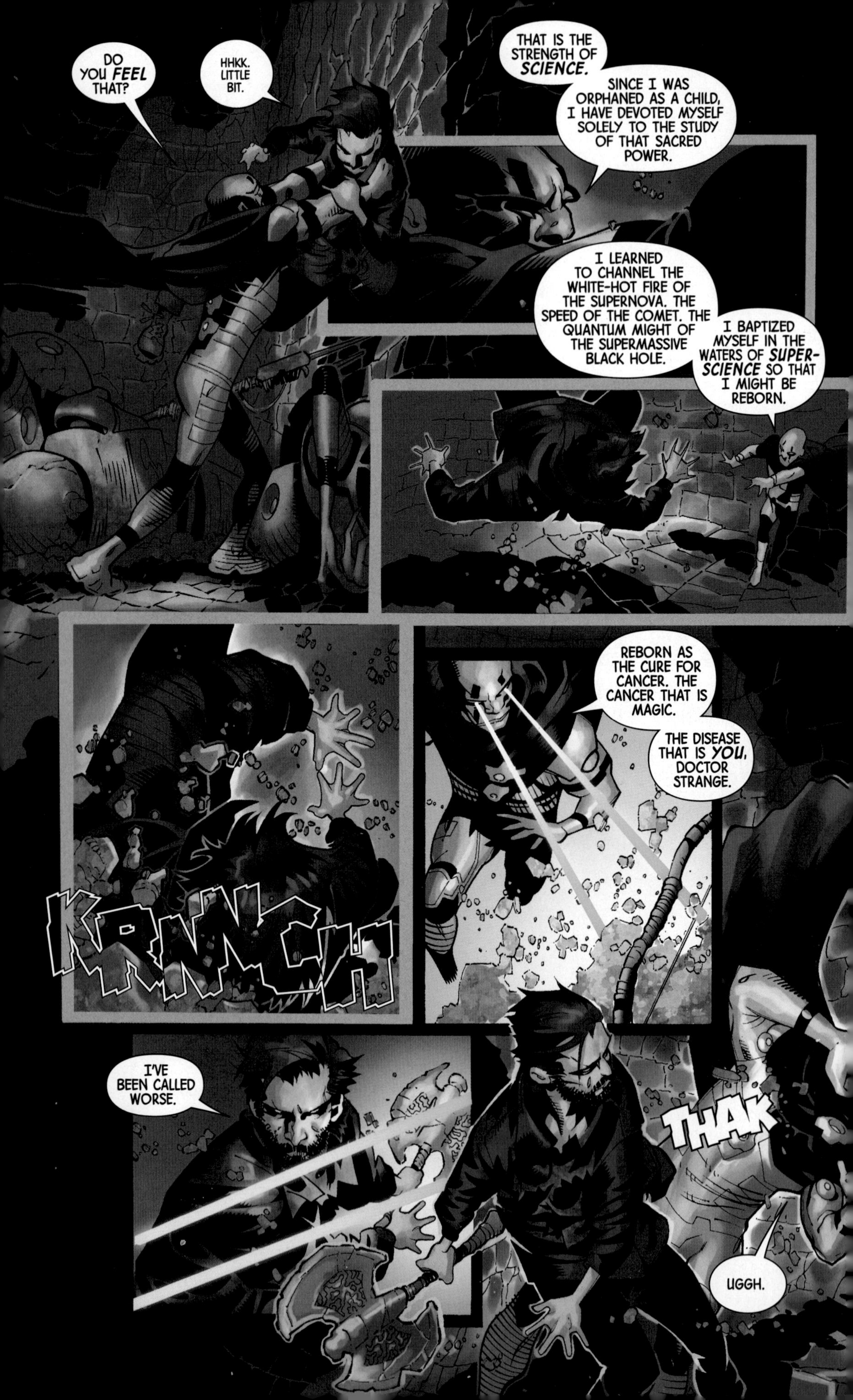
DO YOU FEEL THAT?
HHKK. LITTLE BIT.
THAT IS THE STRENGTH OF SCIENCE.
SINCE I WAS ORPHANED AS A CHILD, I HAVE DEVOTED MYSELF SOLELY TO THE STUDY OF THAT SACRED POWER.
I LEARNED TO CHANNEL THE WHITE-HOT FIRE OF THE SUPERNOVA. THE SPEED OF THE COMET. THE QUANTUM MIGHT OF THE SUPERMASSIVE BLACK HOLE.
I BAPTIZED MYSELF IN THE WATERS OF SUPER-SCIENCE SO THAT I MIGHT BE REBORN.
KRNNCH
REBORN AS THE CURE FOR CANCER. THE CANCER THAT IS MAGIC.
THE DISEASE THAT IS YOU, DOCTOR STRANGE.
I'VE BEEN CALLED WORSE.
THAK
UGGH.

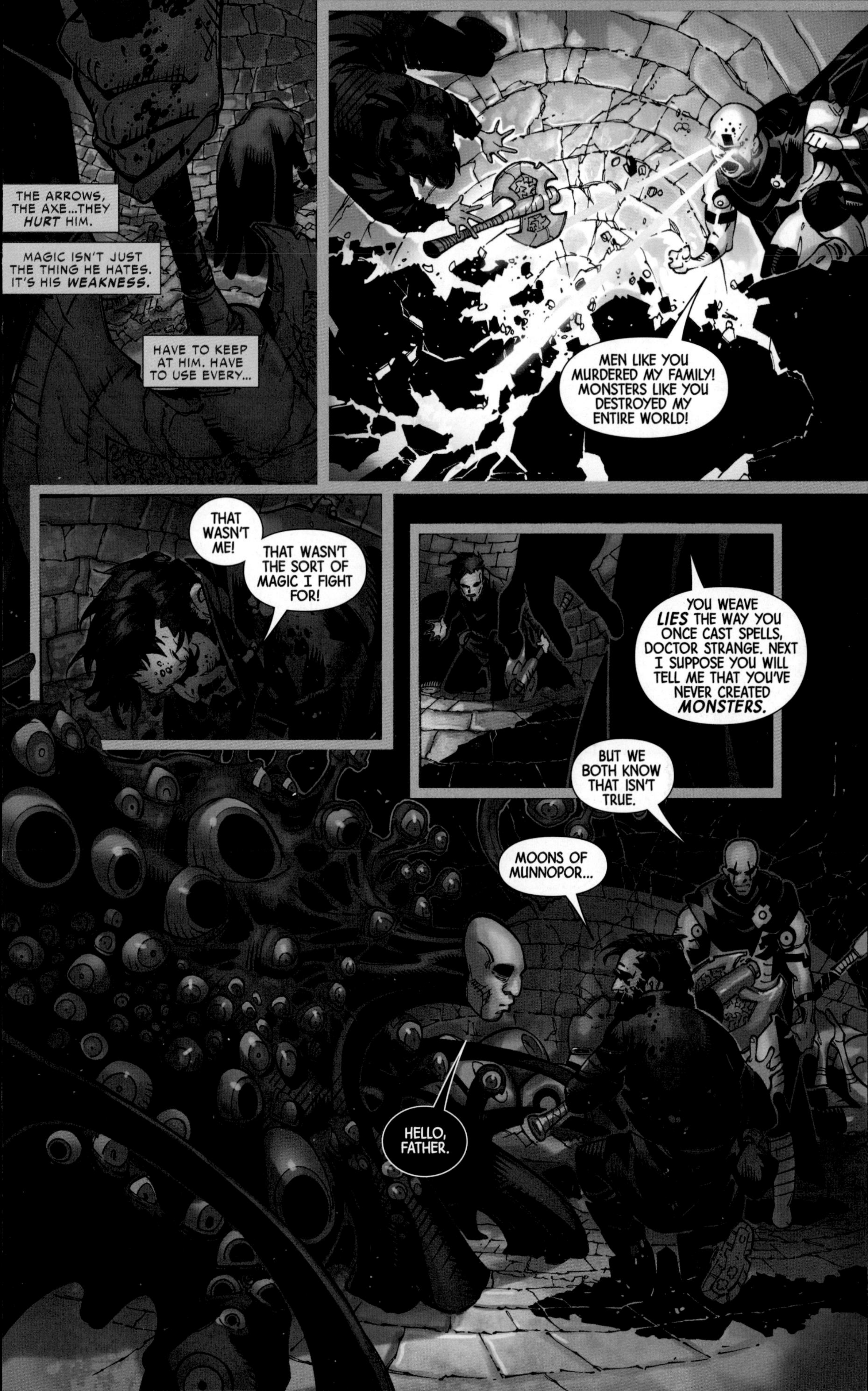
THE ARROWS, THE AXE...THEY *HURT* HIM.
MAGIC ISN'T JUST THE THING HE HATES. IT'S HIS *WEAKNESS.*
HAVE TO KEEP AT HIM. HAVE TO USE EVERY...
MEN LIKE YOU MURDERED MY FAMILY! MONSTERS LIKE YOU DESTROYED MY ENTIRE WORLD!
THAT WASN'T ME!
THAT WASN'T THE SORT OF MAGIC I FIGHT FOR!
YOU WEAVE *LIES* THE WAY YOU ONCE CAST SPELLS, DOCTOR STRANGE. NEXT I SUPPOSE YOU WILL TELL ME THAT YOU'VE NEVER CREATED *MONSTERS.*
BUT WE BOTH KNOW THAT ISN'T TRUE.
MOONS OF MUNNOPOR...
HELLO, FATHER.

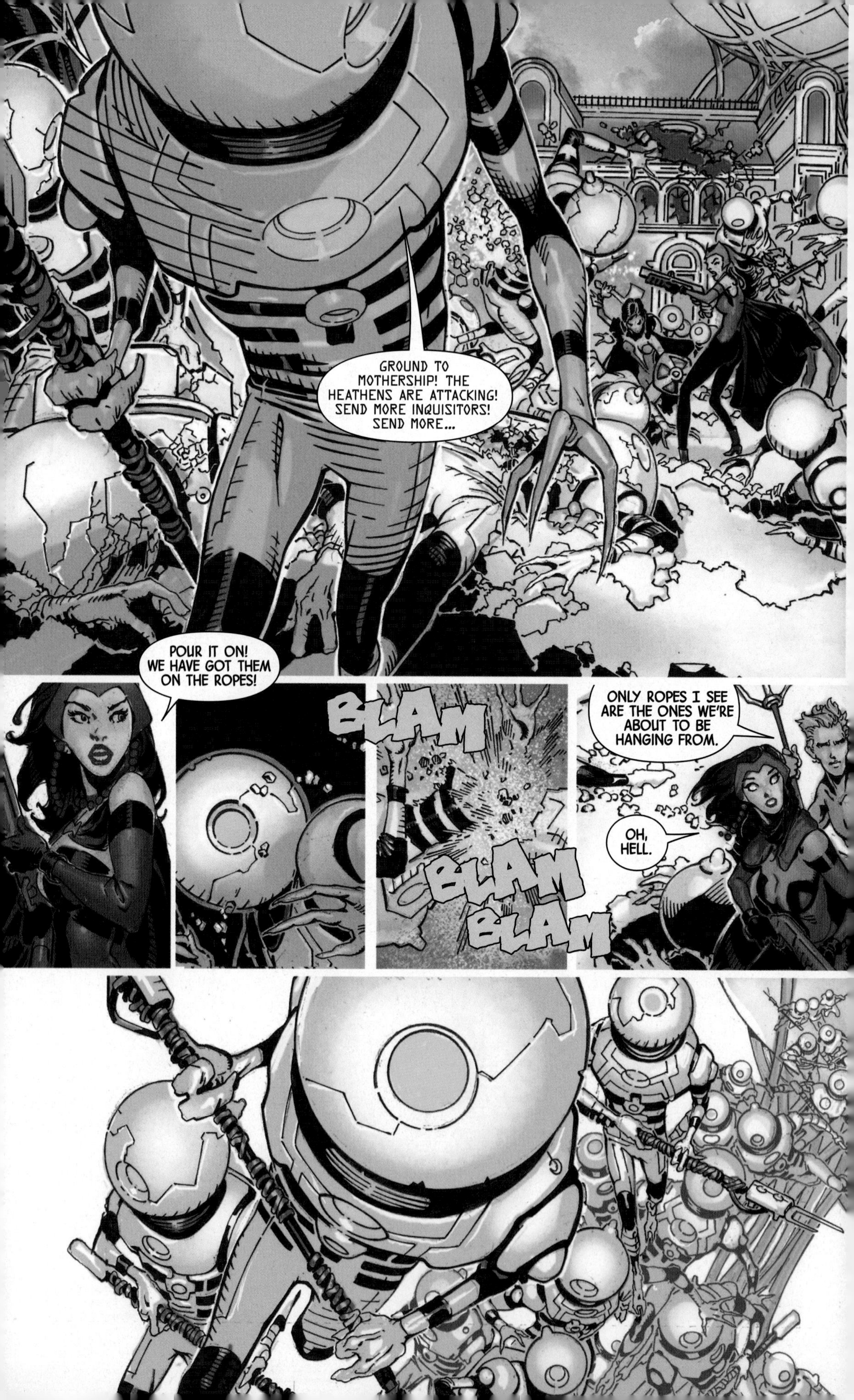

GROUND TO MOTHERSHIP! THE HEATHENS ARE ATTACKING! SEND MORE INQUISITORS! SEND MORE...
POUR IT ON! WE HAVE GOT THEM ON THE ROPES!
BLAM
BLAM
BLAM
ONLY ROPES I SEE ARE THE ONES WE'RE ABOUT TO BE HANGING FROM.
OH, HELL.

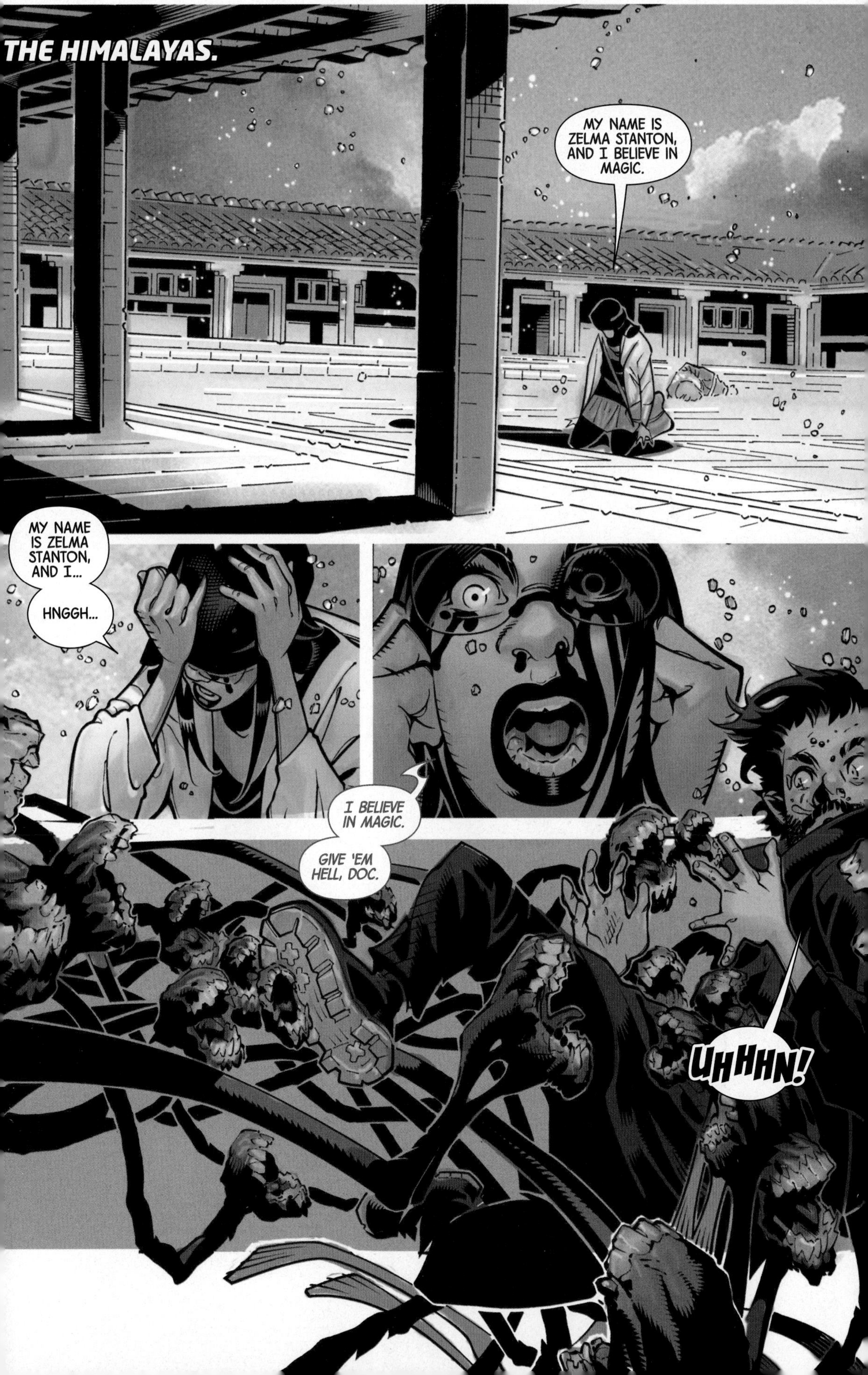

THE HIMALAYAS.
MY NAME IS ZELMA STANTON, AND I BELIEVE IN MAGIC.
MY NAME IS ZELMA STANTON, AND I...
HNGGH...
I BELIEVE IN MAGIC.
GIVE 'EM HELL, DOC.
UHHHN!

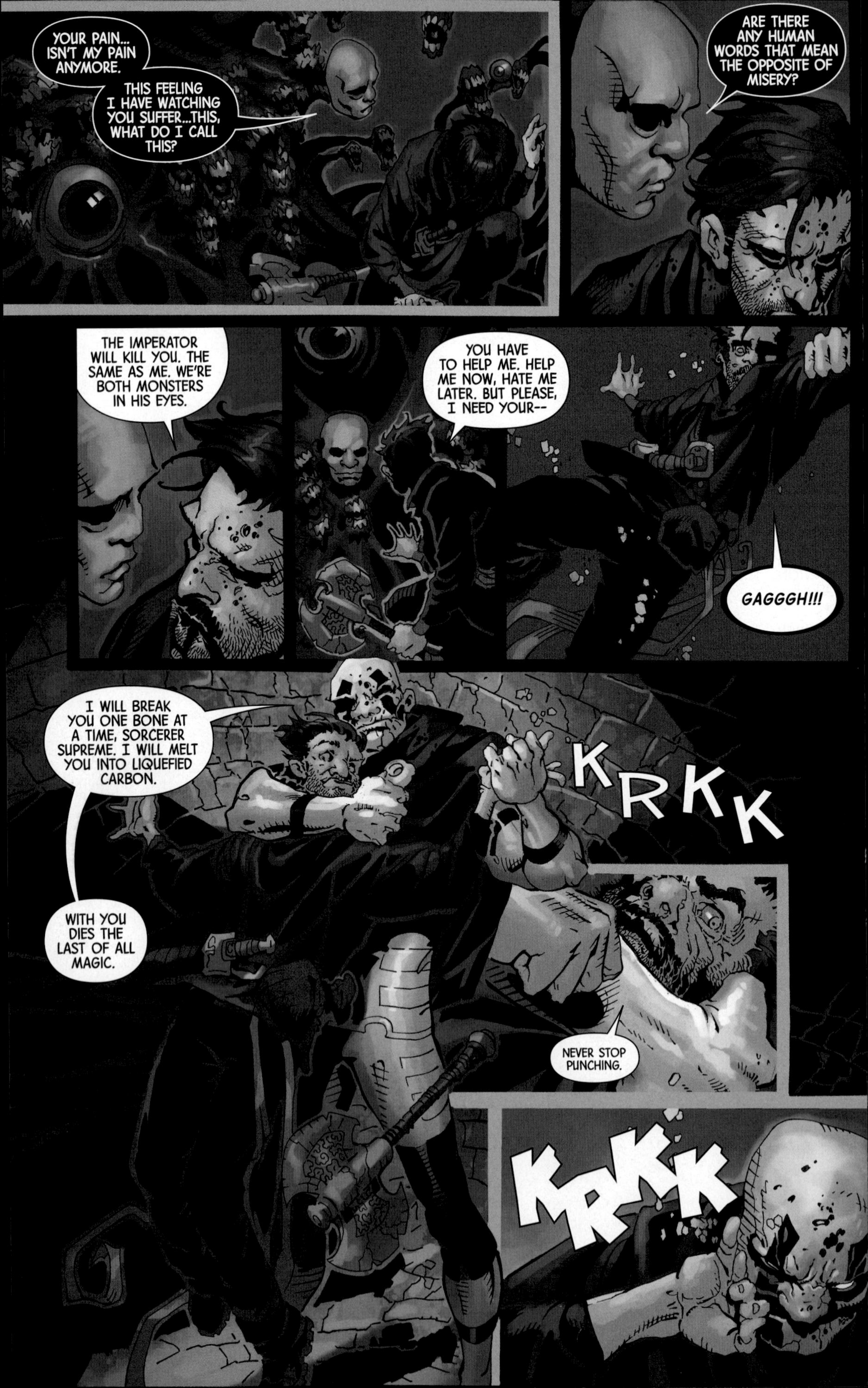
YOUR PAIN... ISN'T MY PAIN ANYMORE.
THIS FEELING I HAVE WATCHING YOU SUFFER...THIS, WHAT DO I CALL THIS?
ARE THERE ANY HUMAN WORDS THAT MEAN THE OPPOSITE OF MISERY?
THE IMPERATOR WILL KILL YOU. THE SAME AS ME. WE'RE BOTH MONSTERS IN HIS EYES.
YOU HAVE TO HELP ME. HELP ME NOW, HATE ME LATER. BUT PLEASE, I NEED YOUR--
GAGGGH!!!
I WILL BREAK YOU ONE BONE AT A TIME, SORCERER SUPREME. I WILL MELT YOU INTO LIQUEFIED CARBON.
KRKK
WITH YOU DIES THE LAST OF ALL MAGIC.
NEVER STOP PUNCHING.
KRKK

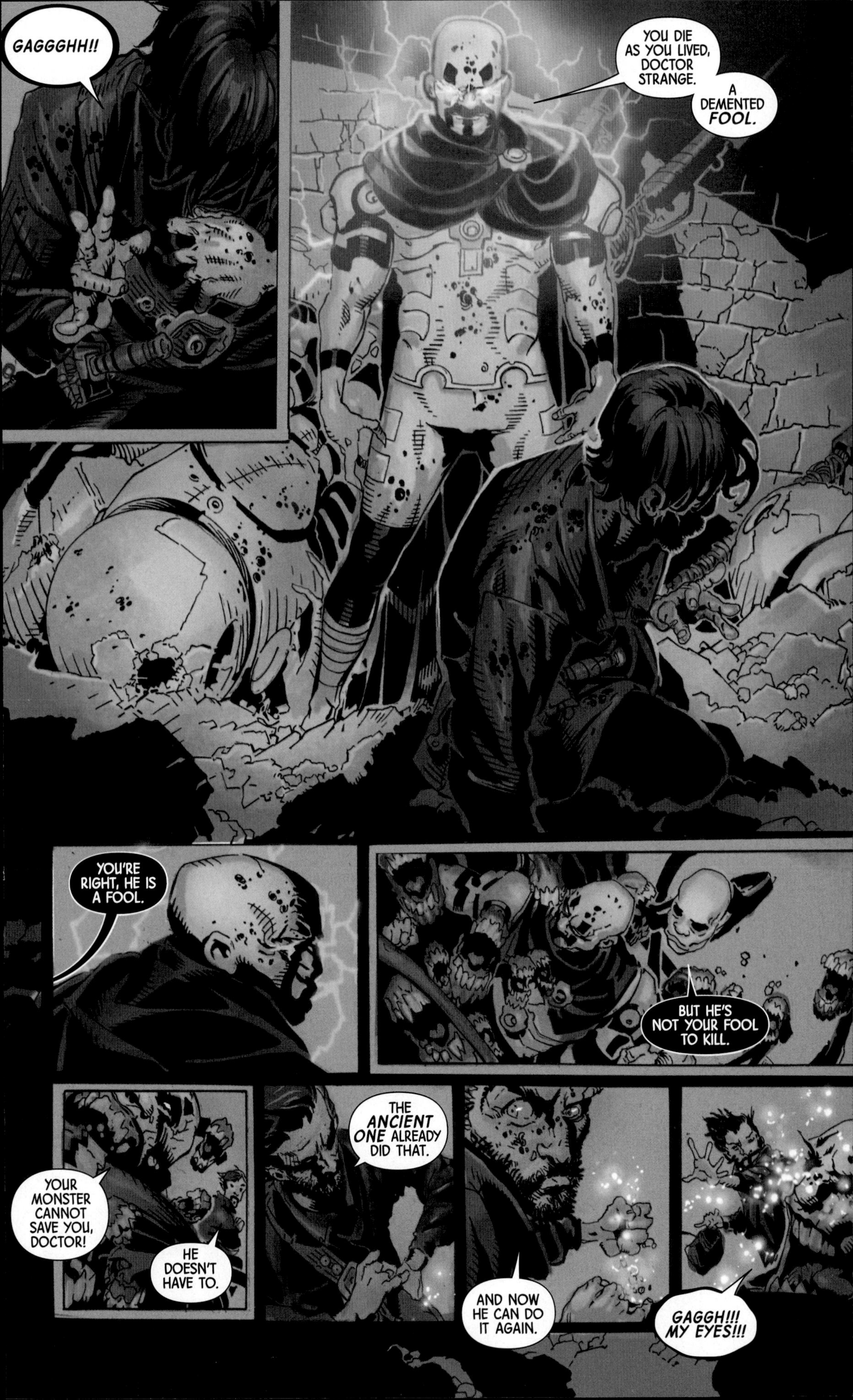
GAGGGHH!!
YOU DIE AS YOU LIVED, DOCTOR STRANGE.
A DEMENTED FOOL.
YOU'RE RIGHT, HE IS A FOOL.
BUT HE'S NOT YOUR FOOL TO KILL.
YOUR MONSTER CANNOT SAVE YOU, DOCTOR!
HE DOESN'T HAVE TO.
THE ANCIENT ONE ALREADY DID THAT.
AND NOW HE CAN DO IT AGAIN.
GAGGH!!! MY EYES!!!

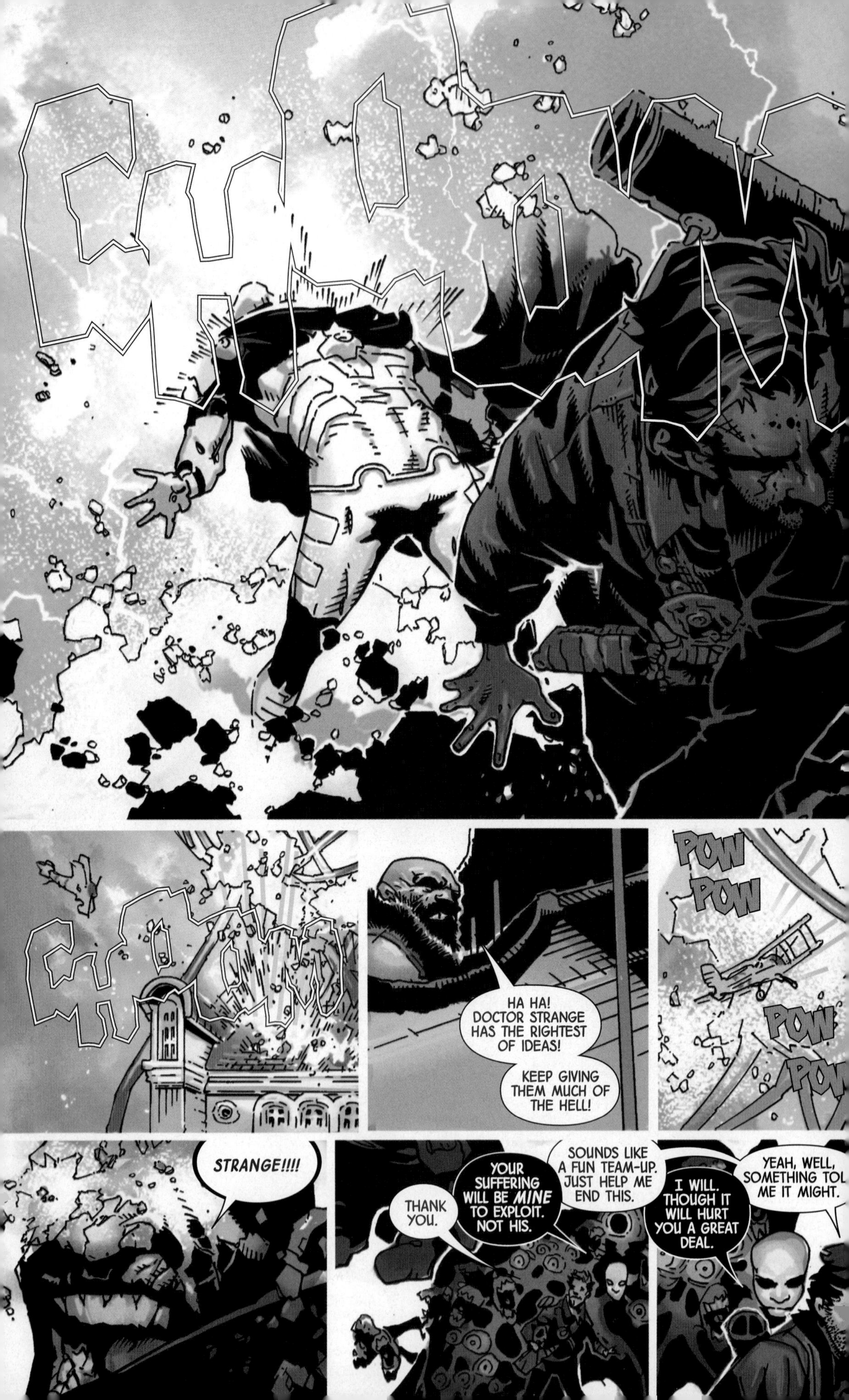
POW
POW
POW
POW
HA HA! DOCTOR STRANGE HAS THE RIGHTEST OF IDEAS!
KEEP GIVING THEM MUCH OF THE HELL!
STRANGE!!!!
THANK YOU.
YOUR SUFFERING WILL BE MINE TO EXPLOIT. NOT HIS.
SOUNDS LIKE A FUN TEAM-UP. JUST HELP ME END THIS.
I WILL. THOUGH IT WILL HURT YOU A GREAT DEAL.
YEAH, WELL, SOMETHING TOL ME IT MIGHT.

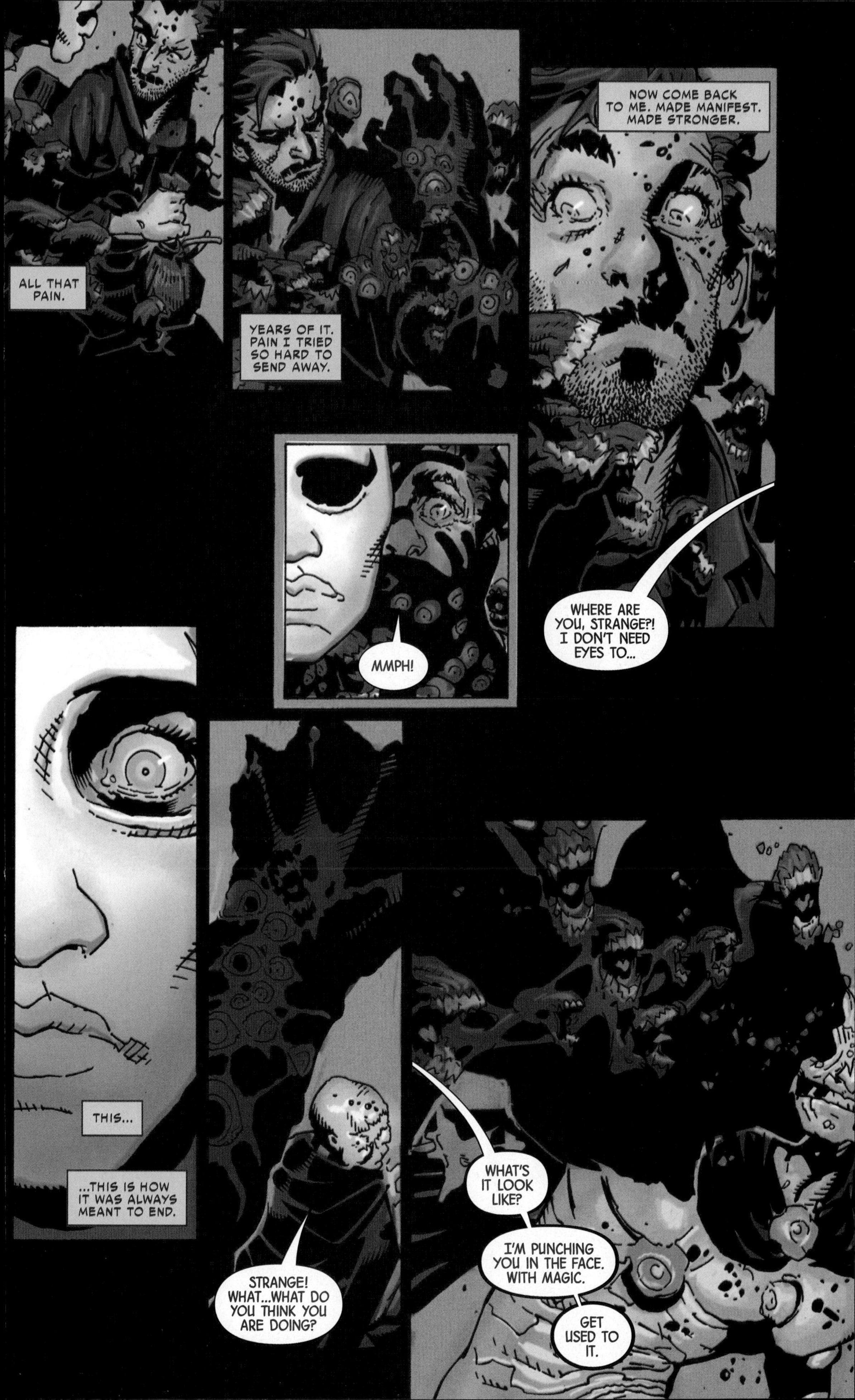
ALL THAT PAIN.
YEARS OF IT. PAIN I TRIED SO HARD TO SEND AWAY.
NOW COME BACK TO ME. MADE MANIFEST. MADE STRONGER.
MMPH!
WHERE ARE YOU, STRANGE?! I DON'T NEED EYES TO...
THIS...
...THIS IS HOW IT WAS ALWAYS MEANT TO END.
STRANGE! WHAT...WHAT DO YOU THINK YOU ARE DOING?
WHAT'S IT LOOK LIKE?
I'M PUNCHING YOU IN THE FACE. WITH MAGIC.
GET USED TO IT.

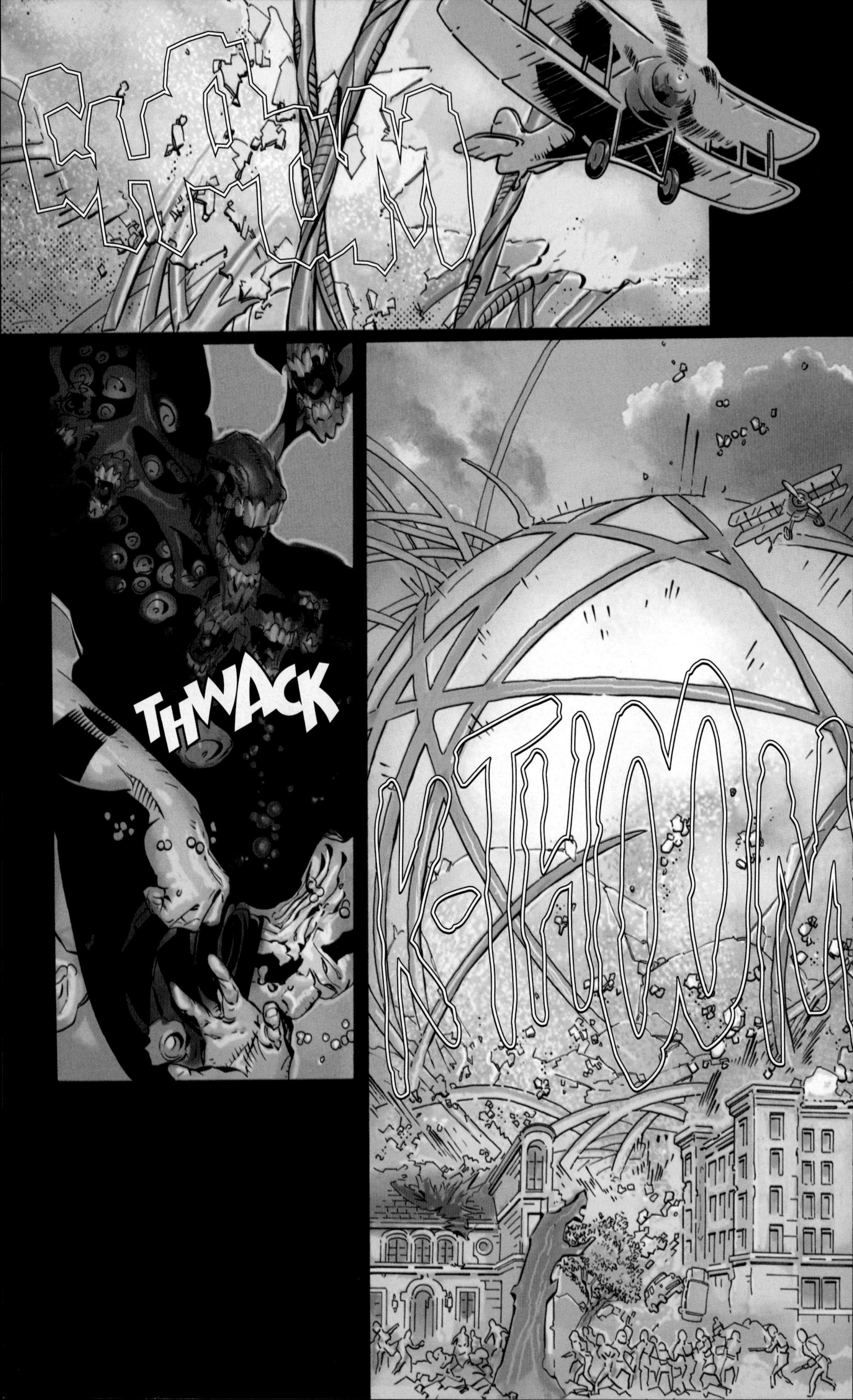
THWACK
K-THOOM

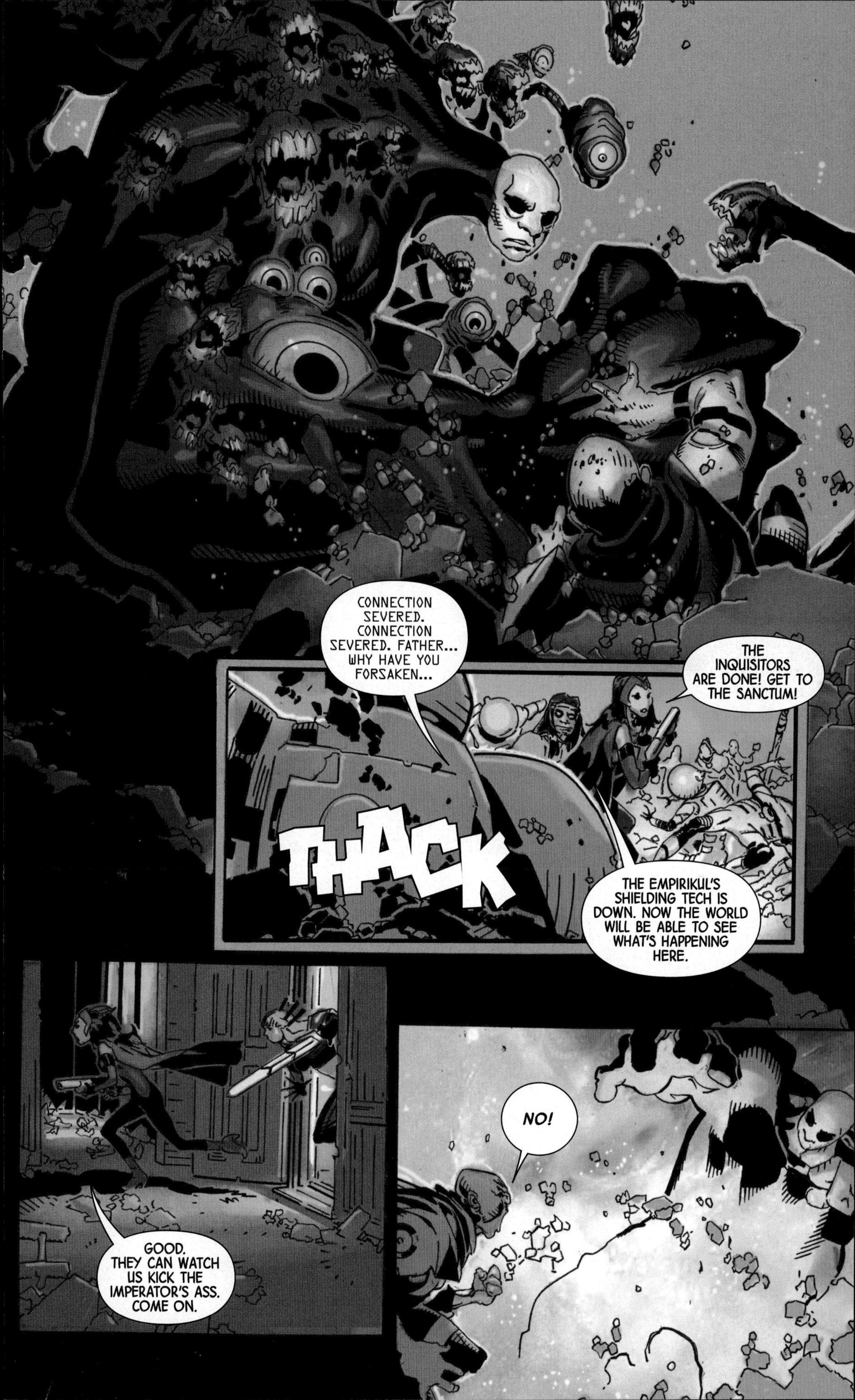
CONNECTION SEVERED. CONNECTION SEVERED. FATHER... WHY HAVE YOU FORSAKEN...
THE INQUISITORS ARE DONE! GET TO THE SANCTUM!
THACK
THE EMPIRIKUL'S SHIELDING TECH IS DOWN. NOW THE WORLD WILL BE ABLE TO SEE WHAT'S HAPPENING HERE.
GOOD. THEY CAN WATCH US KICK THE IMPERATOR'S ASS. COME ON.
NO!

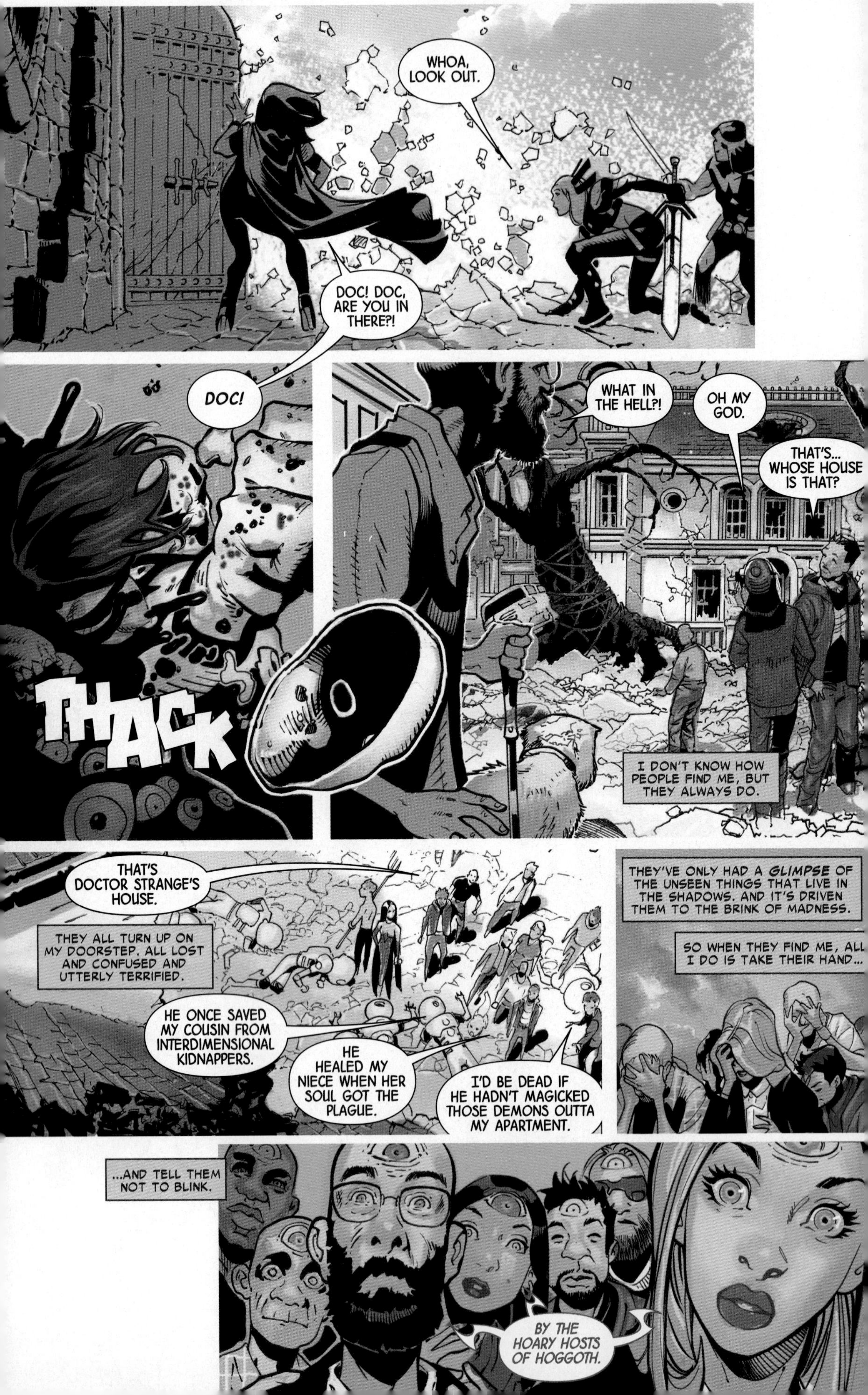
WHOA, LOOK OUT.
DOC! DOC, ARE YOU IN THERE?!
DOC!
THACK
WHAT IN THE HELL?!
OH MY GOD.
THAT'S... WHOSE HOUSE IS THAT?
I DON'T KNOW HOW PEOPLE FIND ME, BUT THEY ALWAYS DO.
THAT'S DOCTOR STRANGE'S HOUSE.
THEY ALL TURN UP ON MY DOORSTEP. ALL LOST AND CONFUSED AND UTTERLY TERRIFIED.
HE ONCE SAVED MY COUSIN FROM INTERDIMENSIONAL KIDNAPPERS.
HE HEALED MY NIECE WHEN HER SOUL GOT THE PLAGUE.
I'D BE DEAD IF HE HADN'T MAGICKED THOSE DEMONS OUTTA MY APARTMENT.
THEY'VE ONLY HAD A GLIMPSE OF THE UNSEEN THINGS THAT LIVE IN THE SHADOWS. AND IT'S DRIVEN THEM TO THE BRINK OF MADNESS.
SO WHEN THEY FIND ME, ALL I DO IS TAKE THEIR HAND...
...AND TELL THEM NOT TO BLINK.
BY THE HOARY HOSTS OF HOGGOTH.

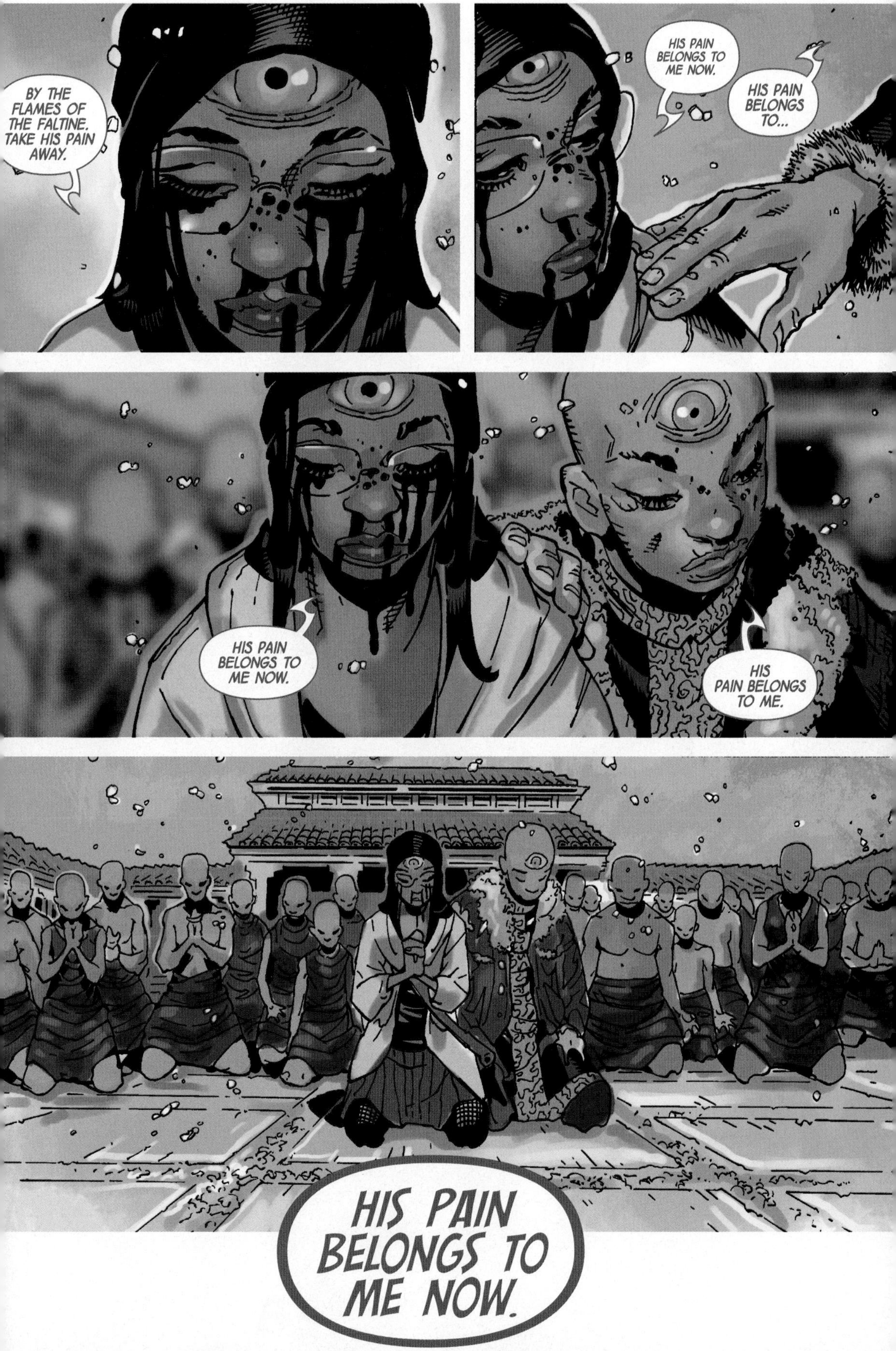
BY THE FLAMES OF THE FALTINE. TAKE HIS PAIN AWAY.
HIS PAIN BELONGS TO ME NOW.
HIS PAIN BELONGS TO...
HIS PAIN BELONGS TO ME NOW.
HIS PAIN BELONGS TO ME.
HIS PAIN BELONGS TO ME NOW.

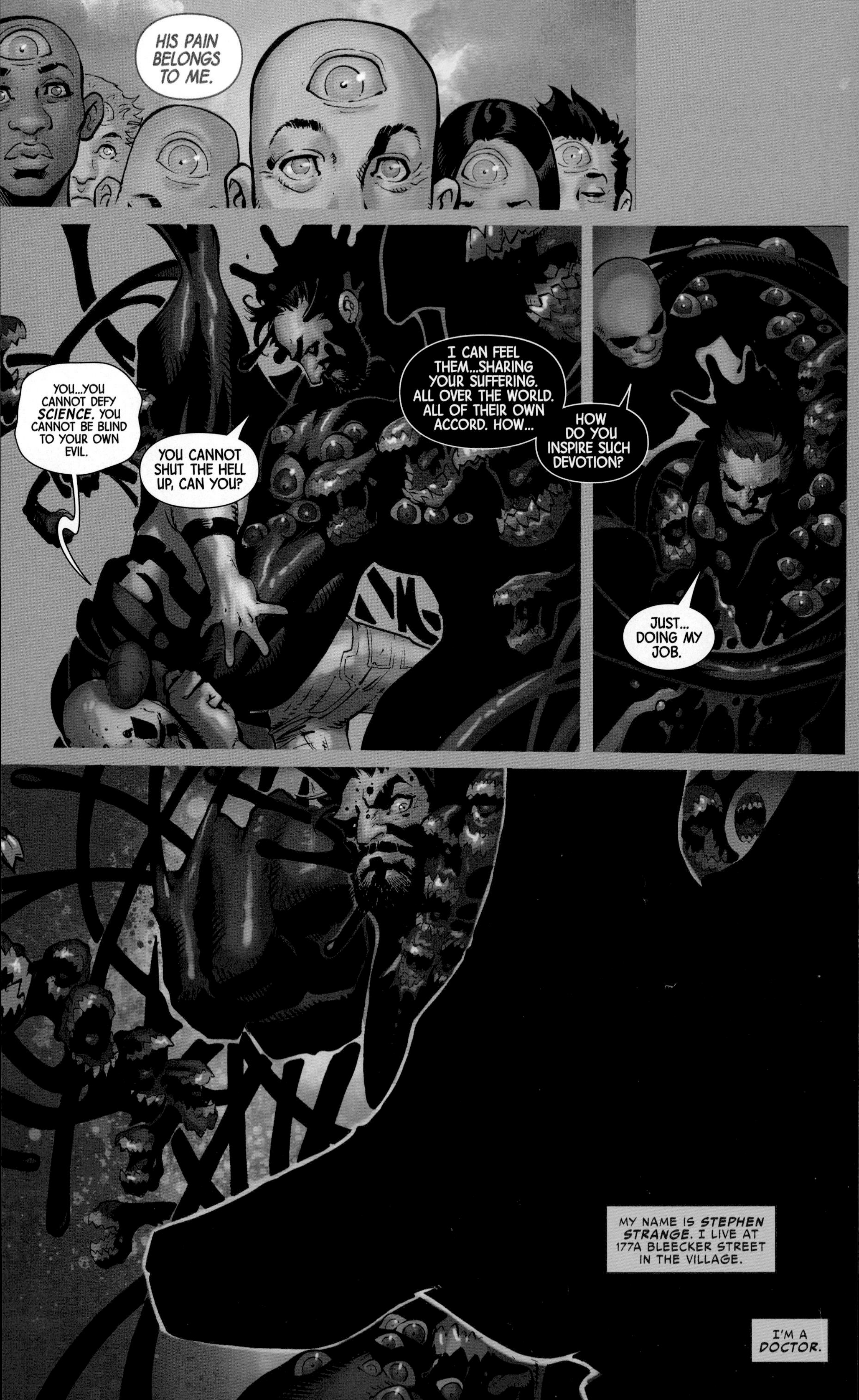
HIS PAIN BELONGS TO ME.
YOU...YOU CANNOT DEFY SCIENCE. YOU CANNOT BE BLIND TO YOUR OWN EVIL.
YOU CANNOT SHUT THE HELL UP, CAN YOU?
I CAN FEEL THEM...SHARING YOUR SUFFERING. ALL OVER THE WORLD. ALL OF THEIR OWN ACCORD. HOW...
HOW DO YOU INSPIRE SUCH DEVOTION?
JUST... DOING MY JOB.
MY NAME IS STEPHEN STRANGE. I LIVE AT 177A BLEECKER STREET IN THE VILLAGE.
I'M A DOCTOR.

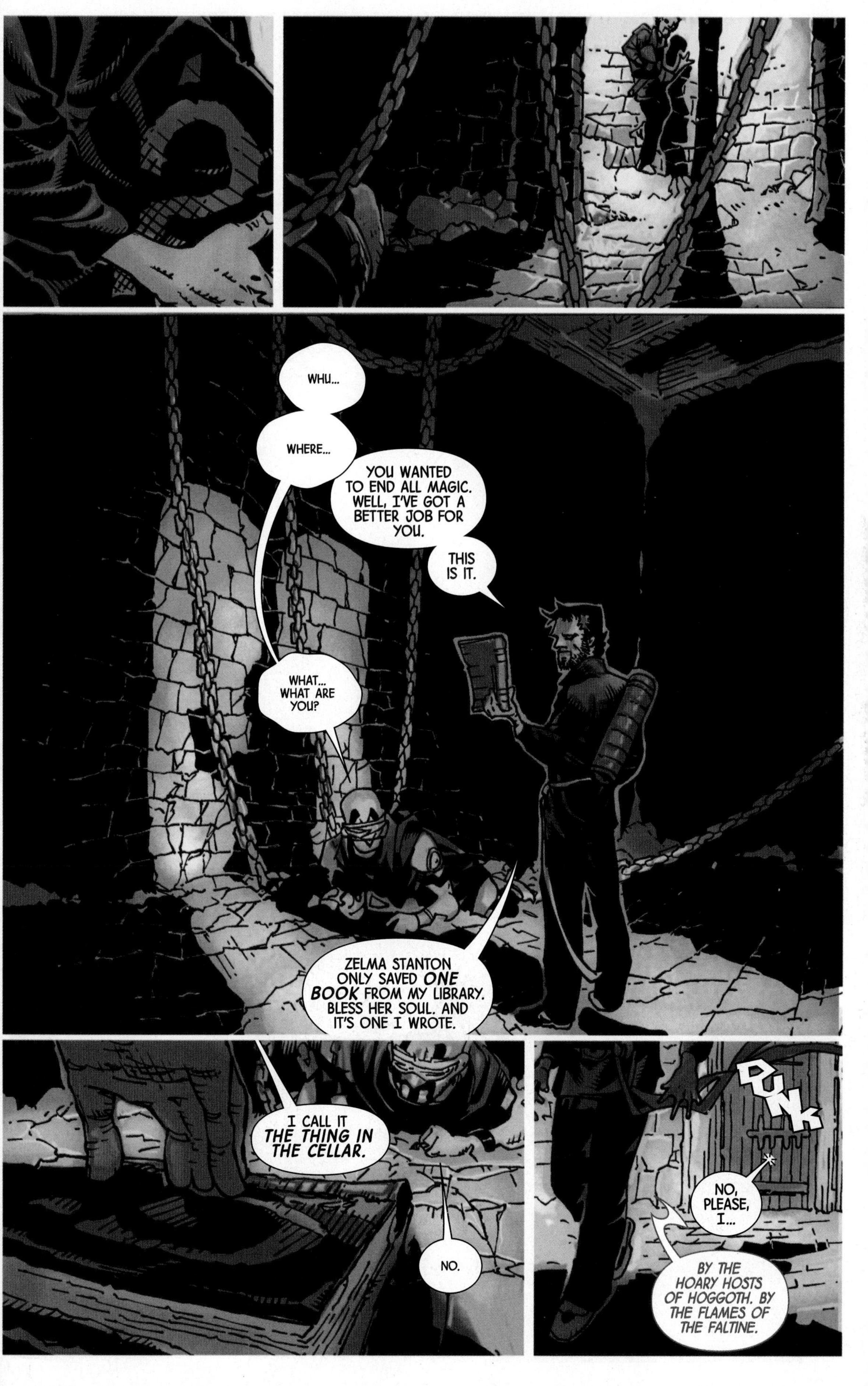
WHU...
WHERE...
YOU WANTED TO END ALL MAGIC. WELL, I'VE GOT A BETTER JOB FOR YOU.
THIS IS IT.
WHAT... WHAT ARE YOU?
ZELMA STANTON ONLY SAVED *ONE BOOK* FROM MY LIBRARY. BLESS HER SOUL. AND IT'S ONE I WROTE.
I CALL IT *THE THING IN THE CELLAR.*
NO.
DUNK
NO, PLEASE, I...
BY THE HOARY HOSTS OF HOGGOTH. BY THE FLAMES OF THE FALTINE.

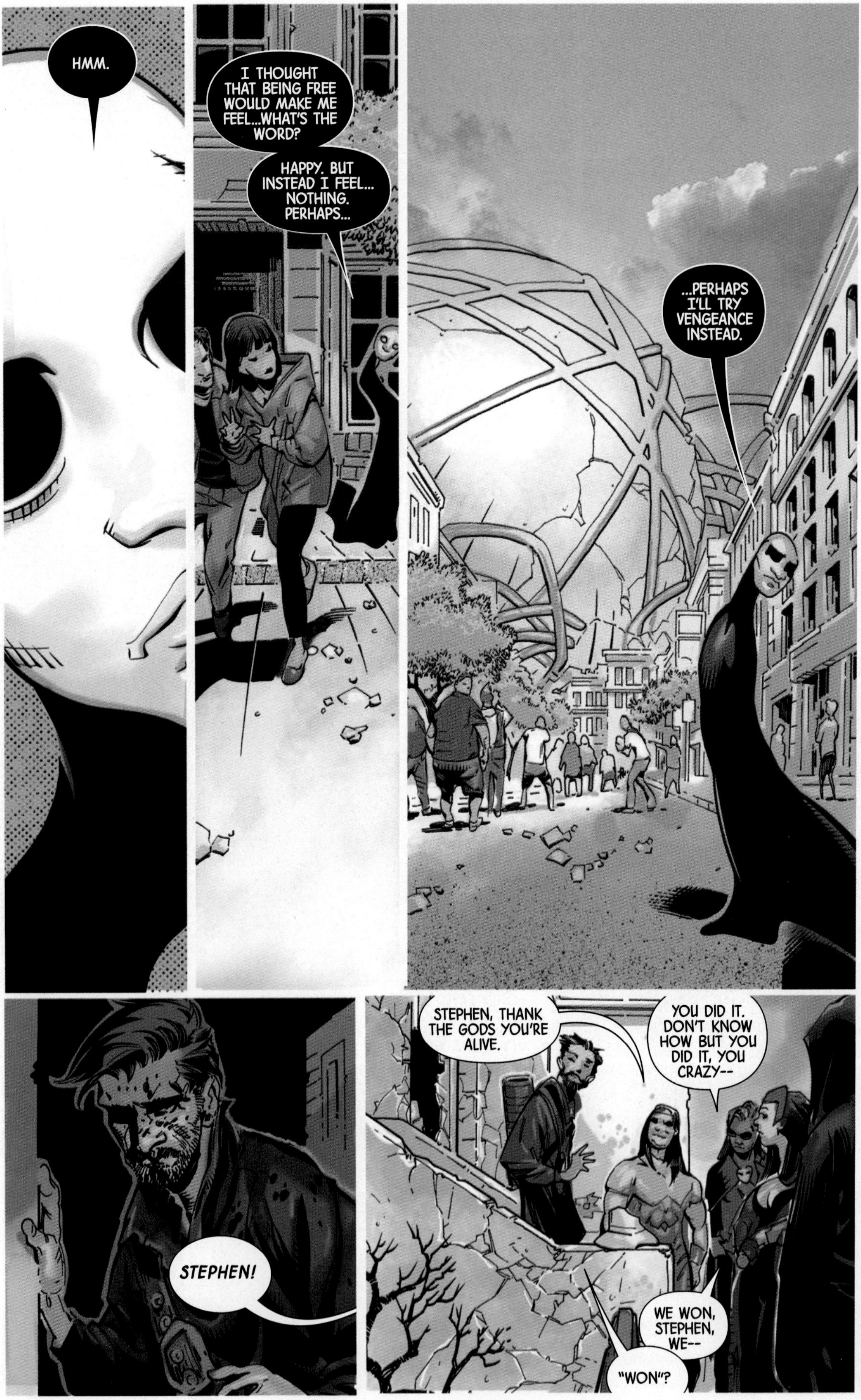
HMM.
I THOUGHT THAT BEING FREE WOULD MAKE ME FEEL...WHAT'S THE WORD?
HAPPY. BUT INSTEAD I FEEL... NOTHING. PERHAPS...
...PERHAPS I'LL TRY VENGEANCE INSTEAD.
STEPHEN!
STEPHEN, THANK THE GODS YOU'RE ALIVE.
YOU DID IT. DON'T KNOW HOW BUT YOU DID IT, YOU CRAZY--
WE WON, STEPHEN, WE--
"WON"?

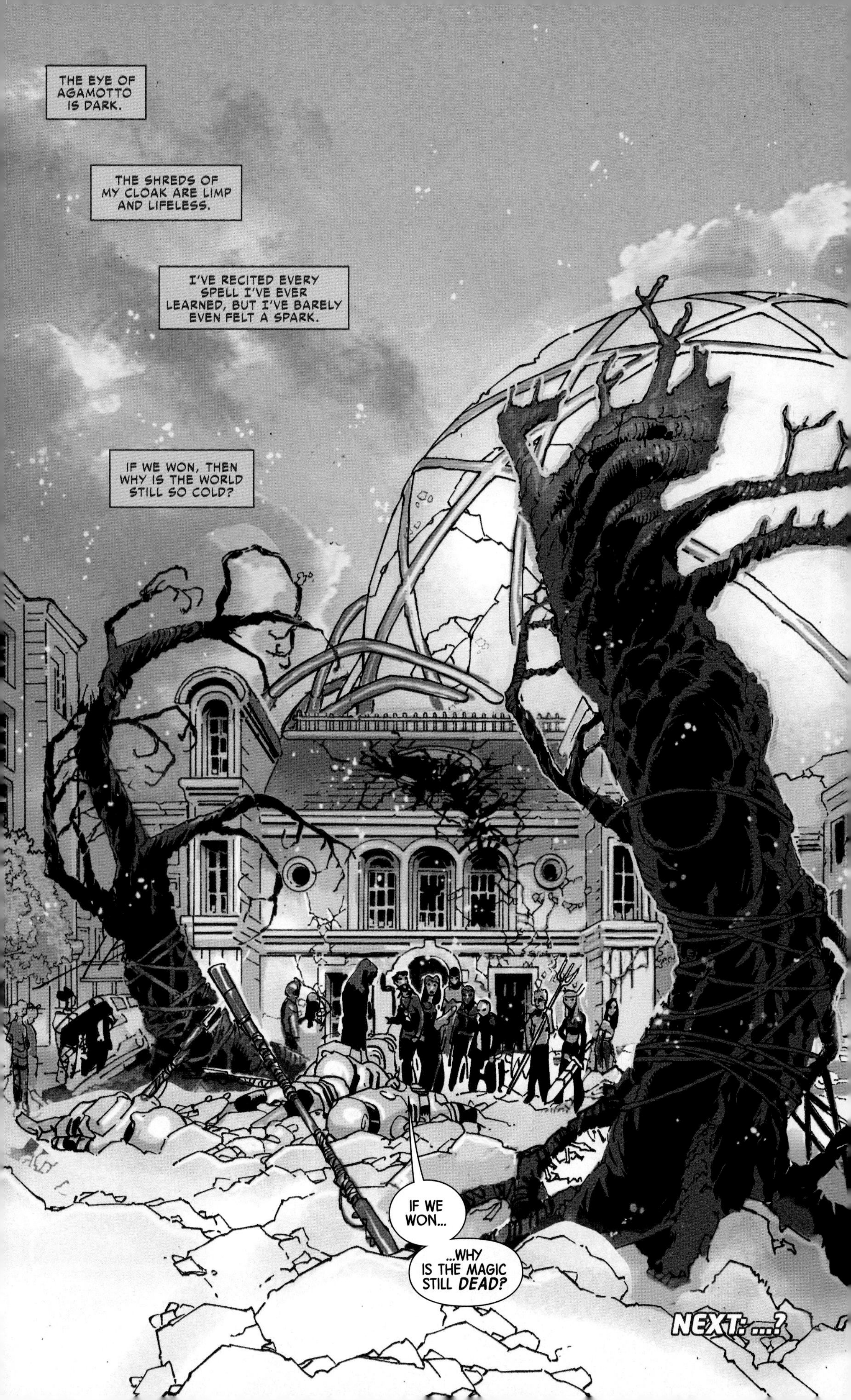
THE EYE OF AGAMOTTO IS DARK.
THE SHREDS OF MY CLOAK ARE LIMP AND LIFELESS.
I'VE RECITED EVERY SPELL I'VE EVER LEARNED, BUT I'VE BARELY EVEN FELT A SPARK.
IF WE WON, THEN WHY IS THE WORLD STILL SO COLD?
IF WE WON...
...WHY IS THE MAGIC STILL DEAD?
NEXT: ...?

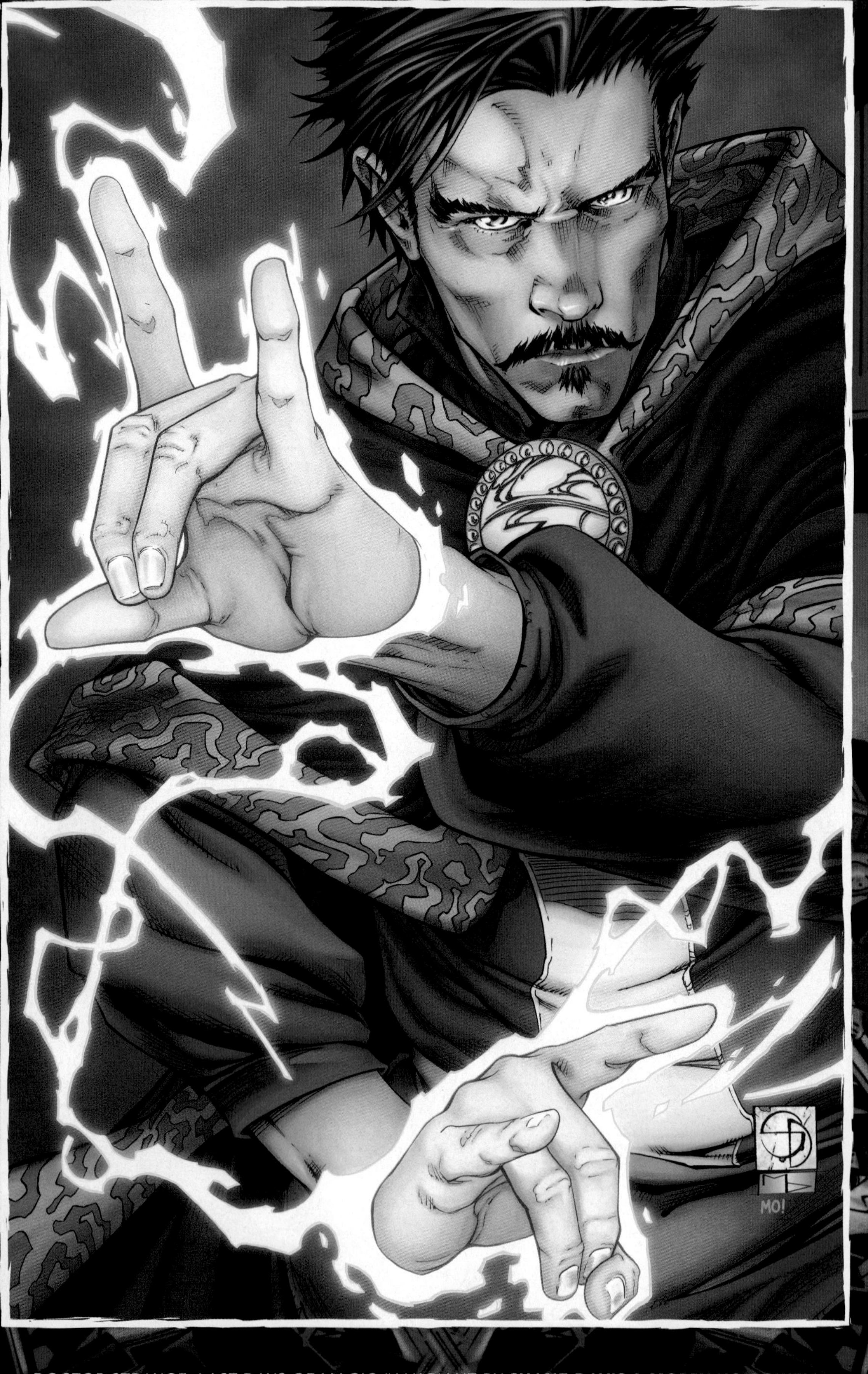
MO!

DOCTOR STRANGE: LAST DAYS OF MAGIC #1 VARIANT BY **SHANE DAVIS** & **MORRY HOLLOWELL**

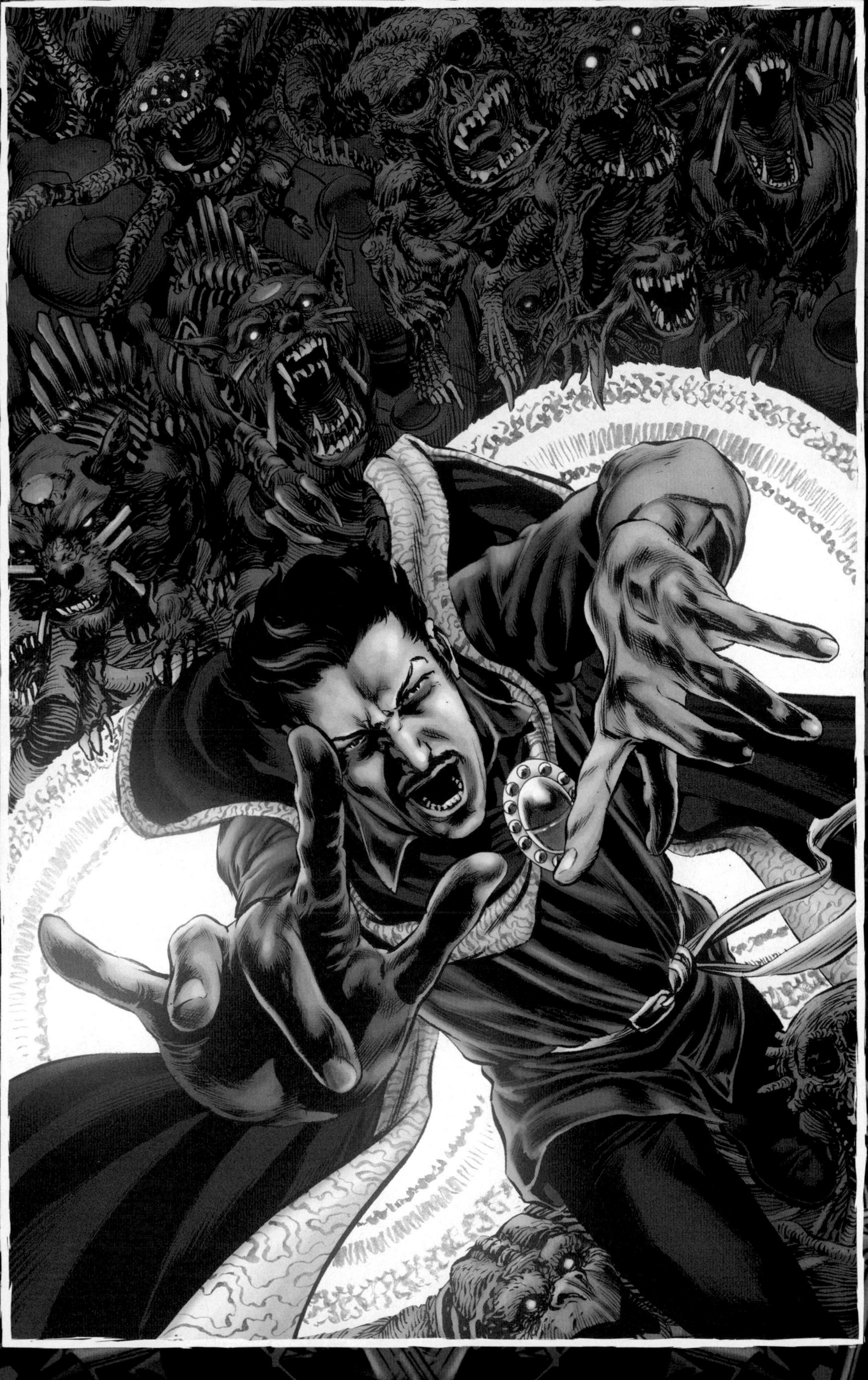

DOCTOR STRANGE: LAST DAYS OF MAGIC #1

(THIS STORY TAKES PLACE BETWEEN ISSUES #6 & #7.)

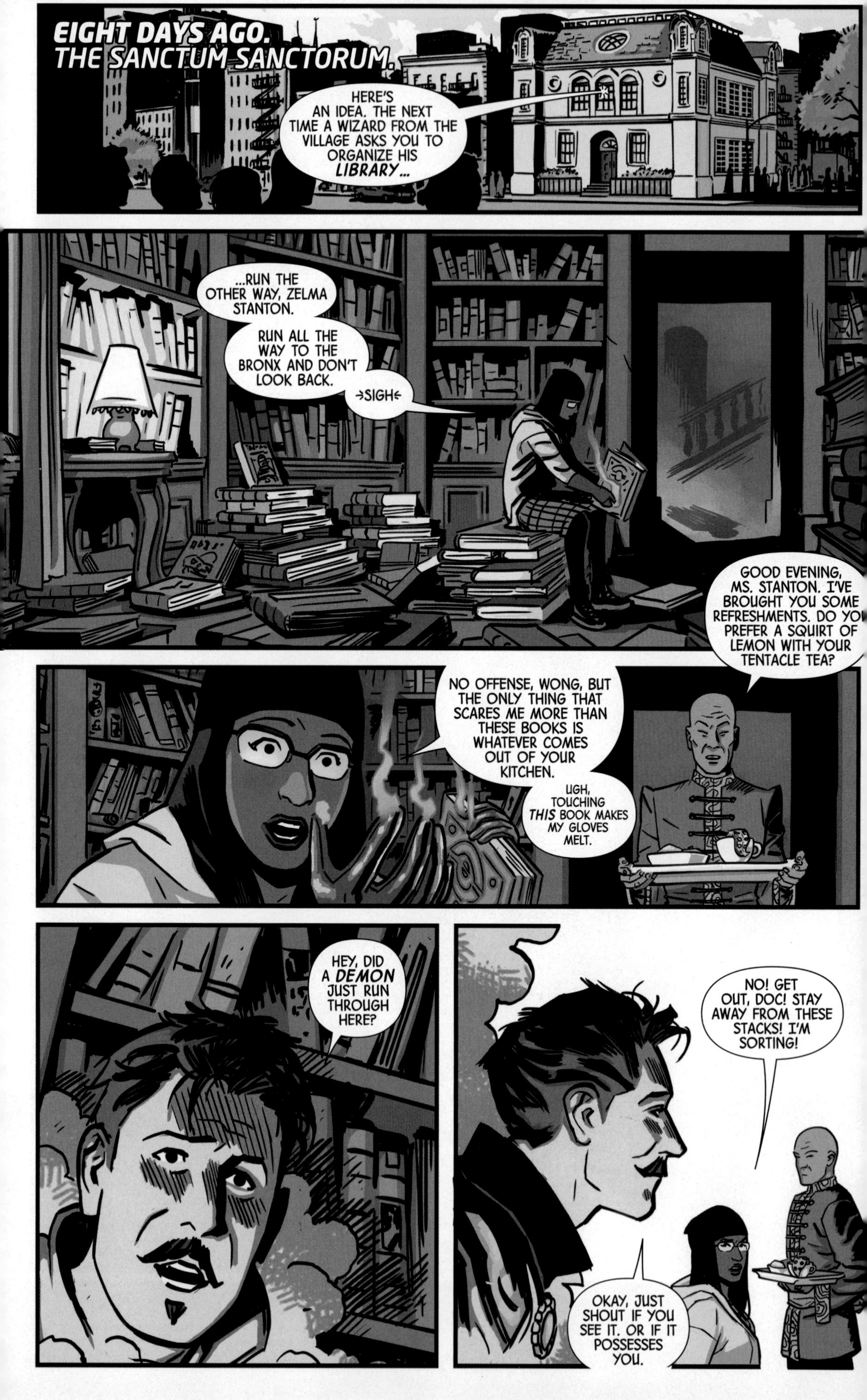
EIGHT DAYS AGO.
THE SANCTUM SANCTORUM.
HERE'S AN IDEA. THE NEXT TIME A WIZARD FROM THE VILLAGE ASKS YOU TO ORGANIZE HIS LIBRARY...
...RUN THE OTHER WAY, ZELMA STANTON.
RUN ALL THE WAY TO THE BRONX AND DON'T LOOK BACK.
SIGH
GOOD EVENING, MS. STANTON. I'VE BROUGHT YOU SOME REFRESHMENTS. DO YO PREFER A SQUIRT OF LEMON WITH YOUR TENTACLE TEA?
NO OFFENSE, WONG, BUT THE ONLY THING THAT SCARES ME MORE THAN THESE BOOKS IS WHATEVER COMES OUT OF YOUR KITCHEN.
UGH, TOUCHING THIS BOOK MAKES MY GLOVES MELT.
HEY, DID A DEMON JUST RUN THROUGH HERE?
NO! GET OUT, DOC! STAY AWAY FROM THESE STACKS! I'M SORTING!
OKAY, JUST SHOUT IF YOU SEE IT. OR IF IT POSSESSES YOU.

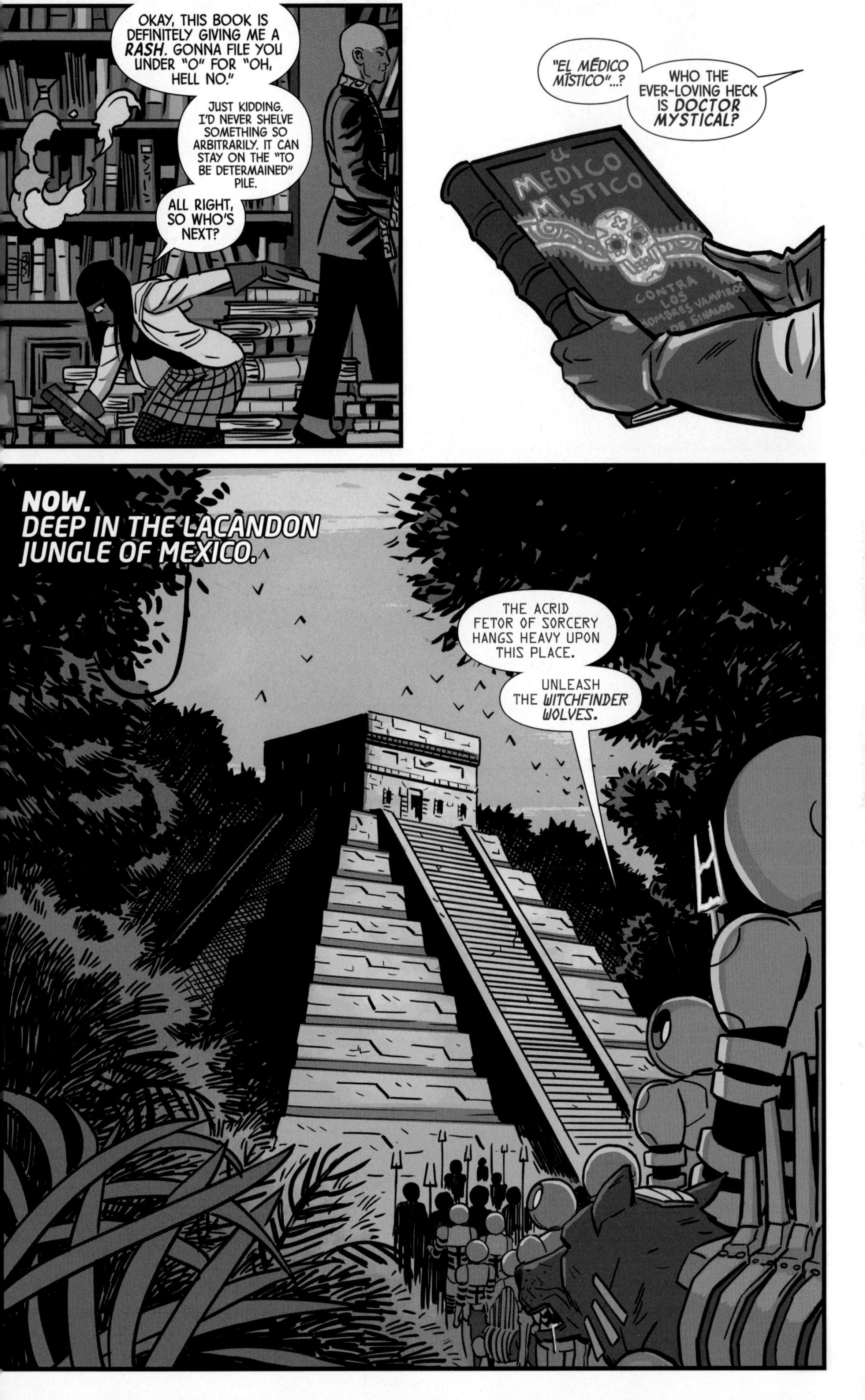
OKAY, THIS BOOK IS DEFINITELY GIVING ME A RASH. GONNA FILE YOU UNDER "O" FOR "OH, HELL NO."
JUST KIDDING. I'D NEVER SHELVE SOMETHING SO ARBITRARILY. IT CAN STAY ON THE "TO BE DETERMINED" PILE.
ALL RIGHT, SO WHO'S NEXT?
"EL MÉDICO MÍSTICO"...?
WHO THE EVER-LOVING HECK IS DOCTOR MYSTICAL?
EL MEDICO MISTICO CONTRA LOS HOMBRES VAMPIROS DE SINALOA
NOW. DEEP IN THE LACANDON JUNGLE OF MEXICO.
THE ACRID FETOR OF SORCERY HANGS HEAVY UPON THIS PLACE.
UNLEASH THE WITCHFINDER WOLVES.

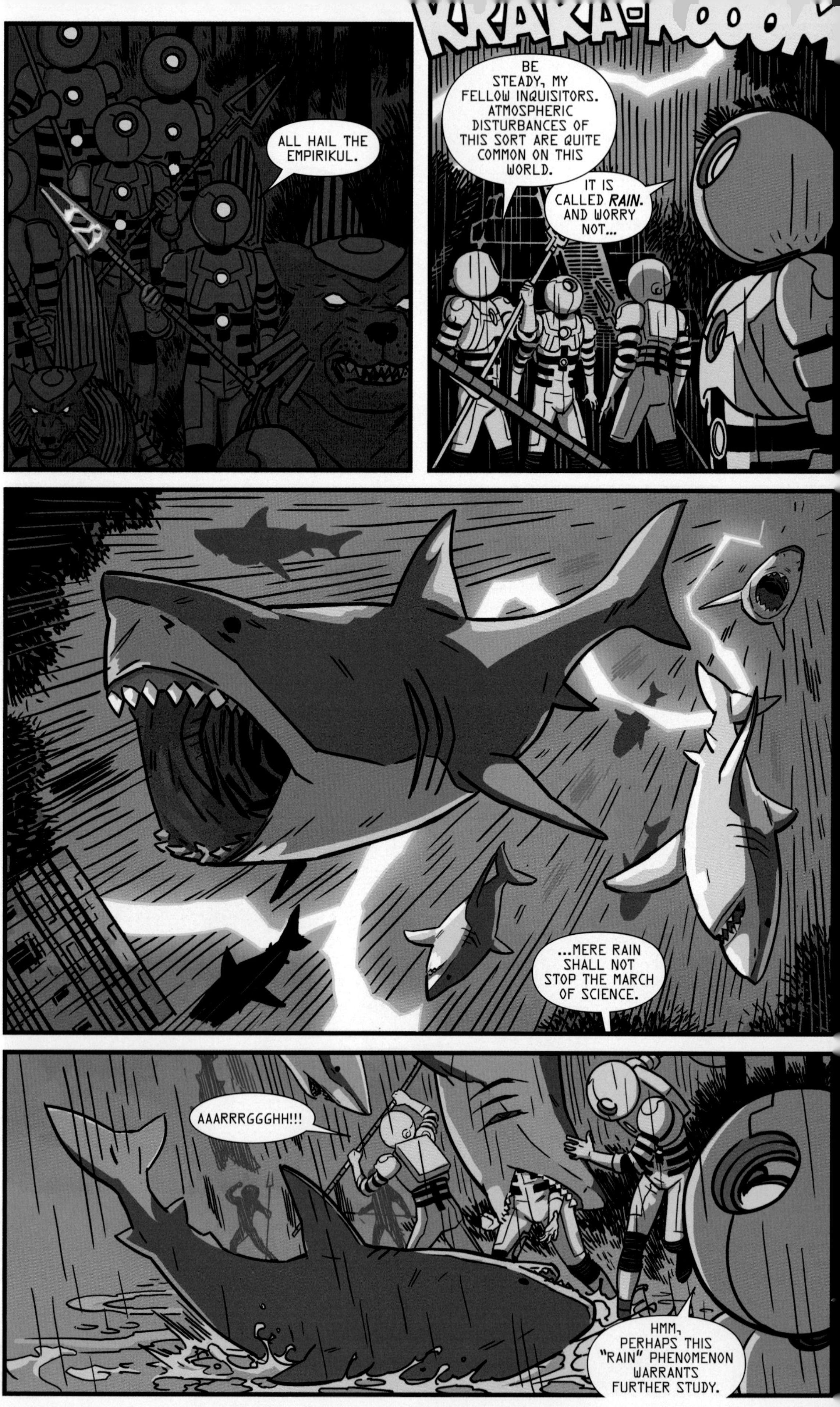
ALL HAIL THE EMPIRIKUL.
KRAKA-KOOOM
BE STEADY, MY FELLOW INQUISITORS. ATMOSPHERIC DISTURBANCES OF THIS SORT ARE QUITE COMMON ON THIS WORLD.
IT IS CALLED RAIN. AND WORRY NOT...
...MERE RAIN SHALL NOT STOP THE MARCH OF SCIENCE.
AAARRRGGGHH!!!
HMM, PERHAPS THIS "RAIN" PHENOMENON WARRANTS FURTHER STUDY.

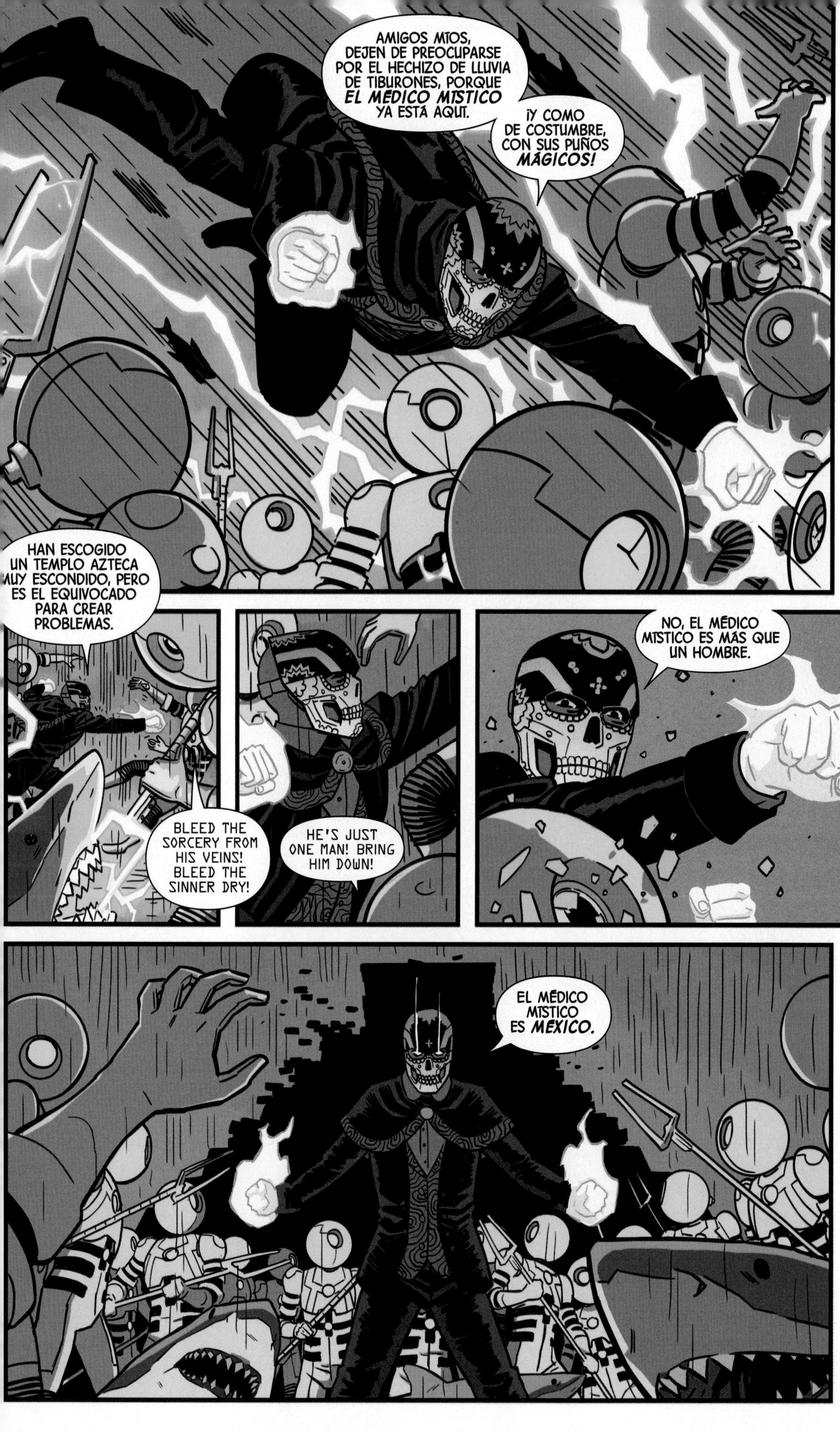

AMIGOS MÍOS, DEJEN DE PREOCUPARSE POR EL HECHIZO DE LLUVIA DE TIBURONES, PORQUE *EL MÉDICO MÍSTICO* YA ESTÁ AQUÍ.
¡Y COMO DE COSTUMBRE, CON SUS PUÑOS *MÁGICOS!*
HAN ESCOGIDO UN TEMPLO AZTECA MUY ESCONDIDO, PERO ES EL EQUIVOCADO PARA CREAR PROBLEMAS.
BLEED THE SORCERY FROM HIS VEINS! BLEED THE SINNER DRY!
HE'S JUST ONE MAN! BRING HIM DOWN!
NO, EL MÉDICO MÍSTICO ES MÁS QUE UN HOMBRE.
EL MÉDICO MÍSTICO ES *MÉXICO.*

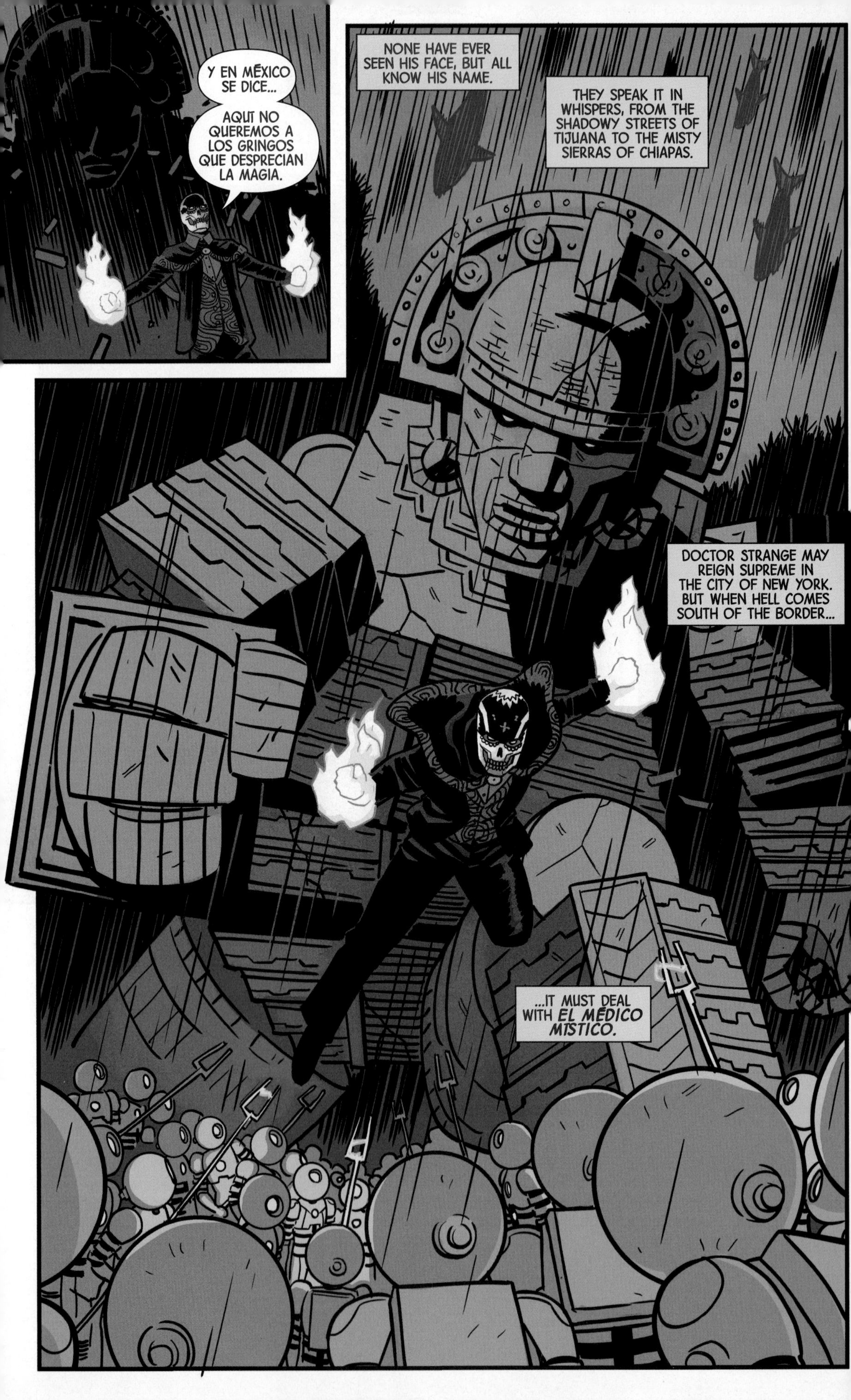
Y EN MÉXICO SE DICE...
AQUÍ NO QUEREMOS A LOS GRINGOS QUE DESPRECIAN LA MAGIA.
NONE HAVE EVER SEEN HIS FACE, BUT ALL KNOW HIS NAME.
THEY SPEAK IT IN WHISPERS, FROM THE SHADOWY STREETS OF TIJUANA TO THE MISTY SIERRAS OF CHIAPAS.
DOCTOR STRANGE MAY REIGN SUPREME IN THE CITY OF NEW YORK. BUT WHEN HELL COMES SOUTH OF THE BORDER...
...IT MUST DEAL WITH EL MÉDICO MÍSTICO.

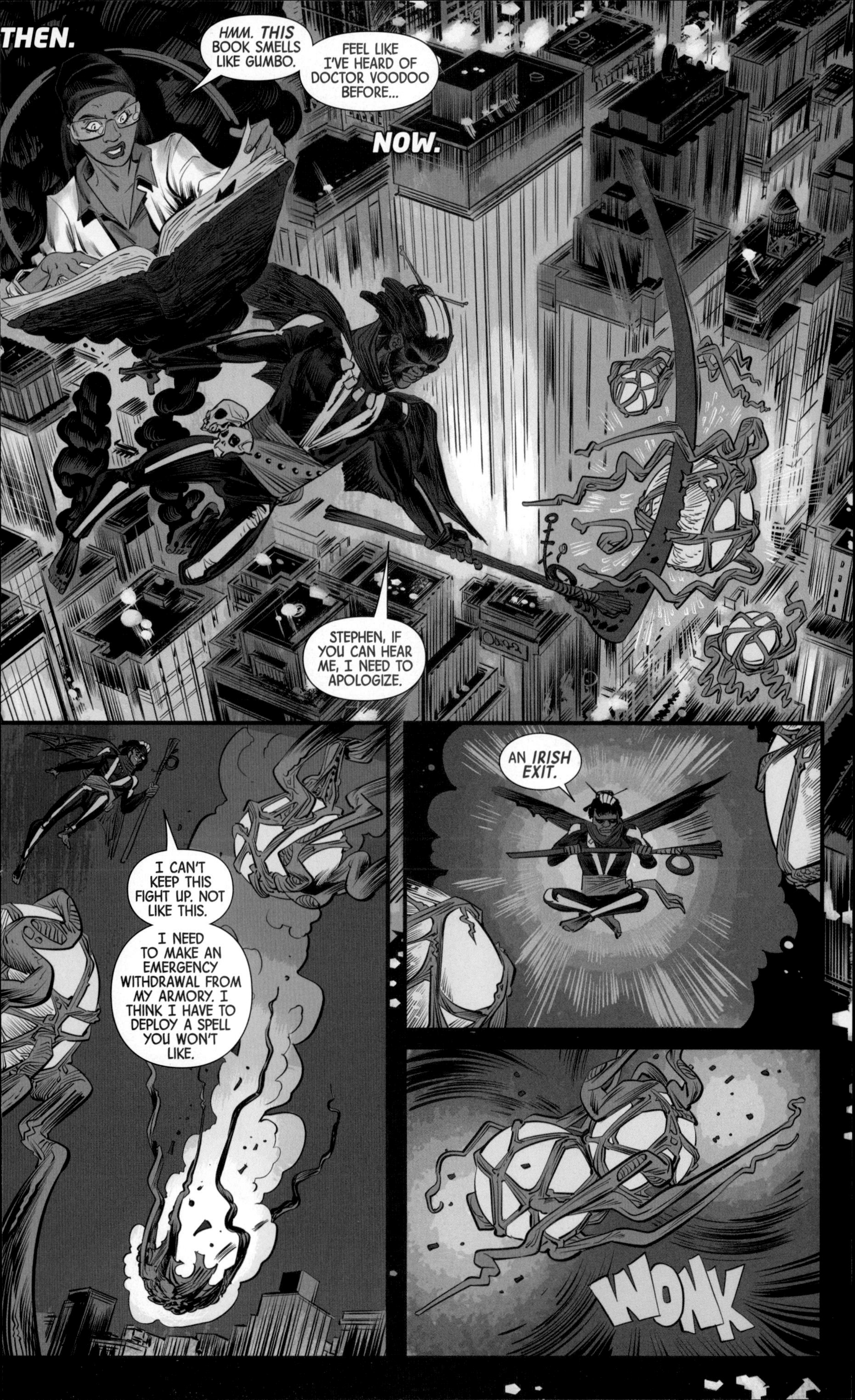
THEN.
HMM. THIS BOOK SMELLS LIKE GUMBO.
FEEL LIKE I'VE HEARD OF DOCTOR VOODOO BEFORE...
NOW.
STEPHEN, IF YOU CAN HEAR ME, I NEED TO APOLOGIZE.
I CAN'T KEEP THIS FIGHT UP. NOT LIKE THIS.
I NEED TO MAKE AN EMERGENCY WITHDRAWAL FROM MY ARMORY. I THINK I HAVE TO DEPLOY A SPELL YOU WON'T LIKE.
AN IRISH EXIT.
WONK

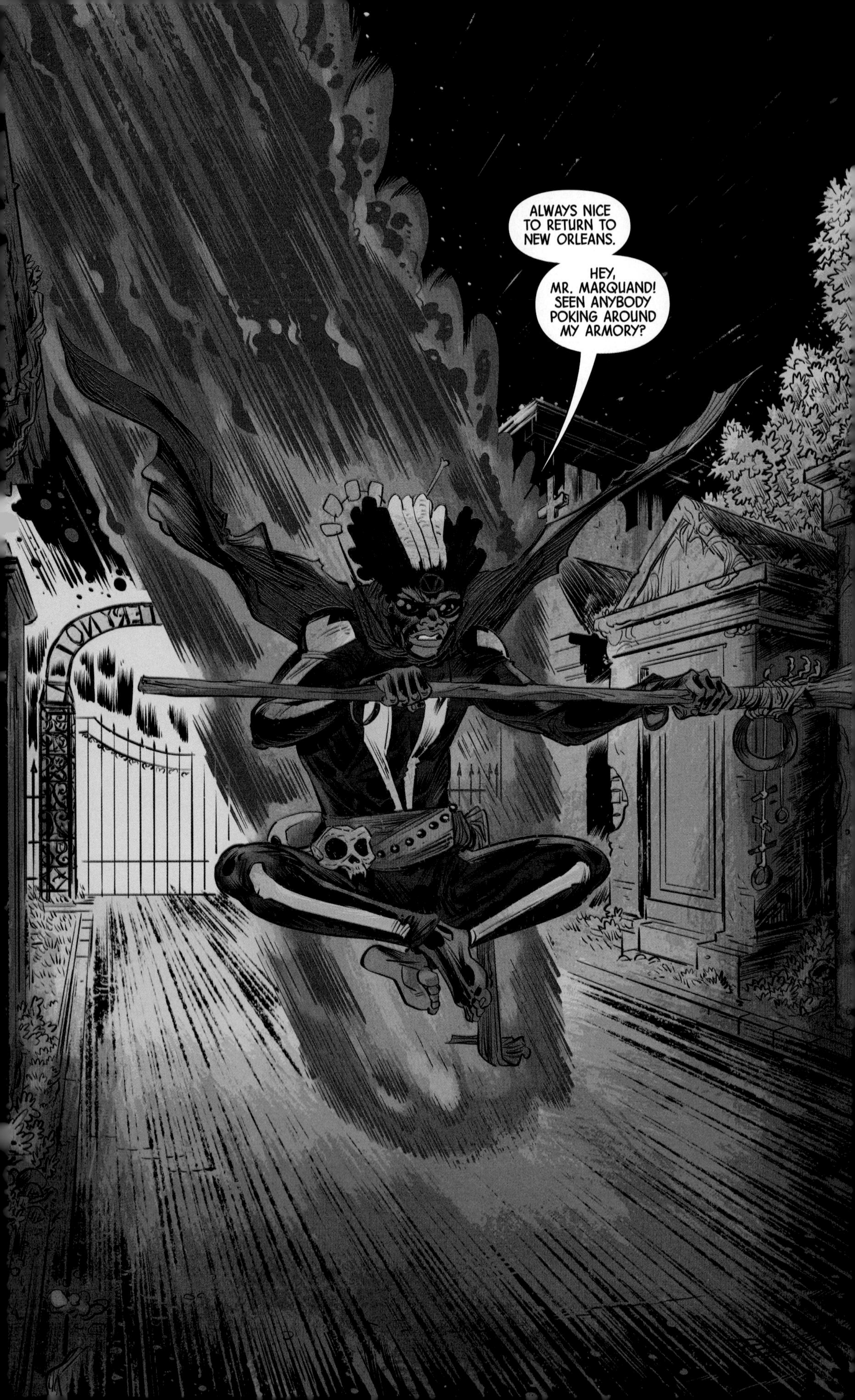
ALWAYS NICE TO RETURN TO NEW ORLEANS.
HEY, MR. MARQUAND! SEEN ANYBODY POKING AROUND MY ARMORY?

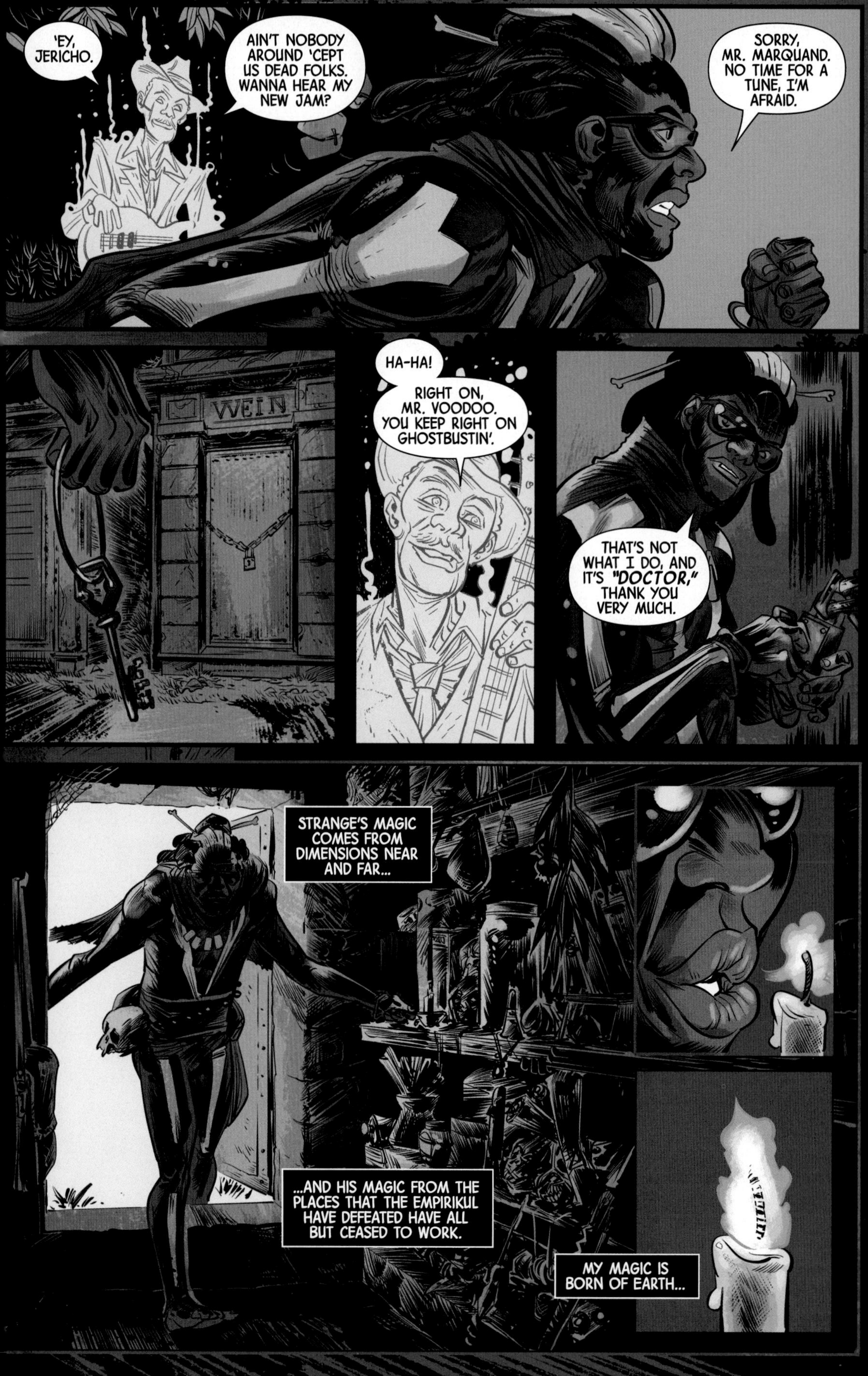
'EY, JERICHO.
AIN'T NOBODY AROUND 'CEPT US DEAD FOLKS. WANNA HEAR MY NEW JAM?
SORRY, MR. MARQUAND. NO TIME FOR A TUNE, I'M AFRAID.
WEIN
HA-HA!
RIGHT ON, MR. VOODOO. YOU KEEP RIGHT ON GHOSTBUSTIN'.
THAT'S NOT WHAT I DO, AND IT'S "DOCTOR," THANK YOU VERY MUCH.
STRANGE'S MAGIC COMES FROM DIMENSIONS NEAR AND FAR...
...AND HIS MAGIC FROM THE PLACES THAT THE EMPIRIKUL HAVE DEFEATED HAVE ALL BUT CEASED TO WORK.
MY MAGIC IS BORN OF EARTH...

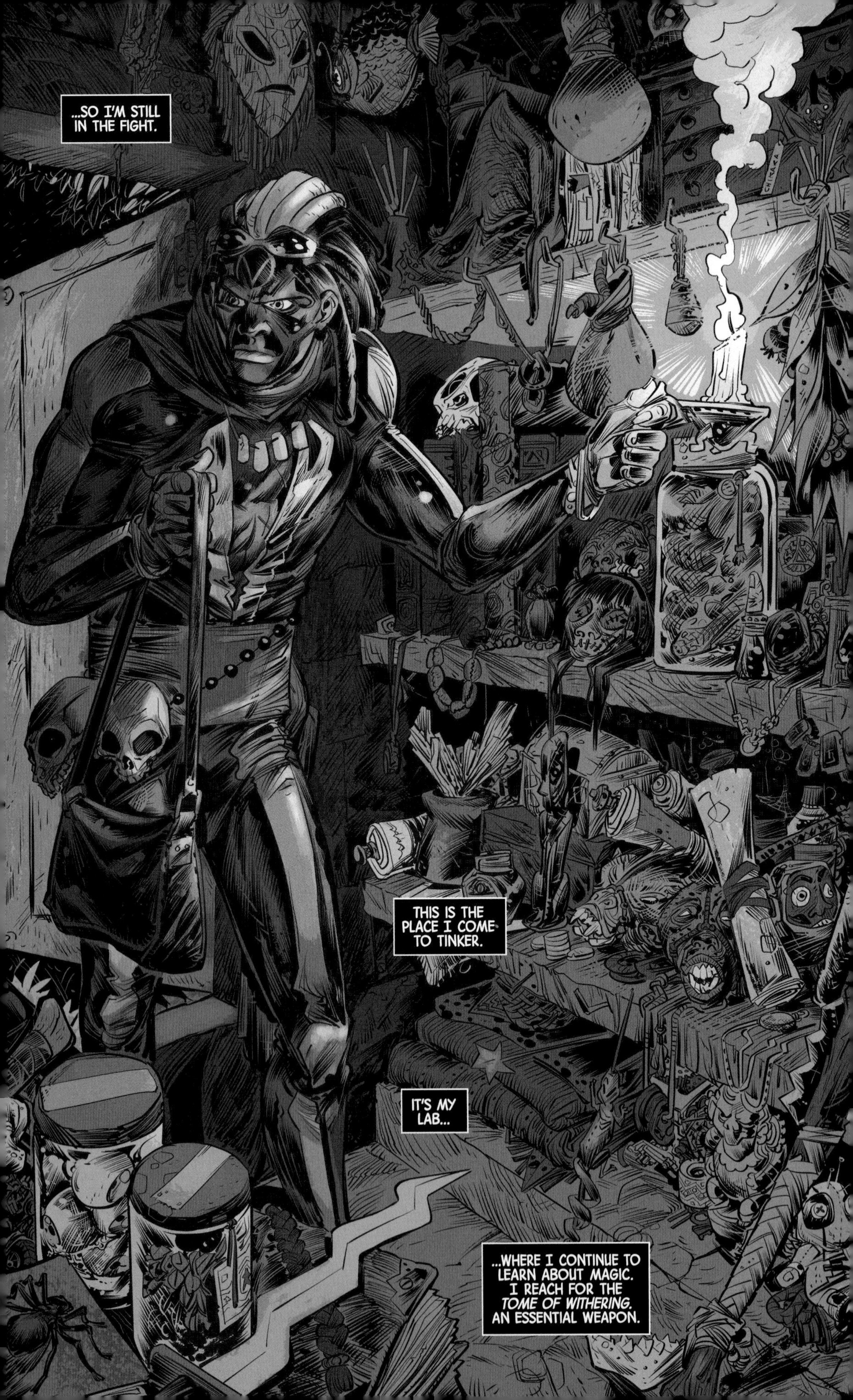
...SO I'M STILL IN THE FIGHT.
THIS IS THE PLACE I COME TO TINKER.
IT'S MY LAB...
...WHERE I CONTINUE TO LEARN ABOUT MAGIC. I REACH FOR THE *TOME OF WITHERING.* AN ESSENTIAL WEAPON.

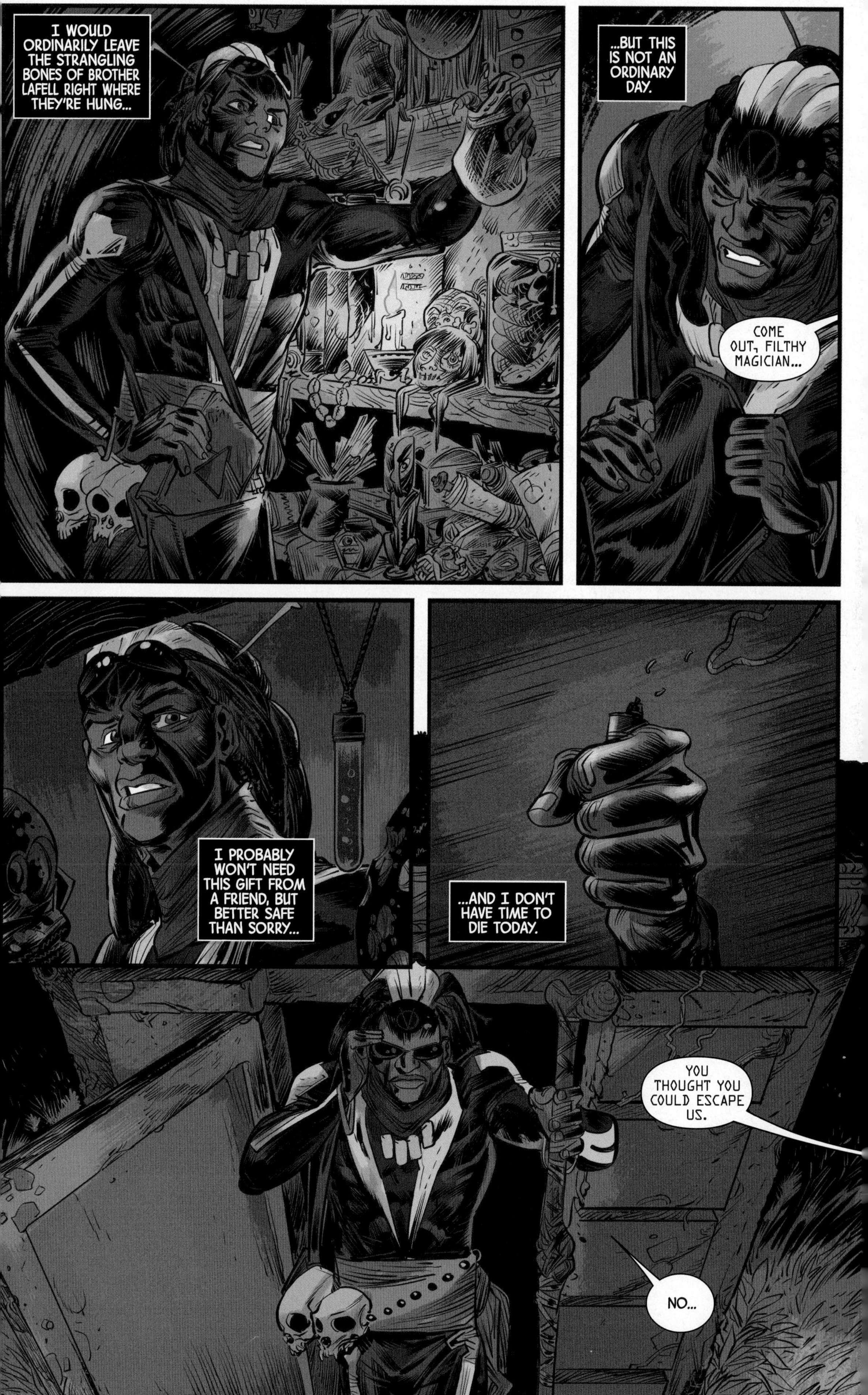
I WOULD ORDINARILY LEAVE THE STRANGLING BONES OF BROTHER LAFELL RIGHT WHERE THEY'RE HUNG...
...BUT THIS IS NOT AN ORDINARY DAY.
COME OUT, FILTHY MAGICIAN...
I PROBABLY WON'T NEED THIS GIFT FROM A FRIEND, BUT BETTER SAFE THAN SORRY...
...AND I DON'T HAVE TIME TO DIE TODAY.
YOU THOUGHT YOU COULD ESCAPE US.
NO...

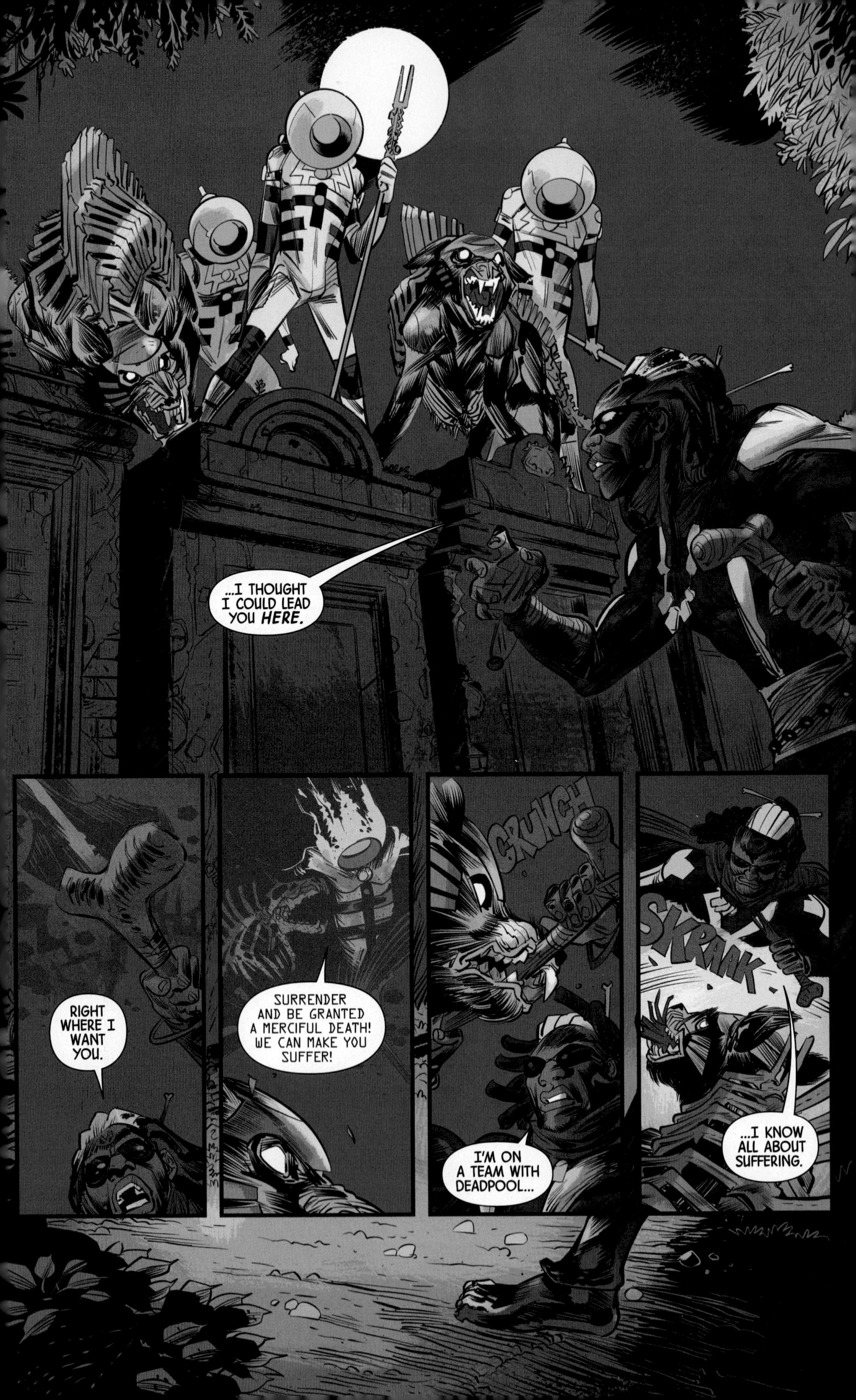

...I THOUGHT I COULD LEAD YOU *HERE.*
RIGHT WHERE I WANT YOU.
SURRENDER AND BE GRANTED A MERCIFUL DEATH! WE CAN MAKE YOU SUFFER!
CRUNCH
I'M ON A TEAM WITH DEADPOOL...
SKRAAK
...I KNOW ALL ABOUT SUFFERING.

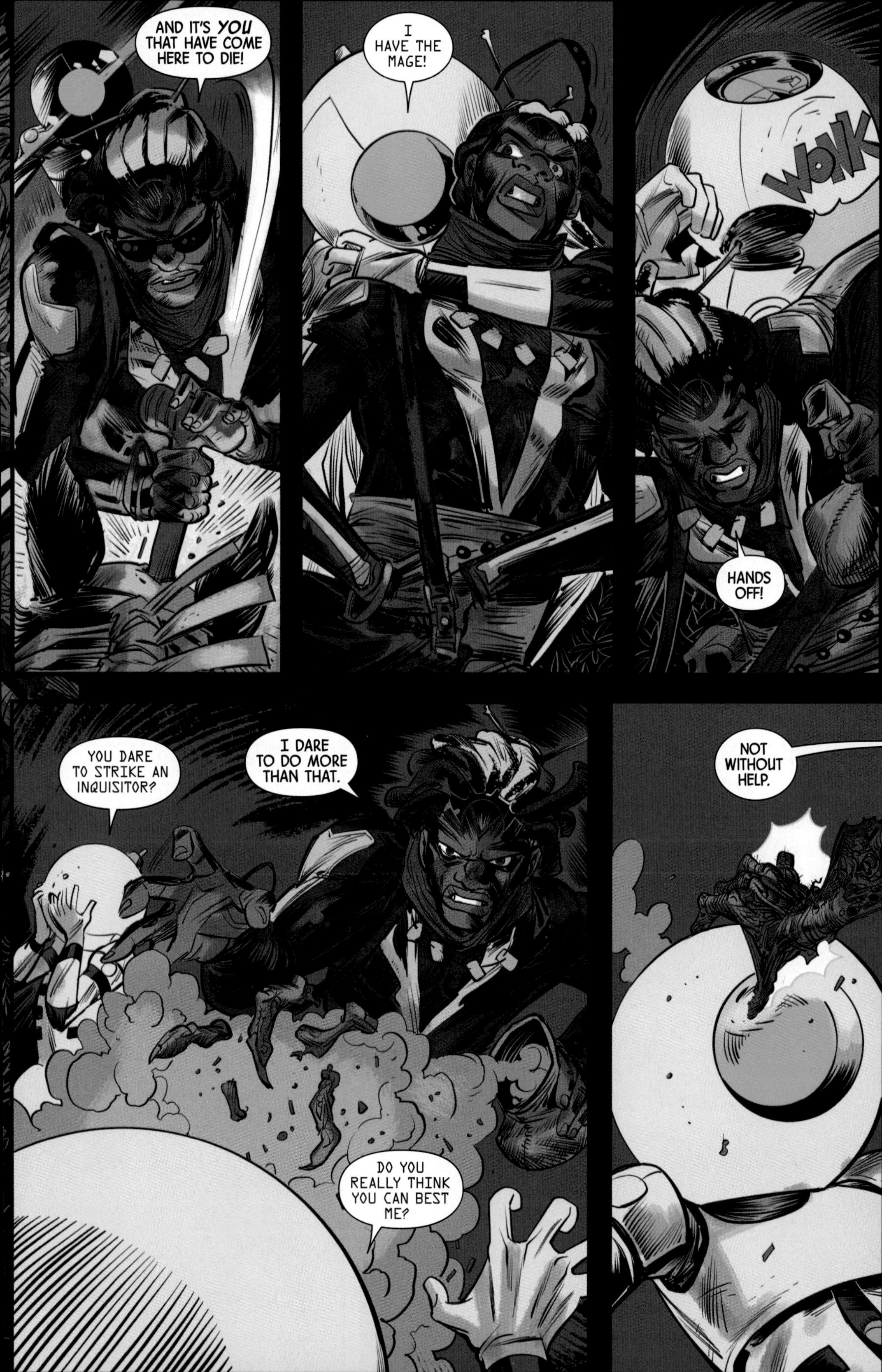
AND IT'S *YOU* THAT HAVE COME HERE TO DIE!
I HAVE THE MAGE!
WONK
HANDS OFF!
YOU DARE TO STRIKE AN INQUISITOR?
I DARE TO DO MORE THAN THAT.
DO YOU REALLY THINK YOU CAN BEST ME?
NOT WITHOUT HELP.

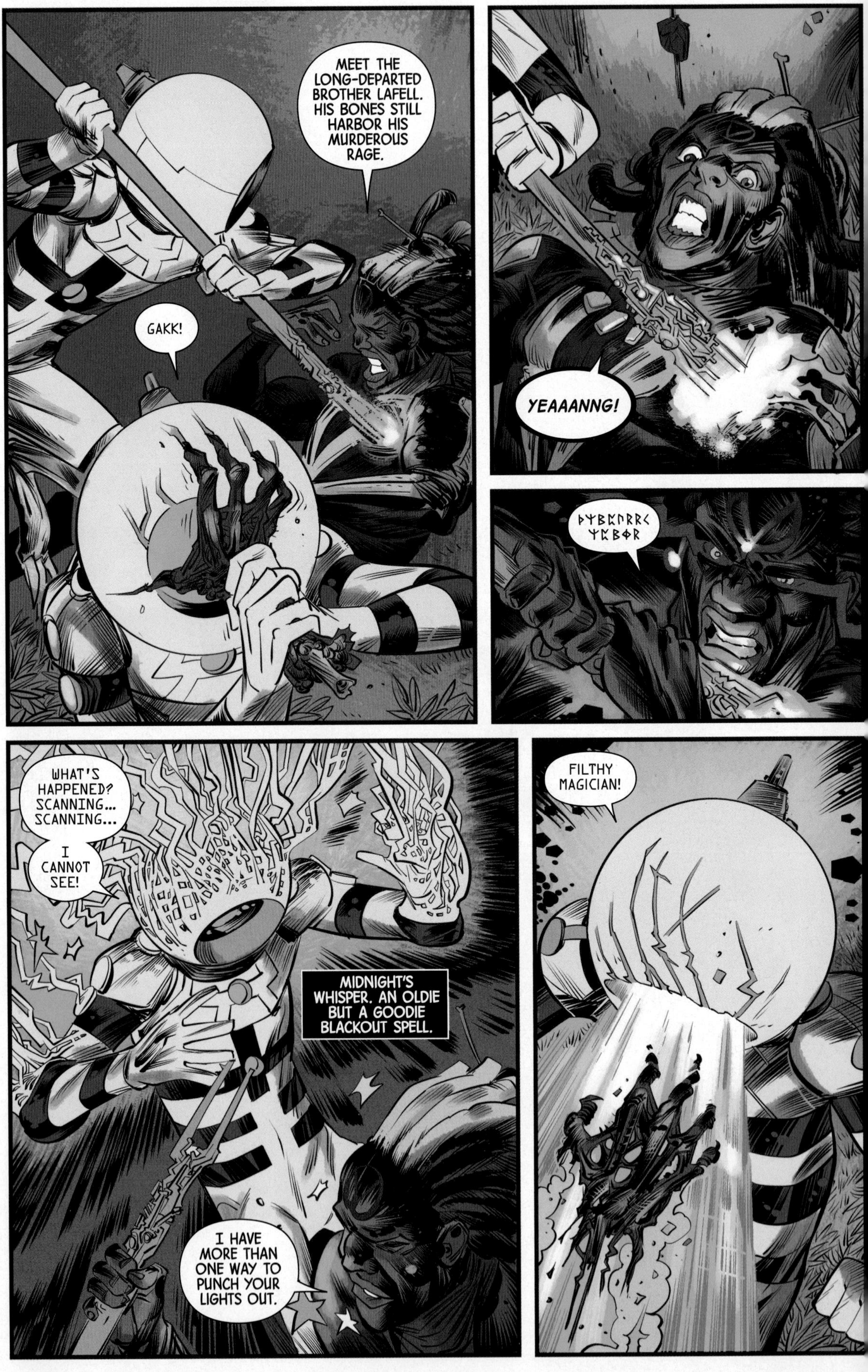
MEET THE LONG-DEPARTED BROTHER LAFELL. HIS BONES STILL HARBOR HIS MURDEROUS RAGE.
GAKK!
YEAAAANG!
WHAT'S HAPPENED? SCANNING... SCANNING...
I CANNOT SEE!
MIDNIGHT'S WHISPER. AN OLDIE BUT A GOODIE BLACKOUT SPELL.
I HAVE MORE THAN ONE WAY TO PUNCH YOUR LIGHTS OUT.
FILTHY MAGICIAN!

SORRY TO BEAT THE HELL OUT OF YOU AND RUN, BUT--

YOU'LL GO NOWHERE!

DAMMIT! DON'T KNOW HOW YOU STOPPED MY TELEPORTATION SPELL BUT YOU CAN'T STOP--

ᚴᚤᛮᛘᛉᚱᛒ ᛒᚤᚴᚴᚠᛢᛌ ᚴᚱᛌᚤᛢᚠᚠᚱ

THE EMPIRIKUL WILL NOT PREVAIL, WE'LL--

PUFF

OH, NO!

HOW COULD MY MAGIC FAIL?! THAT MEANS--

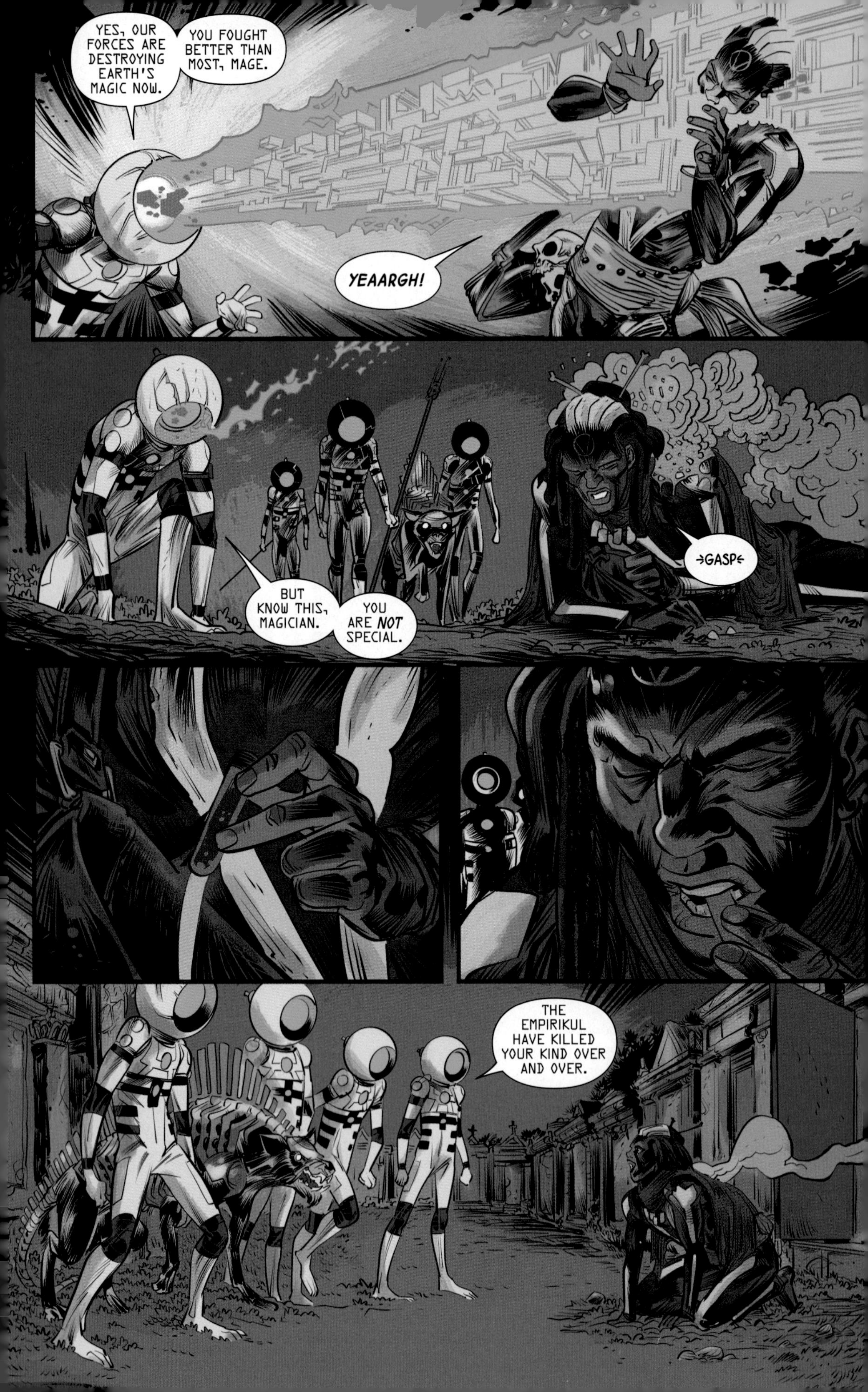
YES, OUR FORCES ARE DESTROYING EARTH'S MAGIC NOW.
YOU FOUGHT BETTER THAN MOST, MAGE.
YEAARGH!
BUT KNOW THIS, MAGICIAN.
YOU ARE NOT SPECIAL.
GASP
THE EMPIRIKUL HAVE KILLED YOUR KIND OVER AND OVER.

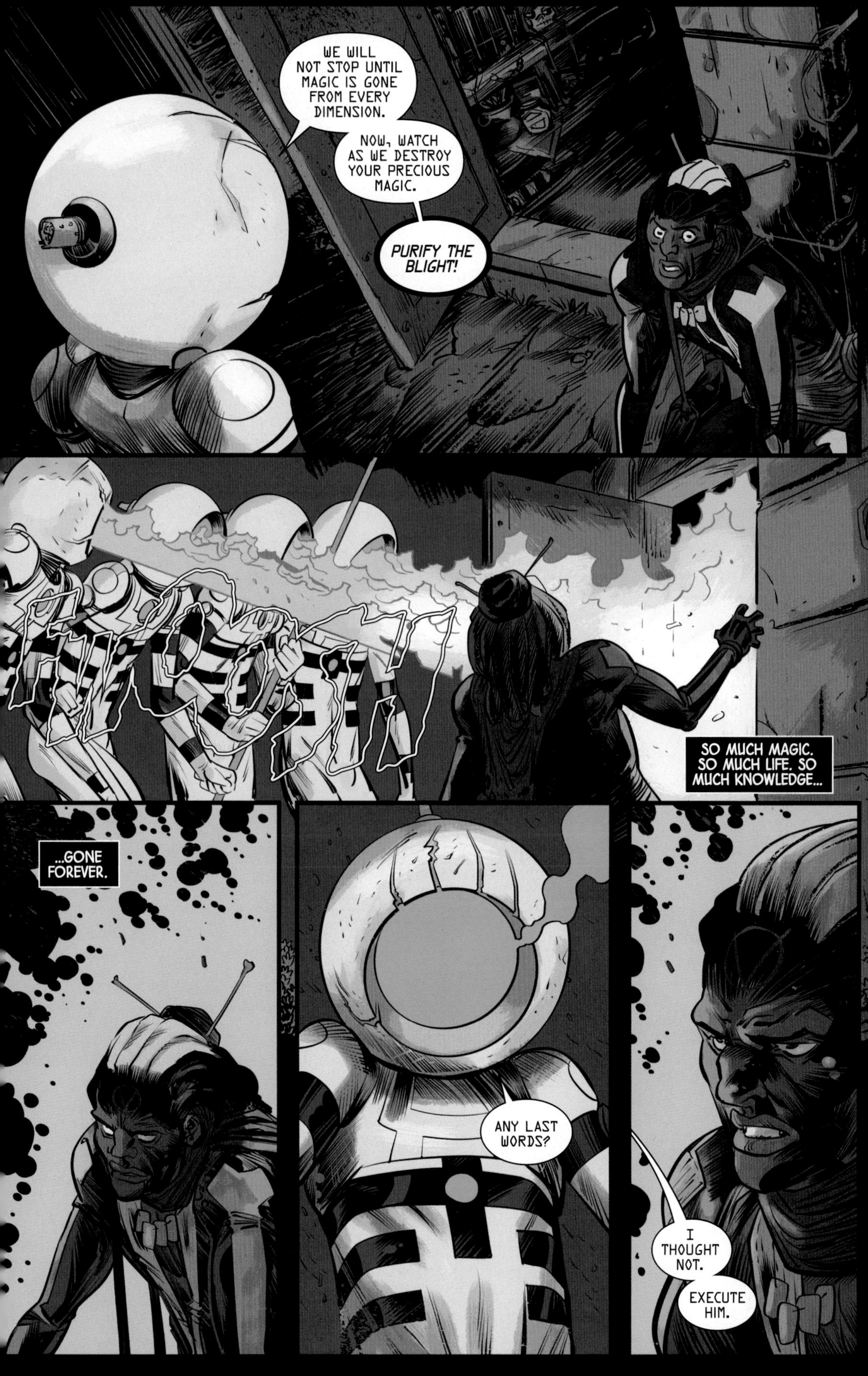
WE WILL NOT STOP UNTIL MAGIC IS GONE FROM EVERY DIMENSION.
NOW, WATCH AS WE DESTROY YOUR PRECIOUS MAGIC.
PURIFY THE BLIGHT!
FWOOSH
SO MUCH MAGIC. SO MUCH LIFE. SO MUCH KNOWLEDGE...
...GONE FOREVER.
ANY LAST WORDS?
I THOUGHT NOT.
EXECUTE HIM.

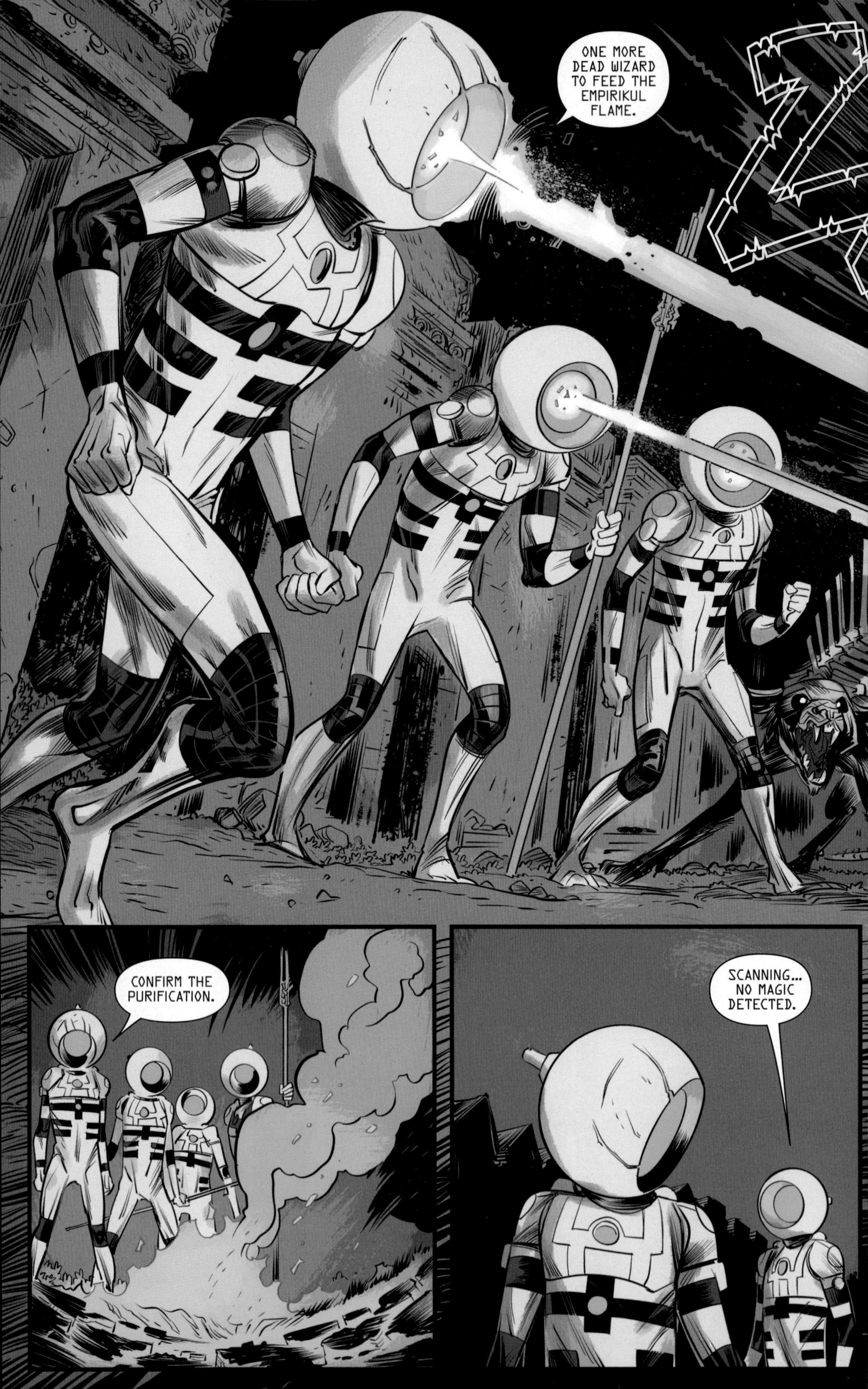
ONE MORE DEAD WIZARD TO FEED THE EMPIRIKUL FLAME.
CONFIRM THE PURIFICATION.
SCANNING... NO MAGIC DETECTED.

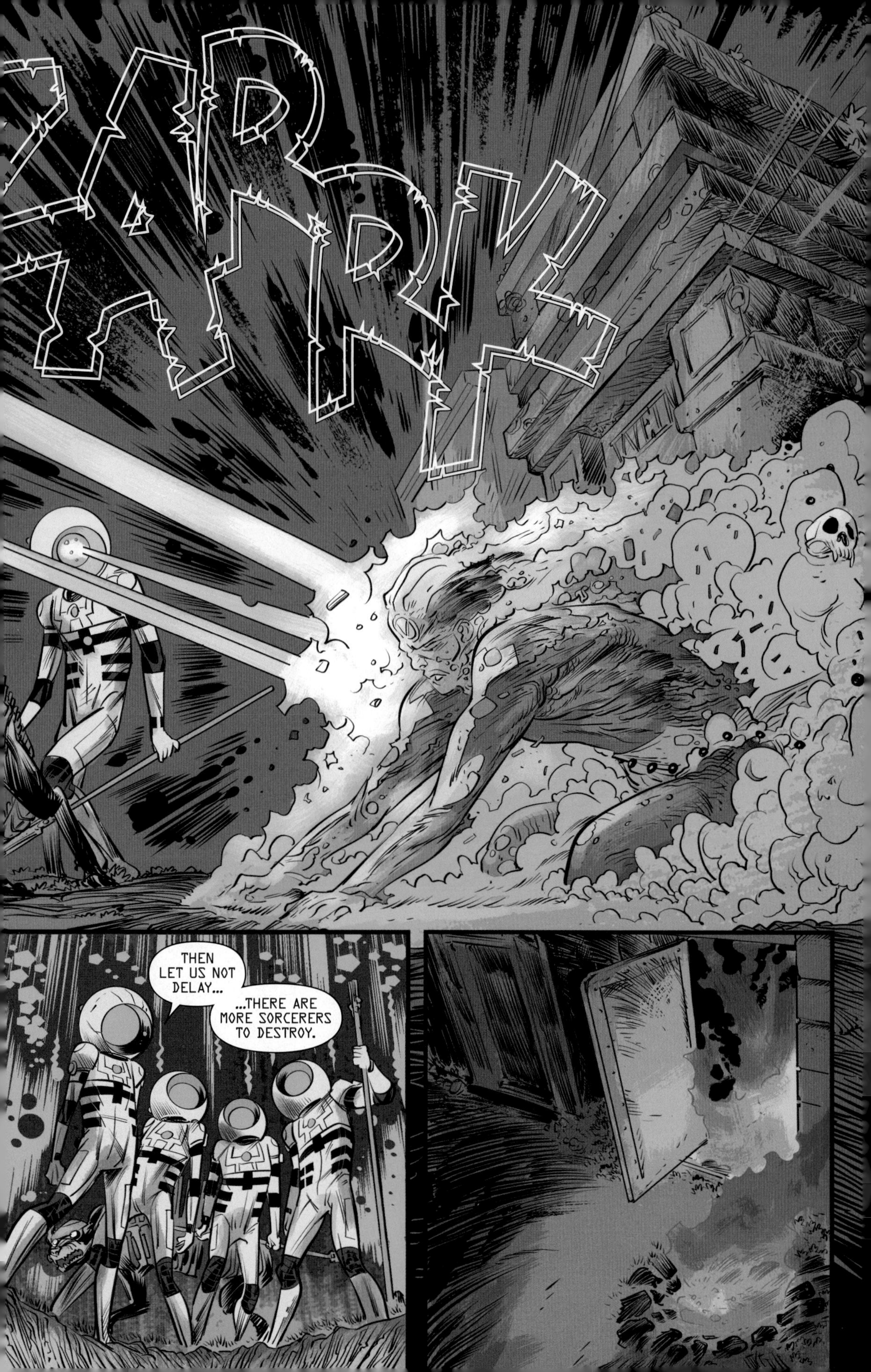
THEN LET US NOT DELAY...
...THERE ARE MORE SORCERERS TO DESTROY.

MY BEST SPELLS ARE DESTROYED. MY STAFF IS SPLINTERED.

I SHOULD BE DEAD...

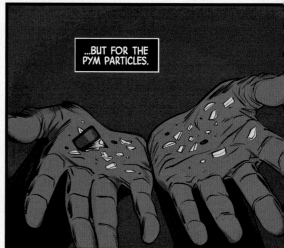

...BUT FOR THE PYM PARTICLES.

I ASKED HANK FOR A SAMPLE SO THAT I COULD STUDY THE EFFECTS OF MAGIC IN THE MICROVERSE. I NEVER GOT AROUND TO THE STUDY. PROCRASTINATION SAVED MY LIFE.

I SHOULD BE HAPPY TO BE ALIVE, BUT INSTEAD...

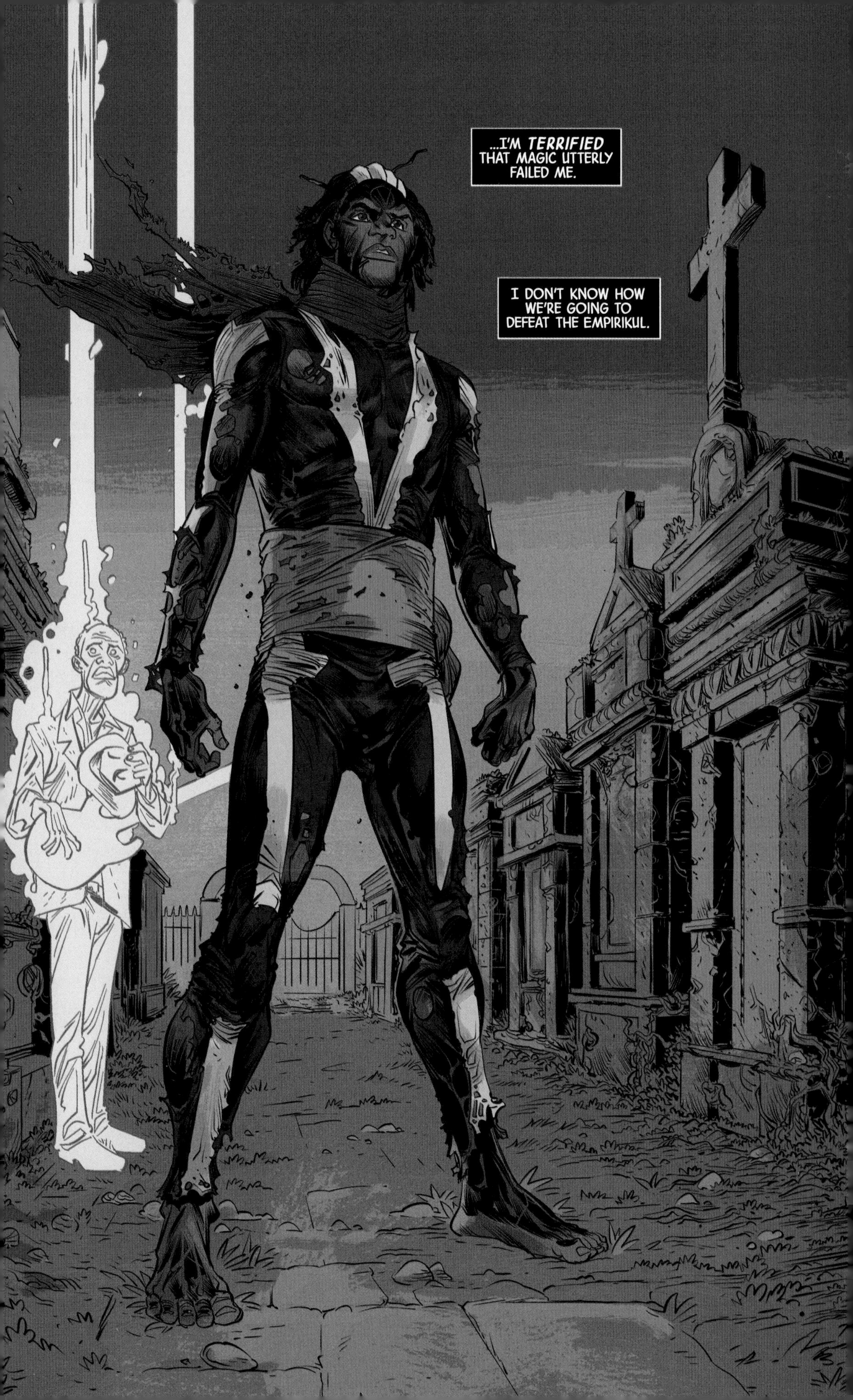
...I'M TERRIFIED THAT MAGIC UTTERLY FAILED ME.
I DON'T KNOW HOW WE'RE GOING TO DEFEAT THE EMPIRIKUL.

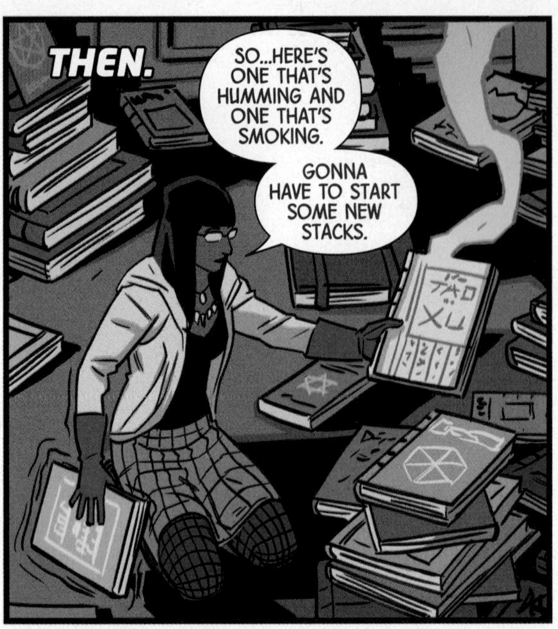
THEN.
SO...HERE'S ONE THAT'S HUMMING AND ONE THAT'S SMOKING.
GONNA HAVE TO START SOME NEW STACKS.

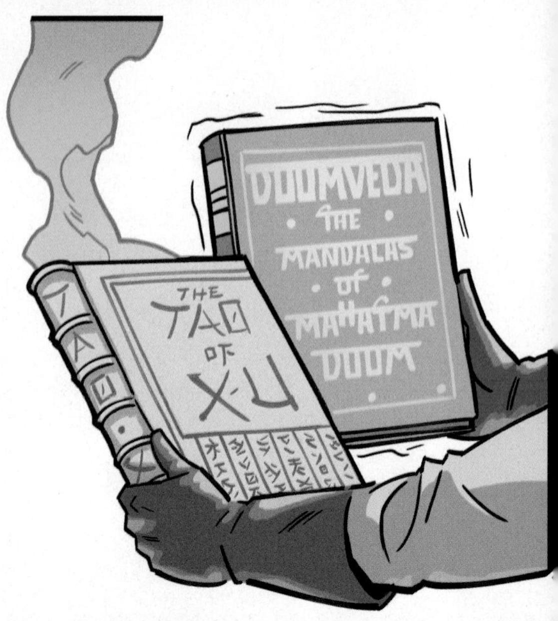
DOOMVEDA
THE MANDALAS OF MAHATMA DOOM
THE TAO OF XU

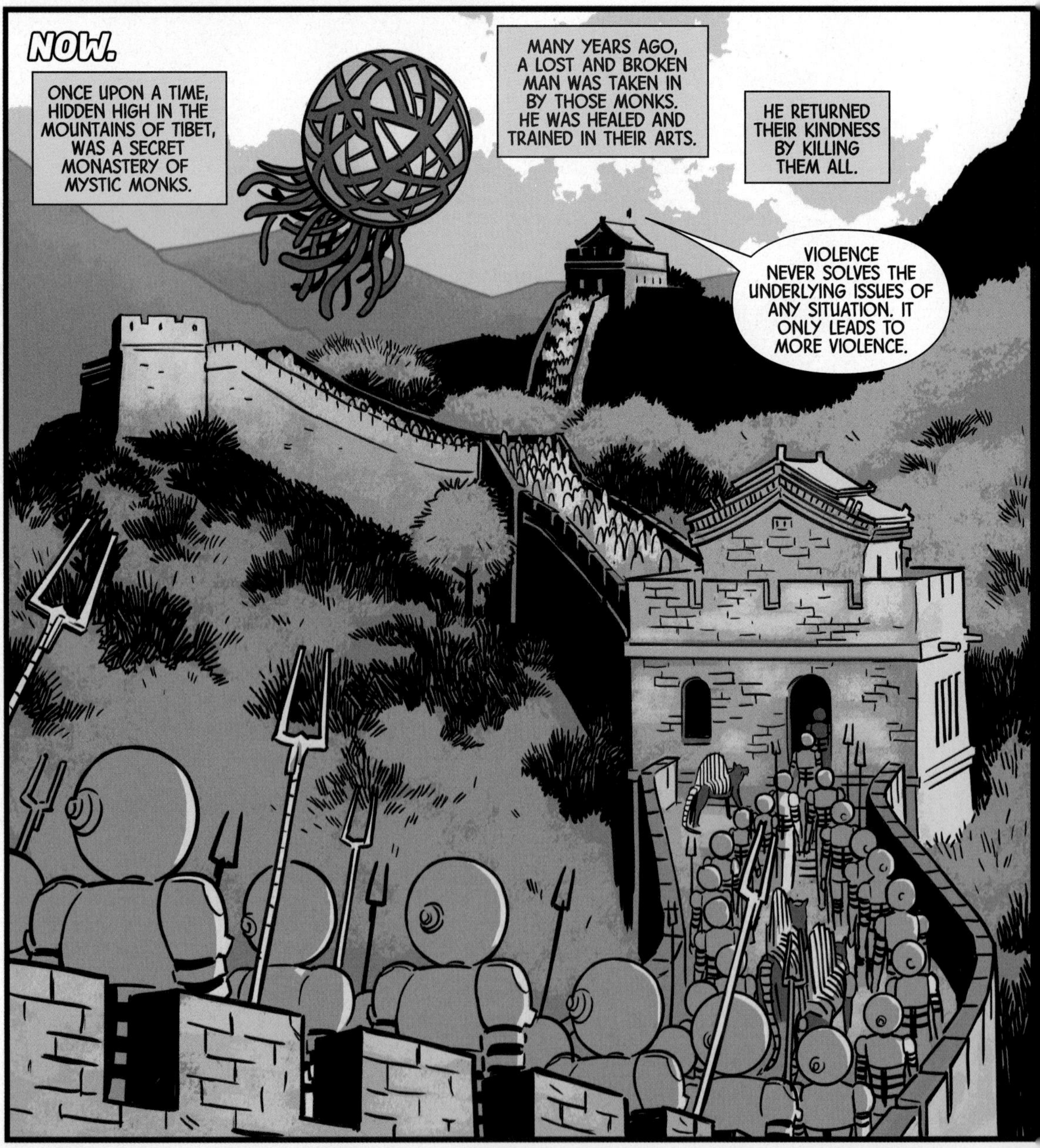
NOW.
ONCE UPON A TIME, HIDDEN HIGH IN THE MOUNTAINS OF TIBET, WAS A SECRET MONASTERY OF MYSTIC MONKS.
MANY YEARS AGO, A LOST AND BROKEN MAN WAS TAKEN IN BY THOSE MONKS. HE WAS HEALED AND TRAINED IN THEIR ARTS.
HE RETURNED THEIR KINDNESS BY KILLING THEM ALL.
VIOLENCE NEVER SOLVES THE UNDERLYING ISSUES OF ANY SITUATION. IT ONLY LEADS TO MORE VIOLENCE.

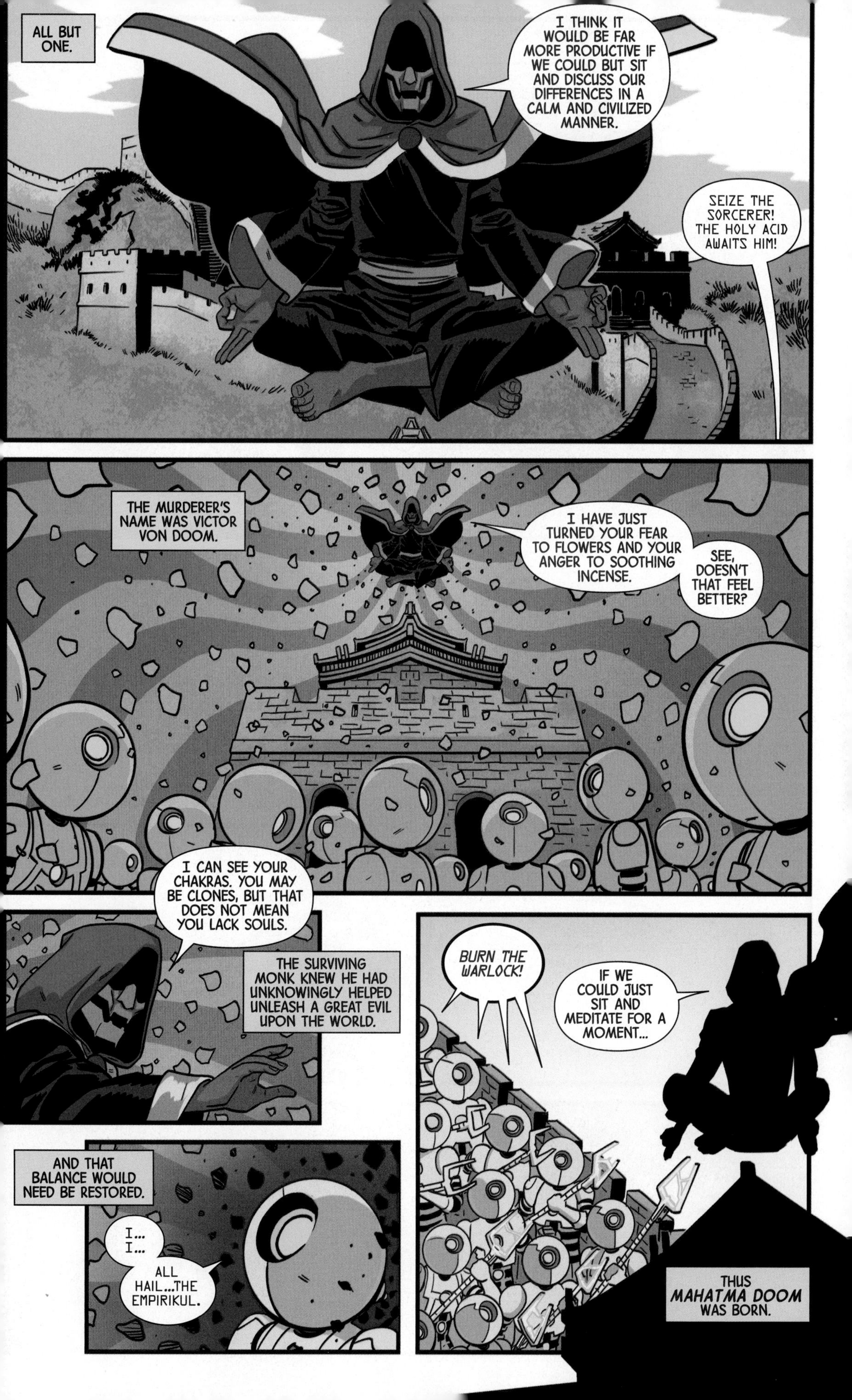
ALL BUT ONE.
I THINK IT WOULD BE FAR MORE PRODUCTIVE IF WE COULD BUT SIT AND DISCUSS OUR DIFFERENCES IN A CALM AND CIVILIZED MANNER.
SEIZE THE SORCERER! THE HOLY ACID AWAITS HIM!
THE MURDERER'S NAME WAS VICTOR VON DOOM.
I HAVE JUST TURNED YOUR FEAR TO FLOWERS AND YOUR ANGER TO SOOTHING INCENSE.
SEE, DOESN'T THAT FEEL BETTER?
I CAN SEE YOUR CHAKRAS. YOU MAY BE CLONES, BUT THAT DOES NOT MEAN YOU LACK SOULS.
THE SURVIVING MONK KNEW HE HAD UNKNOWINGLY HELPED UNLEASH A GREAT EVIL UPON THE WORLD.
AND THAT BALANCE WOULD NEED BE RESTORED.
I... I...
ALL HAIL...THE EMPIRIKUL.
BURN THE WARLOCK!
IF WE COULD JUST SIT AND MEDITATE FOR A MOMENT...
THUS MAHATMA DOOM WAS BORN.

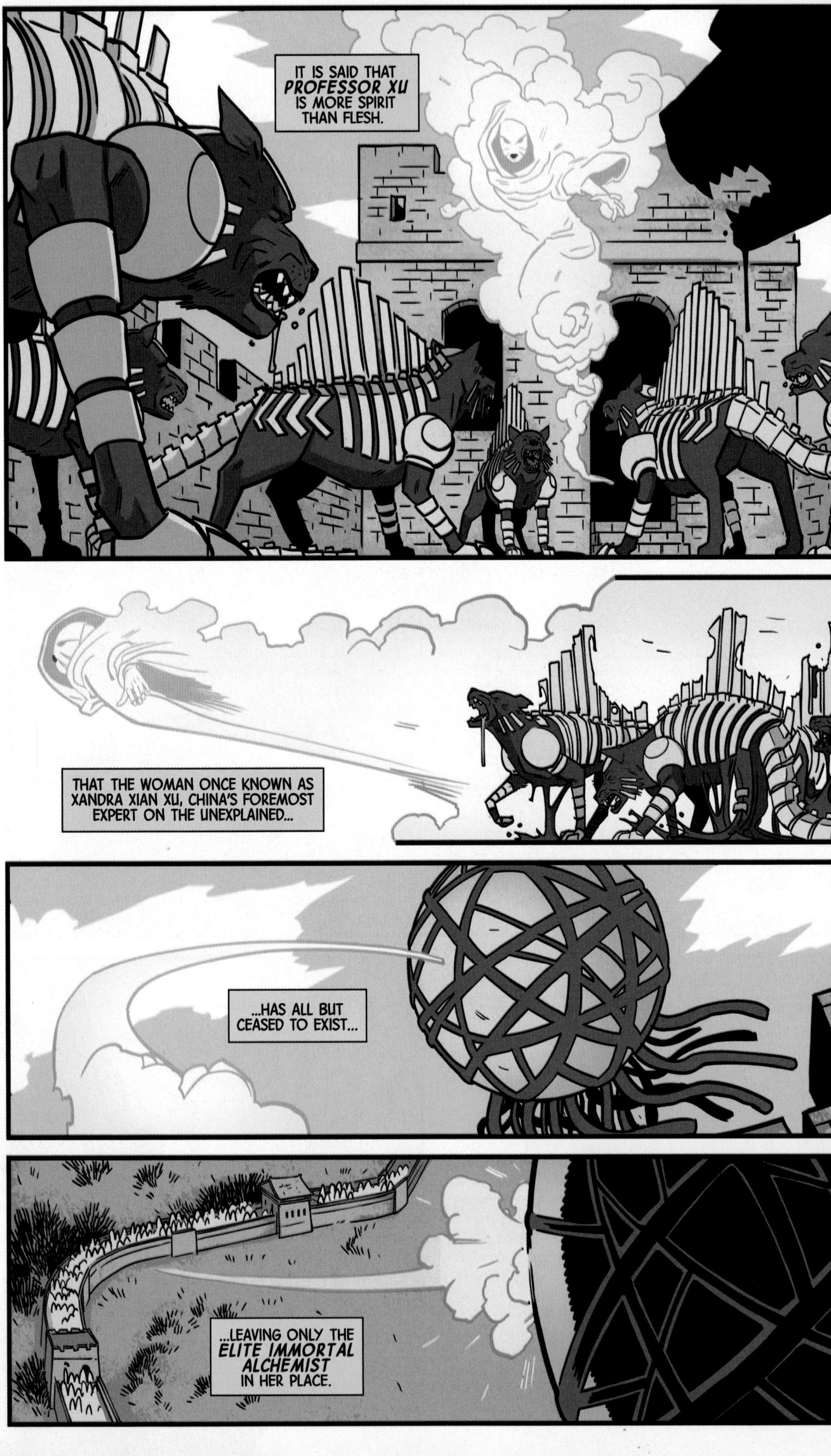
IT IS SAID THAT PROFESSOR XU IS MORE SPIRIT THAN FLESH.
THAT THE WOMAN ONCE KNOWN AS XANDRA XIAN XU, CHINA'S FOREMOST EXPERT ON THE UNEXPLAINED...
...HAS ALL BUT CEASED TO EXIST...
...LEAVING ONLY THE ELITE IMMORTAL ALCHEMIST IN HER PLACE.

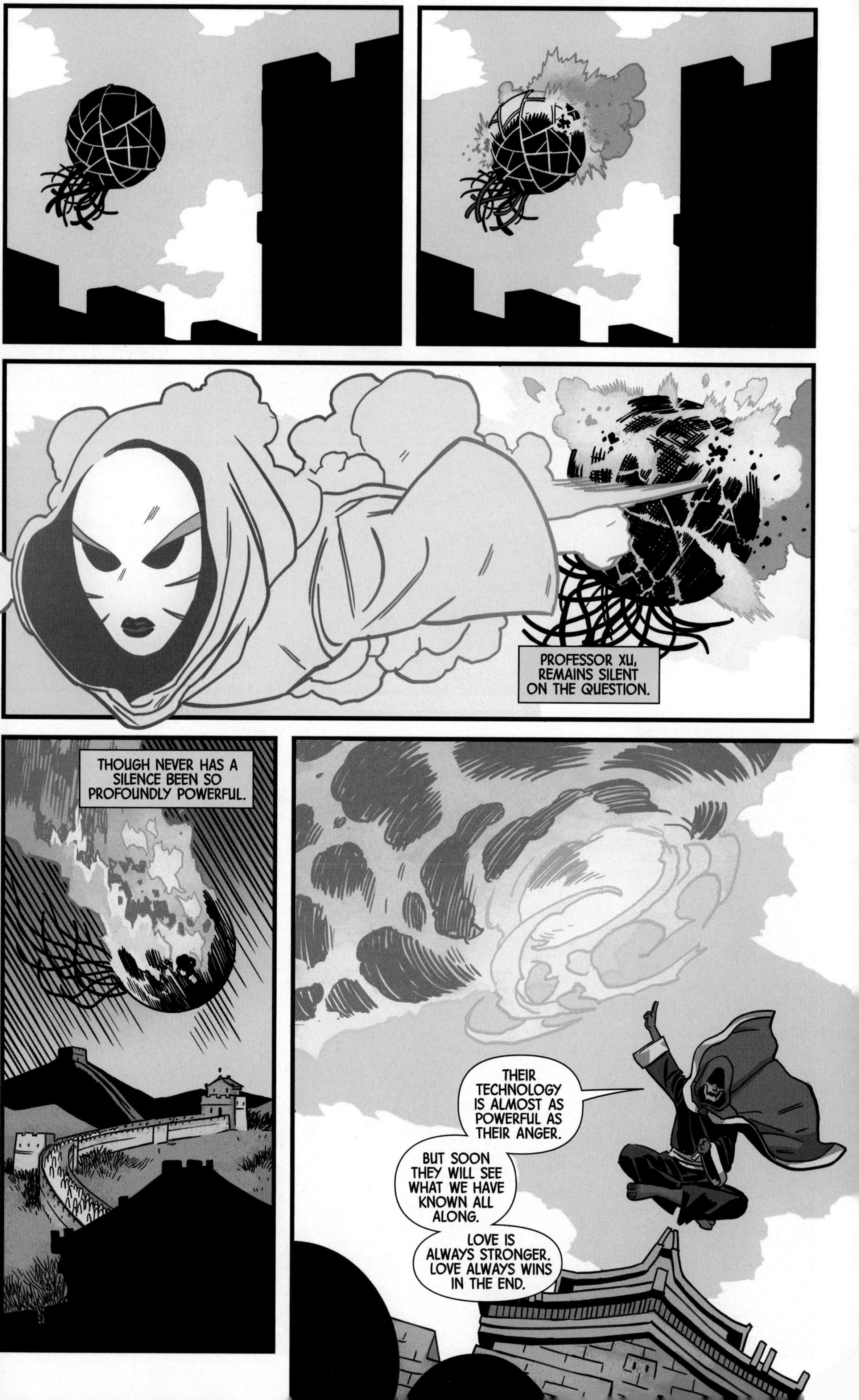
PROFESSOR XU, REMAINS SILENT ON THE QUESTION.
THOUGH NEVER HAS A SILENCE BEEN SO PROFOUNDLY POWERFUL.
THEIR TECHNOLOGY IS ALMOST AS POWERFUL AS THEIR ANGER.
BUT SOON THEY WILL SEE WHAT WE HAVE KNOWN ALL ALONG.
LOVE IS ALWAYS STRONGER. LOVE ALWAYS WINS IN THE END.

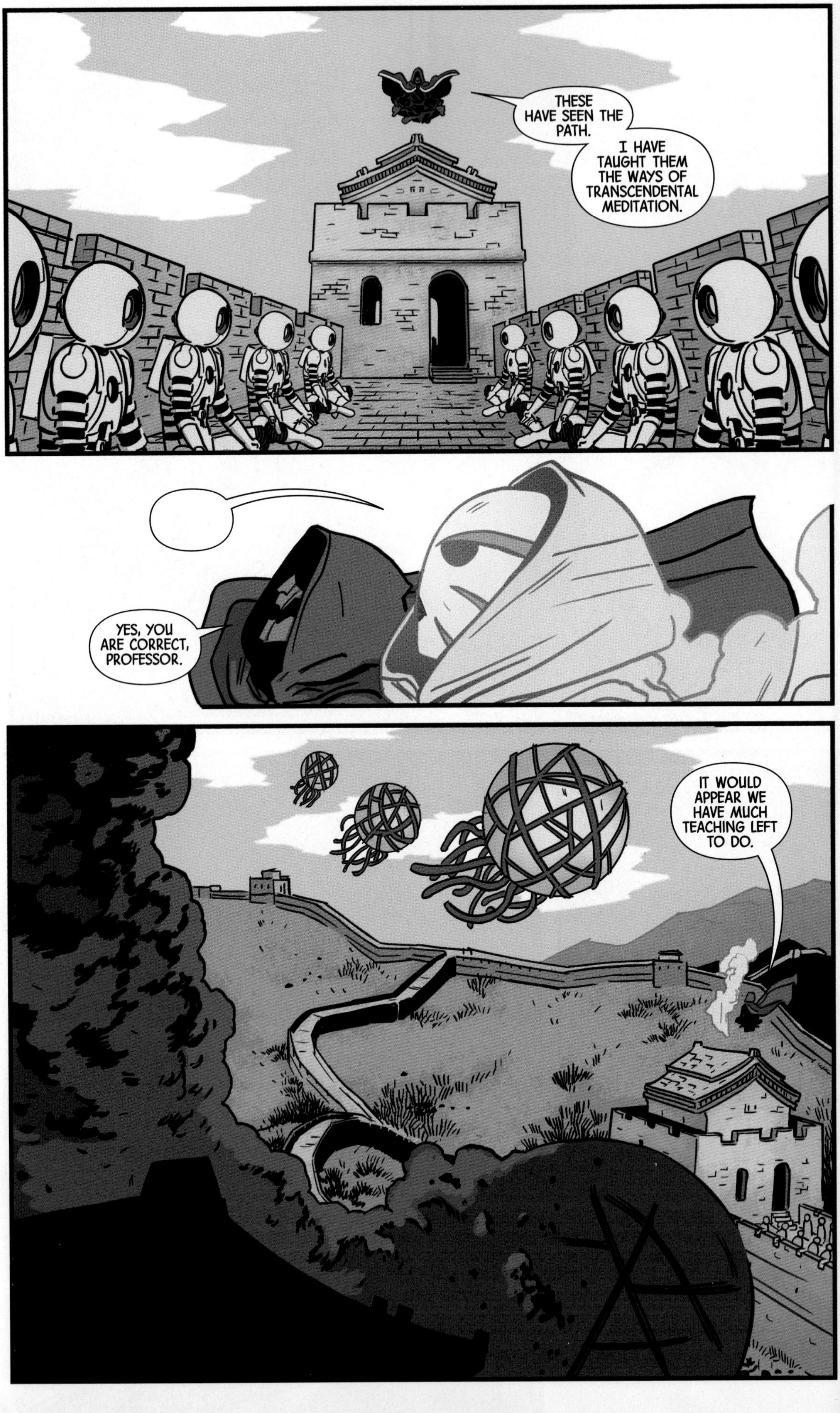
THESE HAVE SEEN THE PATH.
I HAVE TAUGHT THEM THE WAYS OF TRANSCENDENTAL MEDITATION.
YES, YOU ARE CORRECT, PROFESSOR.
IT WOULD APPEAR WE HAVE MUCH TEACHING LEFT TO DO.

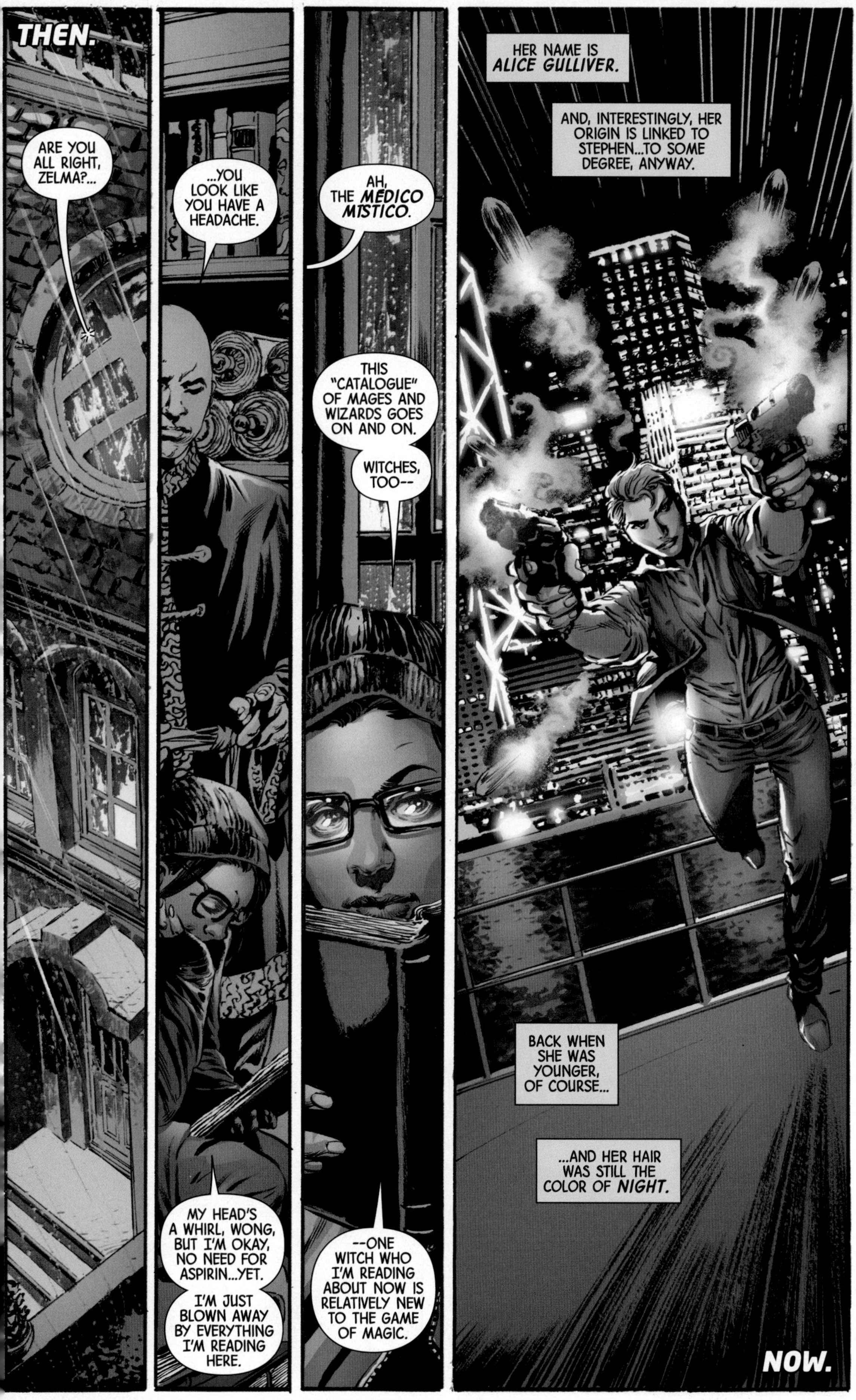
THEN.
ARE YOU ALL RIGHT, ZELMA?...
...YOU LOOK LIKE YOU HAVE A HEADACHE.
MY HEAD'S A WHIRL, WONG, BUT I'M OKAY, NO NEED FOR ASPIRIN...YET.
I'M JUST BLOWN AWAY BY EVERYTHING I'M READING HERE.
AH, THE MEDICO MISTICO.
THIS "CATALOGUE" OF MAGES AND WIZARDS GOES ON AND ON.
WITCHES, TOO--
--ONE WITCH WHO I'M READING ABOUT NOW IS RELATIVELY NEW TO THE GAME OF MAGIC.
HER NAME IS ALICE GULLIVER.
AND, INTERESTINGLY, HER ORIGIN IS LINKED TO STEPHEN...TO SOME DEGREE, ANYWAY.
BACK WHEN SHE WAS YOUNGER, OF COURSE...
...AND HER HAIR WAS STILL THE COLOR OF NIGHT.
NOW.

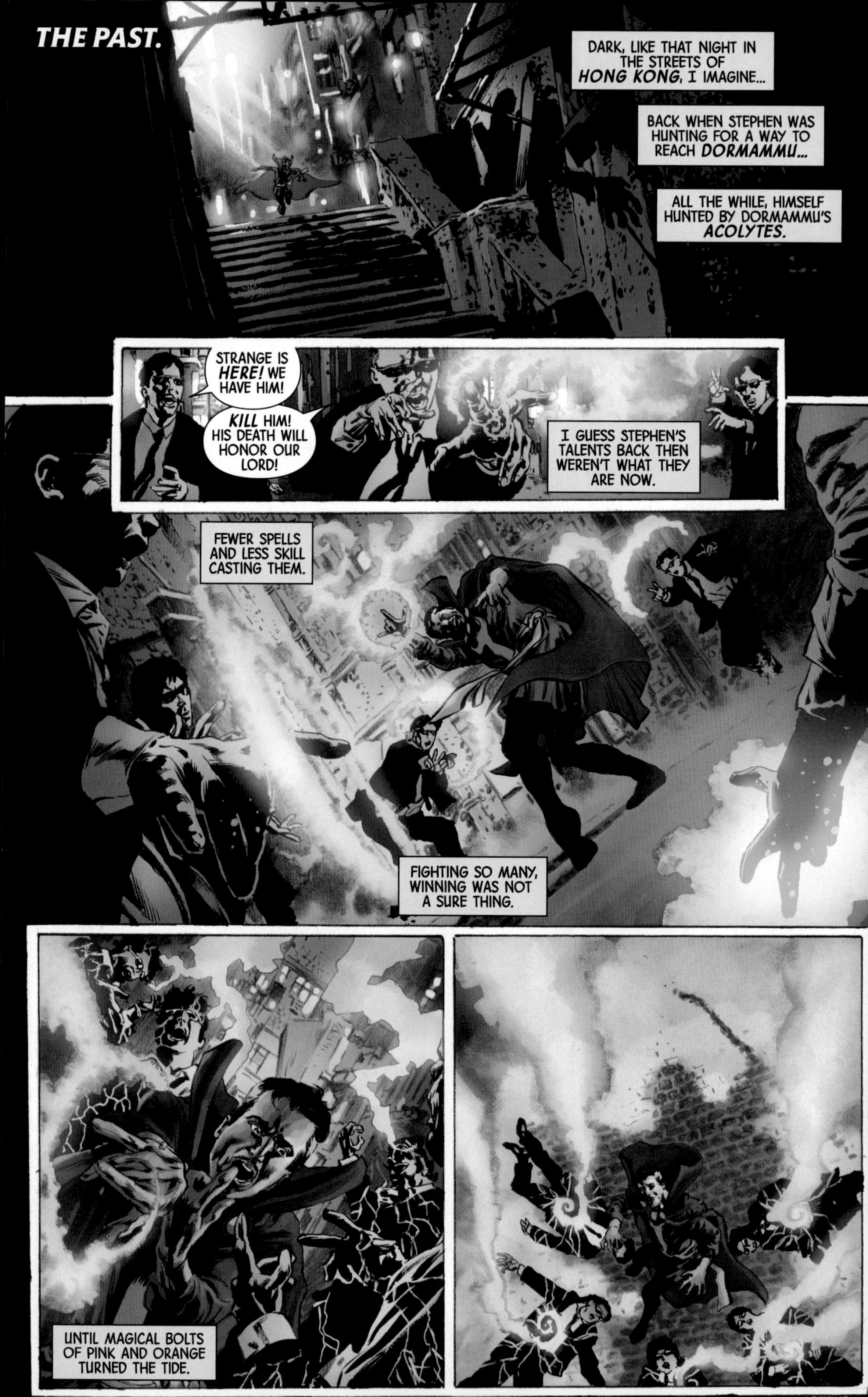
THE PAST.
DARK, LIKE THAT NIGHT IN THE STREETS OF HONG KONG, I IMAGINE...
BACK WHEN STEPHEN WAS HUNTING FOR A WAY TO REACH DORMAMMU...
ALL THE WHILE, HIMSELF HUNTED BY DORMAMMU'S ACOLYTES.
STRANGE IS HERE! WE HAVE HIM!
KILL HIM! HIS DEATH WILL HONOR OUR LORD!
I GUESS STEPHEN'S TALENTS BACK THEN WEREN'T WHAT THEY ARE NOW.
FEWER SPELLS AND LESS SKILL CASTING THEM.
FIGHTING SO MANY, WINNING WAS NOT A SURE THING.
UNTIL MAGICAL BOLTS OF PINK AND ORANGE TURNED THE TIDE.

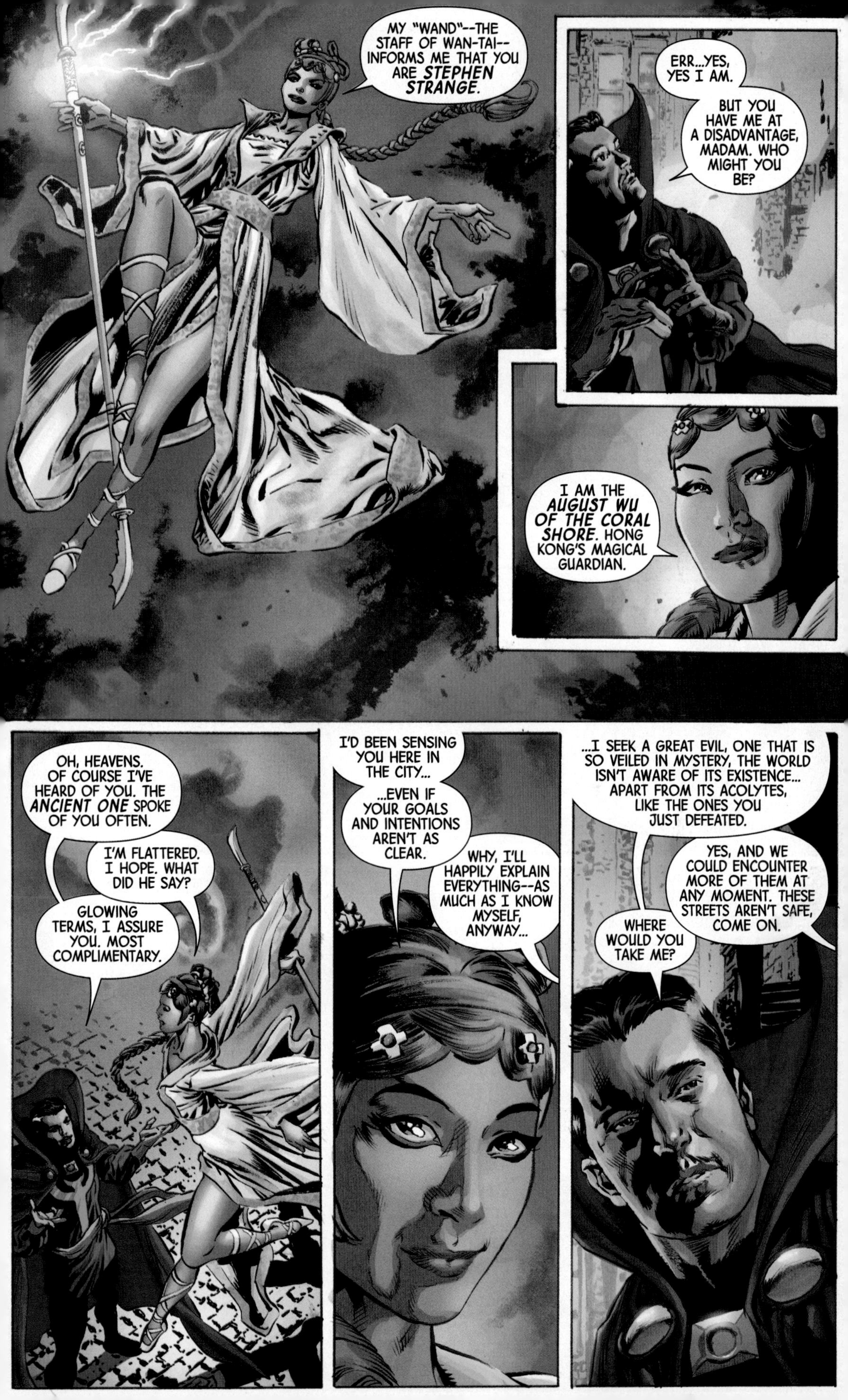

MY "WAND"--THE STAFF OF WAN-TAI--INFORMS ME THAT YOU ARE STEPHEN STRANGE.
ERR...YES, YES I AM.
BUT YOU HAVE ME AT A DISADVANTAGE, MADAM. WHO MIGHT YOU BE?
I AM THE AUGUST WU OF THE CORAL SHORE. HONG KONG'S MAGICAL GUARDIAN.
OH, HEAVENS. OF COURSE I'VE HEARD OF YOU. THE ANCIENT ONE SPOKE OF YOU OFTEN.
I'M FLATTERED. I HOPE. WHAT DID HE SAY?
GLOWING TERMS, I ASSURE YOU. MOST COMPLIMENTARY.
I'D BEEN SENSING YOU HERE IN THE CITY...
...EVEN IF YOUR GOALS AND INTENTIONS AREN'T AS CLEAR.
WHY, I'LL HAPPILY EXPLAIN EVERYTHING--AS MUCH AS I KNOW MYSELF, ANYWAY...
...I SEEK A GREAT EVIL, ONE THAT IS SO VEILED IN MYSTERY, THE WORLD ISN'T AWARE OF ITS EXISTENCE... APART FROM ITS ACOLYTES, LIKE THE ONES YOU JUST DEFEATED.
WHERE WOULD YOU TAKE ME?
YES, AND WE COULD ENCOUNTER MORE OF THEM AT ANY MOMENT. THESE STREETS AREN'T SAFE, COME ON.

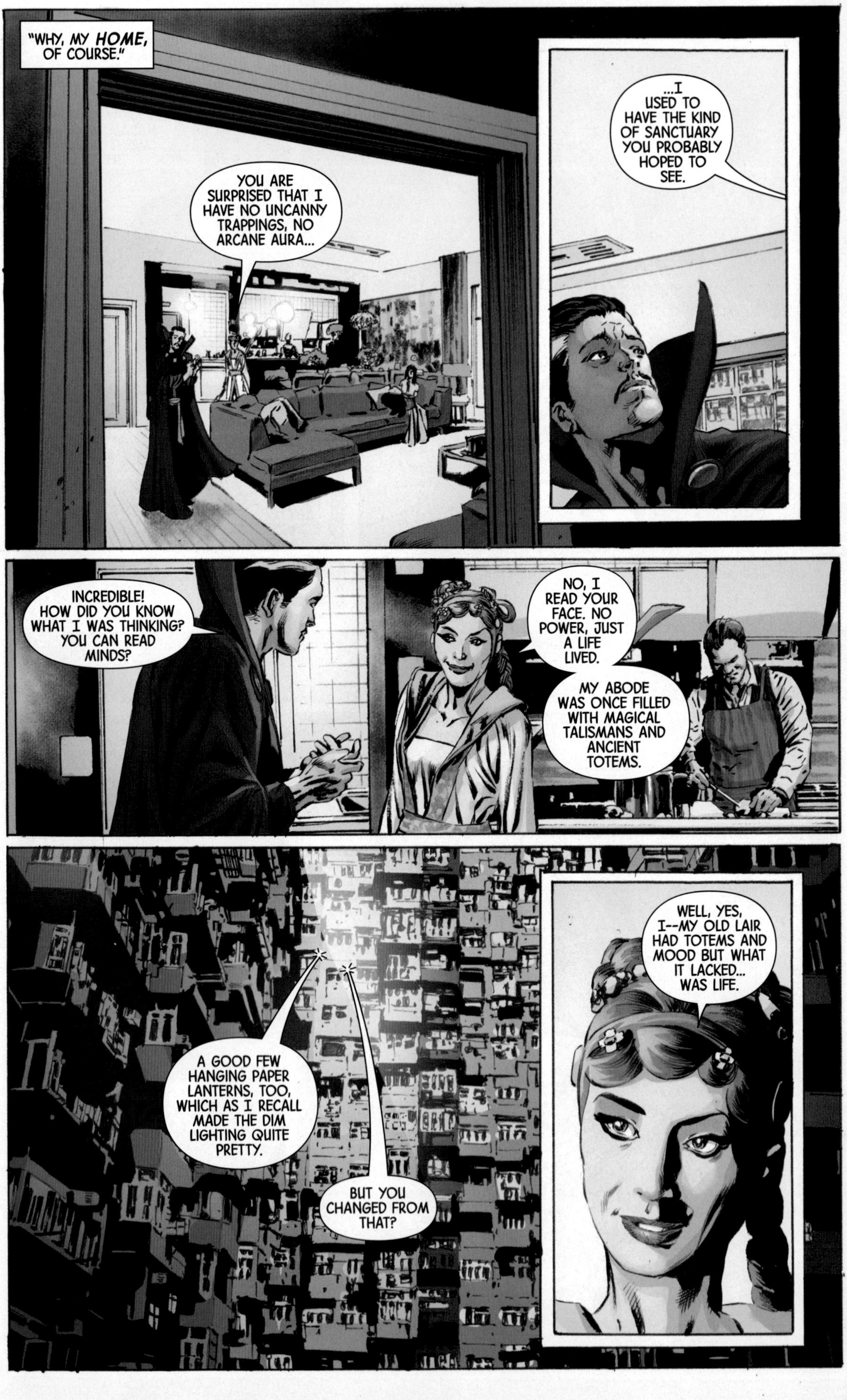
"WHY, MY HOME, OF COURSE."
YOU ARE SURPRISED THAT I HAVE NO UNCANNY TRAPPINGS, NO ARCANE AURA...
...I USED TO HAVE THE KIND OF SANCTUARY YOU PROBABLY HOPED TO SEE.
INCREDIBLE! HOW DID YOU KNOW WHAT I WAS THINKING? YOU CAN READ MINDS?
NO, I READ YOUR FACE. NO POWER, JUST A LIFE LIVED.
MY ABODE WAS ONCE FILLED WITH MAGICAL TALISMANS AND ANCIENT TOTEMS.
A GOOD FEW HANGING PAPER LANTERNS, TOO, WHICH AS I RECALL MADE THE DIM LIGHTING QUITE PRETTY.
BUT YOU CHANGED FROM THAT?
WELL, YES, I--MY OLD LAIR HAD TOTEMS AND MOOD BUT WHAT IT LACKED... WAS LIFE.

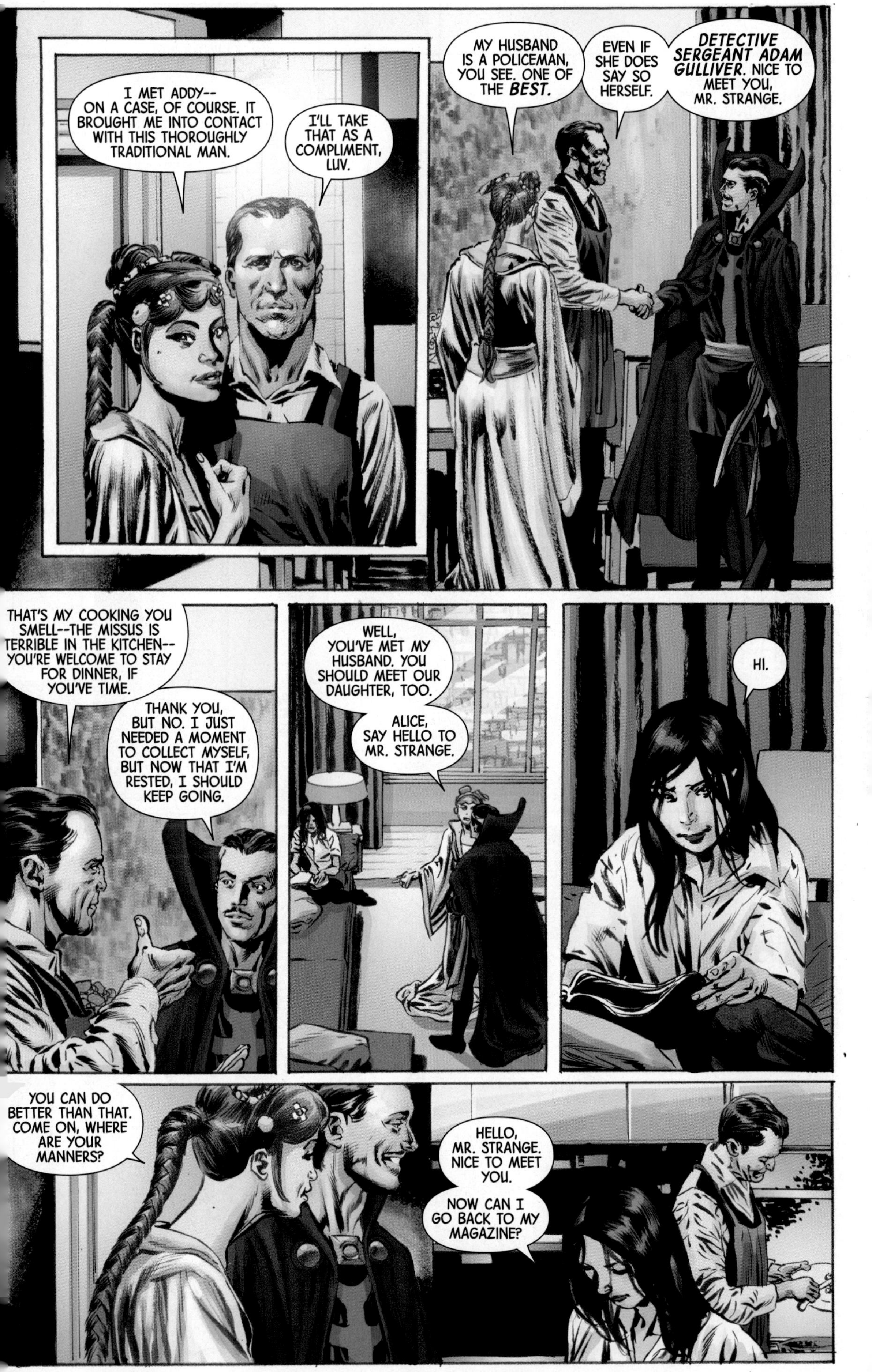
I MET ADDY-- ON A CASE, OF COURSE. IT BROUGHT ME INTO CONTACT WITH THIS THOROUGHLY TRADITIONAL MAN.
I'LL TAKE THAT AS A COMPLIMENT, LUV.
MY HUSBAND IS A POLICEMAN, YOU SEE. ONE OF THE BEST.
EVEN IF SHE DOES SAY SO HERSELF.
DETECTIVE SERGEANT ADAM GULLIVER. NICE TO MEET YOU, MR. STRANGE.
THAT'S MY COOKING YOU SMELL--THE MISSUS IS TERRIBLE IN THE KITCHEN--YOU'RE WELCOME TO STAY FOR DINNER, IF YOU'VE TIME.
THANK YOU, BUT NO. I JUST NEEDED A MOMENT TO COLLECT MYSELF, BUT NOW THAT I'M RESTED, I SHOULD KEEP GOING.
WELL, YOU'VE MET MY HUSBAND. YOU SHOULD MEET OUR DAUGHTER, TOO.
ALICE, SAY HELLO TO MR. STRANGE.
HI.
YOU CAN DO BETTER THAN THAT. COME ON, WHERE ARE YOUR MANNERS?
HELLO, MR. STRANGE. NICE TO MEET YOU.
NOW CAN I GO BACK TO MY MAGAZINE?

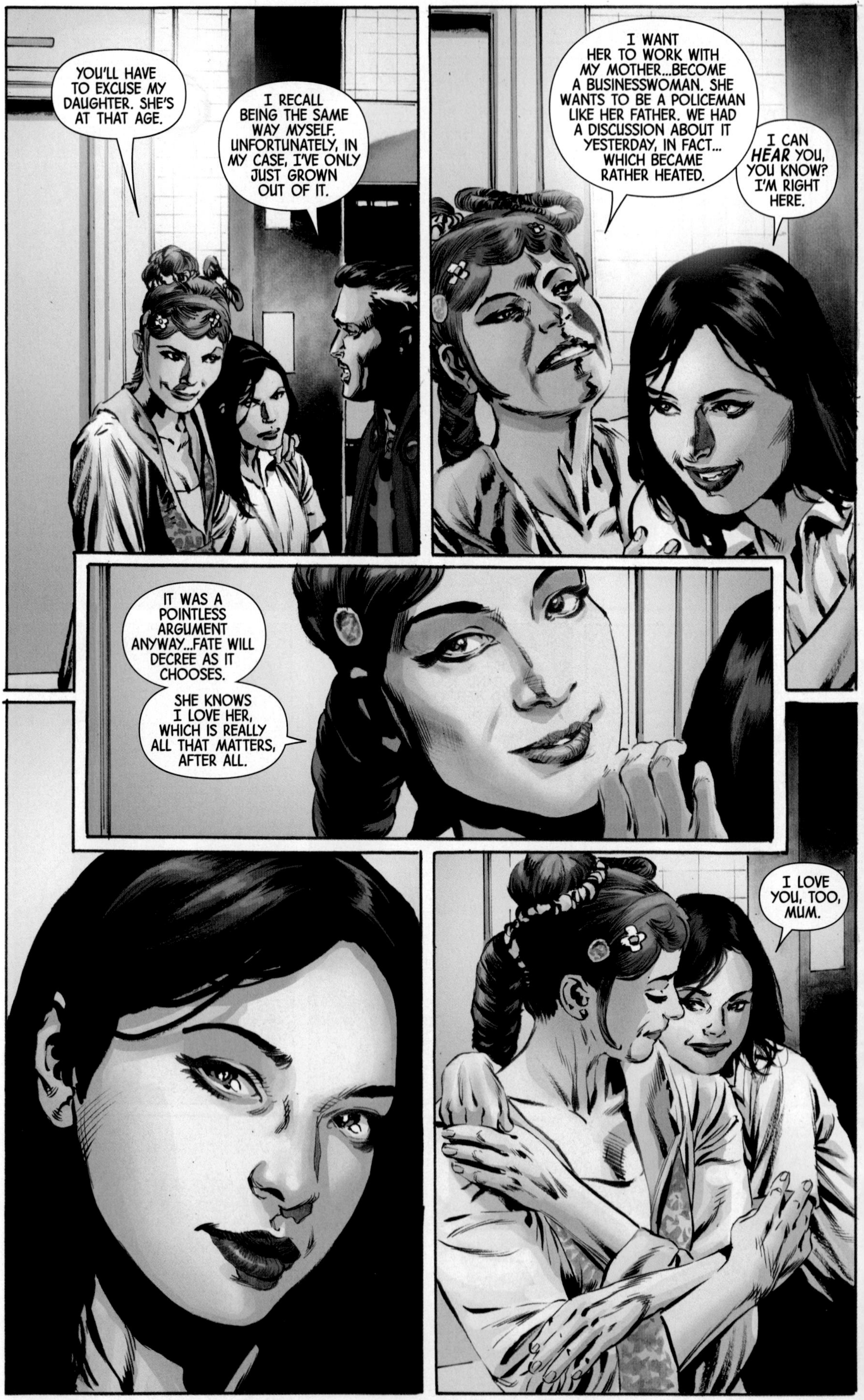
YOU'LL HAVE TO EXCUSE MY DAUGHTER. SHE'S AT THAT AGE.
I RECALL BEING THE SAME WAY MYSELF. UNFORTUNATELY, IN MY CASE, I'VE ONLY JUST GROWN OUT OF IT.
I WANT HER TO WORK WITH MY MOTHER...BECOME A BUSINESSWOMAN. SHE WANTS TO BE A POLICEMAN LIKE HER FATHER. WE HAD A DISCUSSION ABOUT IT YESTERDAY, IN FACT... WHICH BECAME RATHER HEATED.
I CAN *HEAR* YOU, YOU KNOW? I'M RIGHT HERE.
IT WAS A POINTLESS ARGUMENT ANYWAY...FATE WILL DECREE AS IT CHOOSES.
SHE KNOWS I LOVE HER, WHICH IS REALLY ALL THAT MATTERS, AFTER ALL.
I LOVE YOU, TOO, MUM.

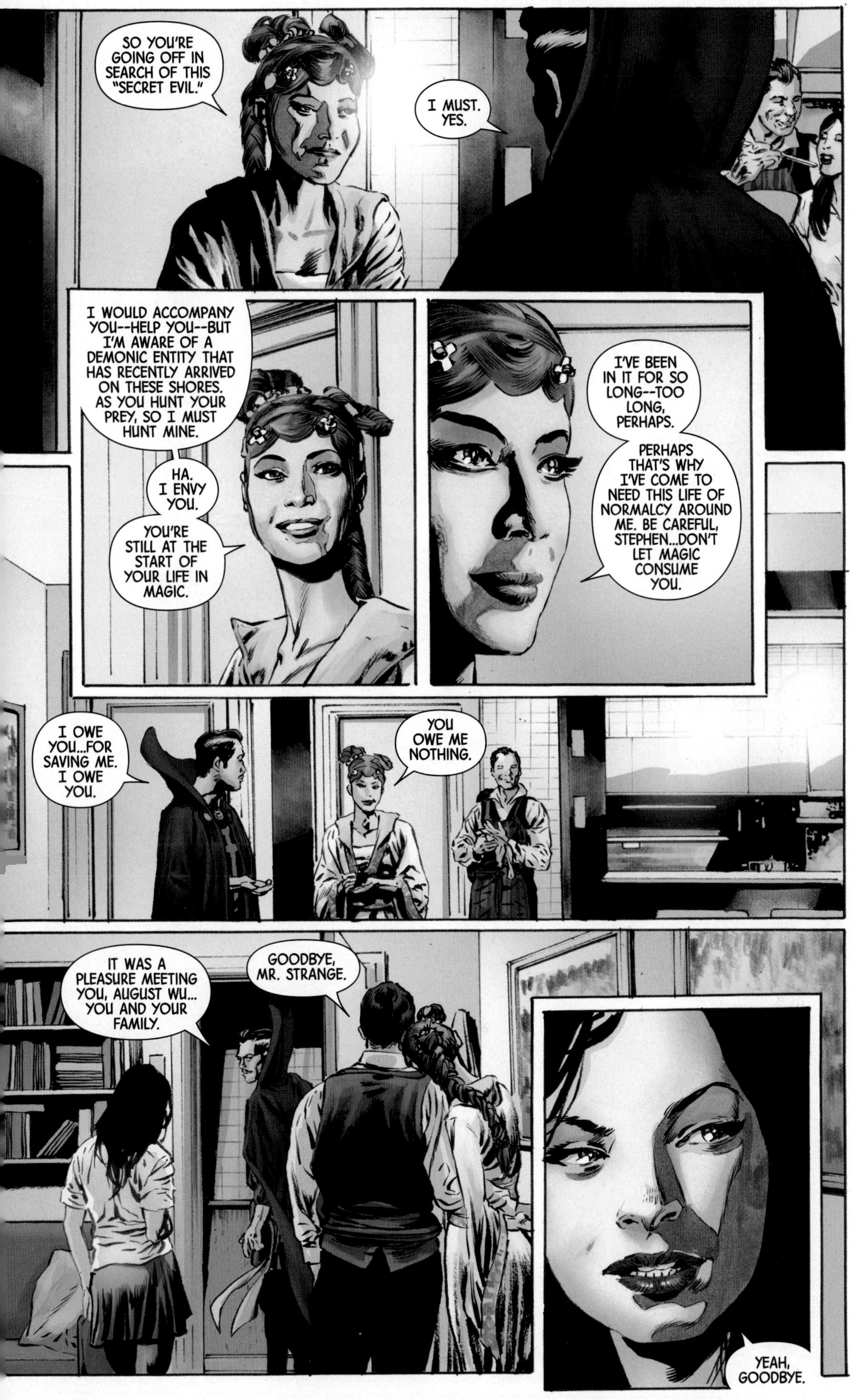
SO YOU'RE GOING OFF IN SEARCH OF THIS "SECRET EVIL."
I MUST. YES.
I WOULD ACCOMPANY YOU--HELP YOU--BUT I'M AWARE OF A DEMONIC ENTITY THAT HAS RECENTLY ARRIVED ON THESE SHORES. AS YOU HUNT YOUR PREY, SO I MUST HUNT MINE.
HA. I ENVY YOU.
YOU'RE STILL AT THE START OF YOUR LIFE IN MAGIC.
I'VE BEEN IN IT FOR SO LONG--TOO LONG, PERHAPS.
PERHAPS THAT'S WHY I'VE COME TO NEED THIS LIFE OF NORMALCY AROUND ME. BE CAREFUL, STEPHEN...DON'T LET MAGIC CONSUME YOU.
I OWE YOU...FOR SAVING ME. I OWE YOU.
YOU OWE ME NOTHING.
IT WAS A PLEASURE MEETING YOU, AUGUST WU... YOU AND YOUR FAMILY.
GOODBYE, MR. STRANGE.
YEAH, GOODBYE.

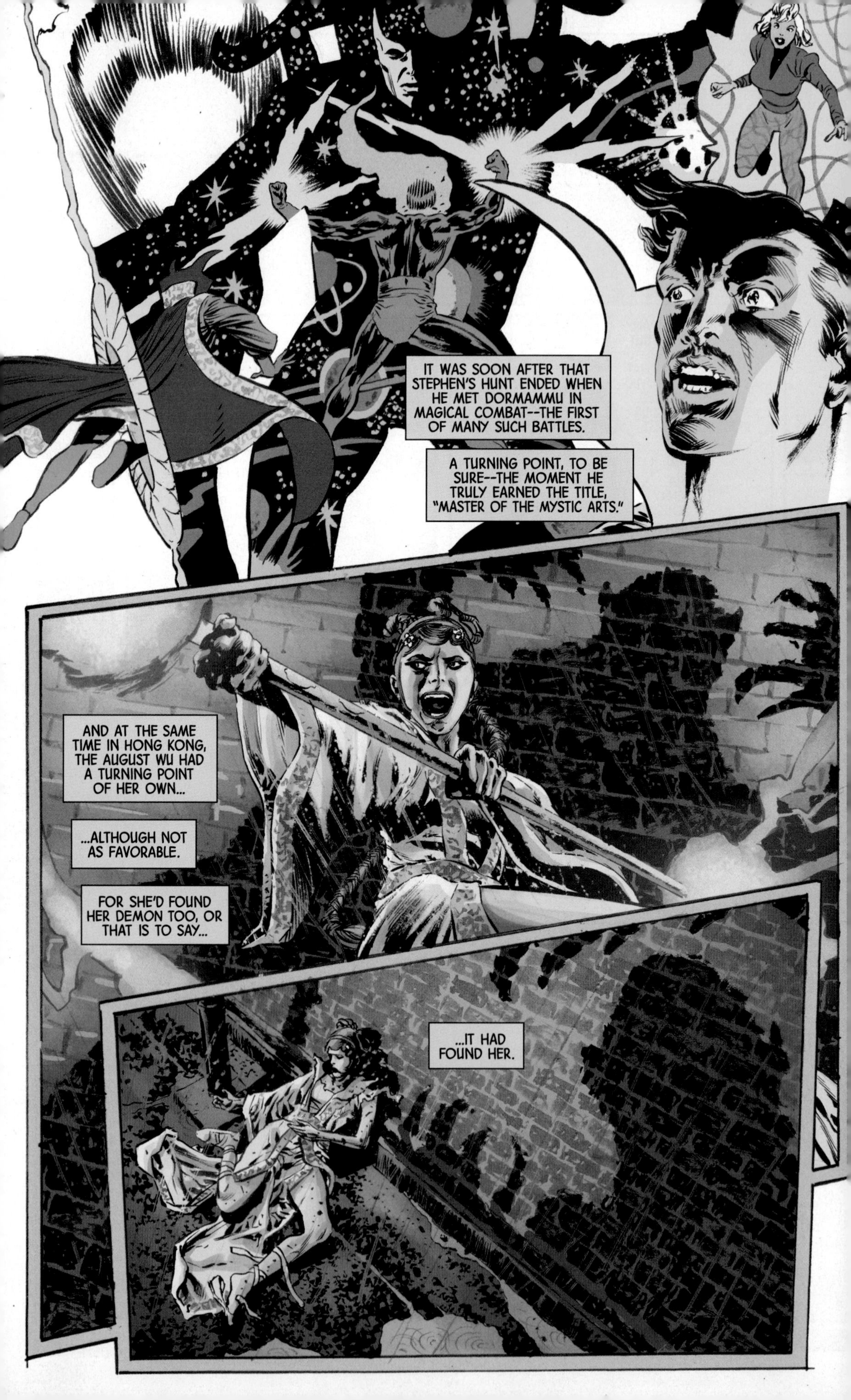
IT WAS SOON AFTER THAT STEPHEN'S HUNT ENDED WHEN HE MET DORMAMMU IN MAGICAL COMBAT--THE FIRST OF MANY SUCH BATTLES.
A TURNING POINT, TO BE SURE--THE MOMENT HE TRULY EARNED THE TITLE, "MASTER OF THE MYSTIC ARTS."
AND AT THE SAME TIME IN HONG KONG, THE AUGUST WU HAD A TURNING POINT OF HER OWN...
...ALTHOUGH NOT AS FAVORABLE.
FOR SHE'D FOUND HER DEMON TOO, OR THAT IS TO SAY...
...IT HAD FOUND HER.

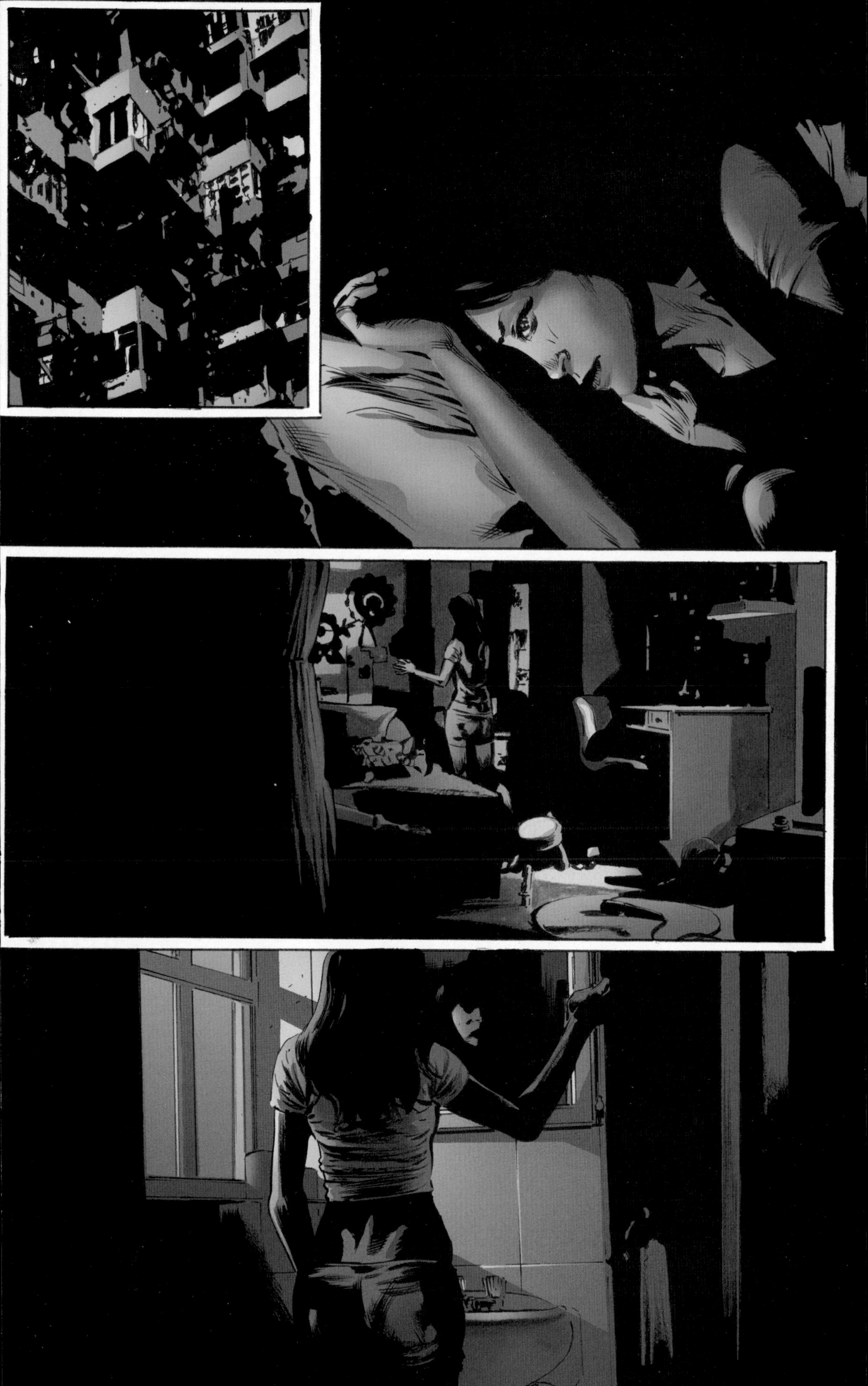

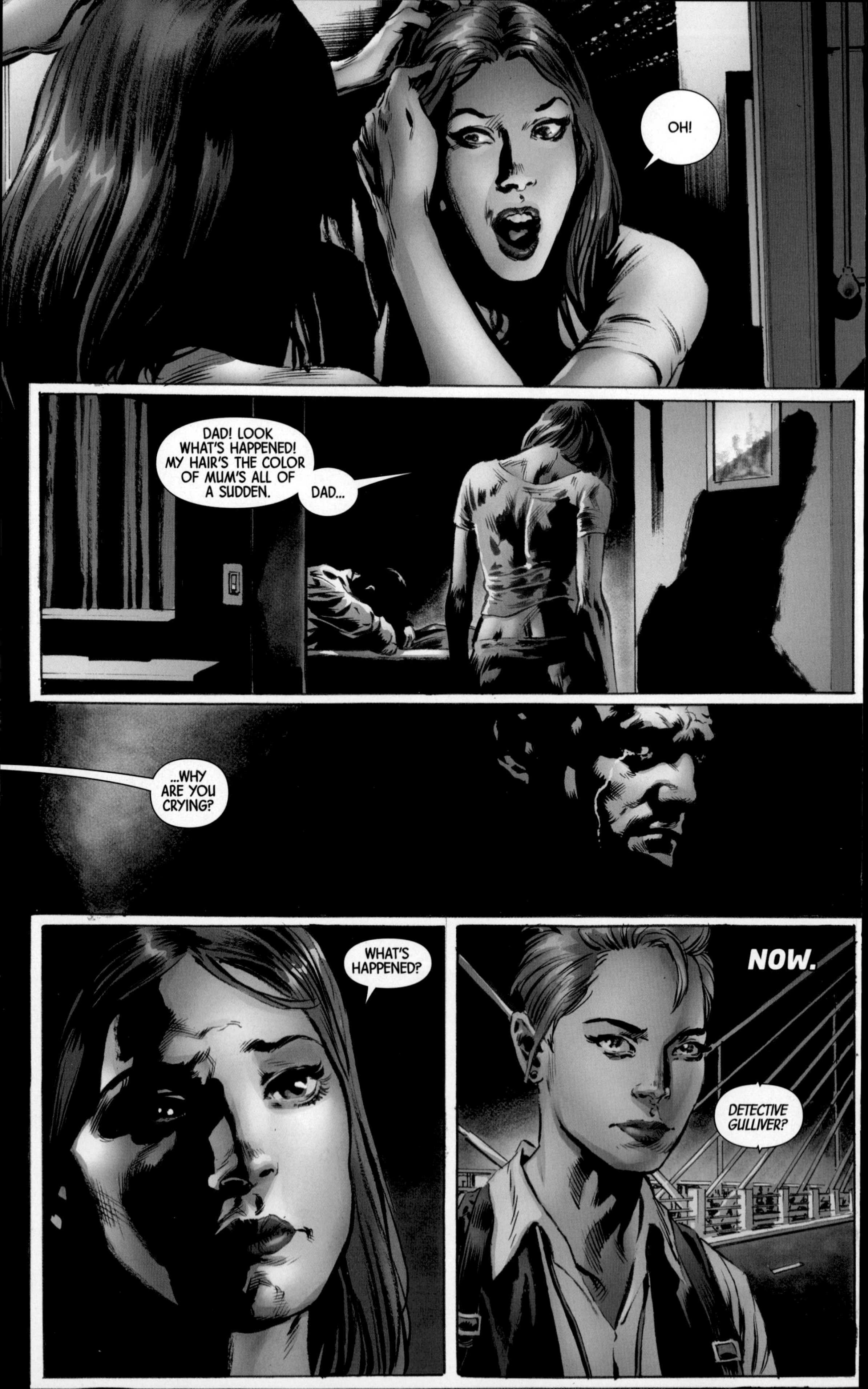
OH!
DAD! LOOK WHAT'S HAPPENED! MY HAIR'S THE COLOR OF MUM'S ALL OF A SUDDEN.
DAD...
...WHY ARE YOU CRYING?
WHAT'S HAPPENED?
NOW.
DETECTIVE GULLIVER?

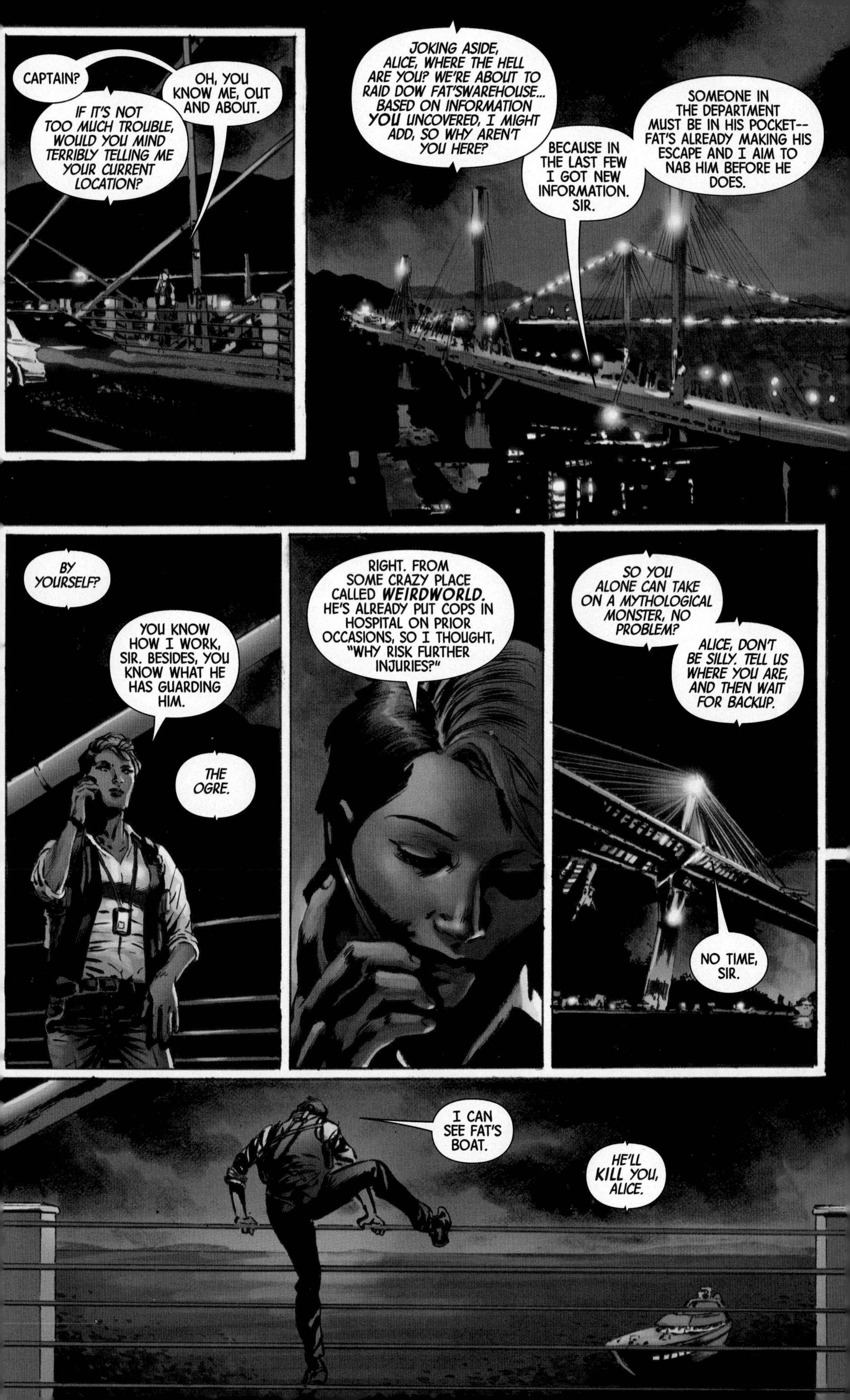
CAPTAIN?
IF IT'S NOT TOO MUCH TROUBLE, WOULD YOU MIND TERRIBLY TELLING ME YOUR CURRENT LOCATION?
OH, YOU KNOW ME, OUT AND ABOUT.
JOKING ASIDE, ALICE, WHERE THE HELL ARE YOU? WE'RE ABOUT TO RAID DOW FAT'SWAREHOUSE... BASED ON INFORMATION YOU UNCOVERED, I MIGHT ADD, SO WHY AREN'T YOU HERE?
BECAUSE IN THE LAST FEW I GOT NEW INFORMATION. SIR.
SOMEONE IN THE DEPARTMENT MUST BE IN HIS POCKET-- FAT'S ALREADY MAKING HIS ESCAPE AND I AIM TO NAB HIM BEFORE HE DOES.
BY YOURSELF?
YOU KNOW HOW I WORK, SIR. BESIDES, YOU KNOW WHAT HE HAS GUARDING HIM.
THE OGRE.
RIGHT. FROM SOME CRAZY PLACE CALLED WEIRDWORLD. HE'S ALREADY PUT COPS IN HOSPITAL ON PRIOR OCCASIONS, SO I THOUGHT, "WHY RISK FURTHER INJURIES?"
SO YOU ALONE CAN TAKE ON A MYTHOLOGICAL MONSTER, NO PROBLEM?
ALICE, DON'T BE SILLY. TELL US WHERE YOU ARE, AND THEN WAIT FOR BACKUP.
NO TIME, SIR.
I CAN SEE FAT'S BOAT.
HE'LL KILL YOU, ALICE.

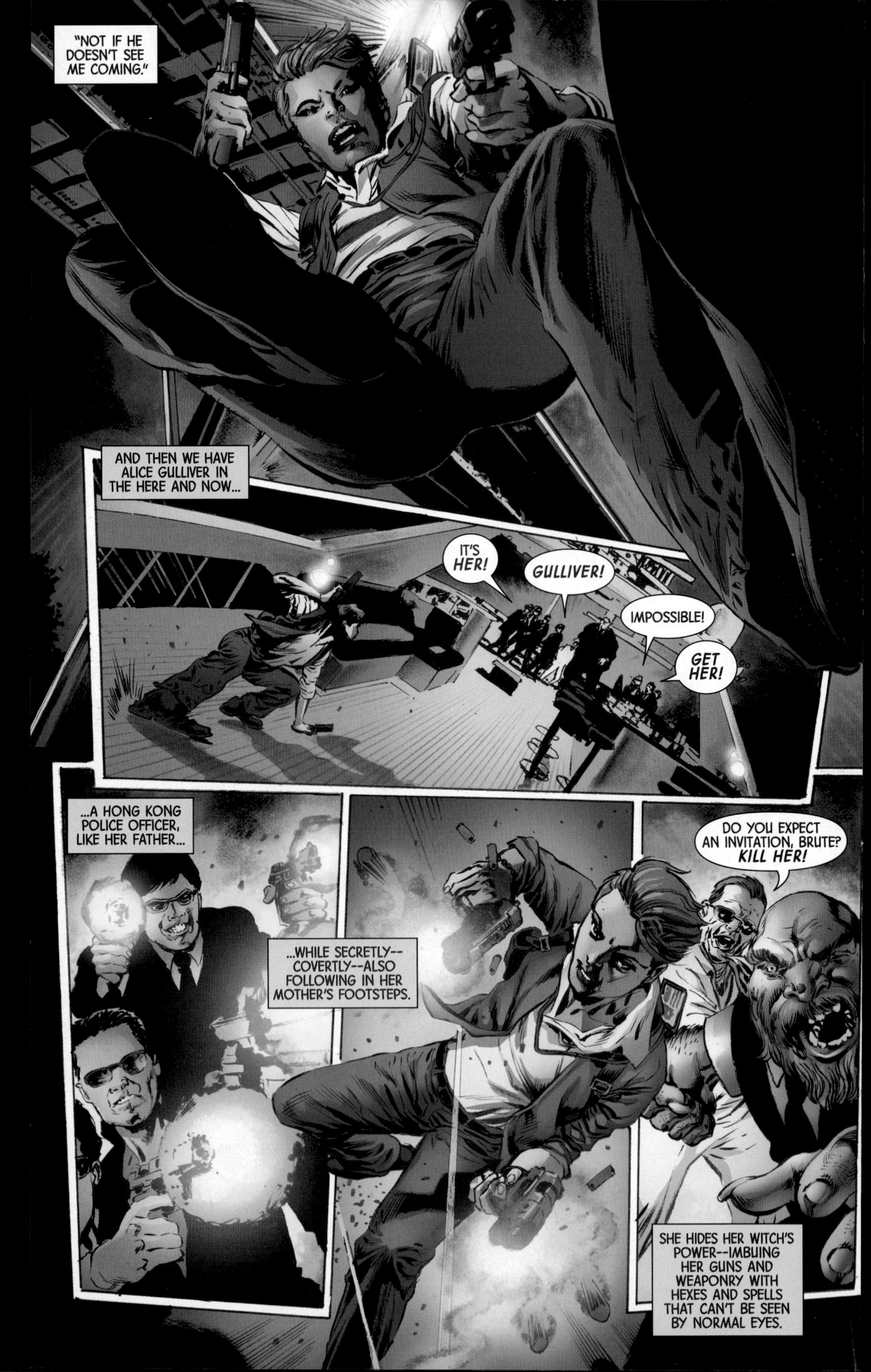
"NOT IF HE DOESN'T SEE ME COMING."
AND THEN WE HAVE ALICE GULLIVER IN THE HERE AND NOW...
IT'S HER!
GULLIVER!
IMPOSSIBLE!
GET HER!
...A HONG KONG POLICE OFFICER, LIKE HER FATHER...
...WHILE SECRETLY--COVERTLY--ALSO FOLLOWING IN HER MOTHER'S FOOTSTEPS.
DO YOU EXPECT AN INVITATION, BRUTE? KILL HER!
SHE HIDES HER WITCH'S POWER--IMBUING HER GUNS AND WEAPONRY WITH HEXES AND SPELLS THAT CAN'T BE SEEN BY NORMAL EYES.

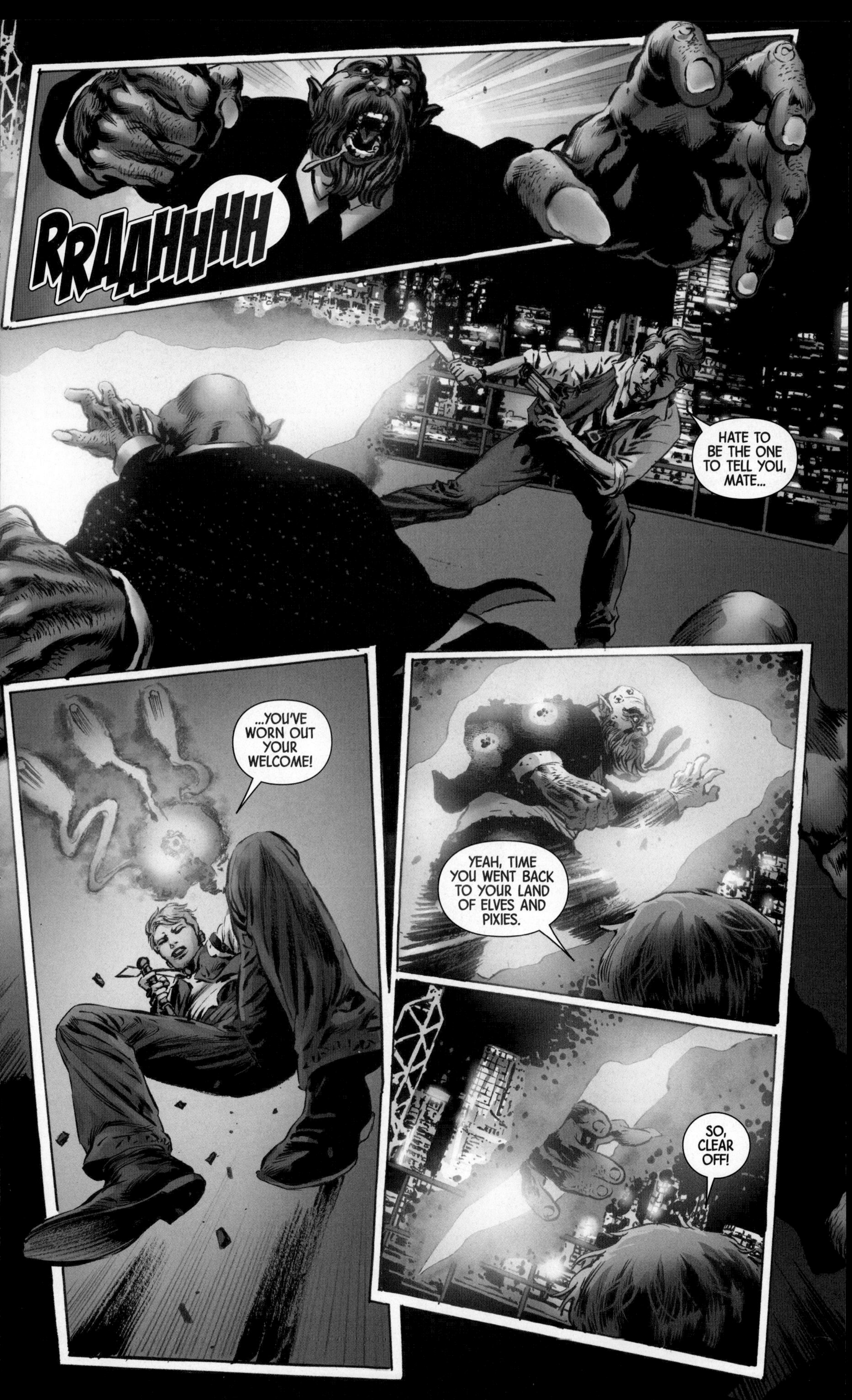
RRAAHHHH
HATE TO BE THE ONE TO TELL YOU, MATE...
...YOU'VE WORN OUT YOUR WELCOME!
YEAH, TIME YOU WENT BACK TO YOUR LAND OF ELVES AND PIXIES.
SO, CLEAR OFF!

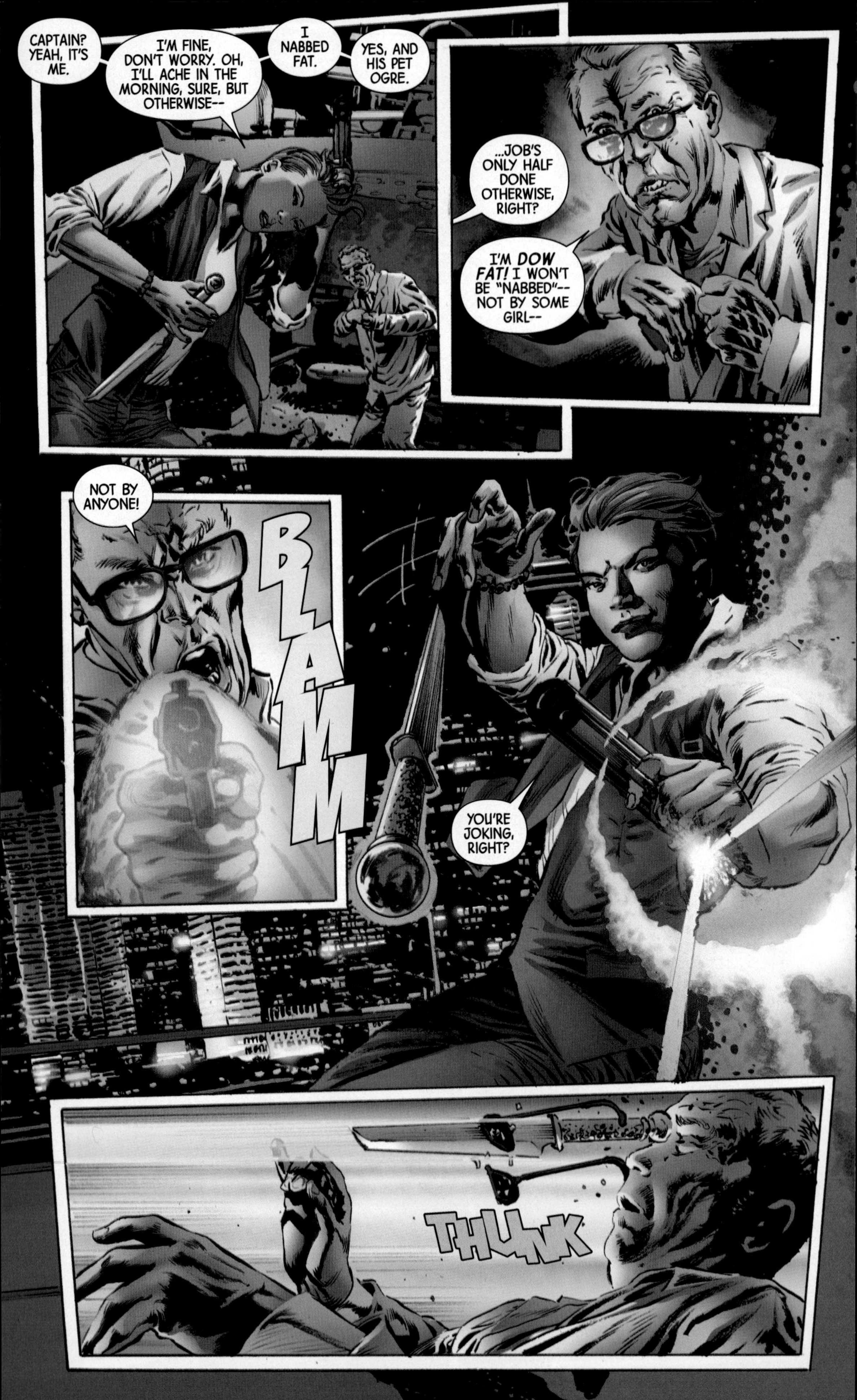
CAPTAIN? YEAH, IT'S ME.
I'M FINE, DON'T WORRY. OH, I'LL ACHE IN THE MORNING, SURE, BUT OTHERWISE--
I NABBED FAT.
YES, AND HIS PET OGRE.
...JOB'S ONLY HALF DONE OTHERWISE, RIGHT?
I'M DOW FAT! I WON'T BE "NABBED"-- NOT BY SOME GIRL--
NOT BY ANYONE!
BLAMM
YOU'RE JOKING, RIGHT?
THUNK

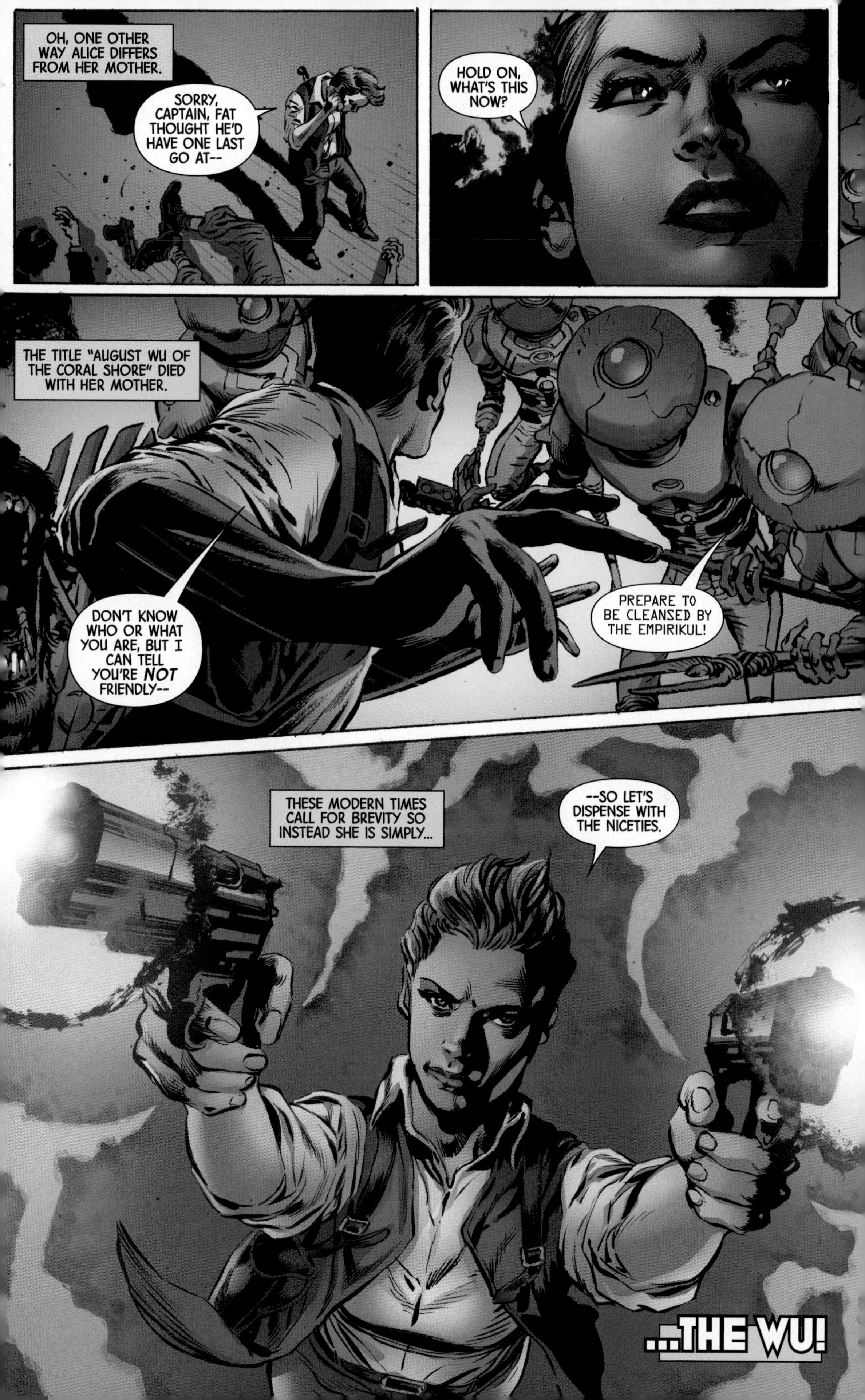
OH, ONE OTHER WAY ALICE DIFFERS FROM HER MOTHER.
SORRY, CAPTAIN, FAT THOUGHT HE'D HAVE ONE LAST GO AT--
HOLD ON, WHAT'S THIS NOW?
THE TITLE "AUGUST WU OF THE CORAL SHORE" DIED WITH HER MOTHER.
DON'T KNOW WHO OR WHAT YOU ARE, BUT I CAN TELL YOU'RE NOT FRIENDLY--
PREPARE TO BE CLEANSED BY THE EMPIRIKUL!
THESE MODERN TIMES CALL FOR BREVITY SO INSTEAD SHE IS SIMPLY...
--SO LET'S DISPENSE WITH THE NICETIES.
...THE WU!

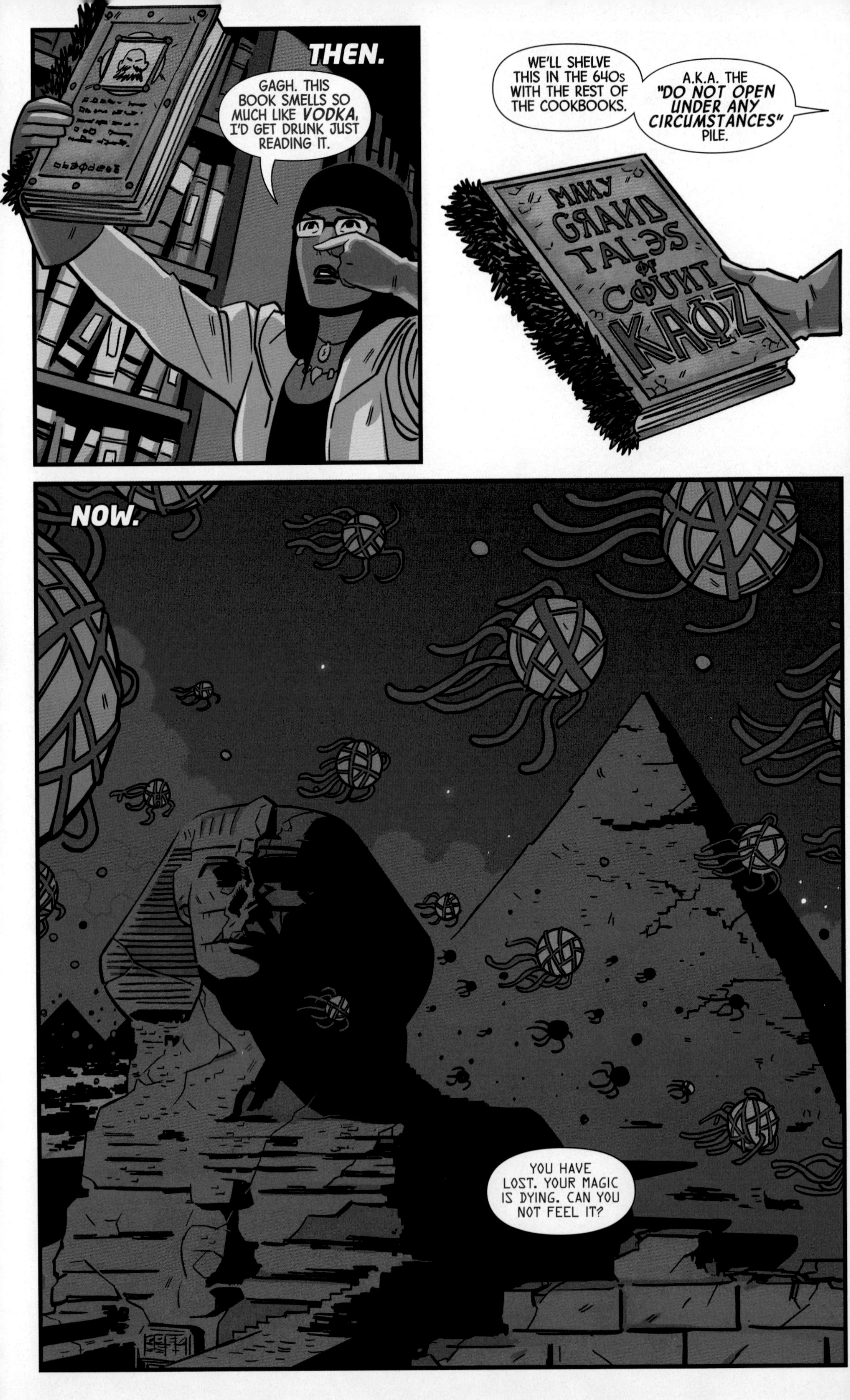
THEN.
GAGH. THIS BOOK SMELLS SO MUCH LIKE VODKA, I'D GET DRUNK JUST READING IT.
WE'LL SHELVE THIS IN THE 640s WITH THE REST OF THE COOKBOOKS.
A.K.A. THE "DO NOT OPEN UNDER ANY CIRCUMSTANCES" PILE.
MANY GRAND TALES OF COUNT KAOZ
NOW.
YOU HAVE LOST. YOUR MAGIC IS DYING. CAN YOU NOT FEEL IT?

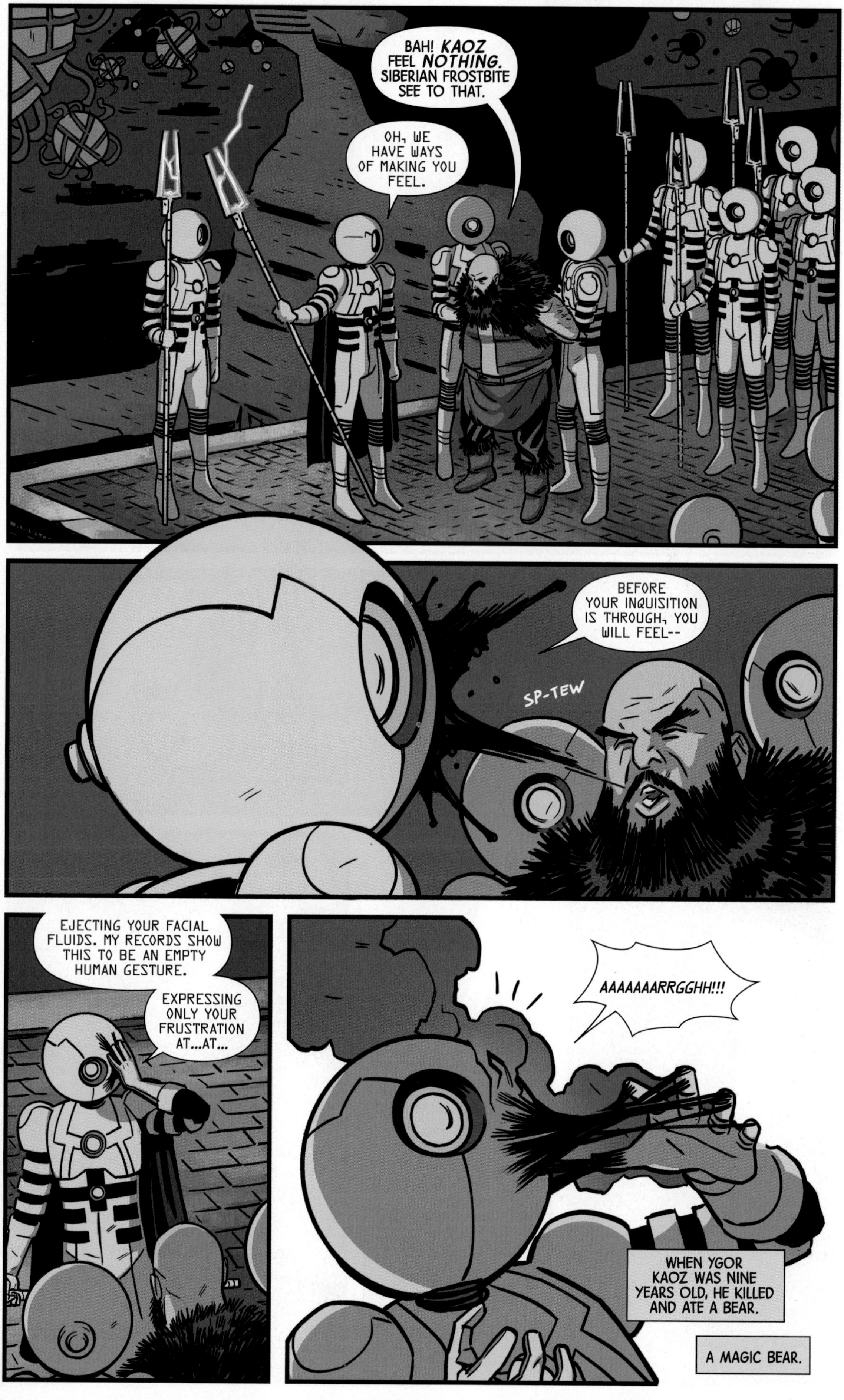
BAH! KAOZ FEEL NOTHING. SIBERIAN FROSTBITE SEE TO THAT.
OH, WE HAVE WAYS OF MAKING YOU FEEL.
BEFORE YOUR INQUISITION IS THROUGH, YOU WILL FEEL--
SP-TEW
EJECTING YOUR FACIAL FLUIDS. MY RECORDS SHOW THIS TO BE AN EMPTY HUMAN GESTURE.
EXPRESSING ONLY YOUR FRUSTRATION AT...AT...
AAAAAAARRGGHH!!!
WHEN YGOR KAOZ WAS NINE YEARS OLD, HE KILLED AND ATE A BEAR.
A MAGIC BEAR.

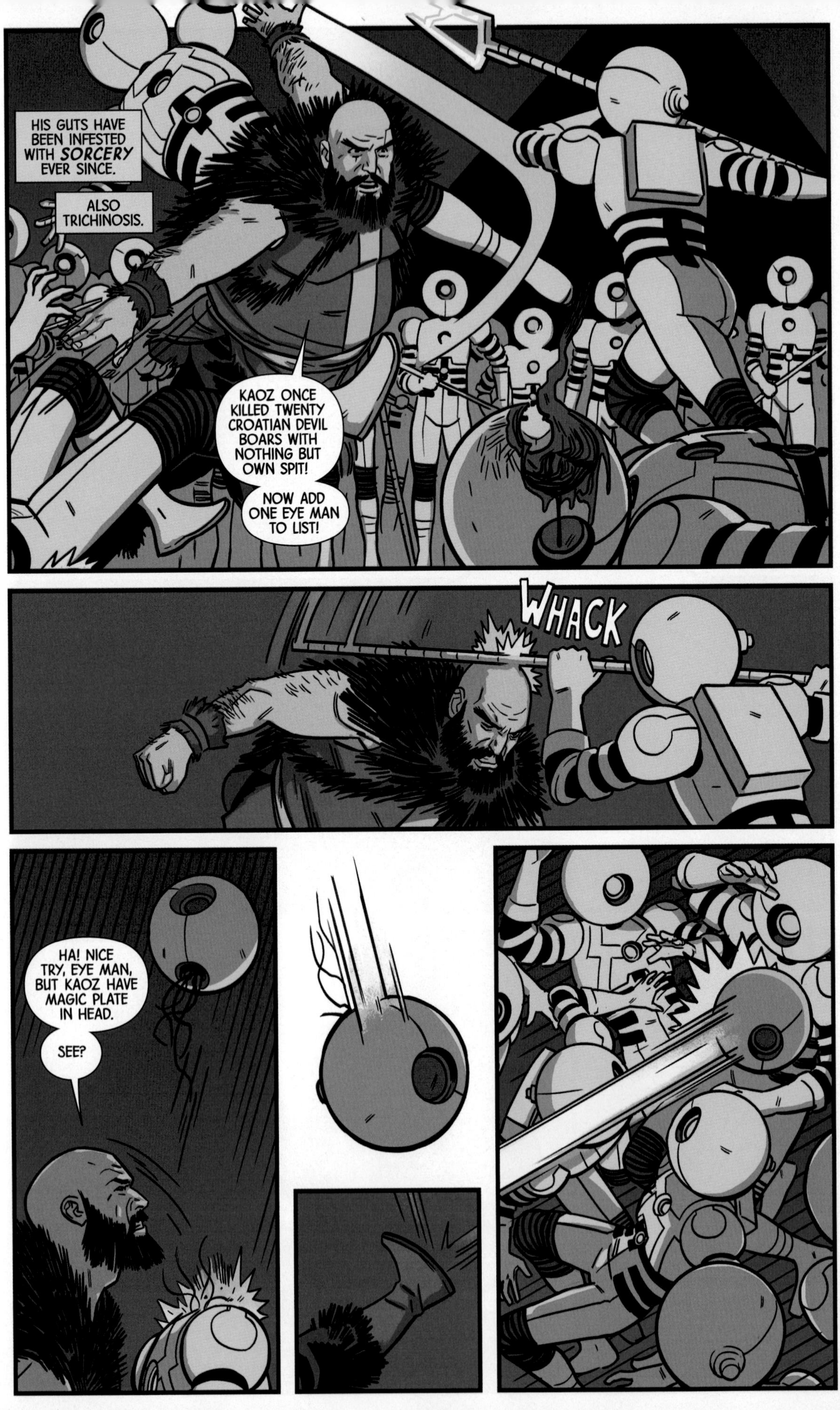

HIS GUTS HAVE BEEN INFESTED WITH SORCERY EVER SINCE.
ALSO TRICHINOSIS.
KAOZ ONCE KILLED TWENTY CROATIAN DEVIL BOARS WITH NOTHING BUT OWN SPIT!
NOW ADD ONE EYE MAN TO LIST!
WHACK
HA! NICE TRY, EYE MAN, BUT KAOZ HAVE MAGIC PLATE IN HEAD.
SEE?

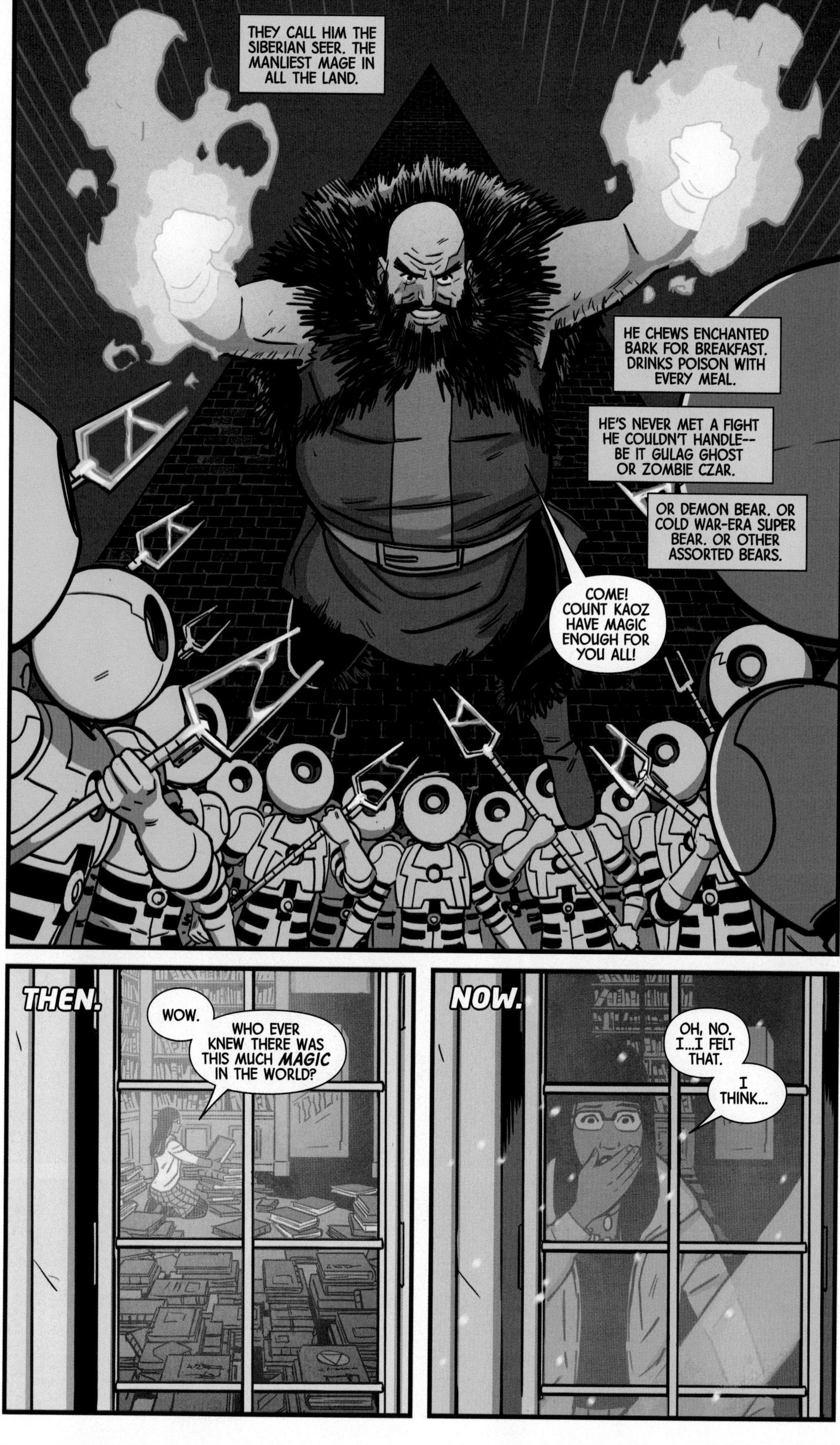

THEY CALL HIM THE SIBERIAN SEER. THE MANLIEST MAGE IN ALL THE LAND.
HE CHEWS ENCHANTED BARK FOR BREAKFAST. DRINKS POISON WITH EVERY MEAL.
HE'S NEVER MET A FIGHT HE COULDN'T HANDLE-- BE IT GULAG GHOST OR ZOMBIE CZAR.
OR DEMON BEAR. OR COLD WAR-ERA SUPER BEAR. OR OTHER ASSORTED BEARS.
COME! COUNT KAOZ HAVE MAGIC ENOUGH FOR YOU ALL!
THEN.
WOW.
WHO EVER KNEW THERE WAS THIS MUCH *MAGIC* IN THE WORLD?
NOW.
OH, NO. I...I FELT THAT.
I THINK...

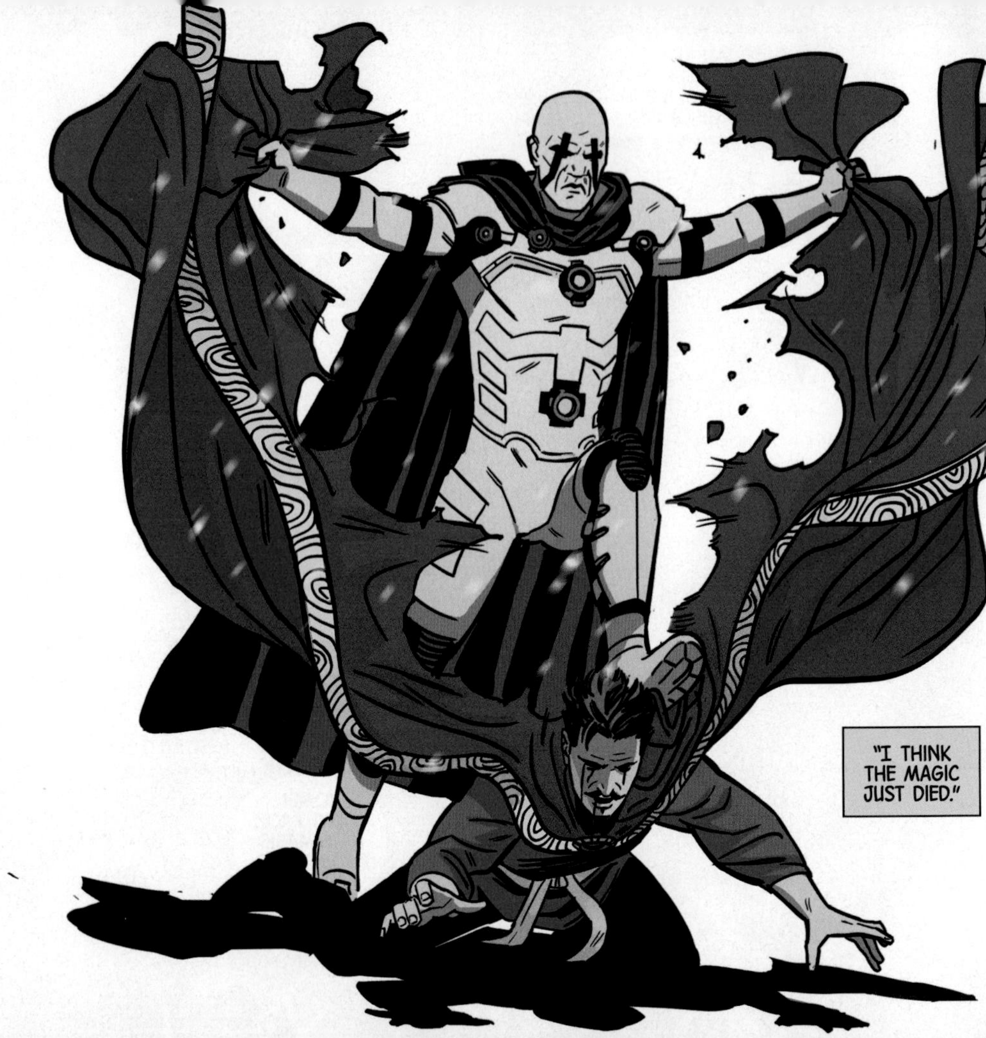
"I THINK THE MAGIC JUST DIED."

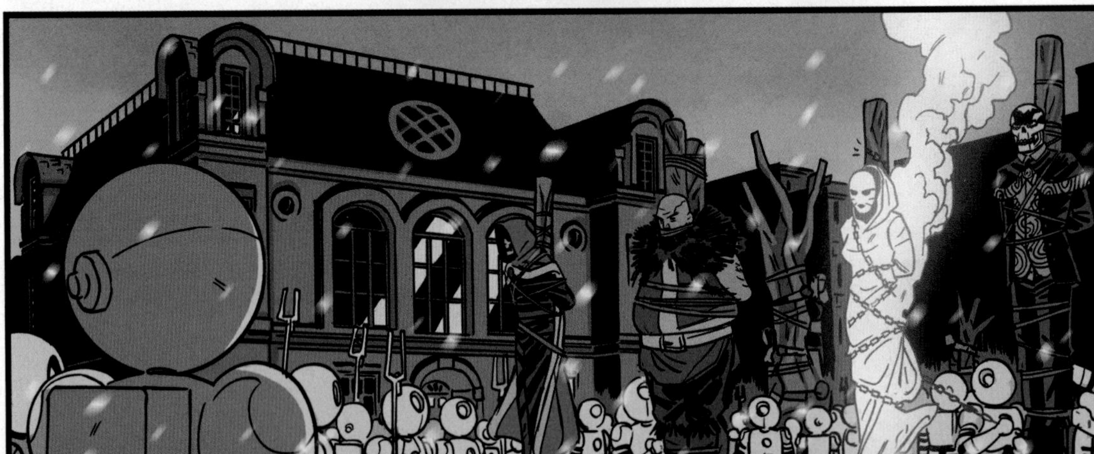

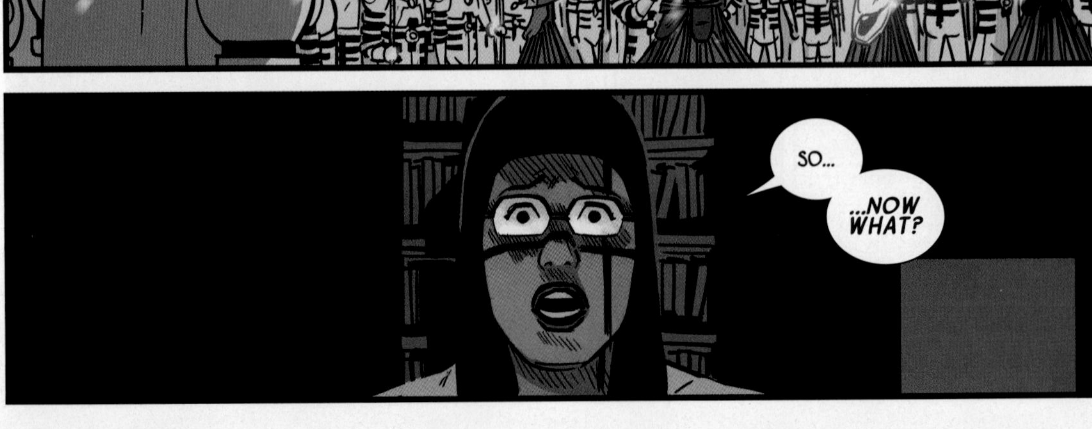
SO...
...NOW WHAT?

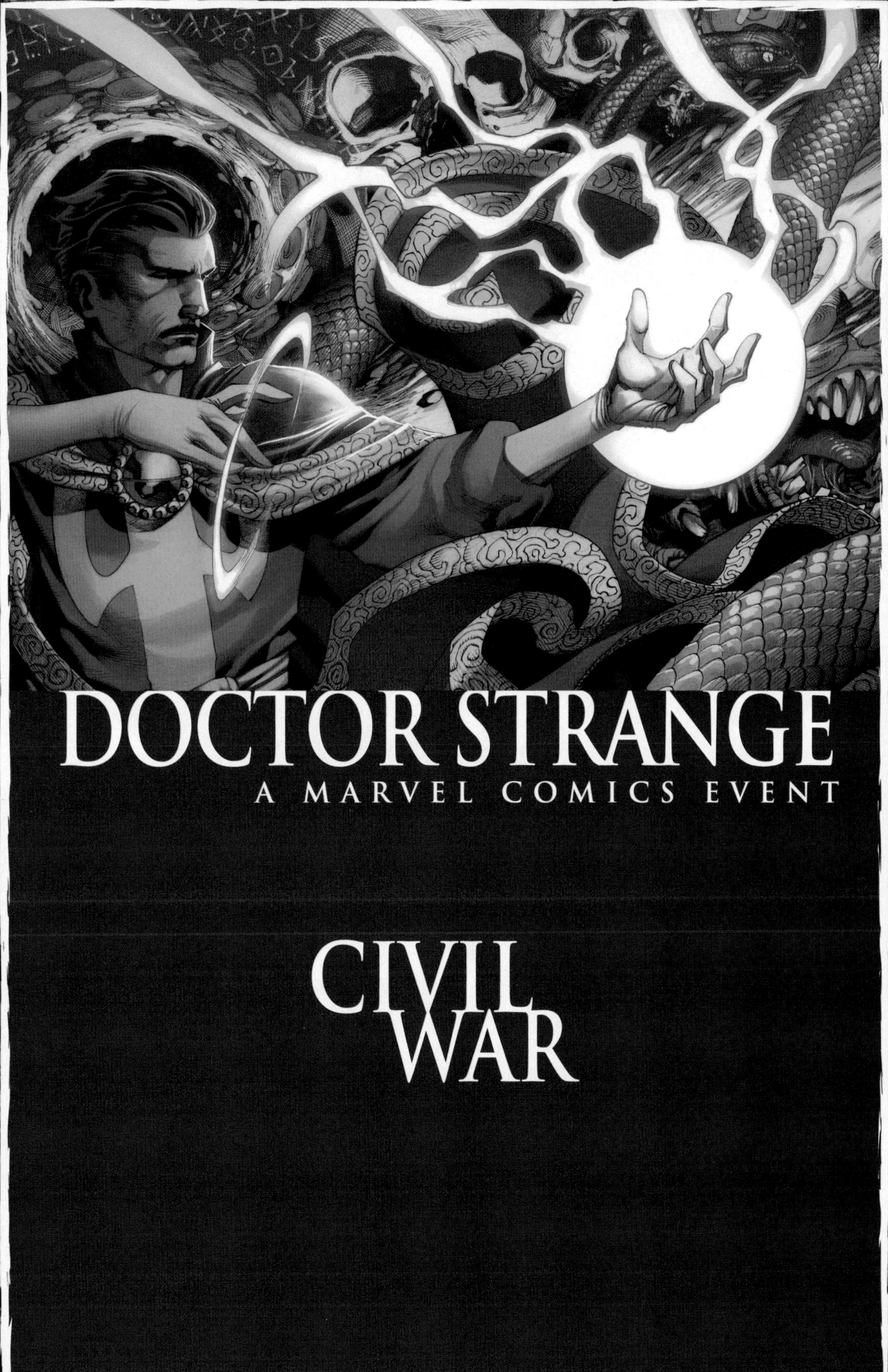
DOCTOR STRANGE
A MARVEL COMICS EVENT
CIVIL WAR

#7 CIVIL WAR VARIANT BY **CHRIS STEVENS**

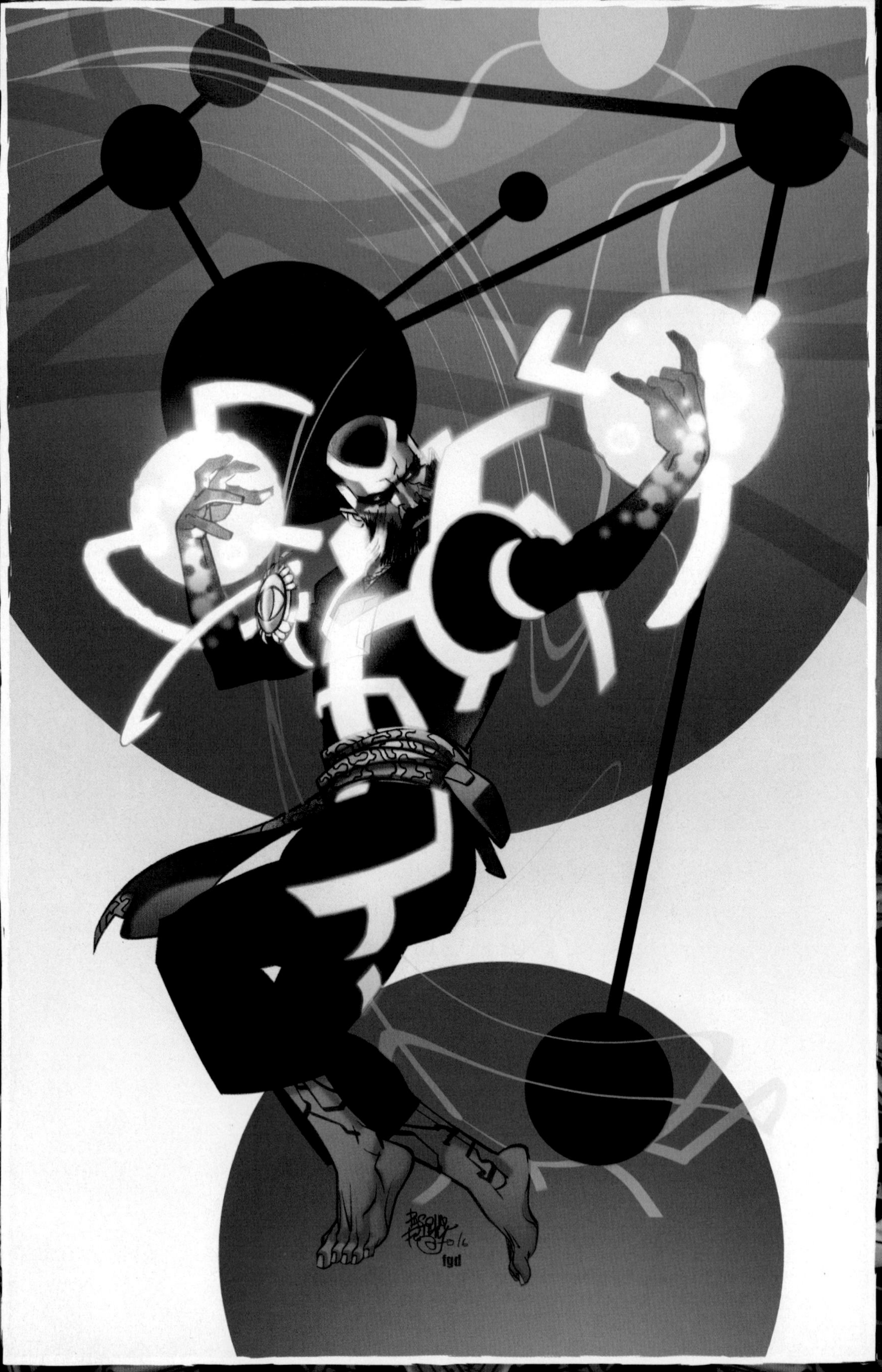
fgd

#8 AGE OF APOCALYPSE VARIANT BY **PASQUAL FERRY** & **FRANK D'ARMATA**

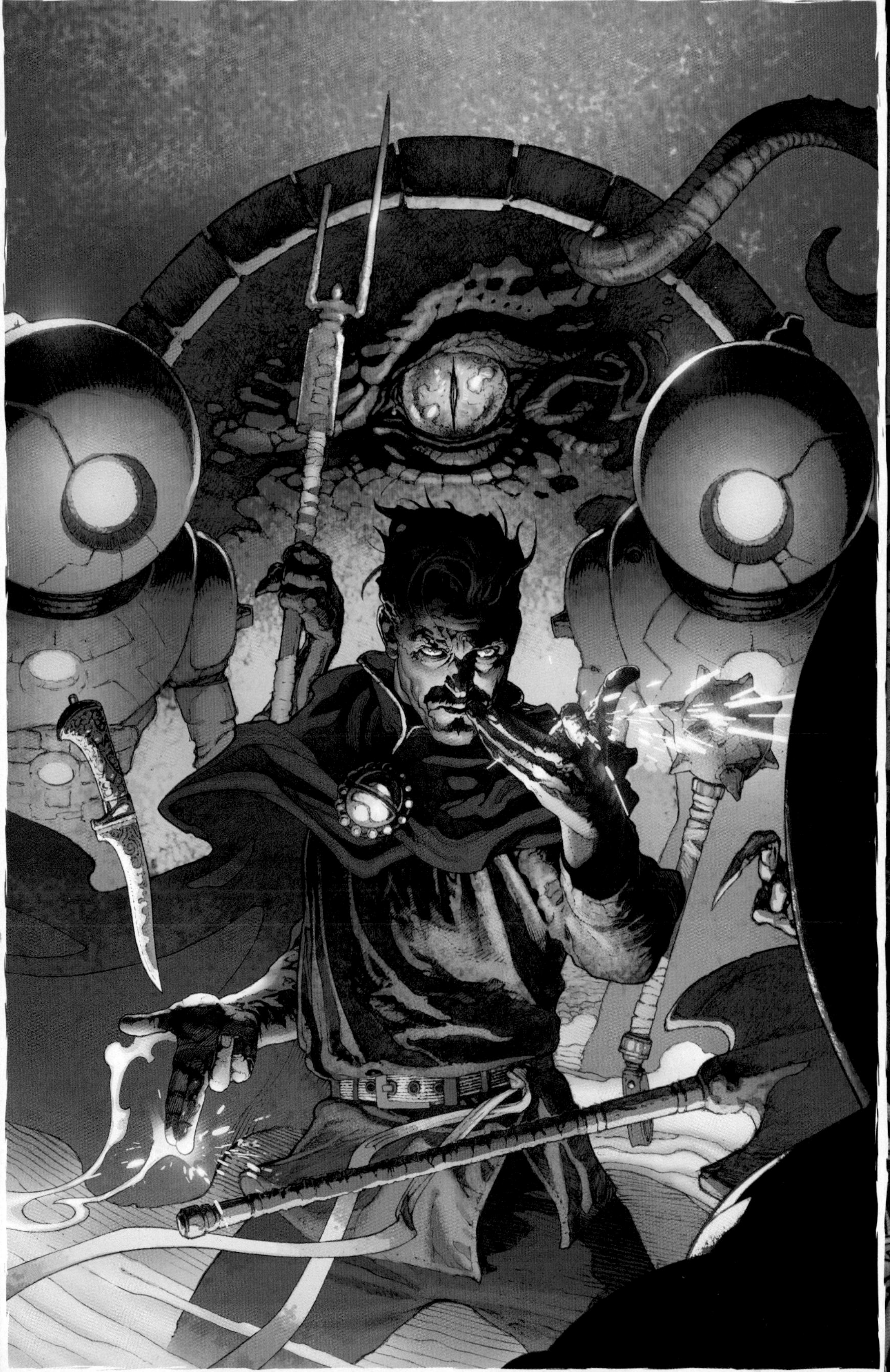

DOCTOR STRANGE: LAST DAYS OF MAGIC #1 VARIANT BY **ANDY BRASE**

Free Digital Copy

TO REDEEM YOUR CODE FOR A FREE DIGITAL COPY:

1. GO TO MARVEL.COM/REDEEM. OFFER EXPIRES ON 10/5/18.
2. FOLLOW THE ON-SCREEN INSTRUCTIONS TO REDEEM YOUR DIGITAL COPY.
3. LAUNCH THE MARVEL COMICS APP TO READ YOUR COMIC NOW.
4. YOUR DIGITAL COPY WILL BE FOUND UNDER THE 'MY COMICS' TAB.
5. READ AND ENJOY.

YOUR FREE DIGITAL COPY WILL BE AVAILABLE ON:
MARVEL COMICS APP FOR APPLE IOS® DEVICES
MARVEL COMICS APP FOR ANDROID™ DEVICES

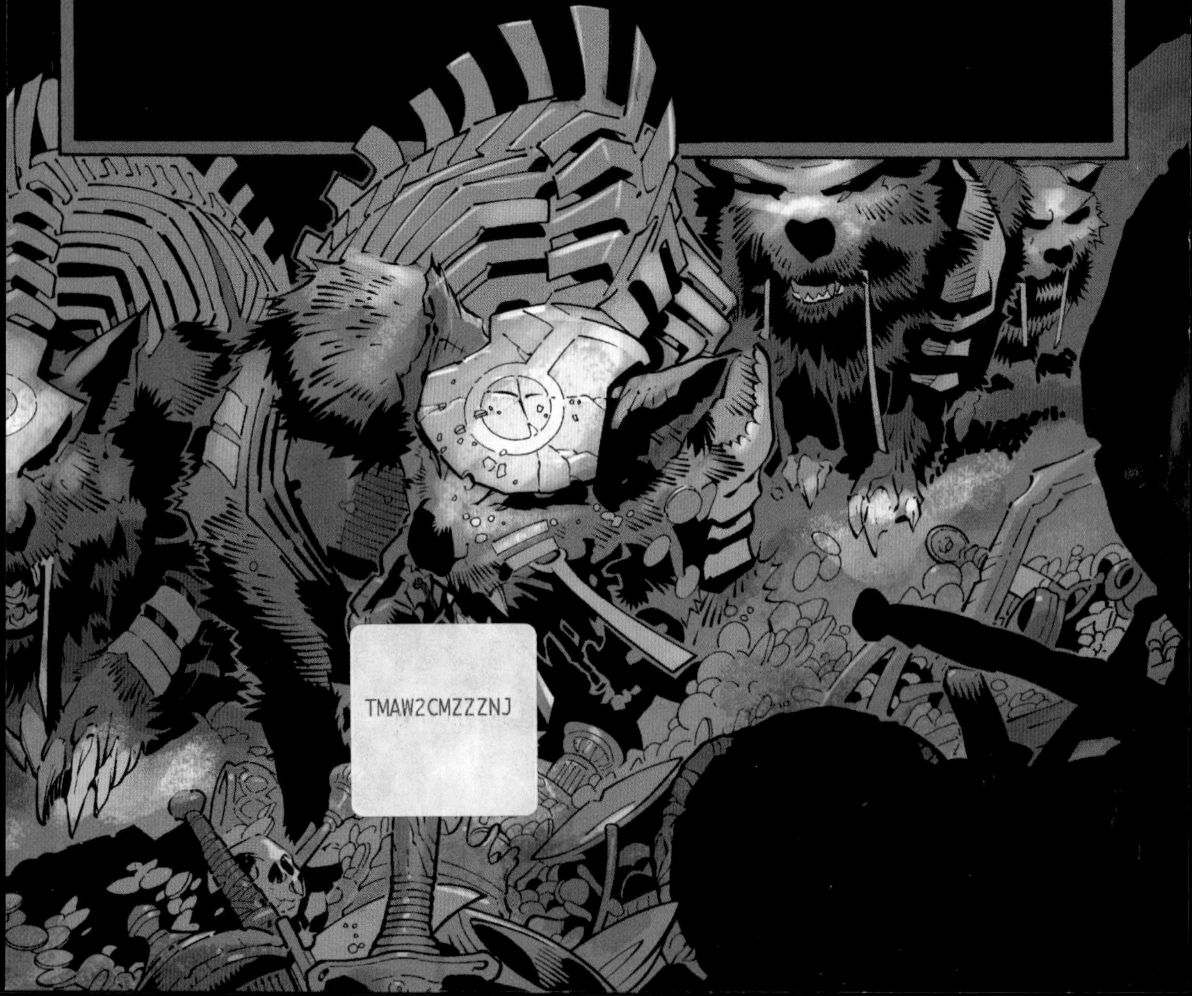

TMAW2CMZZZNJ